Conversation With God

Answers to the Important Questions of Life

Conversation with God

Cruzian Mystic Books
P.O.Box 570459
Miami, Florida, 33257
(305) 378-6253 Fax: (305) 378-6253

First U.S. edition 2007

All rights reserved. No part of this book may be used or reproduced in any manner whatsoever without written permission (address above) except in the case of brief quotations embodied in critical articles and reviews. All inquiries may be addressed to the address above.

The author is available for group lectures and individual counseling. For further information contact the publisher.

Ashby, Muata
ISBN: 1-884564-68-2

Library of Congress Cataloging in Publication Data

1 Mysticism 2 Spirituality 3 Egyptian Philosophy 4 Yoga 5 Self Help.
6 Egyptian Mysticism 7 African spirituality & Mysticism

Also by Muata Ashby

Egyptian Yoga: The Philosophy of Enlightenment.
Initiation Into Egyptian Yoga: The Secrets of Shedy.
Egyptian Proverbs: Tempt Tchaas.
The Egyptian Yoga Exercise Workout Book.

For a complete listing of titles send for the catalog in the back of the book.

Mystical Answers to the Important Questions of Life

Sema Institute of Yoga (Founded 1995)

Sema (☥) is an ancient Egyptian word and symbol meaning *union*. The Sema Institute is dedicated to the propagation of the universal teachings of spiritual evolution which relate to the union of humanity and the union of all things within the universe. It is a non-denominational organization which recognizes the unifying principles in all spiritual and religious systems of evolution throughout the world. Our primary goals are to provide the wisdom of ancient spiritual teachings in books, courses and other forms of communication. Secondly, to provide expert instruction and training in the various yogic disciplines including Ancient Egyptian Philosophy, Christian Gnosticism, Indian Mystical Philosophy and modern science. Thirdly, to promote world peace and Universal understanding.

A primary focus of our tradition is to identify and acknowledge the yogic principles within all religions and to relate them to each other in order to promote their deeper understanding as well as to show the essential unity of purpose and the unity of all living beings and nature within the whole of existence.

The Institute is open to all who believe in the principles of peace, non-violence and spiritual emancipation regardless of sex, race, or creed.

About the author and editor:
Dr. Muata Ashby

Mr. Ashby began studies in the area of religion and philosophy and achieved a doctorate degree in these areas while at the same time he began to collect his research into what would later become several books on the subject of the African History, religion and ethics, world mythology, origins of Yoga Philosophy and practice in ancient Africa (Ancient Egypt/Nubia) and also the origins of Christianity in Ancient Egypt. This was the catalyst for a successful book series on the subject called "Egyptian Yoga" begun in 1994. He has extensively studied mystical religious traditions from around the world and is an accomplished lecturer, musician, artist, poet, painter, screenwriter, playwright and author of over 40 books on yoga philosophy, religious philosophy and social philosophy based on ancient African principles. A leading advocate of the concept of the existence of advanced social and religious philosophy in ancient Africa comparable to the Eastern traditions such as Vedanta, Buddhism, Confucianism and Taoism, he has lectured and written extensively on the correlations of these with ancient African religion and philosophy.

Muata Abhaya Ashby holds a Doctor of Divinity Degree and a Masters degree in Liberal Arts and Religious Studies. He is also a Teacher of Yoga Philosophy and Discipline. Dr. Ashby is an adjunct professor at the American Institute of Holistic Theology and worked as an adjunct professor at the Florida International University.

Dr. Ashby has been an independent researcher and practitioner of Egyptian Yoga, Indian Yoga, Chinese Yoga, Buddhism and mystical psychology as well as Christian Mysticism. Dr. Ashby has engaged in Post Graduate research in advanced Jnana, Bhakti and Kundalini Yogas at the Yoga Research Foundation.

Since 1999 he has researched Ancient Egyptian musical theory and created a series of musical compositions which explore this unique area of music from ancient Africa and its connection to world music. Dr. Ashby has lectured around the United States of America, Europe and Africa.

Mystical Answers to the Important Questions of Life

Through his studies of the teachings of the great philosophers of the world and meeting with and studying under spiritual masters and having practiced advanced meditative disciplines, Dr. Ashby began to function in the capacity of Sebai or Spiritual Preceptor of Shetaut Neter, Ancient Egyptian Religion and also as Ethics Philosopher and Religious Studies instructor. Thus, he took the title of Sebai and the acronym of his African/Kemetic and western names is MAA (Sebai MAA). He believes that it is important to understand all religious teachings in the context of human historical, cultural and social development in order to promote greater understanding and the advancement of humanity.

Karen Clarke-Ashby ("Dja") is the wife and spiritual partner of Muata. She is the author of *De-stressing 101, Tools for Living a Stress Free Life*, co-author of *Egyptian Yoga Exercise Work Out Book: Movement of the Gods and Goddesses*, and contributing author of *Kemetic Diet*. She is also an independent researcher, practitioner and certified teacher of Yoga, a Doctor in the Sciences and a Pastoral Counselor, the editor of *Egyptian Proverbs* and *Egyptian Yoga* by Muata.

Sema Institute
P.O. Box 570459, Miami, Fla. 33257 (305) 378-6253,
Fax (305) 378-6253
©1995-2007

Table of Contents

INTRODUCTION: 13
    Question: Privacy between teacher and students? 14

WHAT IS IT ALL ABOUT? 15
    Question: What is a Conversation with God? 16
    Question: What is Shetaut Neter? 17
    Question: What is the Temple of Shetaut Neter and are you affiliated with any other Kemetic organizations? 18
    Question: Real knowledge or just relative knowledge? 19

HOW TO BECOME A TRUE SEEKER, A SPIRITUAL ASPIRANT, AND MOVE FORWARD IN LIFE, WHAT NEEDS TO BE DONE? 20
    Question: What does it Take to Be a Successful Aspirant? 21
    Question: what is the purpose of being a spiritual teacher? ... 24
    Question: How to practice Devotion to God? 26
    Question: What does it mean when an aspirant sees the Spiritual Preceptor in a dream? 28
    Question: How to maintain good association? 29
    Question: Can I change the chants I practice daily? 32
    Questions: Is the Spiritual Battle Between Differentiated and Undifferentiated Consciousness? 33
    Question: could you please provide insight into the science of chanting? 35
    Question: How can I receive a spiritual name? 37
    Question: can I get several names and initiations? 38
    Question: Am I practicing the Postures Correctly? 39
    Question: How does the discipline of the postures operate on the physical plane? 41
    Question: Should I leave my family and go live closer to the spiritual teacher? 42
    Question: What is too much talking? 45
    Question: Why have I become agitated since I started practicing the teachings? 47
    Question: How to raise the Serpent Power? 50
    Question: what musical instruments would be helpful in awakening the neters? 52
    Question: how should an aspirant be like the Sage? 53

Mystical Answers to the Important Questions of Life

WHO AND OR WHAT IS GOD? **54**
  Question: What is the Kemetic concept of God? 55
  Answer 55
  Question: What is the Kemetic concept of God, the difference between religion and spirituality? 56
  Answer 56
  Question: Who translated the Ancient Egyptian Religious texts? 59
  Question: How can God be intimately personal, one who listens to your prayer, while at the same time be transcendental? 60

WHAT IS THE SOUL, WHAT IS THERE AFTER DEATH AND HOW DOES IT RELATE TO MIND AND GOD CONSCIOUSNESS? **63**
  Question: What is the difference between the spirit and the soul? What is "Human and Mankind" 64
  Question: Please what are explain waking, dream and sleep and the means to wake up in those planes? 70
  Question: How to prove the passing of the soul between planes of existence? 76
  Question: How should I handle a death in the family? 79
  Question: Is fear an Illusion? 80
  Question: why is the God Amun called the bull of his mother. 82
  Question: are the BA & KA different from the SPIRIT & SOUL 83

QUESTIONS ABOUT HISTORY, RELIGION, MYTH AND SPIRITUAL PHILOSOPHIES? **84**
  Question: What are Freemasonry and Mythology? 85
  Question: what is the proper way to understand mythology? 87
  Question: Were Ancient Egyptians Africans and did the Bible originate in Egypt? 89
  Question: Where does the tradition of the Baptism come from? 90
  Question: Should I become a Baptist? 91
  Question: Did Jesus really exist? 93
  Question: Is the Kingdom of Heaven within as it says in the Christian Bible? 94
  Question: Is the Trinitarian philosophy included in the Neterian Creed? What is true religion? What is Faith-based Religion? 95

Questions: Did the Ancient Egyptians and Atlantians Self-destruct and did the Serpent Power teaching come from Asia to Egypt? 103

Question: Are the miracles discussed in the book Autobiography of a Yogi true? 106

Question: What is Avatarism? 108

Question: Should Saints and Sages Charge for their services? 109

Question: Is Neterian religion and its priesthood only for black/African people? 114

Question: is it possible to have a meeting with all Kemetic teachers? 117

Question: How to use the Tutelary divinity? 119

Question: who was Imhotep? 120

Question: Is the year 2012 the end of the world? 121

Question: Where there any "fighting yogis"? 123

HANDLING FAMILY AND RELATIONSHIP ISSUES 124

Question: I feel bad I cannot help my family, what should I do? 125

Question: How to handle family entanglements? 127

Question: How to handle family gatherings? 130

Question: Why do I like to be in love and then fight with my lovers? 134

IN CHAPTER 4 OF THE PMH ENTITLED "THE WISDOM OF THE SECRET IDENTITY OF THE GODS AND GODDESSES" IT IS STATED THAT, ... 136

Questions: Why does my relationship seem to be failing? 140

Question: Why is it that many people get bitter, ornery or depressed as they get old? 142

Question: Why am I losing my friends since we started following the Kemetic path? 144

Question: how does romantic love fit with the spiritual teachings? 145

Question: Why did God create Creation? What is the use of Sexuality? 147

Question: Is it necessary to have children in order to attain spiritual awakening? 150

Question: How much sex is enough? 153

Question: Is Homosexuality bad? 156

Mystical Answers to the Important Questions of Life

 Question: How to control sex desire?..................................... 158
 Question: Is Polygamy allowed in Egyptian religion?................ 160
 Question: How to maintain family relations with closed-minded Christian relatives?... 161
 Question: How to rejuvenate my passion for this marriage?. 163

HOW TO BECOME A HEALTHY PERSON AND PURIFY MIND, BODY AND SOUL IN ORDER TO BE READY TO ATTAIN HIGHER CONSCIOUSNESS? 165

 Question: on methods concerning mental and physical purification... 166
 Question: How to promote brain enhancement?...................... 167
 Answer... 167
 Question: How to handle my diet?... 169
 Question: How to handle my diet after achieving success in the teachings and growing older?... 170
 Question: What should I eat?... 171
 Question: How to take care of the Skin without poisonous chemicals?... 173
 Question: why do you recommend taking vitamins?............... 175

HOW TO DEVELOP ETHICAL CONSCIENCE AND PURITY OF HEART? .. 177

 Question: Should I focus on the Maat Path?.......................... 178
 Question: How does the concept of Judgment work in Neterian spirituality?... 179
 Question: What is the difference between Ari (Karma) and the Divine Plan, also what is the relation of the soul with Life Force energy?.. 180
 Answer... 180
 Questions: Can Hip Hop be a Righteous Path as I study the Teachings?.. 184
 Question: How to Change my Life?.. 188
 Question: If I kill insects am I a killer and will my spiritual evolution suffer?... 190
 Question: How can meditation cleanse Karmic seeds if all deeds must be judged by Maat?... 194
 Question: Does Neterian religion & philosophy promote forgiveness of enemies – Part 1?.. 197
 Question: Does Neterian religion promote forgiveness of enemies – Part 2?... 203

Question: What is Meskhent and Where does the term: "Know Thyself" come from?... 213
Question: What should I do about my insatiable desire for winning?.. 218
Question: Is violence ever justified in the name of righteousness?.. 223

HOW TO CONTROL AND CULTIVATE THE MIND IN ORDER TO ACHIEVE SANITY, WISDOM, PROSPERITY AND POSITIVE SPIRITUAL EVOLUTION?
.... **226**

Question: how to positively affect behavior modification?.... 227
Question: How can one best handle anger?................................ 230
Question: how can I break out of the sense of psychological slavery?... 233
Question: how to destroy this ego-based mind that likes to rationalize "wrong thinking"?.. 235
Question: How to control thoughts?... 237

HOW TO HANDLE THE WORLD AND THE DAY TO DAY CHALLENGES OF LIFE AND STILL BE A SUCCESSFUL SPIRITUAL ASPIRANT? **240**

Question: What can I do about my failing daily spiritual discipline?... 241
Question: How much should I work to support myself?.......... 242
Question: is it possible to grow spiritually attaining enlightenment by listening to tapes and reading books and meeting at conferences?.. 244
Question: Is College worth it?... 246
Question: How to become free from Globalization?............... 247
Question: How to protect oneself from evil spells?................. 248
Question: How to handle a rough journey?................................ 252
Question: how to handle a challenge or an adverse situation and make a right decision?... 254
Question: Do you recommend the use of oracles?................... 258
Question: How are oracles to be used?..................................... 259
Question: I don't know what to do, can you help me?............. 261
Question: Why shouldn't I kill myself?.. 264
Question: challenged by the world in difficult ways, will this change?.. 267
Question: How can I deal with my hateful boss?...................... 269

Mystical Answers to the Important Questions of Life

GOVERNMENT, ECONOMICS, SOCIAL ORDER, SOCIAL JUSTICE AND THE IMPORTANCE OF ETHICS? HANDLING SOCIAL AND ECONOMIC PROBLEMS 274

Question: What is our responsibility in assisting others who are in need?.. 275
Question: Is Ancient Egypt the source of the caste system and capitalism?... 278
Question: What Should Neterians do about Racial Violence and Suffering?... 282
Question: Should I stay in the Military?... 284

HOW TO BECOME SPIRITUALLY ENLIGHTENED BY UNDERSTANDING THE MYSTICAL WISDOM TEACHINGS OF THE SAGES AND THE METAPHYSICAL DISCIPLINES FOR ATTAINING HIGHER CONSCIOUSNESS? 287

Question: What is meant by integration of the meditative experience?.. 288
Question: Is the self controlling the self or the self controlling the personality?.. 291
Questions: How to handle the bodiless state?................................... 292
Question: What are these Meditative sensations?............................. 293
Question: Does enlightenment bring back memories from previous lives?... 294
Questions: Can an enlightened person be wicked? Can an unenlightened person be righteous?... 296
Question: If I Feel like a detached witness is this an illusion?. 299
Question: How can a person be enlightened and not know it? 301
Question: How do I know when I have Enlightenment?............. 303
Question: If there is no mind can there be illusion?..................... 304
Question: is Enlightenment equal to Civilization?.......................... 306
Question: What is the Path of Divine Love and How does it Lead one to Spiritual Enlightenment?.. 308
Question: Am I ready to study the Book of the Dead?............. 310
Question: Have I attained the goal of the teaching? Am I ready to be a Spiritual Preceptor?.. 311
For Q & A on the subject: Science, Faith or The Transcendental? The Debate over Creationism or Evolution and other Related Issues see the book "The Limits of Faith" by Sebai Dr. Muata Ashby 314

INDEX... *315*
OTHER BOOKS FROM C M BOOKS **324**
MUSIC BASED ON THE PRT M HRU AND OTHER KEMETIC TEXTS **338**

Mystical Answers to the Important Questions of Life

INTRODUCTION:

Greetings,

The following is a grouping of some of the questions that have been submitted to Sebai Dr. Muata Ashby. They are efforts by many aspirants to better understand and practice the teachings of mystical spirituality. There is a very special quality about the Q & A process that does not occur during a regular lecture session. Certain points come out that would not come out otherwise due to the nature of the process which ideally occurs after a lecture. Having been to a certain degree enlightened by a lecture certain new questions arise and the answers to these have the effect of elevating the teaching of the lecture to even higher levels. Therefore, enjoy these exchanges and may they lead you to enlightenment, peace and prosperity.

Some of the questions asked in this volume are asked using to Kemetic (Ancient Egyptian) terms. Where these occur a brief explanation has been included. However, their application is universal as the reader will discover.

Peace

Sebai Dr. Muata Ashby

Conversation with God

Question: Privacy between teacher and students?

Greetings, I have a question. When we as aspirants send questions via email are they shared with other aspirants?

Answer

Greetings,

As a priest I have a fiduciary[1] responsibility to maintain confidentiality in all communications between individual aspirants. So no personal information is disseminated to other aspirants. Sometimes I deem it beneficial to share answers to questions that apply to aspirants generally as when a widely applicable question is asked in our group gatherings. In that case the names of aspirants are removed from any materials that are shared in order to maintain the confidentiality but at the same time benefit other aspirants. In that way indirectly the aspirant who asks the original question gains merit through the Shedy and service processes. So presenting your questions is good for you and it is a way of your service to humanity through the work of the teacher.

Peace and Blessings!

Sebai MAA

---

[1] One, such as an priest(ess) or legal counsel, that stands in a special relation of trust, confidence, or responsibility in certain obligations to others.

Mystical Answers to the Important Questions of Life

What is it all about?

Conversation with God

Question: What is a Conversation with God?

Answer

Greetings,

First we must understand what a "conversation with God" is versus an ordinary conversation. A conversation with God can be thought of in different ways. To most people they would understand that as a conversation from a person to a Spirit and many think that that Spirit should look like an old man with a long beard, a flowing robe, etc. or if there is no form it should be just a voice, a burning bush or perhaps a tree or just a presence. All of those have in common, one thing, they are all between two individuals, them and God. It is important to understand that praying to god is not the same as having a conversation with God; meditating on God is not the same either; neither is having faith in God. None of those practices are the same as a Conversation with God. From the standpoint of mystical religion, communication with God is seen as direct contact with the essential source and reality of existence. That can occur when a human being achieves higher consciousness. At that point they can communicate directly with that essential being; But that communication is not between two personalities but rather a communication of oneness, being of one mind, one existence, with the Supreme and ultimate and transcendental being.

If that direct communication is not possible another form of indirect communication with God is possible, through the writings or recordings of someone who is or was in direct contact. But the higher contact is with a living person who has or has had that contact and understands the philosophical interpretation of it for communication purposes with others who are interested, but the highest is when one can commune directly without the intermediary. The role of a sage, someone who has done the spiritual work that has allowed them to have direct contact with the Supreme, is to act as a conduit for transmitting the divine wisdom to the physical plane. Those people who are advanced enough to value such contacts will benefit from the sagely wisdom until the day they will be able to have direct contact themselves. So in this sense, a conversation with God is an exchange of beingness that is achieved when a human being grows in spiritual insight and has cleansed the personality through ethical conscience and physical purity in order to discover the deeper mystery of their own essential nature. From time immemorial, the sagely wisdom has been passed on, rediscovered by sages and kept alive so that when people are ready to listen and stud they may have not only the wisdom teaching available but enlightened personalities who can teach it and help them understand how it should by applied in life. Thus, look to the great writings of the world, the masters who discovered the mysteries of life and who recorded their thought and if you are fortunate to meet one who is versed in this contact listen to them closely and learn how to discover that glory for yourself. And when you do, be a beacon for others and in so doing join the legacy of light that enlightens all humanity.

Peace and Blessings!
Sebai MAA

Mystical Answers to the Important Questions of Life

Question: What is Shetaut Neter?

Answer

Shetaut Neter is the name that the Ancient Egyptians (also referred to as "Kemetans," or "Kamitans") called their mystical religion; it has also been referred to more commonly as the *Egyptian Mysteries*. "Kemet" is the ancient Egyptian name for the land now called Egypt. The words *Shetaut Neter* mean "Hidden Divine." It refers to a process of growing to discover the hidden Divinity within oneself and within Creation. One who grows to develop that understanding attains Nehast, that is, one becomes an awakened being. This terminology is akin to the concept of "Enlightenment." Shetaut Neter is the first known organized and developed mystical religion in human history. The earliest archeological/geological evidences of its existence occur at c. 10,000 B.C.E. You can read more on this in our book, *The African Origins of Civilization, Religion, Yoga Mysticism and Ethics Philosophy*. It incorporates special disciplines called *sema*, which includes meditation, as well as other disciplines generally referred to today as "yoga," to enhance the process of spiritual evolution.

Shetaut Neter is also practiced as a religion by the Sema Institute. It is the source of great mystical wisdom, and it is a religion for men and women alike. Also, even though it originated in Ancient Africa by Africans, it is a universal religion for all humanity, not unlike Buddhism, Hinduism, Christianity, Islam, etc. Shetaut Neter is referred to as "Neterianism" by members of Sema Institute.

Peace and Blessings!

Sebai MAA

Conversation with God

Question: What is the Temple of Shetaut Neter and are you affiliated with any other Kemetic organizations?

Answer:

The Temple of Shetaut Neter is also known as Sema Institute. It is not affiliated with any other Kemetic studies group, Rosicrucians, Masons, Freemason, Illuminati, or Greek Sororities or Fraternities. Those organizations are latecomers that seek to affiliate themselves with the glory and wisdom of the ancients but those organizations were created in modern times (mostly within the last 400 years) along lines other than Neterian Mystical spirituality such as Christianity, Islam, or Judaism and incorporate some teachings of Ancient Egyptian religion but not the full mysteries of the mystic arts of Ancient Egypt. Shetaut Neter is an indigenously originated religion of Africa and is not affiliated with Arab culture, European culture, Christianity, Judaism or Islam, Bahaism, Hinduism or Buddhism.

While there are some similarities with other Kemetic Spirituality organizations we are not associated with any other organization. Our use of terminology and definitions emanates from our own translations and interpretations of the Neterian teaching, based on our own insights derived from the initiatic tradition.

Peace and Blessings!

Sebai MAA

Mystical Answers to the Important Questions of Life

Question: Real knowledge or just relative knowledge?

Greetings, Muata Ashby

If and when you have the time, I would like your opinion on some information that I have come across on nexus.com.

These are a few excerpts from some authors.

The evidence for ancient atomic warfare by David Hatcher Childress. *Bloodline of the holy grail.* by sir Laurence Gardner. *Realm of the ring lords.* by sir Laurence Gardner

Tell me what you think about their information that they feel that is so true. It saddens me how western academia speaks so highly of logical science and what nature applies by evidence, but yet they write misleading information to the public.

Peace

Answer

Greetings,

As often happens, the movement of darkness is interrupted by flashes of light and this intermittent light is mistaken for full understanding. This is like believing that one understands the universe by examining our planet and extrapolating "logically" what the rest of the universe is. In reality, the problem stems from the logical reasoning that occurs in the absence of higher knowledge. Recall how throughout history science has had to continually revise its findings and continues to do so even today because they have not arrived at absolute truth, but only varying levels of relative truth, the truths that operate in the realm of time and space under given circumstances.

As long as the minds of scientists are caught in the illusion that their experiments of logical thinking can circumscribe reality, so long the absolute and transcendental truth will elude them. Thus, aspirants are trained to work within the physical laws of the physical world, but also to understand and work within the higher laws of the cosmic essence, thereby out-stepping, going beyond the illusion of physical reality and realizing the higher nature of Self.

Peace and Blessings!

Sebai MAA

How to become a true seeker, a spiritual aspirant, and move forward in life, what needs to be done?

Mystical Answers to the Important Questions of Life

Question: What does it Take to Be a Successful Aspirant?

Dear Mr. Ashby,

I just began reading what I believe is the first book in your series "Egyptian Yoga, The Philosophy of Enlightenment." I have been on a journey all of my life that has culminated within the last few years with my reading much material on spirituality. Books on Indian Spirituality, Books by African American authors on spirituality, and anything else that my spirit led me to purchase for what I thought I had been looking for. I was especially interested in information about Kemetic studies. I have believed for quite some time that a thorough study of their teachings was the path that I ultimately needed to follow for enlightenment. I had no basis for believing this other than my "gut" feeling. I read quite a few books on Kemetic studies but found them to be either to theoretical or too simplistic in that it was clear that the author him or herself did not truly have an understanding of the culture and religion of Kemet.

For the last couple of months I have realized that even with the most reading that one could do, I know that reading is not enough. I believe that I also need a teacher or guide myself to truly obtain enlightenment. That is when I found your book and began reading it.

I am writing this e-mail because you may be able to help me in my quest for enlightenment. Maybe you are the answer to my prayers. I am looking for someone (master) who can help guide me on my path to oneness with God.

Maybe you can help.

Thank You,

Answer

Greetings,

Thank you for the kind words and your interest. What does it take to be a Successful Aspirant? The following injunctions from the Ancient Egyptian sages have some insights that give us a place to begin.

FROM: THE STEALE OF ABU:

"Be chief of the mysteries at festivals, know your mouth, come in Peace (peace), enjoy life on earth but do not become attached to it, it is transitory."

FROM THE STEALE OF DJEHUTI-NEFER:

"Consume pure foods and pure thoughts with pure hands, adore celestial

Conversation with God

beings, become associated with wise ones: sages, saints and prophets; make offerings to GOD."

-Ancient Egyptian Proverbs

Many people proceed in their search for higher knowledge with an erroneous concept of what it means to be an authentic spiritual aspirant and also what it takes to succeed on the spiritual path. Many are overwhelmed by the plethora of spiritual traditions and scriptures available now due to modern technology. Others are overwhelmed by their vices and cannot partake fully in any teaching due to their own failings or incapacities, despite their honest desire to grow spiritually. Most people think they are more advanced than they really are and that factor atrophies their ability to receive instruction. Many are deluded due to their overemphasis on intellectual capacity and others by their emphasis on miracles or other misconceptions about the teachings and what is expected of aspirants as well as an authentic spiritual preceptor. They have come to believe that since they have many books or can quote from many scriptures that this makes them automatically more elevated. Sometimes this makes those people arrogant and conceited. They look down on others and this "spiritual" egoism is actually clouding their higher intellectual capacity. You must realize that you have four main aspects of the personality (intellect, emotions, physical body, and will). If you develop any one of these at the exclusion of the others, then your attainment will be lopsided like a four legged table with one leg or two legs or three legs missing. What is such a table worth?

One cannot achieve anything on the spiritual path without humbling to a Spiritual Preceptor. Think about it, you cannot even learn to walk without your mother and you cannot get a trade without a mentor or a college degree without a teacher, etc. You cannot achieve anything in this world without a teacher, so how is it that people have come to believe that they can achieve spiritual enlightenment without an authentic Spiritual Preceptor? Many people, especially in the "new age" circles, have latched on to notions like "its all within me" or "all I need to do is look within" or "God is everywhere." All of these notions are true in a sense but having a realization of their deeper, transcendental reality is a different matter. This is why people can be going around singing "God is everywhere, God is everywhere" and the next minute they may be cursing someone who took a book without their permission or getting upset over the death of a loved one, who are all God; if it is all God. This is called living in a fanciful notion of reality or in short, it is a delusion. A Spiritual Preceptor helps to dispel these and so many other incorrect ideas, allowing the aspirant to really understand the teachings and then blossom into true spiritual enlightenment.

The aspirant must work closely with the preceptor, attending his/her classes and also assisting them in the sacred work they are involved in. This is the highest form of selfless association, service and worship which lead to positive spiritual evolution. Many people want to get books but books cannot answer your questions when the books says something you don't understand, or tell you when you are mistaking what you have read, or guide you as to how to solve problems not directly discussed in the book! The book cannot assist in your application of the teaching in the physical world! The book gives you only a mental/intellectual framework; the application of the teaching, critical

Mystical Answers to the Important Questions of Life

thinking (right reasoning), problem solving, purification of body, mind and soul and personality integration are something else; these require feeling and feeling can only be imparted through a book in a limited fashion. How would you like to go to a hospital for surgery and have a doctor operating on you who never operated before or was never supervised by another doctor who only just read a book on how to do surgery? Would you live in a tall building built by someone who learned from a book or heard lectures about building tall buildings? That is ridiculous, is it not? So too it is ridiculous to think that you can truly understand the three levels of religion and mystical philosophy, which is more difficult and subtle than brain surgery or rocket science (physics and engineering), without competent guidance. Methods like watching video lectures, listening to audio tapes, calling the preceptor via telephone or writing letters are extensions of the book, but are also limited. Ideally you need to be in the same city as the teacher and serve the teachers needs, which in turn serves you as well as humanity. Books are an entry into higher knowledge, but not a total path. For that a living, breathing teacher is essential.

You need to dedicate yourself with honesty and forthrightness, and not seeking to make the teaching in your own image. There are many aspirants who have an erroneous notion as to how a Spiritual Preceptor should look or act. The teachings of Maat provide the guidelines. So if the so-called teacher violates these, then you know what you are dealing with. Conversely, if the teacher meets the criterion set out by the teaching, but does not meet the aspirant's expectations of how a preceptor should look, then the aspirant should adjust their expectations. Sometimes people have elevated themselves in one area but not in others. They may be adequate teachers of what they know, but not adequate to act as preceptors of the whole path. You may learn something from them and then move on, but be careful of what you learn. Until you find an authentic teacher, use the scripture as your guide. You will not have a full understanding but if you are sincere, you will receive sufficient guidance and inspiration until you find your teacher.

Along with this you must of course practice the disciplines of Kemetic (Integral) Yoga daily. Many people have come to believe that simply being in the company of an authentic teacher is enough to enlighten them. While there is an illuminating radiation, this is still not enough. The preceptor (Sebai) cannot enlighten you if you are not ready and/or if you do not apply yourself to the disciplines instructed. You must follow the path and enlighten yourself.

For more on this see the book Initiation Into Egyptian Yoga.

Peace and Blessings!

Sebai MAA

Conversation with God

Question: what is the purpose of being a spiritual teacher?

Greetings. While reflecting in the temple today, the following ideas dawned upon me, please let me know if they are correct.

It is said that everyone's destiny, eventually, is spiritual enlightenment. It is also said that one's karma (self-effort, ari) is what will lead an individual toward this ultimate goal, so you can turn blue in the face spreading the teachings yet if a person is not ready they will not understand. When I put these two thoughts together, I wondered what is the purpose of being a spiritual teacher? And then the following insight dawned upon me.

This is why a true spiritual preceptor does not have extensive advertising of his or her teachings and does not go around looking for students, recognition, etc. (Just like you). And then your comment from last Sunday's lecture crystallized: You said at one point, to those aspirants who turn away from the teachings, "ok go ahead, go out into the world. I and the world are partners; the world is always going to refer customers to me."

So then, does that mean that the world will refer customers to you only when they have bought enough objects, experienced enough frustrations in the world-process (only when they are ready).

I pray that I have understood this profound teaching.

Peace.

Answer

Greetings,

Your assessment is partially correct. Never forget that a spiritual preceptor works for God and not for self. This means that he or she works to promote spiritual enlightenment in society and this is its own reward, doing God's work, to serve humanity. It is God's desire to provide a means for human beings to become enlightened. This means is the spiritual teacher. There can be no learning of the philosophy without an authentic spiritual teacher; just as you cannot even learn how to walk, talk, eat, etc., without a mother, father, or guardian, so too human beings are helpless in spiritual matters without the teacher. A person has the POTENTIAL to become a human, being but that potential will not be realized unless another adult shows the way, just as a spiritual aspirant has the POTENTIAL to attain enlightenment, but that will not happen without someone to show the way.

Mystical Answers to the Important Questions of Life

There are always elevated personalities around, but there can only be a teacher when there is a qualified student, and therefore teachers are there when human beings are ready for the teaching, when they recognize the wise ones in the world around them, hence the saying:

When the student is ready the master appears!

Peace and Blessings!
Sebai MAA

Conversation with God

Question: How to practice Devotion to God?

Greetings Sebai Maa,

I've been trying to get into some type of devotion to God. I am feeling that I need to get into some sort of routine. Could you tell me a little bit more about the Glorious Light Meditation, a) What it accomplishes, b) Is it safe, c) Can I substitute any of the Hekau (I have your *Egyptian Proverbs* book by Dr. Ashby which has other Hekau. d) Can I use some of my own personal affirmations and the like, e) How much freedom do I have to deviate from the original devotional prayers (some of the affirmations don't apply, yet or everyday)...Do you understand where I'm going with this?

Thanks a lot.

Answer

Udja-Greetings,

Think of devotional practice as a bouquet of flowers you are going to offer to God. That requires flowers. They may be of different length, color, fragrance, etc., but, yet there is a constant- they are flowers. You may offer different Hekau, different affirmations, etc., those are the variations. Variations add spice and excitement to the devotional program. However, the basic elements of the practice should remain constant. For example, as far as Hekau (chants), use the daily chant list as prescribed, in the order prescribed, but you may add others to that afterwards. Have one main system of meditation even if you practice others. As for the practice of meditation, keep one regular time and system for practice -keep the routine. Do not mix and match practices from different religious traditions as that will lead to scattered practice and lack of focus and sometimes also confusion.

The *Glorious Light Meditation (GLM) System*, developed by the sages of Ancient Egypt in c. 1,350 B.C.E. (before Buddhism, Hinduism, Taoism, etc.) relates to the practice of certain physical, mental and psychological disciplines that allow a practitioner to discover the Higher Self (the Glorious Light) within. It has certain advantages. It is the oldest known system of formal meditation in human history. It is designed for laypersons and clergy alike. It is safe and effective. It promotes peace and harmony as well as intellectual brightness and enlightenment. It has specific Hekau designed for use with the GLM so that should not be changed. But the Hekau used in devotions, worship, rituals prior to the meditation practice may be adjusted according to your feeling. From a higher perspective, Hekau from different religions should not be used by aspirants since that mixing can produce conflicted feelings, intellectual confusion and or erratic energetic productions (the practice of music, chanting and meditation produces specific forms of psychic energies that work in harmony with other disciplines that are energetically matched to them). However, an aspirant should have competent guidance when engaging any

Mystical Answers to the Important Questions of Life

spiritual practice as the problems arise most often from psychological issues born of egoistic complexes due to lack of mental integration rather than from the meditation practice itself.

Peace and Blessings!

Sebai MAA

Conversation with God

Question: What does it mean when an aspirant sees the Spiritual Preceptor in a dream?

Hi Dr. Ashby,
My friend met you this summer at the conference. She and her husband were present the night that you spoke at the program. She has just recovered from triple bypass surgery. While she was ill in the hospital, she saw you in her dream. She wanted me to tell you that. You made a very strong impression on her. .

Answer

Greetings,

Having visions of those who have caused a strong impression is a normal feature of the human mind, but when a strong impression is left by a spiritual personality, it is an auspicious event. It signals the Higher Self within is pointing towards the need in which the soul wants to direct life. When we have problems and adversities in life it is due to our going in a direction other than what the inner self, the soul, God, wants. This causes stress and disease. We must look towards what is fruitful and glorious as opposed to what is leading to inner disharmony. The bypasses can take care of the immediate problem, but the source of the problem is not with the heart or the blood vessels or even diet. Although these things must be changed, these are only effects of misdirection in life. The true cause of the problem is denying the higher need of the inner self. Disease is the soul's way of letting us know that we must change direction in our lives. The lifestyle as well as the purpose of life must change and this will lead to health, prosperity and inner peace. This and more is explained in our book *Kemetic Diet*. You may convey to her that I remember her and have prayed for her speedy recovery.

Peace and Blessings!

Sebai MAA

Mystical Answers to the Important Questions of Life

Question: How to maintain good association?

Greetings,

I have two questions. Since I will be moving away, I have been thinking of how I will maintain good association. I know that along with spiritual inquiry, serenity, and contentment, good association is one of the most important practices for an aspirant. I feel I could practice the first three, but how can I keep good associations in a place foreign to me with no friends or relatives for support?

Also, how is it that sometimes people who seem very into the mystical teachings and practices seem to stop practicing the disciplines and begin to lead a very worldly, and sometimes even a negative, life? Why does this happen, and is there anything we could do to help?

Thank you.

Answer

Greetings,

As for your first question, you are going away to pursue a righteous goal. This first of all is a great stride in the pursuit of good association because people of a higher caliber (intellectually) will make your acquaintance. You will have an opportunity to exercise your intellect and develop concentration in order to perform your duties. This will in turn help you to practice reflection and meditation on the teachings that will enable you to move further. What you must do is exercise caution in selecting those whom you associate within the new group that you will meet, taking care to interact with those who are sincere and honest while steering away from those who are selfish and greedy. Having intellectual capacity does not automatically make one a righteous personality. Many con artists and unethical business and political personalities have high intellectual capacities and even greater will to concentrate on unrighteous actions. Therefore, seek out those who display Maatian virtues (truthfulness, sincerity, honesty, selflessness, continence, self-control, temperance, moderation, spiritual consciousness, etc.) even if they have not practiced advanced spirituality (Sema {Yoga}). The next thing you can do is start your own study group. It need not be anything fancy, just open your own practice to others. You will be very busy with your studies however, you should endeavor to never cease in your daily practice of yoga exercise, meditation and study of the teachings – keeping up with the teachings will be facilitated if you get the taped lectures. This is your direct access to good association. If you are able, seek out spiritual centers in your area or authentic teachers in your area to practice with. Further, if you do your daily practices in the morning, place a notice on the student board letting others know who you are and what you are doing. Those interested will call and join you and you will be able to create extended good association. You may eventually want to lead a class and even discussions on the teachings. Thus, you will create your own good association wherever you may be now that you have a firm foundation to build on.

As to your second question, the reason why spiritual aspirants are admonished to keep a daily spiritual schedule that is regular and unbroken and to keep good association is so that they may be able to maintain a distance from the world. It is very difficult especially for young (in age) aspirants, to practice the teachings, because the impetus and vitality of youth is to experience life and satisfy self with great intensity. This means that the world is a great pressure in the form of media, peers, pent up unconscious desires, etc. What often happens is that a period of intense interest and practice will lead to some advancement but the deep-rooted unconscious impressions of worldliness still remain. If these are not dealt with through the spiritual practice, they emerge and distract the aspirant and draw them back into the world. Often when this happens, the worldly experience is more intense (in positives and negatives) than the worldliness before the yoga practice. This is because having elevated the mind and glimpsed the higher, an aspirant in falling seeks to grasp on to that higher feeling in the world. Being unable to do so, there will be greater entanglement and frustration with the world. This may be seen as a setback, however, it is still part of their spiritual path. They will eventually learn from the world the same lesson they already learned from the yoga class and eventually they will be drawn back to the spiritual practice. In the mean time, such aspirants are to be prayed for and presented with the spiritual ideal by the example of others such as yourself and attending ongoing spiritual programs. People will come and go until they are firmly rooted in the Self within. Then they will never again fall back down to the world. This is the stage in which enlightenment is assured and there is no turning back or falling back. Until that point is reached, the practice of the daily spiritual disciplines (study wisdom teachings, offer devotional offerings, practice ethical living, practice meditation) should not cease. In fact, the perfection of spiritual practice is to make every aspect of your entire life a spiritual practice (walking down the street and practicing spiritual reflection, studying and practicing spiritual reflection, eating and practicing spiritual reflection, talking and practicing spiritual reflection, etc.). You should learn to practice yoga at all times, no matter what you are doing and wherever you may be. In this manner, the sprouting unconscious impressions of the mind are continuously cleansed and prevented from leading the mind into worldly entanglements and ignorance, no matter what the internal state of mind (depression, elation, desire, greed, lust, hatred, satisfaction, contentment, righteousness-unrighteousness, uplifted-degraded, etc.) or external conditions may be (good association available or not, adversity or prosperity).

Indeed, the struggle of an aspirant is often referred to in the spiritual scriptures as a battle. In Ancient Egypt, Heru fought Set; in Christianity, Jesus fought the Devil; in Hinduism, Krishna fought Kamsa, and Rama fought Ravana, etc. It is a battle between good and evil, righteousness and unrighteousness, that is waged in the heart of every individual. It is ultimately a battle between ignorance and enlightenment. The only way to defeat the ego and stop it from rearing its head is to attain enlightenment, to know oneself, to discover one's identity beyond the ego personality. This is accomplished through the practice of the teachings: good association, practice of righteousness, meditation, prayer, chanting, exercise, etc., until enlightenment is fully discovered. Until then there should

Mystical Answers to the Important Questions of Life

be ceaseless, regular and relentless practice of the spiritual disciplines. This is the way to keep the ego in its place (prevent falls and setbacks) and to insure the final victory of the Higher Self. The main obstacles to spiritual enlightenment are misunderstanding the teachings, irregularity in practice, distractions, not attending class faithfully. Success may be measured in direct proportion to the level of practice mentioned above. Intermittent practice (such as people who attend class every once in a while) yields poor results in a person's ability to control the ego and transcend it to attain enlightenment; they are still caught in the world. Moderate practice yields moderate results. A person here may have some successes but also some downfalls as well. Intense practice yields advanced results sooner. Intense practitioners are able to control the ego even before attaining enlightenment and the chances of a fall are minimized. They understand the importance of the teachings above all other worldly considerations, practice the teachings given by their teacher and follow the teaching closely and attain enlightenment in one lifetime!

May Maat be your constant ally in the battle of life!

Peace and Blessings!

Sebai MAA

Conversation with God

Question: Can I change the chants I practice daily?

Dear Dr. Muata Abhaya Ashby

I have read all the main books in the Egyptian Yoga series and I am applying the three steps of listening, reflecting, and meditating. I have chosen Asar theology for my path. I have been doing the daily chants for two years now. Can I substitute the Journey to the Duat meditation presented in Resurrecting Osiris in place of the Daily Chants. It was said in Goddess path that Ushet Rekhat could be done instead of Daily Chants, but can this be done for the former ritual?

Peace

Answer

Greetings,

Now that you have invested 2 years in effort, you should continue the same way, using the daily chants as your main discipline. The others may be added but should not take the place of the main discipline. If you have discovered some resonance with the other techniques that is OK, so those may be added to your overall practice. For example, you may practice them directly after the main regular discipline. In this way the depth and structure and foundation you have created will be a strong foundation for your next level of practice.

Peace and Blessings!

Sebai MAA

Mystical Answers to the Important Questions of Life

Questions: Is the Spiritual Battle Between Differentiated and Undifferentiated Consciousness?

Udja,

it has been written that the undifferentiated state of consciousness is Heru. In the myth, Heru battles Set to regain the throne.

Query:

Our job then is to reach the state where undifferentiated consciousness guides us at all times correct? And this is achieved by the integrated practice of the teachings with deep meditation correct?

If this is so, then, the battle is actually a battle between differentiated and undifferentiated consciousness being in control.

Answer

Your thought process does follow a generally logical course but it is not fully grounded in a logical foundation. The foundation or starting point influences the thought process and leads to certain conclusions so it is important to be properly founded. Also, logic can lead to error if it is not based on all the possible information and just on available information (i.e. the truth). It can be based on reality but reality is not necessarily true, but only real in a relative (conditional circumstance). The foundation would be that while undifferentiated consciousness may be seen as an opposite to differentiated consciousness that view is from the perspective of the differentiated mind but not from spirit. Think in terms of the following diagram

Conscious ➤ differentiated soul ⬌ undifferentiated ◀ spirit

From the perspective of the spirit anything other than spirit is illusorily differentiated but not in actuality. From the perspective of the soul the undifferentiated and spirit look lie another or the other. Yet that viewpoint is illusory. The point is that the differentiation occurs from the perspective of conscious soul and its battle is with the other than itself. Undifferentiated consciousness may seem as part of that other but it is actually neutral. Thus the fight is within the differentiated and itself. Heru is that part that is real, the spirit, undifferentiated or not. Heru is enlightened soul and ego is personality, Set. Both exist as differentiated aspects. When mind is undifferentiated both Heru and Set dissolve.

Conversation with God

Query:

Is this so? I mean is my understanding correct?

It has been written that the longer one experiences the undifferentiated state of consciousness, the more the mind reorganizes and begins placing that state in rulership over the self replacing the ego.

Answer

Yes in a manner of speaking, correct.

Query:

Is my understanding of the writing correct?

If so, does this mean, that the road to Nehast actually begins to be experienced when Heru COMPLETELY takes over the throne of Egypt?

Answer

Enlightenment occurs in degrees, so with each battle won by Heru there is more experience of expansion, more control, more peace, more transcendence, until one day the threshold is reached, the dawning comes, the caterpillar becomes the butterfly, the tadpole becomes the frog, the larva becomes the fly, graduation day comes, etc., well you get the picture!

Peace and Blessings!

Sebai MAA

Mystical Answers to the Important Questions of Life

Question: could you please provide insight into the science of chanting?

Greetings,

Today, through reading and listening to Sebai Maa, I came to the realization of not only the importance of chanting, but also the meditating of the meaning of the chant while chanting. For example, while chanting Om Asar Aset Heru, I am thinking, feeling and seeing myself moving or transforming from the Physical to the Astral to the Causal and then to the Absolute; these are the teachings I believe I am getting from you Sebai Maa, please guide me if I am wrong.

What initiated this communication is that ever since I was introduced to Sebai Maa's teachings, I felt that there were so many different paths that if I focus on Om Asar Aset Heru, everything else would fall into place. When I read *Serpent Power* book, it confirmed the embedding of this chant within my subconscious mind. But for some reason, when I woke up this morning I was subconsciously chanting *Om Amun Ra Ptah*. I know that we are working within the spiritual realm and wherever or however the Om Amun Ra Ptah came to me is good and welcomed. Please, I beg of you, let me know if I am wrong. I believe within the guidance of this synchronizing I can become closer to being One with the Father.

Peace....

Answer

Greetings,

Your questions are most welcome.

The science of chanting was instituted by the sages to assist the aspirant in concentrating the mind and infusing it with cleansing vibrations that will lead them towards a spiritual realization. All words of power given by the sages of all authentic traditions can be effective if the aspirant is honest, pure and if the effort is sustained over time and augmented with wisdom- insight into the teaching. This means that the words of power are in reality reflections of the higher truth that can be realized if they are chanted long enough and if the philosophy behind them and the overall teaching is correctly understood. After a while of chanting, the vibrations create new "grooves" in the mind, and it becomes spontaneous. There is energy built up with it and this energy is the redirected Life Force, sublimated towards the Divine Self. At this level, there is spontaneous higher vibration and this cleanses the negative "*ariu*" (karmic deeds) of the past. There is no need to suppress a righteous chant, just as there is no need to suppress a righteous thought. All positive vibrations have their effect and are helpful towards the spiritual evolution. However, while it is all right to use different chants at different times

Conversation with God

and to sing divine songs, there should be one main chant for the overall spiritual discipline and this should not be changed. Otherwise, if you changed chants frequently, it would be like digging a deep hole to reach the center of the world (God), only to stop digging that hole and begin another, before you reached the center. Proceeding this way, you will never reach the center, because each time you would get close, you would be abandoning that hole and starting over anew. Similarly, changing your main chant frequently will create mental distraction each time, and will not allow you to build up the concentration and one pointed focus that is necessary to penetrate and transcend the mind/thoughts, to experience your essential nature. In the same way, one may also drink from the waters of other teachers and be nourished, but there should be one main teacher to guide one on the path. Otherwise, because different teachers have different methods of teaching and teachers respond to aspirant's questions about the practical world and applying the teachings in practical day-to-day life slightly differently, due to the different levels of aspirants, there is bound to be confusion and waste of time, leading to frustration and discontent with the teaching. Different teachers or spiritual philosophies can have some nuances of difference or concentrations in particular areas and still have the same ultimate goal. Likewise, there should be one path even though all authentic paths lead to the same ultimate reality. An aspirant should decide which path and teacher are most in harmony with their sensibility, and then follow that path. Read the book *Initiation Into Egyptian Yoga* for more details.

Peace and Blessings!

Sebai MAA

Mystical Answers to the Important Questions of Life

Question: How can I receive a spiritual name?

Hotep Sebai Maa,

I feel very privileged to have you respond to me personally. I have been closely studying the books you have authored throughout this entire year, and you deserve great respect. The divine Kemetic energies you have expressed are a powerful link for us as a Great People. One thing that I feel deeply about is that the potential of every Black Leader and Spiritual Master is in great need, in so far as, more links between our Black leaders Really needs to be made. *What exactly is required for one in my position to receive a spiritual name?*

Answer

Greetings,

It is true that there are a few individuals espousing the Kemetic spiritual teachings but just as in ancient times, there are schools which promote the teachings from different angles. A spiritual aspirant needs to understand that just as people can look up in the sky from different countries and see the same sun, so too spiritual philosophies can have some nuances of difference or concentrations in particular areas and still have the same ultimate goal. With this view, it is possible to understand that the spiritual teachings are interconnected and that there is in reality no conflict in the higher perspective.

If it is divinely ordained, these groups may physically come together in the future in order to promote a more united front, but this would be for the benefit of society, because if they are genuinely working towards the dissemination of the teachings and the promotion of spiritual enlightenment, they are already working together, because they are indeed working towards the same goal already.

In our tradition we emphasize the monastic and mystical aspects of the teachings for individual spiritual enlightenment, while others emphasize traditions, others rituals and still others history or religious practice. An aspirant should learn to choose the right denomination for himself/herself. This process can be conducted through counseling by a qualified spiritual preceptor, and by properly guided study and reflection upon the true purpose of religion. As stated earlier, the initiation process is most effective when it is performed by an authentic spiritual preceptor. This establishes a subtle connection between the student and the teacher and the teaching, and it establishes a psychological impetus which helps the aspirant develop devotional feeling towards the Divine, the teaching and the preceptor. This devotional feeling allows the faculty of understanding to blossom. The spiritual name is formally given at the initiation ceremony by the spiritual preceptor to those aspirants who have demonstrated a serious inclination towards the teachings.

Peace and Blessings!
Sebai MAA

Conversation with God

Question: can I get several names and initiations?

Peace Sebai Maa,

This is a follow up to the previous question. I agree with you totally about our Kemetic Schools and Degrees coming from different angles, but having the same goals. I recognize that Egyptians had many names, even the Neteru. So by me receiving different spiritual names from different degrees, it will help me to overstand my True Nature. I was already given one spiritual name: _____, and with another one, perhaps I can learn more.

Peace

Answer

Greetings,

Although you are well intentioned, be careful not to make the mistake that some aspirants make, like sick people who sometimes figure, "well if one pill is good, several should be better."

In reality, all it takes is one authentic path, one authentic teacher and one righteous aspirant. Otherwise, there is a chance of confusion and distraction, which will impair the ability to progress. So stay with one path - at least one at a time, until you discover the path with which you really resonate. This does not mean you cannot read the writings of other teachers, but initiation and the initiatic process itself means that you are following one path, teacher and teaching. This one-pointedness leads to spiritual wisdom and realization.

May god bless you and illumine your path.

Peace and Blessings!

Sebai MAA

Mystical Answers to the Important Questions of Life

Question: Am I practicing the Postures Correctly?

Greetings Dr. Ashby

I've been practicing the movement of the gods and goddess postures and I had a question. When I'm doing the headstand pose, everything is feeling alright. There is no strain or pressure on my neck, but when I lay down on my back to let the blood recirculate to the rest of my body, I feel a pressure in my neck. I wonder if I'm doing it wrong or is this natural until the body gets used to the position.

Thank you

Answer

Greetings,

As for your question about the postures, the strain you feel in your neck area when you are laying down could be several things. It is possible that your positioning is incorrect, which is why the postures should be learned under the guidance of certified teachers. In addition, you should check with your health care practitioner about this, or perhaps even a chiropractor to see if you have any spinal problems. This is generally advised before beginning one's practice of the postures, because oftentimes persons may have degenerative spinal conditions that manifest when the spine is now bent and stressed in ways it is not used to, and which can aggravate a spinal injury or degenerative condition that has been dormant. In addition to the neck discomfort possibly being due to incorrect practice of the posture or a spinal problem, it could also be due to muscle strain, once again because of the use of muscles that you have not used previously in this manner, and therefore they are not developed and capable of handling the movements of this posture or your weight.

One needs to practice the postures in accordance with the physical capacity of the physical body, allowing the body to adapt, adjust and develop to the postures gradually, over a period of time, without strain and without pain which may signal injury. The neck area is an especially delicate area, and you need to be extra cautious. So, for example, before attempting the headstand posture, you can position yourself in the posture, up until the point where you would raise your legs up into the air, and remain there only for a short time initially, but lengthening the time gradually, so as to allow the muscles in the neck area to adapt to this posture. After a period of time of practicing this, you can then raise the legs up off the floor, but keeping the knees bent which puts less stress on the neck; if you feel neck strain, continue to practice without raising your legs up for a longer period of time. Once you are able to remain with your legs up, but knees bent, without feeling neck discomfort, then you can try to straighten the legs. Again, practice for a short period of time initially, and go back to the previous practices if you feel any strain on your neck.

So you should plan to receive instruction by a qualified teacher - they are listed on the web site or you may plan to attend a conference. And you should also consult a chiropractor and or your health care practitioner.

Peace and Blessings!

Sebai MAA

Mystical Answers to the Important Questions of Life

Question: How does the discipline of the postures operate on the physical plane?

Greetings Dr. Ashby

If the soul doesn't exist in the human body but on higher levels of being, how does it operate on the physical plane? When we tap into the soul level of our being, we are actually elevating ourselves to higher levels of existence or consciousness? I think it was in the book *Initiation Into Egyptian Yoga* that you said that the spirit gets sent through the soul to the astral body to the physical body. Could you explain this further please?

Answer

Greetings,

This is a detailed subject that requires more explanation than is possible in this short missive since it involves many aspects of study and spiritual practice that are needed to render your personality pure and your intellect subtle so that you may understand the answer. However, in brief, the Spirit operates through various layers of grosser energies. One of these levels is the soul, another the astral body, yet another the physical body. The soul is your individual consciousness, a piece of Spirit, as it were, and it sustains your personality by lending it consciousness and life force energy. The consciousness sustains the individual human capacity for awareness (which may be enlightened or ignorant). The life force sustains the capacity of the personality to live and move in time and space, i.e. sustain a relative existence.

The soul interacts with the astral body and this astral body in turn interacts with the subtle nervous system (*Sefech Ba Ra*) -seven life force energy centers- and the subtle nervous system interacts with the physical nerves and these energize the brain and allow it to perceive perceptions of the physical body and impel its movements.

For more details on this subject you need to enter into the deeper study and practice as suggested in the *Initiation Into Egyptian Yoga* book - find a qualified Spiritual Preceptor and receive teachings from that person as you practice privately also and not only will you discover the deeper meaning of what has been explained here, but also you will experience it and this is the higher form of understanding - beyond all intellectual explanations and limited missives.

Peace and Blessings!

Sebai MAA

Conversation with God

Question: Should I leave my family and go live closer to the spiritual teacher?

Greeting Sebai Maa and Seba Dja,

I have been studying the teachings for a year and a half now. The main thing that has sunk into my heart is that the teacher is of the utmost importance. I am serious about moving to the support center to be taught and to help run the center. I have to wait six months to a year to get my ID situation resolved because I moved here from out of the country, and things haven't gotten worked out since then. I have a three year old daughter and my mate has agreed to take on full responsibility of the child. The only thing is that she doesn't make enough money to take care of her by herself and I wanted to know if I did qualify to move to the yoga center would there be any way if I could earn any income with the sole purpose of sending it back home for the support of my daughter. I have given up all other aspirations except for enlightenment. Could you please let me know at your earliest convenience where I stand on this issue?

ankh, udja, senab

        Sincerely

Answer

Greetings and Blessings,

I was pleased to see your letter and also encouraged by your desire to continue studying the teachings. I am also pleased to see you understand the importance and necessity of a teacher. And now I tell you that the greatest teacher is useless to the unqualified aspirant since they cannot understand the advice given to them or at least trust in it and follow it. Even if they do understand there are obstacles to their acting on it, obstacles of their own making. Therefore, read the following and then search yourself, reflect inwardly and see if you have faith in yourself and the teaching and in me. For if you think you are ready to make an important move like leaving your family to move here, then you should be capable of following instructions that will lead you to success.

Over the years I have had other aspirants contact me in the same manner and with the same desire, to devote themselves to the teaching and perhaps even move to the center. Some are truly sincere while others are seeking to escape their situations. However, up to this time I have not sanctioned anyone to move to the center. There are several reasons for this.

Firstly, aspirants may move to be closer to the center in order to volunteer their service to increase the capacity of the center, as they attend classes, but they will need to take care of their own expenses and accommodations since the center cannot support that yet.

Mystical Answers to the Important Questions of Life

Therefore, I suggest that you contact other aspirants with your same interest and see how it may be possible to cooperate with them by pooling resources and effort to develop conditions that will be conducive to having a center that can sustain fulltime spiritual workers. Other groups have developed in that way and in time we may also. An example of this which I have spoken of previously is the case of the Sikh community. People who came to the USA with nothing literally and worked in the city, pooled their resources and purchased land and businesses to hire and support each other. If this were done there would be a financial basis not only to support the center but a community based on Neterian principles of life. This would be a powerful facility to study and disseminate the teachings and to serve the cause of uplifting the culture.

In any case, spiritual evolution can occur with or without a center, provided the aspirant is willing to work harder to overcome the pressures of the world and in applying him/her self to the teachings and that there is contact with the teacher.

Nevertheless, some aspirants have moved here to be close by and attend classes in person. They found it difficult to make ends meet and practice the teachings and became distracted.

Speaking generally, before I could accept anyone as a candidate for residency near the center and to work at the center they would have to be qualified aspirants. This means that family responsibilities, financial issues, legal problems, inability to hold a job or irresponsibility on the job, mental disease or defect, etc., disqualify an aspirant because these issues become a burden by distracting and stressing the spiritual work. These issues must be satisfactorily handled. One of the main reasons why it is enjoined for aspirants not to have children is that childbearing can cause a burden in life especially where there is financial insufficiency. Aspirants should not become overburdened with mortgages, bills, properties or anything that will cause them to be constantly needing to pay attention to worldly endeavors they cannot afford. In a sustainable community, there is a place for people who are dealing with serious issues but we do not yet have a sustainable community and what we need now are intelligent, hard-working and devoted people who are free of major unresolved entanglements to support and help the teaching grow.

Giving up worldly aspirations for spiritual pursuits is enjoined by the teachings but so too is taking care of responsibility and family. If you have developed worldly entanglements, they need to be resolved adequately so they will not be a burden in the mind. This means righteously. In your case if you could properly support your family and if they were to be cared for properly while you were away this could be an acceptable action. However, most aspirants are not financially free and this limitation is also by divine dispensation. Your situation, you have created it, and it is up to you to resolve it but a child cannot be raised at a distance. If you have a partner and or child, they were acquired by your desire and now you must resolve that desire and handle its consequences. Then you will be true material for spiritual transformation.

Do not feel you are in an especially burdened situation however. Even single and unattached aspirants have developed attachments and entanglements they must resolve.

Conversation with God

Unattached aspirants often think they are ahead in the path but they only have different attachments. These prevent them from following the path fully also. They are attached to the world but in a different way. This makes their movement slower. With your financial situation the dissemination and practice of the teaching is more challenging but not impossible especially if there is cooperation and coordination of our efforts.

Thus, another way for you to proceed might be to work while supporting your family and at the same time deepening your studies until one day you will have no burdens or fewer burdens and be completely free to follow the path that God will lay out for you. Resolve that from this day on you will take on no more entanglements and that you will face the ones you have. Take care of the practical realities by working any job you can get while working to improve your income capacity, perhaps by getting a technical school degree; work as a mechanic, appliance repairman, air conditioning repairman, deliveries, etc. Acquire a trade you can work at anywhere. Go where the work is if need be. Use the resources of social services while necessary but do not rely on these. If possible allow your partner to work also; do not overburden yourself and live within your means.

Are you up for that challenge? It is difficult indeed but the rewards are worth it; peace with the world and enlightenment of the spirit. This is a path that will lead you to a place where you would be able to move more freely. Resolve your immigrant status, provide for your family, and continue your studies and work to make the situation of your spiritual aspiration come true. Day by day trust in my words and in the Divine; place yourself in her hands and accept your situation as it is but working to improve it, while meditating daily, studying daily, listening to the teachings and reading them daily, teach them to your family and your daughter, who came to you not by chance but to receive the glory of the teaching through you. While it is a harder path, this is what you have chosen and need at this time. In teaching them you will learn the teaching in a more qualitative manner. Attend our conferences. Join the services online. Have them join you or at least your daughter partake with you. Thereby allow your dispassion for the world and desire for the teaching to develop in time into a blazing fire, the Sekhmit fire that destroys all ignorance and opens the doors of supreme Nehast (awakening).

I will know you are ready when you have followed these instructions. We need to teach our families, love them and care for them as the Goddess teaches, sustains and loves us. In doing so we elevate them and ourselves and there is no greater social duty than this and it is the means by which the teaching is transmitted from generation to generation. This is also the essence of Maat Philosophy, the underpinning of Shetaut Neter. With this as the foundation we open up the mystic doors of inner transformation and spiritual awakening for others but mostly for ourselves. Thus, by serving others we lead ourselves to enlightenment; so do not pass up your opportunity, for if you do not take advantage of it, what you need to learn will not be learned and you will not progress to the next level of instruction.

Peace and Blessings!

Sebai MAA

Mystical Answers to the Important Questions of Life

Question: What is too much talking?

Dear Seba Maa,
Greetings!

It is my understanding that excessive talking is not good for the mind or the soul. It helps to maintain and create more desires. It is my understanding that one of the purposes behind not talking too much is to create an internal environment that will not allow new worldly thoughts to become planted in the subconscious that will materialize again in the future.

If my understanding is correct, how do you balance this with speaking to people whose only reality is the world? I am finding that people want to go on and on about things that are only creating agitation in their minds. "I don't know what I want to do with my life," "I wish I had more money," "my spouse gets on my nerves," "I want new furniture," " How come my boss doesn't like me." I understand how these conversations keep one tied to the world. I also understand how this creates agitation in the mind. I do not want to identify with the so-called reality of the world. I want to permanently identify with the "Spirit." I have had to fight the urge to be frustrated with people who want to engage in these types of conversation because it is not directed towards my goal.
Of course I must be in control of my thoughts and actions. Maybe these are my tests. Yet I still have to live in the world and my family and loved ones must be dealt with. This has been difficult as of late because many times I do not want to talk at all. Many times I am concentrating on seeing everything as the primeval ocean. This effort towards one pointed concentration on my goal takes a lot of work as you know. It is difficult enough not knowing if you are practicing the teachings correctly in the first place. Jesus was able to live in the world but not be of the world. I can tell he was a sage. I know it takes much work to get to that level, but are there any technique(s) that I can utilize that will help me engage in conversation while keeping my thoughts on a higher level? Or is this simply a matter of just keeping in mind that the "Self" is my master at all times and that the ego must be subordinate to it and just keep on practicing the teachings?

Thank you for reading.

Peace!

Answer

Greetings,

The balance is sought by following the injunctions of the teachings. Avoid argument and confusion and worldly company when possible, but in the course of life this is not always possible. Further, it would not be beneficial to be completely removed from the challenges of life since these interactions provide opportunities for aspirants to test their application of the teachings. When in the company of worldly people, first do not indulge

Conversation with God

in their worldliness but rather simply acknowledge them. If they ask for advice or ask why you seem distant or unaffected tell them it is because of the philosophy you are studying that has given you insight into the way of life that enjoins balance, detachment, peace and introspection. At that point they will: either leave you alone and look at you strangely or they may want to know more. In that latter case, introduce them to the books. In any case be patient for the interaction will pass in a short time and you will be on your way.

Being in the world and not of the world consists in a mental shift and not a necessarily physical separation. However, a disciplinary and temporary separation from the world is enjoined to study and practice the teaching in peace, without distractions, and then one may return to the world as needed to fulfill ones duties. Do not strain to maintain the awareness of Self while you are in worldly situations. Rather intensify your practice while doing the disciplines in private and this will automatically have an increasing residual effect when you return to the world. It took thousands of years for you to develop your personality failings and virtues. Do not expect to change overnight but have faith, patience and continue to work on yourself. In time you will see changes that will eventually become major transformations. Forgive yourself as you would a sick person who has done or said something negative due to the sickness and delirium and KNOW that the Divine Self is with you on the journey to Enlightenment, to sanity and health. Do not pressure yourself with lofty goals of sagehood. Rather, continue practicing the teachings but in balance, accepting the teaching and accepting the responsibilities and trials you must face in the world. See them as a help and not a hindrance to your evolution. See the worldly as well as the wise people in your world as manifestations of the Divine, some acting out of ignorance and some out of knowledge, but all seeking to find their way, as you are; but also they are both teachers, the worldly show you the folly of egoism and the wise show you the glory of spiritual evolution. Let them both be your inspiration to practice the disciplines more diligently. Thus love that same Divine Self within yourself and extend that love to others, who also carry that same Divine Self within them even if they do not know it. This is the golden road, the RASTAU path that leads to the supreme abode of peace and enlightenment.

Peace and Blessings!
Sebai MAA

Mystical Answers to the Important Questions of Life

Question: Why have I become agitated since I started practicing the teachings?

Greetings:

    I would like some advice please. Actually I am in need of some advice. I have now been practicing the teachings to the best of my ability and understanding for about 17 months. Before I started practicing I was really laid back. I never let anyone see me get upset about anything and I showed very little emotion. In fact I did not think that anything really bothered me at all. At the time I thought that I was a person who did not let things bother me. I thought that people who could not control their emotions were weak, and I thought that things really had no affect on me. Since I have been practicing the teachings, while I have attempted to control my thoughts and actions, and master my emotions, the exact opposite has happened. I have begun to take things personally, people get on my nerves (especially my family), I blow up and get angry quickly and it seems like I am becoming the person who I did not like previously. Even after meditation, it seems like it takes very little to set me off. This happens about once a week and I wind up having a foul disposition. This disposition lasts 2-4 days sometimes. I don't stop my Shedy but I do sometimes forget to practice control. My wife has even commented that ever since I have been studying I have become more "sensitive" to things and irritable, which makes me get upset which was not the case previously.

    I don't get it. It is my understanding that progress in the teaching is measured in one's ability to detach from the world and not be affected by it. It seems like I am becoming more affected by it. The only thing I can think of is that my practice and understanding of the teaching must be off because the opposite is happening to me.

    Any advice? I do the breathing exercises, prayer, chanting, Tjef Neteru exercises and Meditate in the mornings and do the same except for the exercises 3-4 times a week during the evenings. I really would like some advice.

Peace

Answer

Greetings,

Take heart, what you are describing is a natural stage on the spiritual path. Actually it is a sign that you are practicing the teachings and indeed making progress. How is this possible? Consider that when a person turns to a healthy vegetarian diet after consuming meat, there is a cleansing reaction. The good food causes a cleansing effect and the person appears to get sick from the good food. In reality, a cleansing process is going on because the good food is pushing out the poisons ingested previously. That person may have appeared to be healthy but internally there were many toxins in the body. This is the detoxification process. For the Ka and Ba (mind and soul) there is also a cleaning process that must occur. You are now only learning that your supposed previous peace and calm was like a person who cleans house by sweeping dust under the rug instead of picking it up and throwing it out of the house; in other words, you were not facing issues but rather ignoring them. You are also learning that your idea of being more advanced in the teachings and of having mastered some lower levels was a misconception, an illusion. It is good for you to realize this. And yes, in the short term, you will become more sensitive and because you are in a householder environment, your challenge is more difficult than someone living alone or in a temple.

Family relations are more intense because the involvement with family members is very complex and more intimate than with strangers or on the job or in the temple. Nevertheless, as you continue to practice the teaching, these complexes will be resolved and transcended. Yet consider that your progress will be faster than the person living alone because your failings will be exposed more efficiently by your family, and you no longer have the illusions about the world to fall back on that most people have (since you are a follower of the teaching). You cannot just "kiss and make up" because you know the illusoriness of life. Further, realize that 17 months is a short time and hearing the teaching and interacting with the teacher is more powerful than reading books alone or practicing the teaching on your own. Books and self-taught practices are prone to error and you may be experiencing the strong effect of attending classes, which you were not exposed to before. What you are going through is called "personality integration." It is the necessary process whereby you are challenged, then you must reflect and come to terms with your experiences. Do not wonder why, simply rest assured that it is necessary and that the outcome will be for your ultimate benefit. The Divine Self has made things this way for a reason; have faith.

However, do not keep yourself in a pressure cooker all the time; relax from the teachings as it were. Take your family to a positive movie, eat with them (vegetarian food). Show them you care, but internally work to care with the higher vision, with less sentimentality. Take breaks also by going on retreats so that you may reflect and meditate on the teaching, thereby you can have true recreation and bolster your personality's strength to handle the world. Constant pressure is not necessary or advised to promote enlightenment. The personality needs time to make sense of the experiences and how to integrate them into the new understanding of life; this goes for the stresses as well as the pleasures. It often leads to an imbalanced personality and this is counterproductive, causing strife, anger etc., especially because the feeling comes in that you have failed in attaining the level you thought you were at, etc. Leave these thoughts behind.

Yet there needs to be a balance in life even for the advanced aspirants. Seek this balance by having faith and trust in these words. Next accept the negative that seems to be coming forth from the deeper levels of the personality and allow it to be cleansed. Do not own it, but simply marvel at the complexes and thank goddess Maat for assisting you to see them because they would have been obstacles to enlightenment had they remained hidden. Even when an episode of anger or irritability occurs, remember these words and they will help you to return to calm. If need be, remove yourself from the situation until you are calm and then return. Go to your meditation area, utter some chants, read some of the text or read this letter again and again and you will find solace and peace. Realize that the negative actions are born of the egoistic impressions of the mind due to previous

Mystical Answers to the Important Questions of Life

ignorance. Offer those actions to the Divine just as you should offer the positive actions as well. Try to follow Maat, but do not own the outcomes of your actions or their consequences. Let the goddess handle those. You work to purify yourself and the rest will come together in time. Continue the daily disciplines and judge your progress by how fast you return to normalcy and balance, how fast you return to self-control. If the negative disposition now lasts 2-4 days sometimes, see if it goes to 1-3 days, then to 1 day, then to ½ day, then to hours and even minutes. This is mastery of the feelings and emotions. In this mastery they are controlled, made slaves and are no longer masters over you, controlling your personality, making you angry against your will, etc.

Soon you will develop deeper sensitivity and you will know when anger is entering the mind and you will be able to stop it there before it comes to the surface, and if you can control it before it expresses you will have a better chance to overcome it and the trouble that its consequences produce in your environment. In any case, seek to follow Maat. Maat says, "I have not allowed myself to become angry without cause." Sometimes there is just cause for anger and sometimes it is necessary even for sages to show anger. If a child is in some imminent danger, it is appropriate to angrily stop her from injuring herself, or if some injustice is done, it may be appropriate to show anger to convey the emotional content needed to reach and impress the person perpetrating the injustice or others who can help stop that person from hurting others. But in sages these emotions are controlled and harnessed. Sages do not internally really become angry or hate anything even if they appear to be. The emotions do not control the sages. Examine the cause of your anger. If it is justified (needed to achieve a goal), show it to the extent it assists to get the point across. If it is not justified, proceed as outlined above.

Remember that to reach the sagehood level, the sages had to practice control as you are today. The fire of worldly situations is the forge that molds sages, but in order for this process to work there must be a blacksmith to shape the aspirant; this is the teacher. The soul is the iron to be shaped, the teaching is the anvil upon which the soul is worked by the sage and the fire of life are the worldly situations. However, if the fire is too hot (too much stress all the time) the metal melts away. If it is too cold (not enough challenges) there is no way to bend the metal. The metal cannot shape itself on its own by studying books or imagining things. So there must be challenge and stress but this is to be managed in doses and not constant. The teacher must help the student to apply the right amount of pressure, striking with the hammer at the right times and placing the iron in the fire or water at the right times. An aspirant must learn to relax and accept the imperfections of the personality even while working towards perfection in a balanced manner. This is the path of Ari m Hetep/Hotep ("actions in peace" -Yoga of right actions). You can see how magnanimous and advanced this philosophy is and how its deeper insights cannot come from only reading books on Maat or simplistic ideals such as do good and be good or be balanced. Aspirants grow when they go through the process of life, being led by the authentic teacher and an authentic teaching.

Peace and Blessings!
Sebai MAA

Conversation with God

Question: How to raise the Serpent Power?

Peace and blessings upon you. I'm interested in raising the kundalini. I've tried standing pose and the qigong beginning stance, but what I've yet to do is dive deep in the practice because I've not an active guide, e.g. a reader or logos of method inspired through light or realization. This I seek justly. When I attempt to bury the stance to enhance my dance of light, my root chakra or sphincter shuts and the whisper felt below grows silent. I ask of you, kind words of advice, be it books, organizations, arts, what you feel inspired to emit to me.

From my deepest desire,

Answer

Greetings,

Thank you for your inquiry. The ancient Egyptian discipline of Arat Sekhem (Serpent Power) is for cultivating the inner Life Force so that it becomes dynamic enough to push consciousness from the lower levels (waking, dream and unconscious states of mind) to transcend time and space and the universe, unite the lower self with cosmic consciousness, the Higher Self, the Divine. The discipline involves a specific philosophy and psychological discipline as well as vegetarian diet for cleansing the body, mind and the main spiritual energy centers which we call *Sefech Ba Ra* – "seven spheres" (what the Indians of India call "chakras"). It involves a special regimen of mental and physical cleansing.

However, I am not allowed to provide you with the advanced knowledge that you seek because the Arat Sekhem (Serpent Power) discipline can be dangerous if practiced wrongly. This is reserved for students who receive the teaching in person and only after at least two years of mental and physical cleansing. If you desire to continue without direct guidance you should proceed slowly in whatever experiments you decide to undertake. In our book *The Serpent Power,* I have outlined the philosophy but not the advanced disciplines but only the preparatory ones. If you are able to discern well you will glean much of the advanced philosophy and advanced discipline, though. Use this book to prepare yourself for the time when you meet a proper teacher to advise you more directly.

Realize also that the integral practices of the Shedy disciplines (Devotion, Maat {righteousness and selflessness}, Wisdom and Meditation all facilitate the rising of Kundalini (awakening of the Serpent Power), in a gradual and safe manner as they cleanse and integrate the personality. Engaging in specific practices that only focus on raising the Kundalini when the personality has not been cleansed and is thus not properly prepared to handle energy is like prying open a rose and forcing it to bloom when it is just in its budding stage and closed; the petals will be damaged if you manually force it to

Mystical Answers to the Important Questions of Life

open. So, it is safer and better to practice the disciplines in an integral fashion, and allow the lotus petals of the chakras (*Sefech Ba Ra*) to open in a natural manner as you purify and integrate the mystical teaching into your personality.

Peace and Blessings!
Sebai MAA

Conversation with God

Question: what musical instruments would be helpful in awakening the neters?

What musical instruments would be helpful in awakening the neters, the gods and goddesses of Ancient Egypt?

Answer

Greetings,

The question is not so much which instruments, but what kind of music is helpful towards spiritual evolution?

The musical theory of ancient Egypt is almost unique in its primary teaching and the intent with which it was instituted. Music should not be employed to excite the mind or as mindless entertainment. It should be soothing, harmonious and oriented towards a spiritual feeling. Otherwise, it leads the mind towards the base levels of human feeling, emotion and thought; in other words, downwards instead of upwards. This was the primary lesson that the early Greeks learned from ancient Egypt. The writings of Pythagoras, Plato and Strabo confirm this. However, the Greeks did not practice this precept perfectly and music was thus used for entertainment and later western society developed the use of music as a theatrical entertainment and the spiritual aspects were virtually lost. In ancient times, the professional musicians were employed by Temples and devoted their lives and their music towards extolling the glory of the Divine in its various forms (gods and goddesses). As long as music is used for entertainment only, it will not serve to awaken the Higher Self (neters).

The ancient Egyptian musical theory held that music should be improvised within the spiritual parameter as opposed to rigid formalization. Thus, it served as a means for expressive devotional feeling and an inducement to a meditative state. Also, there is a scientific system of diatonic sound for bringing the personality into harmony with the cosmic sound.

The ancient Egyptians used several instruments such as the Nefer – longneck lute, Tar – hand-drum, sistrum, harp etc.

Peace and Blessings!
Sebai MAA

Mystical Answers to the Important Questions of Life

Question: how should an aspirant be like the Sage?

Greetings! Thank you for the practical and spiritual insights to my situation. Last Sunday when you said that I must be like you, I think I understand. The ultimate modeling that I will do is think like you, and that means not thinking. Since I feel that a sage is not thinking using an ego-based mind, but spontaneously allowing the divine to express and manifest itself through them (their nervous system).

Peace!

Answer

Greetings,

It is certainly true that enlightened sages operate out of a spontaneous wisdom derived from the Spirit. An aspirant should learn to live in this manner as well, and thereby become enlightened as well. However, until such enlightenment is attained, the aspirant should be guided by the teacher as well as the scriptures. This process is also emulating the path of the sage's own spiritual evolution. The aspirant should follow the instructions of the sage, also the aspirant should emulate the principles that the sage lays out for standards of living, following ethical culture, diet, hygiene, etc. The aspirant should spend as much time as possible with the sage to observe how he/she handles the world and carries on with the struggle of life. Very important is that the aspirant should attend classes offered by the sage so as to imbibe the wisdom directly along with subtle energy emanations of the sage that purify the personality, just as the sunrays purify the ground and engender life on earth. If this process is engaged effectively, the aspirant will undoubtedly attain enlightenment and of course all who may be close to such a personality will be benefited greatly.[2]

Peace and Blessings!
Sebai MAA

---

[2] for more details see the book *Initiation Into Egyptian Yoga*

Who and or what is God?

Mystical Answers to the Important Questions of Life

Question: What is the Kemetic concept of God?

Dear Sebai Maa

Just writing in request of a few questions, that I would like to be answered by you. The first question: "What was the ancient Egyptian concept of God?

Peace

Answer

Greetings,

The Western language and culture tends to see "God" as a male figure and as a phenomenal Creator who exists as part of time and space. In Kamitan religion the term Neter does not necessarily signify male or female but "The Divine" transcending but including gender. So the term "Pa Neter" is properly translated as "The Divine". The Ancient Egyptian concept of God is that God is the source and sustenance of all that exists. This is explained through a concept, referred to in religious studies, as "Henotheism": There is one Supreme Being from whom the neteru or gods and goddesses emerge. God is the source and the neteru are Creation itself and all life. For more details, see the book *Egyptian Yoga: The Philosophy of Enlightenment.*

Peace and Blessings!

Sebai MAA

Conversation with God

Question: What is the Kemetic concept of God, the difference between religion and spirituality?

Dear Sebai Maa

Is there a difference between religion and spirituality? If there is please explain?

Peace

Answer

Greetings,

The way religion is practiced in modern times it is often not spiritual. From a political perspective, it is often used as a tool to control others. In the field of religious studies many scholars approach religion as a spiritual activity without ultimate purpose, besides being a social pastime. Many practitioners of religion in the masses follow their religions as a faithful endeavor not requiring ethical conscience. The English term "religion" is derived from the Latin "relegare" ("re-link," or "link back"), meaning a process for human beings to re-link (reconnect) with God (a deity, divinity) or whatever a people consider to be a Supreme Being or cause behind existence. Theology is the study "ology" of "theism," a belief in a divinity as opposed to atheism which is disbelief in the existence of a god, deity or divinity. In its full form, religion has three steps: Mythology, Rituals and Metaphysics. Most people know something about the myths and rituals of their religion, but not about their true meaning. When mysticism, the third step of religion, is not practiced, religion becomes degraded and loses its spirituality.

The African definition would be similar in that religion is a process of reconnecting with the "Higher Self" the Supreme Being. However, while the Supreme Being concept of western religion is monotheistic, and relating to a phenomenal[3] divinity, the African, East Asian, and Native American are based on a Henotheistic[4] conception. In the higher perspective of the African, Indian, Buddhist as well as Native American practice of religion, the Supreme Divinity is not just a phenomenal personality as in Western monotheism, but rather a phenomenal and transcendental divinity; this means that God appears as a personality, as nature, and also transcending forms and names, beyond Creation itself; so religion is a process for attaining spiritual development by re-linking one's soul with God, or the Divine. In Ancient Egyptian terminology, the term "Shetaut Neter" means "Hidden (mysterious) Divine Essence" this term has been rightly interpreted as the "religion" of the Ancient Egyptians. However, in the strict application of the grammatical meaning, the term "Shetaut Neter" is a name of a religion while the

---

[3] Existing in time and space and appearing with name and form
[4] There is a Supreme Divinity with lesser gods and goddesses that emanate from it.

Mystical Answers to the Important Questions of Life

term "religion" is a noun referring to a process. In Ancient Egyptian language, the term "Shedy" is more applicable as it means: process of penetrating the mysteries (i.e. the "Hidden {mysterious} Divine Essence).

The term "Spirituality" is defined as: that which pertains to what is incorporeal or pertaining to the supernatural as distinguished from the physical nature: *a spiritual approach to life*. "Spiritology" is the study of the spiritual aspects of the soul and or of life (aspects that transcend the physical). However, in popular culture "spirituality" has been applied to mean something pertaining to sacred things or matters; religious; devotional; the sacred or the spirit or soul.

So the term religion specifically relates to a theistic[5] perspective on spirituality: it relates to the soul and a Divinity. The term "spirituality" may or may not relate to a Divinity and may relate to incorporeal matters or concerns with non-physical matters. Religion without the three steps may be considered spirituality, but in the strict interpretation it is not true religion. Thus, while true religion (religion that contains the three steps or levels of practice) will incorporate spirituality, we cannot say that all spirituality is religious, related to a Divinity (theistic) or even that it is enlightening. In the strictest terms, we cannot say that a person worshipping a tree is practicing religion since religion is worshipping a Supreme Divinity unless that tree is an access point to the Higher Divinity. We cannot say that a person had a religious experience if they had an out of body experience. The OB experience may be spiritual but not specifically religious unless it relates the person to the Supreme.

The term "mystical" is similarly misinterpreted by the popular culture just as the term "spiritual" is automatically confused with something sacred, altruistic, or sometimes even as a belief system or practice that is better or even purer than religion, etc. Mysticism relates to the achievement of consciousness wherein the individuality is evolved into universality, a oneness of soul with the Divine, like a river uniting with the ocean. So one cannot say that one had a "mystical" experience by "going to a movie," "falling in love," "traveling," "seeing a celebrity" or "having a child," as is expressed often in modern culture, unless one means that those experiences have led one to discover higher consciousness by transcending one's physical reality, time and space and becoming one with the universe and what transcends it!

What is the proof that religion is a reality? In other words, what is the substantiation that there is a Supreme Being and that we are to reconnect with that Divinity? Proof lies in the experience of those who have reconnected through the process enjoined by religion (myth, ritual, mysticism) and who have reported about that reconnection to those who have not yet reconnected. It is derived from the experience of those who have reconnected, that there is an ultimate agency or Being that is responsible for the existence of souls and Creation, and that there was an original connection between that Being and the souls of human beings that was disconnected and needs to be reconnected so that a human being may find peace, contentment and completeness.

---

[5] Belief in a god or goddess

Conversation with God

Disbelieving in religion (atheism) without engaging in the process enjoined by religion does not constitute proof of the invalidity of religion or non-existence of the Divine. Also, having faith in religion without engaging in the reconnection process does not constitute the authentic practice of religion. Faith in the existence of a Divinity is not religion in and of itself; it is part of the myth aspect or stage of religion, but alone may only be considered as theism or spirituality until the full course of a reconnection process is engaged. To be clear here, in order to be considered a religion, the discipline or tradition needs to incorporate as its goal the objective of reconnection of the soul to the High God or Goddess, the Supreme Being or ultimate agency causing and sustaining existence; Those practices that do not incorporate this goal may not be included as part of the definition of religion, but would more aptly be included in the definition of spirituality.

Peace and Blessings!

Sebai MAA

Mystical Answers to the Important Questions of Life

Question: Who translated the Ancient Egyptian Religious texts?

Greetings,

Who translated the Ancient Egyptian texts, like the *Virgin of the World* and others, into English? Thanks.

Answer

Greetings,

There are various texts that are included under the heading of "Kemetic Philosophy" ranging from the Pyramid Texts (5,000 B.C.E.) to the Hermetic and Gnostic texts (around the year 300 A.C.E.). Texts such as the *Virgin of the World* were translated by G.R.S. Mead, a European student of the Mysteries and specialist in Hermeticism, and published as part of a larger work called "Thrice Greatest Hermes." Hermes of course is the ancient Greek name given to the Ancient Egyptian God Djehuti. The texts from "Thrice Greatest Hermes" are actually called Hermetic texts. They are from the period just before Christianity when the Greeks had conquered Kemet (Ancient Egypt) and had adopted the Ancient Egyptian mystical philosophy. In essence, the Hermetic texts may be compared to the English translations of the Hebrew texts of the Bible. Though they are updated versions of the original texts, they were translated from the original teachings of Ancient Egypt. As far as the main principles, they follow the teachings learned by the early Greek philosophers from the Ancient Egyptian Sages. Thus, exact and close parallels can be found between the Hermetic texts and the Ancient Egyptian Texts such as the Pert m Heru and the Pyramid Texts and others. In fact, the Hermetic texts openly acknowledge their origins in Ancient Egypt.

Peace and Blessings!

Sebai MAA

Conversation with God

Question: How can God be intimately personal, one who listens to your prayer, while at the same time be transcendental?

Greetings. I just read an article by another spiritual master on The Power of Prayer that is posted on the internet and my mind is confused...

How can God be intimately personal, one who listens to your prayer, while at the same time be transcendental? How can he be immanent and transcendental without a dualist philosophy? If soul and Absolute Self are really one, then what is the purpose of praying to a God who in reality is our own self? Please help me understand the deeper mystical meaning behind praying to the Divine?

Peace.

Answer

Greetings,

The sages have devised different terminologies to explain the nature of the Divine for people at different levels of spiritual development. The dualistic concept envisions that there are two entities, either a supreme and transcendental one or the humanoid incarnation type, a god or goddess with humanlike characteristics. There is another form of philosophy, the Henotheistic, in which there is a Supreme Being who emanates gods and goddesses like a sun emanates rays, in order to touch the physical world and interact with life on earth. This theological conception may be thought of in the context of pantheism, that there is Divinity in nature but also transcending nature (Creation) as well. God has two aspects, the time and space aspect and the transcendental absolute aspect. The time and space aspect is called *bes* or "image" while the other is *an ran – an bes* or "without name" "without form." God manifests in time and space as the gods and goddesses and in fact as Creation itself, which is the temporary or "illusory" appearance. So God may be known through the cosmic force(s) that emanates from God or directly by internal realization of the Divine as the essence of your being. But let us expand the definition of God further, God can be male or female and also androgynous, i.e. transcending gender, even though genders arise from God and are aspects of her.

The dualist philosophy is really a road which leads to the realization of non-dualism. This means that God is first understood as somebody who is apart from you, and accessible, operating as a personality in time and space, caring for souls. Then the aspirant learns that there is a closer relationship between himself or herself and God, i.e., God is in my heart (soul); the two are somehow together, related. Then the aspirant learns that he or she and God are one, i.e. I and God are one (my soul and the spirit of God are really the same essence).

Mystical Answers to the Important Questions of Life

However, the final non-dualist realization is really not a philosophy but an experience: *Nehast*, the spiritual awakening, i.e. "Enlightenment." Even though a Sage may speak in dualistic terms in an effort to break down the explanation of the nature of the Divine, they are always also referring to a higher reality, but this can only be reached through mind, and mind operates in words and concepts and these are by definition dualistic instruments in themselves. Therefore, the higher goal of spiritual practice is to go beyond words in order to experience the non-dualistic reality that is beyond dualism. In an effort to reach that goal, a sage may speak in terms that seem contradictory or paradoxical in an effort to confound the time and space logical mind and enable it to fathom the depths of transcendental reality beyond dualism, wherein there is no more soul and no more God.

As an aspirant you must learn to distinguish when dualist philosophy is being spoken and what its purpose is. In the Neterian teaching, there is the *ua-ba* (individual soul) and the *Un-Ba* (universal soul). Also, there is *Neberdjer* (all-encompassing Divinity, i.e. Absolute Self). When talking about God you can only talk in dualistic terms even if you are using non-dualist philosophy (transcendental wordings). The time and space "relative" forms of God, seeing God as a personality like Heru, Krishna, Buddha, etc., and the religions containing myths about God's incarnation as a human being on earth or appearing as a god are like crutches for those who need assistance in discovering God within the self, within Creation and transcending Creation. When the aspirant has direct access to the Divine, that help from the crutches is no longer needed. Then the myths and varied forms of gods and goddesses are no longer needed, for they have been realized within oneself; this is why it is said: *Men and women are mortal gods and goddesses, the gods and goddesses are immortal men and women.*

In the Asarian Resurrection epic of Ancient Egypt, the Goddess Aset teaches Heru that "sex is a thing of bodies, not of souls." This means that duality as expressed through gender is a peculiarity of physical existence and not of soul or higher existence beyond the physical plane. The statement that the soul is non-dual essentially must be profoundly understood, even as it operates through a male or female body. The soul in men or women is essentially the same, only the body they are manifesting through appears to be different; yet the souls are not only of the same nature, but of the same origin and the same essence, in the same manner as a ray of sun shining on a blade of grass in China originates from the same sun that emanates another ray shining on a blade of grass in England. The two rays are united in the sun, just as the souls are united in the Spirit. The ignorance of the higher reality of the souls leads to dualistic interactions among human beings that lead to conflict.

Dualism has its purpose in promoting spiritual evolution. You asked "How can God be intimately personal?" See the divine as operating through a god or goddess form that is most appealing to you and communicate with that personality through an image, a statue, etc. Share your intimate feelings and concerns with that aspect. Allow your friendship with that divinity, your tutelary, to grow and blossom into friendship and perhaps also lover and beloved. This relationship allows the mind to grow in devotion and kinship with the Divine, thereby promoting greater understanding of the Divine and conversely, the nature of self. Thus, God manifests as and may be approached in terms of duality in

Conversation with God

accordance with how a person who is ego conscious (identifies with the ego as individual, finite and limited and God as a separate entity) needs to relate to God.

When you are ready you can proceed to the other aspect of divine worship. Begin by changing your perspective; see through the eyes of the non-dualist teaching and not through the ignorance of dualistic egoistic desire: to view the world as an individual, soul and god, me and the other. Move away from the notion of "God" as just a male entity. God may be female, animal or cosmic (any of the cosmic forces-gods and goddesses). See whichever form of the Divine you have chosen as an aspect, an image, a manifestation of a transcendental reality. Allow the androgynous nature of God/Goddess to come into your mind and your heart (feelings). Then reflect upon the sexless nature of the soul and the spirit. Finally reflect and realize that spirit (God/Goddess) and soul are one and the same.

So God manifests as duality and non-duality at the same time; thus God can be all things that an aspirant needs at any given time. When you are ignorant, God is dual and you pray TO God; when you become wise, God is non-dual and you are one with God, the transcendental and eternal. The individual ba (soul) is discovered to be a manifestation of the Universal Ba. Isn't that wonderful?

Peace and Blessings!
Sebai MAA

Mystical Answers to the Important Questions of Life

What is the Soul, What is there after death and How does it relate to Mind and God Consciousness?

Question: What is the difference between the spirit and the soul? What is "Human and Mankind"

What is the difference between the Spirit and the soul and do all people have souls? Western society coined the terms "Human" and "Mankind" My question is, why two terms and not just one: Human Society? I thought we all were human or one family.

Answer

Spirit is the ocean and soul is a drop of water from that ocean. All people have souls. But few have Spirit. Soul consciousness is the awareness and identification of oneself as an individual, limited and mortal being, even though the soul is innately a part of the vast, immortal and eternal Spirit. Spirit is God Consciousness, universal transcendental awareness of self as All and transcending All. The enlightened souls who have attained *Nehast*, the Great Awakening (Enlightenment) are the ones who have discovered their true ocean like nature.

As far as I know there is one humanity, and all people are included. The word "kind" refers to a group and the word "society" refers to a subset of socially organized people, a part of the whole humanity.

Peace and Blessings!

Sebai MAA

Mystical Answers to the Important Questions of Life

Question: How does the brain work, what is the soul in me and what do blind people see in their dreams?

Greetings, Peace and Blessings,

My daughter asked me this question a few weeks ago and I was stumbled a bit, probably a big bit. She asked, "what do blind people see in their dreams?" I have never actually thought of that and it intrigued me.

Be blessed in Ankh, Udja and Senab!

Answer

Greetings,

In order to understand the answer to this question, we need to understand the nature of the mind. The mind is actually a complex of several aspects of consciousness that interact with and relate to the objects of the world, which are themselves a form of modified consciousness of God's mind. But where does the human mind come from?

The human mind is like a conglomerate of subtle elements that are illuminated by a spark from a fire; the fire is the all-pervasive Spirit i.e. God. The spark of individuality is the soul. When a soul interacts with a physical body and nervous system that allow it to have sensory experiences in the realm of time and space with objects of its desire in the realm of time and space, it associates itself with objects of its desire in the realm of time and space. The senses perceive objects. The perception of the objects is recognized by instinctual mind. The mind holds the perceptions for the intellect which cogitates over them and relates them to its identity, the ego or the soul (will be explained later). When the identity reacts to the perceptions, the intellect decides how to respond. Then the mind engages the organs of action (hands, eyes, mouth, legs, etc.) to take an appropriate action in relation to the perception. All during this experience a certain residue of feeling-memory (what we call *ariu*) remains associated with the identity in its unconscious level of mind. In the future, when confronted with the object again the reaction will be based on the feeling-memory of the last time. If the feeling-memory of the past was positive, then the intellect-thought will tend towards desire. If the feeling-memory of the past was negative, then the intellect-thought will tend towards repudiation. In a person who identifies himself/herself with his/her ego consciousness, the lower nature that sees itself as an individual, limited, mortal person, the feeling-memory will relate to "I," "me," "mine"; anything that threatens the desires of the "I," "me," or "mine" will be seen as a threat to the happiness of the ego identity, so it will eventually be repudiated and hated. A person who identifies himself/herself with his/her Divine consciousness, the higher nature that sees Itself as a universal, transcendental, immortal and eternal being, then the feeling-memory will relate to magnanimousness, virtue, detachment, peace, balance, universal love, etc. A person's view of the world determines his/her feelings, thoughts and actions. So it is important to know the difference between if you are identifying your

"I," "me," or "mine" with your "who" or your "what". What you are is a personality composed of physical and subtle matter and thoughts and desires based on egoism and ignorance. Who you are essentially is like the drop which is none other than a portion of the ocean, for all water everywhere is part of the total vast quantities of water everywhere. A person who wants to discover the mysteries of life should not promote identification with the little, transient and mortal "I," "me," or "mine" but with the immortal, transcendental "I," as the ocean like Spirit. When the identification is with the lower "I," the tendency is towards vice, ignorance, constriction and closing off from understanding the mysteries. When the identification is with the Higher "I," the tendency is towards virtue, wisdom and self-discovery; so the task is to turn towards the higher "I" identification through study and practice of the wisdom teachings and disciplines.

Consciousness is the subtle essence of existence, the creation as well as awareness of existence itself; universal all-pervasive consciousness is synonymous with the transcendental Divine, the Absolute, the Supreme Being, etc. Universal Consciousness is like a clear sky. The individual mind of a human being is like a small portion of clear sky that is encircled by clouds; the clouds seem to be defining and limiting the sky, making it appear small and limited, but in reality it is not. The mind of an individual human being uses a portion of consciousness which is called the soul. The mind acts as a projector of and screen for the *ariu* or unconscious impressions drawn from previous actions as well as their imaginations and aspirations which a person has allowed to be lodged into his/her unconscious. *Akhu* (spirit-clear sky) is the light that shines in the mind and that light illumines the thoughts that arise in the mind of the blind and the sighted alike. Thoughts and images occur in the mind of the blind and the sighted. All sentient beings including dogs, cats, cows, etc. have thoughts and dreams. However, in a human being, the form-manifestations of those thoughts are determined by a combination of concepts previously learned and the *ariu* (past life experiences) of the person through many lives, modified (clouds in the sky) by the intellectual capacity and belief system adopted by the person, which constitutes the modifications of the consciousness a person uses to be aware of their reality. We should remember that people can retain some subtle memory from previous lives in which they had physical sight. Also, a person who develops the faculty of clairvoyance can use the subtle senses to see things in the physical as well as astral worlds. Both blind and sighted persons may develop the subtle seeing capacity.

People have the advantage over animals of being able to cognize about the thought forms in the mind and relate them to their ego or soul (identity- essential nature). Animals feel pain and pleasure as well as perceive friend or foe, but cannot relate thoughts and objects in the world to their soul; they can think about "I" as a subject and their individual instinctual desires or needs (mind) but they cannot relate these to the nature of existing as a person who can control their destiny or create and reflect upon intellectual disciplines such as those needed to create, for example, science and engineering. Animals also cannot reflect upon life philosophically or otherwise ponder about the meaning of life and what lies beyond tomorrow or for that matter beyond death. Animals are limited by the capacity of their nervous systems, so they also have limited intellectual capacity.

Mystical Answers to the Important Questions of Life

Human beings have the nervous system architecture and therefore the potential to think about the meaning of life, but their egoistic desires act as clouds that atrophy their intellects, which causes their intellectual capacity to be limited; this is called ignorance, the absence of knowledge of higher reality. The clouds that condition the mind are the concepts and limited ideas of self as an individual mortal being. When a human being grows beyond the concept of individuality and intuitionally realizes his/her being as transcending the body and concepts of the mind, he/she is referred to as an awakened/enlightened/liberated/saved being.

Concepts are vehicles which the mind uses to coalesce ideas on. The form-manifestations of those thoughts are aided by objects seen with physical vision, but physical sight is not essential for the thought process to occur. The illumination from the spirit allows thoughts to be "seen" in the mind and manipulated by the thought process (reflection, intellectualized). Thus, blind persons can also use the phrase, "I see what you mean," meaning they intellectually understand the person is telling them. If a person has never seen anything in this lifetime, the thought process will be more abstract but also relying on the other faculties like words, sound and touch for the creation of form-manifestations of those thoughts in the mind-based ideas which are drawn from concepts. Concepts make use of words (naming) to concretize the concepts and allow them to be manipulated, compared and reflected upon (looked at objectively, relative to the soul {subject personality [ego or soul][6]} which is separate) as an object (content) in the mind; but it is the soul (*Amun*) which observes and is aware of them. Thus, concepts allow ideas to be formulated and the ideas relating the concepts operate as thoughts. So words, thoughts and forms in the mind are the means by which the mind thinks (manipulates ideas) and relates them to the individual self. This is the level of operation referred to as the intellect–this level of mental operation draws on relative time and space experiences to derive indirect knowledge. When the mind knows how a concept fits into reality, it relates that to the individual (soul) and the world, and can figure out how to use the concept and apply it to reconstruct, manipulate or work with objects in the world by using the concepts in new ways not specifically learned, but based on previous knowledge; it is called understanding. When the mind does not need to reflect on concepts in order to have insight into the nature of an object in the world or a concept in the spiritual realm, and one knows the essence of an idea, that is, becomes one with the idea without having to think or reflect, then the concepts and the scaffolding (support, framework) of the concepts (words, forms, reflections, etc.) and the ideas used to compare and reflect upon the concepts are no longer needed; at that time the mind holds the essence devoid of qualification or modification. This level of mental operation is called intuition; the mind, intellect, and ego separation between concept and soul breaks down and the soul experiences the reality directly –this is called direct knowledge. Thus, the more vocabulary (names and definitions) a person has that contains substantive concepts about the theories of the nature of existence, the more that person can explore the intellectual ideas and philosophies of life and the nature of self by giving expression to the essential

---

[6] A person acting out of individuality and mortal consciousness is acting out of their ego conscience. A person acting out of self-knowledge as one with transcendental Self is acting out of Soul. However, it is the Soul that sustains either the identity as ego conscience or the identity as enlightened conscience.

nature of the higher identity-Self. Conversely, generally the more a person's vocabulary is limited by lack of education and lack of culture, composed of mundane or worldly concepts, the more difficult it is for them to cognize about spiritual philosophy and the more there is a tendency for them to gravitate towards the lower practice of religion at the level of myth and ritual, which concentrates on dogma, orthodoxy and exclusivity, literalism and ritualism, instead of the full practice of religion (myth-ritual-mysticism {metaphysical – philosophical}). For this reason, it is important for a person to be instructed in the lower mysteries (grammar, mathematics, art, liberal arts, humanities, etc.) before pursuing the higher (the religious mysteries, mystical philosophy). Yet, the deeper the knowledge, the more subtle it is, and thus the less definable it is through gross intellectual definitions. The subtler the definition of Self goes, the more intuitional and less circumscribable the definition becomes, like the clouds (defining, circumscribing factors in the mind) being dispersed from the sky.

If a person has lost sight during the present life, those manifestations in thoughts or dreams may take the shape of the images from memory of this life as well as input from the other senses, imaginations and/or past life memories OR the intuitions of spirit (Higher Self) but without specific objectified forms. If the person has been born without any sight at all, or has lost sight very early in childhood, the projections may be based on the input from the other senses, imaginations and or past life memories OR the intuitions of spirit (Higher Self). Manifestations of physical (natural) or psychological disabilities reflect a mental disability (astral body {Ka}) disability. If a blind person should overcome the astral disability, they may regain physical sight if the disability is only psychological. If it is physical, they may not regain physical vision but through mystic disciplines regain astral vision, the same that is gained by mystics. This is the subtle sense of sight (upon which the physical sight is based) through which the astral plane is discerned and the essence of physical nature is perceived and thereby rendered transparent, revealing the underlying nature or essence as the Divine.

The physical world is after all, as the Ancient Egyptian Harper's Song goes, "illusory." Therefore, the physical reality is not the ultimate reality and this is why an aspirant is admonished to withdraw the senses from the world. Upon reducing the pressure of the physical senses, the inner and subtler reality is more accessible. In this sense, the aspirant temporarily blinds herself/himself to the world. Yet a physically blind person can be as ignorant as a sighted person if there is no turning towards the teaching. Those who see the world and believe it is real are as blind as one who cannot see the world and yet would like to see.

"The Soul that hath no knowledge of the things that are or knowledge of their nature,
is <u>blinded</u> by the body's passions and tossed about.
The wretched Soul, not knowing what it is,
becomes the slave of bodies of strange form in sorry plight,
bearing the body as a load; not as the ruler but as the ruled."
—Ancient Egyptian Proverb

Mystical Answers to the Important Questions of Life

Therefore an aspirant should become blind to the world and sighted to the spirit by becoming indifferent (blind) to passions, and impervious to the world's onslaught on the senses. An aspirant should become insensitive to the thorny pricks of the world on the skin, unresponsive (blind) to the cacophony of the world on the ears, impassive (blind) to the odorous flowers of the worlds blossoming personalities, and unsympathetic (blind) to the inner urge to partake in the illusion of life. Then that aspirant will be truly blind for there is no blindness like the blindness of enlightenment towards the world, superlative, transcendental, untouched, unaffected and unmoved by the world. All others, who do not move towards self-knowledge (Nehast), be they blind or sighted, are entangled, engaged, and caught in the world of illusion.

> *"The senses give the meaning from a worldly point of view;*
> *see with the spirit and the true meaning will be revealed.*
> *This is the relationship between the object and its Creator, its true meaning."*
> —Ancient Egyptian Proverb

Peace and Blessings!

Sebai MAA

Conversation with God

Question: Please what are explain waking, dream and sleep and the means to wake up in those planes?

Udja,

I have a question regarding the lecture given on Sunday. I reviewed some of my notes from the 2005 summer conference, and had recorded the following:
Remembering your dreams
　1. Daily practice of the teachings
　2. Utter prayers before going to rest/sleep
　3. Make a conscious decision to remember your dreams

From my understanding dreams are, for the most part, a way to learn what aspects of your being (negative subconscious programs) require additional work or eradication. I also, understand it to be a way to receive messages (especially through the use and understanding of icons and symbols) from the spiritual/casual realm.

During the lecture on Sunday, I recorded that *Dreams are a manifestation of ignorance* (which I attribute to the manifestation of negative subconscious programs mentioned above).

Please help me to understand the following: If both this life (physical realm) and the astral life (astral realm) are different dream states, and the goal of meditation is to be able to go into the astral dream state while conscious (impressing the subconscious), is going into the astral dream state while sleep and becoming conscious (waking up in the dream) just as equally effective since during the dream state we leave the physical realm of consciousness, and go into the astral realm of consciousness as when meditating. And, are such experiences (waking up in the dream state, and receiving messages or visualizations) still manifestations of ignorance?

Htp,

Answer

Udja,

In the Kemetic language we have certain terms that are instructive in this particular study:

Mystical Answers to the Important Questions of Life

ariu- {actions, deeds, unconscious mental impressions that impel the desires of the mind} accumulated over previous years

resu – waking/wake up/stay awake

resut – dream/vision

resui – dream/fancy/illusion

Beq - Lucid, to be bright to see"

umet-ab - "dull, dense, dull of heart."

Neshsh – "agitated, disturbed- bothered, distracted"

Kmn – "Ignorant/ignorance"

rech-i em ib-i - "I know myself" i.e. self-knowledge

nehast – "resurrection-spiritual awakening-enlightenment"

anarudf- "the place where nothing grows, i.e. no thoughts develop"

Firstly, Ka or mind is composed of subtle energy and physical elements. An individual makes use of that subtle energy and physical elements to create concepts and thoughts in the mind. Concepts are coalesced forms which hold certain meaning relative to one's identity. Identity is "who" one "knows" oneself to be. Thoughts are manipulations of concepts in the mind. Mind is a tool used by the identity to perceive and manipulate the world, the physical reality. If a soul identifies it's "self" as the individual person that is a misunderstanding, based on the delusion that the soul is a finite, limited physical individual. If the soul identifies itself as a part of the vast ocean of spirit, like a drop of the ocean, then that is a manifestation of wisdom, lucidity. However, the soul which is clear of delusion does not need to use mind to be aware of itself as the spirit. Lucidity is only necessary when the mind is caught up in ignorance and delusion. In this sense both ignorance and wisdom are aspects of time and space-physical reality (which includes all planes of existence). Being innately transcendental (beyond all planes of existence), a soul that has rediscovered its transcendental nature can have direct experience of its higher nature not requiring mind, concepts or physical time and space references though it may use mind to interact with the world. However, the soul that has not attained that

Conversation with God

awareness manifests its conscious awareness through waking, dream and dreamless sleep states of mind exclusively–until it rediscovers its true nature. This task is the purpose of the mysteries and their disciplines, to promote that rediscovery. One of the means of effecting that process of rediscovery is the study of the philosophy of mind, psychology, waking, dream and dreamless sleep consciousnesses -which follows.

Notice the glyphs above; the term *resui,* dream, includes a sail, symbolizing the wind that blows a ship; in the same way the winds of mind based in ego/ignorance/desires blows the energies and elements of the mind of a person who is ignorant of their higher nature. In such a mind disordered thought processes, imaginations, fancies and delusions easily develop, leading to confusions, agitated existence (inability to be at peace) and self-destructive feelings, thoughts and behaviors. In such individuals, dreams can have varied and confused manifestations just as their waking lives manifest confusion, error and mediocrity. Also, in such individuals, if the negative thought processes and creation of negative *ariu* is not interrupted the buildup of deluded energies can overwhelm the mind, compelling it to pursue certain actions, even though they are based on imaginations, fancies and delusions which can lead to the detriment of the person.

However, dreams can manifest some elements of wisdom through brief or partial insights due to intermittent contact with the higher nature. This occurs because the fog of egoism is temporarily lifted, due to some positive *ariu* (right action, ethical –of the past), allowing more direct experience of the SELF. Nevertheless, dreams are mostly manifestations of delusions due to ego-identity born of ignorance which causes misunderstanding "who am I", and what the world is. The misunderstanding leads to negative feelings, desires, thoughts and actions as well as acceptance of the consequences of those actions and the memory of them as stored impressions in the unconscious level of mind, along with the value of agreeable or disagreeable. Those judged agreeable are pursued through desires, while those that are judged disagreeable are rejected and avoided through repudiation.

The fundamental delusion that there is something agreeable in the world and should be acquired in order to be happy or that there is something disagreeable in the world and should be repudiated in order to be happy that can satisfy the original delusion of misunderstood self-identity (person believing he/she is an ego/finite personality), leads to endless pursuits or projects attempting to find peace and satisfaction in the world of time and space and human activities. Since that is never abidingly possible the mind becomes filled with innumerable layers of memories, desires repudiations and their associated feelings that the mind becomes clouded with the thoughts and emotions related to those desires and feelings. The endless pursuit of satisfaction becomes a virtually endless cycle of frustration and thus suffering occasionally interrupted by brief periods of pleasure or relief from the stress of pursuing the pleasures of life so the brief relief from stress itself is perceived as pleasure –which further deludes the mind into thinking that if some small measure of satisfaction was achieved then logically it should be possible to attain permanent satisfaction somewhere or somehow. Yet the pleasures of the world are not

Mystical Answers to the Important Questions of Life

abiding and all desires depending on worldly pleasures will be eventually frustrated since the world is finite and ever changeable while the soul is abiding and infinite. So theoretically a soul caught up in ignorance could pursue the cycle of suffering -infinitely. But since ignorance itself is a delusion, an outgrowth from thoughts and feelings of misunderstanding about the nature of reality that have been layered over the soul (which is the underlying reality) and not a reality it (ignorance) cannot be infinite but only indefinite– therefore, at some point what is real, the true nature of the soul (already internally satisfied through its all-encompassing nature, which remains but is not recognized by the ignorant soul caught up in the world i.e. deluded) would be realized and the soul would turn from delusion to enlightenment; in other words, the soul would outlast and exhaust the cycle of pursuing worldly satisfaction due to ignorance –but that could take millions or billions of years.

It all depends on the level of enlightenment how the mind of an individual manifests, yet it is the same mind stuff that the ignorance or wisdom is composed of –while it is the conscious awareness, the identity (who one thinks oneself to be), based on the level of self-knowledge (or lack thereof) that directs the mode (modifies / conditions) of manifestation of that undifferentiated consciousness. In other words, one's conscious awareness of one's identity as the Higher Self or the ego, determines the outcome of the manifestations of the mind either through lucidity or ignorance and the experiences that the person will have.

If you look at a copy of the volume African Religion II-Egyptian Yoga Vol. II you will find in it a diagram in the commentary section related to verse 45 called *The Study of Mind*. In that diagram you will see how from wisdom, infinity and eternity the mind becomes narrow through the conditioning process of individuality and confines reality to the physical, concrete and finite.

An ignorant human being's mind uses the same elements as that of a sage but if the mind is caught up in ignorance of the nature of Self the thoughts, feelings and desires manifest as delusions due to ignorance. Delusions are thought processes based on un-reality, ignorance, the absence of the knowledge of self. So the original wisdom then manifests as a negative manifestation of reality in the waking state through egoism and wrong beliefs; in the dream state it manifests as dreams (fancies and imaginations conjured up by thought processes based on ignorant desires arising from prior erroneous mental impressions. This awareness in dream is predominantly based on ego/ignorance self-identity and reduced or obstructed HIGHER SELF-identity, i.e. awareness based on ego conscience. In this sense also an ignorant person is experiencing a dreamlike existence in their physical waking state as well as their astral dream state.

If the mind is made lucid through *shedy*, study of philosophy, ethics and physical purity etc. then the mind no longer obstructs the manifestation of the original wisdom and a human can manifest positive conscience, lucidity in all states of consciousness, i.e. enlightenment in the waking plane and vision in the astral plane.

Conversation with God

So the designation of positive or negative is relative to the underlying and transcendental innate consciousness, NUN, which is neutral, that all possess, but which manifests either negatively or positively in accordance with a person's level of spiritual evolution.

A human being can be so degraded that the mind is so myopic due to the confinement caused by egoistic thoughts, feelings, desires and emotions that a person's conscience and capacity for expansion becomes atrophied or even occluded and they cannot progress or evolve spiritually until the obstructions are removed. The obstructions are manifestations of their own negative *ari* and sometimes it cannot be overcome in one lifetime and may cause insanity and diseases that cause much suffering. Nevertheless, that suffering, once it has run its course, does not cause obstruction and henceforth can allow the person to develop IF they have overcome the errors that led to the negative *ari* and its deleterious effects; otherwise the same suffering can occur again and again indefinitely. The objective of the disciplines is to prepare the personality to experience the wisdom (lucidity/enlightenment/SELF-knowledge) in the Astral plane through final meditative experiences but when that meditative experience has been achieved it expands consciousness eventually so much so that mind remains expanded in wisdom (positive) state in all modes of mind: physical or astral.

The dreamless sleep state of mind is awareness blanketed with NUN (Undifferentiated Consciousness) undifferentiated form but still dominated by ignorance. The awakened-lucid state of mind transcending waking and dream (physical and astral planes) is unformed conscious awareness where there is no development of forms known as *anarudf*. This special place is discovered through *urtihat* –"great stillness of heart in Neter", that is, stopping the mind processes and remaining in Spirit as opposed to engaging in worldly, egoistic or time and space relative awareness.

It is possible to have insights in the dream state but notice how those are often clouded in a fog along with the jumble of other dream material and are often bewilderingly difficult to fathom (if there is anything of value in them at all) except by the most proficient dream interpreters (elevated/advanced souls –i.e. sages). One can "wake up" while within a dream and become "lucid" and thereafter have a vision, with direct and clear communications with divinities and intuitional realizations of the higher reality within oneself which may or may not be translatable into words. Though the lucidity within a dream that is promoted through utterance of prayers or making a conscious decision to remember your dreams does not occur in an orderly, regular, or direct intentional manner; rather that is indirect and only to be considered as an elementary level practice and not an advanced practice for promoting lucid dreaming and self-discovery. That waking up process can happen in a short time deliberately through practice of the disciplines and in meditative practice.

Furthermore, upon attaining higher consciousness in the level of enlightened consciousness (*nehast*), there is no further "waking up" for one is perennially awakened and no longer conditioned or confined by ignorance or delusions. While there is no more

Mystical Answers to the Important Questions of Life

"waking up" consciousness continues expanding to infinity since there is no limit to the SELF which is infinite.

In conclusion:

If the mind experiences wisdom/lucidity in the waking plane of existence it is called enlightenment-this is the positive manifestation of mind in the waking (physical) plane.
If the mind experiences ignorance (egoism) in the waking plane it is called egoism- this is the negative manifestation of mind in the waking (physical) plane.
If the mind experiences wisdom/lucidity in the astral plane it is called vision – this is the positive manifestation of mind in the astral plane.
If the mind experiences ignorance/delusions in the astral plane it is called dream – this is the negative manifestation of mind in the astral plane.

Now, waking up in the spiritual path is engendered from within but occurs from outside in. What I mean is that the process of spiritual enlightenment is engendered by the soul, which experiences brief episodes of lucidity, and unconsciously causes the personality to find itself in situations, relationships, families, the company of certain personalities and learning specific lessons because it wants to grow in self-knowledge. The person may not realize that consciously but they may feel a desire to seek out a preceptor or read a spiritual text, etc. However, the work of spiritual enlightenment is done in the waking state and as the work of new positive *ariu* is performed that engenders positive new *ariu* in the unconscious (so from outside to inside). When the unconscious is cleansed the work is all done. Nevertheless, the work of spiritual enlightenment is pursued on all levels as an aspirant advances, not just working on the waking or unconscious, but in every area. The relative ease or difficulty lies in the amount of negative *ariu* to be overcome, the effort put in during the spiritual practices, the kind of personality (likes to meditate or likes to work in the world, etc.).

I hope this has been useful

Peace and Blessings!

Sebai MAA

Conversation with God

Question: How to prove the passing of the soul between planes of existence?

Greetings,

How can you prove scientifically or logically that when someone passes from the physical plane (death) that:

1. There is energy or a soul that leaves the body?

2. That this energy or soul contains the mind (the essence of the person's being itself)?

Answer

Greetings,

There are several Para-psychological studies that have been done related to this. One has detected an infinitesimal decrease in the weight of the body after death. As for mind, consider that mind is composed of subtle elements and energies. Those elements are the subtle parts of air, water, fire, ether, which compose the periodic table of elements, etc. Thus, if after death we have an intact body that is not animated with less weight than the living animated body, then we should conclude that the lacking part is the animating part, that is, the mind part of the personality. However, I would add that there is an aspect of mind that cannot be measured by any physical scale. Also, science has demonstrated that some matter goes into and out of existence (time and space).

In his 1992 book, **Sick Societies: Challenging the Myth of Primitive Harmony** the author, Robert B. Edgerton writes: *As these relativists have said, it necessarily follows that if peoples' minds vary so much from one culture to another, Western science is only a culturally specific form of ethnoscience, not a universally valid way of verification or falsification. In this perspective, a person from another culture remains the "Other," forever incomprehensible.*

The arrogance or blind acceptance of the idea that the way of investigating the nature of reality by means of what in the west is referred to as science is the only way to discover truth or reality ignores the most fundamental issue related to science itself, that there is no scientific proof that Western science is the only way to discover truth or that western science is the only science. This was the point made by Nobel laureate Alfred North Whitehead who said that *'This position on the part of scientist was pure bluff.'* After all, *if someone claims that science alone can provide valid data, then one is entitled to ask, 'what is your scientific proof of this?'* The answer is *'None.'*

Societies that attain a great measure of material wealth and "scientific knowledge," like Western society, enter into a self-delusion that theirs is the only true way of life and

Mystical Answers to the Important Questions of Life

others are incorrect or primitive and therefore of lesser value. This acts as a catalyst for hubristic feelings and hegemonic tendencies in the society that exacerbate the greed, fascism and dictatorship elements within the Western culture that characterize their relationships with other countries and manifests through political and economic systems such as colonialism, imperialism and globalization.

Western science is deficient, firstly because it itself and the world it purports to define are illusory in and of themselves. In nature, everything is changeable based on circumstances and yet unknown factors. In any case, the scientific or logical proof of any phenomena is deficient if the instruments of measuring are limited. For example, can you smell a person a mile away? A dog can; why can't you? Because their senses are less limited relative to yours. Likewise you cannot expect Western science to have all answers or for all phenomena to be explainable through Western science. Western science can describe life processes of a cell, but cannot explain why the cell lives. What is the value of this science then? Every year Western scientists have to change their understanding of the body or of the universe and new text books need to be revised; if Western science has the definitive answers, why the need for revisions all the time? While Western science is not an absolute determiner of physical reality, it can be a tool to describe and manipulate some of its aspects. For example, Western science cannot be used to understand history, but can be used to explain dates of relative historical events to help us understand their context. Western science cannot create life, but can manipulate it in many cases, to extend or reduce it. So asking Western science to prove the existence of the soul and God is like asking a man to smell dinner from a mile away. Yet the scientific application of certain spiritual disciplines can allow a man, a sage, to perceive realities that are beyond the grasp of the gross physical sciences. This is the science of the Mysteries, Mysticism (Mystical science), that opens the mind to higher realities and self-discovery.

Western/Physical science is an indirect means to perceive reality because it works with instruments and experiments in a universe that even quantum physicists now acknowledge is only an outer appearance of a deeper energetic reality beyond the senses, like an iceberg, with its greater vastness hidden below the unintelligible surface of the unfathomable waters. The "truth" revealed through the Mysteries (Mystical science), the Mystical philosophy, occurs through training the mind to discover and understand reality through inductive reasoning (reasoning from detailed facts to general principles)[7] and deductive reasoning (reasoning from the general to the particular or from cause to effect).[8] Those who study mathematical principles, such as those presented in Geometry, already are practiced in this mental training. In *Logic & Mathematics,* the transitive principle allows expansion of knowledge from the known to the unknown. Transitivity here means *of or relating to a relationship between three elements such that if the relationship holds between the first and second elements and between the second and third elements, it necessarily holds between the first and third elements.*[9] These disciplines of reasoning, when understood and applied properly to the studies of history,

---

[7] *WordNet® 2.1,* © *2005 Princeton University*
[8] *ibid*
[9] *The American Heritage® Dictionary of the English Language, Fourth Edition* Copyright © 2000

nature, human psychology, religion, spirituality and Mysticism then lead to direct perception of the higher reality through intuitional realization of the truth, which surpasses all indirect means. So, non-Mystical science is the beginning of true knowledge by providing workable though conditional, facts upon which to base correct reasoning. Non-Mystical science is not an end in itself, but a tool through which correct reasoning may be developed for correctly understanding reality (i.e., through the practice of Mystical science).

Peace and Blessings!

Sebai MAA

Mystical Answers to the Important Questions of Life

Question: How should I handle a death in the family?

Greetings,

How should I handle a death in the family? Thank you.

Answer

Greetings,

Death is a part of life that most people seldom think about. It is an aspect of existence that everyone will face, but which most people seldom acknowledge in a thoughtful way. Some prefer to think that there is nothing after death, while others think they will go to a heaven. Those who delve deeper into the nature of death realize that it is merely the cessation of awareness of the physical state of consciousness. In reality, there is no death, but only the passing of awareness of the physical existence, like what happens when a person "falls asleep". In other words, the soul becomes aware of a different existence just as you become aware of the dream world after falling asleep and you forget the waking reality. Those who seek to experience this shifting of consciousness and the nature of the other states of consciousness are called spiritual seekers. One who discovers her/his existence beyond the physical personality as an immortal and eternal all encompassing reality is called sage. Sages do not experience anxiety over loss of a family member, but recognize that as a part of the journey of the soul of that person. Though a sage may experience minimal feelings related to the departed, those feelings are like a grain of sand dropped in the ocean as opposed to the loss that a spiritually immature person feels, as if the world has come to an end. So if you have a death in the family you should keep the higher philosophy in mind. You may honor the deceased with your wisdom by reading the special scriptures from the *Pert m Heru* text. You may also console family members with this wisdom if they are willing to listen. But if they are not then do not try to force it on them, simply be there for them; your fortitude and spiritual strength will sustain them and have a subtle effect on them.

You will discover that your suffering over the passing is reduced and that you will be a stable influence on your family, thereby aiding their spiritual evolution.

Peace and Blessings!

Sebai MAA

Conversation with God

Question: Is fear an Illusion?

Greetings Sebai Maa:

Query? If I am understanding correctly and the teaching says that creation really doesn't exist, fear itself must be an illusion. My ultimate fear is death but I also fear getting hurt. I think I understand that creation only exists in the mind, however this understanding is not helping me transcend my fear of death. Is there any technique that will allow one to work on this aspect of one's personality to eradicate it? This seems like a tough cookie to crack but I want to tackle it head-on.

Any advice?

Peace

Answer

Greetings,

The teaching is not that Creation does not exist, but rather that its true nature is misconceived by the ignorant mind. So, in essence, it is illusory and non-existent in terms that the ego defines. It has a different reality, an abiding and true reality that is experienced when higher consciousness is attained. Indeed, overcoming death is the last obstacle to attaining spiritual enlightenment and immortality. Fear is therefore, a psychological obstacle created by the illusion of life. That is, a person perceives they are "living" because they are awake and breathing but yet what can be said about a person who has drowned in an accident or been buried alive and the heart has stopped and there are no brain waves but then they revive? What about being awake and breathing in a dream? A dream seems real and the fear of a dream feels real but it is illusory. But there is something aware, something that experiences the experience when you are awake or when you are dreaming. IT is neither the personality of the dream nor the personality who goes around in the waking world; so what is it? That is what is real; when THAT is discovered then the fears abate.

To overcome death you must understand what life really is and this is what the Prt m Hru text is all about; it is the book of life. The more you cling to the mortal life and the idea that you are an individual with a body and senses and flesh and blood, you will be more fearful of losing that life because this is all you know. And conversely, the more you realize you transcend the limited and finite body and the world of time and space, the more fearless you become and the more exhilarating life becomes. But so far this is all just philosophy; what is needed is for you to put this into practice to make it effective; to allow the philosophy to be experienced and allow you to overcome the egoism originated fears.

Mystical Answers to the Important Questions of Life

First, be steady with the daily spiritual disciplines; next study the teaching closely and next take time to reflect upon it, and then meditate upon it in silence. Apply the teachings of Maat to your day to day life and bring order and stability to your life. Resolve to relinquish fear and insecurity and embrace Spirit and peace, even if it is not forthcoming right away. Bring yourself to balance so that you may practice profound meditation, the kind which will allow you to discover the truth behind the teachings first hand instead of just theoretically, that you are immortal and eternal. Resolve to throw off the illusion that you are limited and feeble and accept the mantle of golden feathers that is bestowed upon those who follow in the footsteps of Heru, the Golden Glorious Spirit within. Repeatedly uplift the mind with the truths of the teaching and counteract the ignorant thoughts each time they emerge. Work to prevent the negative thinking by becoming a keen observer of the mind in a detached fashion. Resolve to leave behind worldly desires and pursue the desire for self-discovery and enlightenment (Nehast). Then you will move away from fear, sorrow, ignorance and delusion. Then you will discover incomparable peace, boundless joy and freedom from fear and ignorance, once and for all.

Peace and Blessings!

Sebai MAA

Conversation with God

Question: why is the God Amun called the bull of his mother

I have the book Egyptian Yoga vol. 2 which speaks about Theban Theology and the god Amun, and would like you to please explain the term *ka-mut-f* in detail. Also why is Amon called the bull of his mother when he is depicted as a ram- headed man. Or am I confusing the attributes of the neters? em hetepu

Answer

Greetings,

As explained in Egyptian Yoga Volume 2, the term "Ka-mut-f" means "Bull-mother-his." This is a profound teaching that metaphorically refers to the fact that God is self-begotten. In other words no one brings the Supreme Being (Amun) into existence. He himself acts as his own mother as it were. He is the source from which Creation emanates. In other words "he" is an androgynous being out of which the male and female aspects arise. He impregnates Creation, which is his female aspect. Ka means impregnator or engenderer. One of the primary symbols of the male capacity to engender and impregnate is a bull. Just as a bull services and impregnates many cows, God impregnates all existence (Cow Goddess – Nut, Hetheru or Aset) with his spirit. It is this same spirit which sustains all life and all existence. Also, the God Asar is also known as the Ka of Amenti (Astral Plane-realm of the dead). Mut means mother and "f" means "he." In this case the he means "he himself" or "his own."

Also Ka is a pun on the term for astral body, which is one of the elements of the human personality. The Ka is also known as the desire body, wherein thoughts, desires and feelings manifest and engender desires and actions in the physical body, the Khat. According to ancient Kemetic mystical philosophy, a human being is composed of nine elements: (Sahu, Ba, Khu, Khaibit, Ka, Sekhem, Ab, Khat and Ren. The physical body is engendered by the Ka or Astral Body. Thus the Ka (desires, subconscious mind) of a human being causes the soul and the other elements to incarnate into physical form. This teaching is given in *Egyptian Yoga Volume 2,* Chapter 3. It is a profound area of study which must be undertaken over a period of time in order to be fully understood.

Peace and Blessings!
Sebai MAA

Mystical Answers to the Important Questions of Life

Question: are the BA & KA different from the SPIRIT & SOUL.

I am currently in the process of reading *Egyptian Yoga vol. 1 & 2*; I really appreciate these two volumes. They are a lot easier to read than other books on Ancient Egyptian spirituality and philosophy. As a matter of fact I'm able to understand them better by reading your books. My question is are the BA & KA different from the SPIRIT & SOUL. I was under the impression that the BA & KA were another name for the SPIRIT & SOUL. Could you please shed some light on the differences and similarities? Thank You, Peace/Peace!

Answer

Greetings,

The Ba may be translated as "soul" but not in the ordinary Western sense. In the Western sense, the soul is an individual unit created by God which has no connection and exists independently from spirit, as an individual being. The Ba is the sustaining essence, which enlivens the personality of a human being. Ra, the Supreme Being, also has a soul but his soul is universal and from it emanates all individual souls, which sustain all forms of life, i.e. the individual souls of every human being, plant and animal, etc. The Ka is the personality, the subconscious mind with its tendencies and desires, which impel a human being to various actions and circumstances. The spirit is Akhu or Khu, a subtler essence of the constitution. It too is a spark from the universal Akhu or part of the Divine. In essence, every aspect of a human being is a microcosmic expression of the macrocosmic Universal Self. The task of mystical spirituality is to discover the source of one's own being, the substratum, which is God, i.e. the Universal Self and not the ego or personality self of each individual. Review Chapter 4 of *Egyptian Yoga Volume 2* for more details on this teaching.

Peace and Blessings!
Sebai MAA

Questions about History, Religion, Myth and Spiritual Philosophies?

Mystical Answers to the Important Questions of Life

Question: What are Freemasonry and Mythology?

Hello

I would like you to help me out by answering a few questions for me.

Question 1.) The Esoteric Information you teach in your books, are these the teachings which are known as the greater Mystery as apposed to the lesser Mysteries? Are theses also the secrets that freemasons claim to know?

Answer

Yes and Yes, though the operative word in your question is "claim." Just because someone claims something does not make it authentic or real. On this basis, we cannot say that those organizations who claimed to have the true philosophy of the Mysteries have demonstrated it in their teachings or actions.

Question 2.) Could you tell me what is the purpose of freemasonry/Secrets societies?

Answer

For the most part, those organizations have become social clubs for the elite of society who control society, where if present, metaphysics are mostly used to develop energies for worldly goals, including control of governments and the world economy. One of the most famous examples of such a group was the "founding fathers" of the United States of America.

Question 3.) Are the stories In Sumer (Asia Minor) about the Annunaki true? Also is this mythology, or did these events actually take place?

Answer

Yes and no- myth is neither real nor unreal; it is supposed to be a language of self-discovery through the wisdom of the myth. The question is not are mythological stories real, but what is the teaching imparted by the myth through the idea of them. Is that an authentic teaching about the nature of human existence and the means to discover the true, ultimate nature of self? Those are the really important questions? If the answer is yes, then you have an authentic myth in terms of mystical philosophy.

Conversation with God

Question 4.) Could you please explain the difference between Spirit and soul?

Answer

Spirit is to soul as the ocean is to a drop.

Peace and Blessings!
Sebai MAA

Mystical Answers to the Important Questions of Life

Question: what is the proper way to understand mythology?

Greetings,

In modern culture we are told that myths are lies and that ancient myths are primitive speculations by primitive people. How should we as spiritual aspirants approach myth and what is the difference between myth, religion and mysticism? I have read your books and others on Kemetic Spirituality, but I am confused as to the meaning of several terms like Nun, Neberdjer, Neter Neteru and Amun.

Answer

Greetings,

Mystical mythology, specifically, Kemetic mystical mythology, is a special language through which the storytellers and sages of a society convey several important aspects of culture to their posterity. One conveyance is the answer to the question: Who are we? The next is: Where do we come from? The next is: Why are we here? And also related is the question: How do we fulfill the "purpose of our existence?" Most world myths, in one way or another (apparent differences are due to the local folklore), convey that we are here because a higher power created us and the universe; we are here to realize the gift of existing and the full experience of our existence. We achieve that by following the path laid out for the protagonist of the myth, meeting similar trials and making similar discoveries, and then finally achieving the same goal: victory and enlightenment. The myths use the characters of humans and divinities who represent special meanings beyond their superficial mundane qualities. By discovering those meanings within ourselves, we can also discover our true essential nature and the meaning of life. This is the language of myth.

Mythology is the study of myths. Religion is a means to follow and worship myths through faith and ritual. Mysticism is a philosophical and metaphysical means to make myth and faith, as well as rituals, effective as tools to transform the personality in order to achieve higher consciousness. Religion is supposed to have three steps: *myth, ritual and mysticism*. Religion may speak of the gods and goddesses of the myth as objects of worship, while mysticism speaks of them as principles to be mastered within oneself. If myth is applied in religion only at the limited level of worship and ritual, it will devolve, because the meaning of the myth is not being explored in its higher esoteric sense, but is only being applied in its mundane sense (exoteric-worldly). At that low level, myth becomes the basis for fundamentalism, orthodoxy and dogmas, that in order to survive, must repudiate all other orthodoxies and the dogmas of other myths, which leads to religious misunderstanding and conflict. Myth is therefore a highly evolved language that speaks to our deepest needs, our deepest feelings, and also contains the seeds of wisdom for us to understand the meaning of life.

Conversation with God

A myth is not to be understood strictly literally, but its truth lies in the fact that it relates to transcendental principles (which are related through the themes and plots and relationships of the characters in the myth) that applied to the ancients, and still applies to us and to those who may come in the future. So it has a value that transcends historicity; it has a psychological, emotional as well as an intellectual value. To those who are empiricists, or who follow faith-based religions, or who are atheists, these values of myth will be insignificant or will be dismissed as irrational rantings of ignorant people, and the deeper meanings and purpose of mystical myths will be lost to such persons. However, in the mystical field, myth is a highly evolved language, that if applied properly (not fanatically, historically), under proper guidance (sages, mythologists), can lead to the higher wisdom of life instead of the worst expressions of religious intolerance, tribalism and war.

You have studied the teachings, but your research is based on an empirical analysis rather than on a mythological and metaphorical basis. This way of research is prone to confusion because it seeks to assign concrete and rigid phenomenological meanings to living and transcendental, though abiding, spiritual principles. One should not apply linear or limited time and space thinking to mythological philosophical studies. What I mean is that the idea of the Neter Neteru (God of Gods), or Nebertcher (All-encompassing Divinity), or Amun (Hidden Witnessing Self), are all referring to the same essential essence, the Supreme Being. However, these terms also refer to different aspects of that Divine Self in the context of their individual theological systems. This is done by the Sages to impart different teachings at different times, or to emphasize a specific aspect or element of a teaching.

The subtlety of the teachings is something that one must develop through studies with a spiritual preceptor and the development of the capacity to see the holistic essence of the Neteru (gods and goddesses) as they relate to the Nun (primeval essence) from which all arises, and how they relate to the Creation and human existence itself.

Further, even when you look at Ancient Egypt, you have different schools or temples wherein the different divinities are worshiped. While all of the main divinities were referred to as Neter-aah (Supreme One, Great One), this does not mean that one is greater than the other or that there is a conflict in the mythology or the philosophy. In the context of their own teaching, they are supreme, and in the contexts of the whole they all have a rightful place and harmony with each other. The art of reading mythology must be learned carefully, and if it is not understood properly, there will be confusion due to the apparent disparities and contradictions or misunderstandings by those who are researching on their own. This can be alleviated by studying an authentic path fully under proper guidance, before venturing to explore other areas that would potentially be confusing.

For more on these issues read my book: *Comparative Mythology*.

Peace and Blessings!

Mystical Answers to the Important Questions of Life

Sebai MAA

Question: Were Ancient Egyptians Africans and did the Bible originate in Egypt?

Dear Sebai Maa

Were the ancient Egyptians distinctly an African people or were they multicultural? Last question: "Did the Bible really originate in Ancient Egypt like Joel A. Rogers stated in his book, *100 Amazing Facts about the Negro*? Please answer these few questions for me. I greatly appreciate it very much so. Again thanks.

Peace

Answer

Greetings,

In the beginning of the civilization the Ancient Egyptians were dark skinned peoples, just like other Africans.[10] They were descendants of the Ethiopians. The early Greek philosophers who saw them confirmed this. Many years later, towards the end of Ancient Egyptian civilization, sometimes through captured Asiatic prisoners or through political intermarriage, they mixed with the Greeks, Asiatics and others and this is why the pictures of the late period reflect many Ancient Egyptians as looking as Europeans or mixed brown or Semitic. Many depictions are from the period when Egypt was conquered by Asiatics and Europeans who made images of themselves with the Egyptian motif.

The origins of Judaism and Christianity come from Ancient Egypt. The Bible itself supports this, saying that Moses knew the wisdom and magic of the Egyptians and that when he led people out of Egypt they were previously Egyptians now following the God of Abraham. The belief in One God, the resurrection, the final judgment and so many more teachings of Judeo-Christianity were all in Ancient Egypt. The Jews took these when they left and the Christians later carried them on.[11]

Peace and Blessings!

Sebai MAA

---

[10] see the book *The Black Acnient Egyptians*
[11] see the books *Mystical Journey from Jesus to Christ* and *African Origins of Civilization Vol. 2* both by Muata Ashby

Conversation with God

Question: Where does the tradition of the Baptism come from?

Dear Sebai Maa:

I have many of your books and I have to say, that you have given me a new understanding on spirituality. I thank you for the wisdom. I'm writing you today because some brothers and I were reasoning about baptism and it seems that the understanding that we have starts with John the Baptist and the baptism of Jesus. I know that this practice started in Kemet, but I don't have the knowledge to share with my brethren. If you have the time to share some of the knowledge it is greatly appreciated. Many Blessings

Answer

Greetings,

If have read the book "Mystical Journey From Jesus to Christ" you have received some details about the emergence of Christianity from the Ancient Egyptian Asarian tradition. Like the Eucharist, other concepts which are seen as fundamental Christian tenets already existed in Ancient Egyptian religion thousands of years before Christianity emerged. Other practices, traditions and rituals of Christianity that are of Ancient Egyptian origin include, the resurrection, the cross symbol, the concept of savior, concept of incarnation of the son, persecution at birth of the son and savior, the concept of Christhood through anointing, and also the baptism. Baptism is based on the ancient Egyptian ritual of bathing before entrance to the temple. It was also used prior to initiations. This is one of the purposes of the Divine Lake that is found attached to the temple. It is a ritual of rebirth through cleansing by water, just as the god Ra (Heru Nefertum) emerged as the new born sun (Solar child *Nefertum*) on the first day and that is the project of every aspirant, to have a rebirth, to be "like Ra on the day of his birth" so as to discover the higher nature of self as that same divinity.

Peace and Blessings!

Sebai MAA

Mystical Answers to the Important Questions of Life

Question: Should I become a Baptist?

I was advised by one of your students to call or email you to aid in my spiritual growth. Right now, in my life I am about to have my Baptism (into the spiritual Baptist religion). However, this instructor thinks that I should have a deep understanding of the steps I am about to make before I get into something that would stop my growth spiritually. But, being Baptist is something that I want to do. Furthermore, I am familiar with the philosophy of your institution and have come to understand the basis of this body. I was wondering what advise would you give me as to my decision and what advice would you give me on my spiritual quest.

Answer

Greetings,

All the choices one makes in life lead to spiritual evolution-eventually. The question is will that evolution be within a few years or within a few lifetimes? All religions have a purpose and they are designed for those who desire to follow its particular quality of spiritual feeling and evolutionary quality. Yet you are having quandaries about the path you are following and the evidence of that is this inquiry that you have sent. Firstly, there are many spiritual paths. However, not all spiritual paths are religious, and not all religions are effective because not all practice the three levels or stages of religion (myth, ritual, mysticism). However, even if a religion were to be followed out of ignorance, that experience would eventually lead to spiritual evolution as the personality grows to understand its true path either trough failure or success in following that religion. Therefore, follow your heart and do so to the best of your ability and you will be led to the right path.

Generally, indeed you should try to select a religion that resonates with your personality's emotional needs; this is taken care of by the myth and ritual stages of religion. However, most people only go through that step and go no further. A person is not just emotions, but also intellect, ethic and will. Therefore, there are other important features that religions should have beyond just serving the emotions of their parishioners through emotionally satisfying services. A religion should be able to lead you to fulfill the highest spiritual aspirations (mysticism) through wisdom, ethical consciousness and development of inner self-discovery. If a religion tells you to not ask questions, just come to church and pray, just surrender to the church and pay your money, or just have faith or you don't need to know that, don't meditate, don't practice yoga, or stay away from reading this or that, listening to this or that other religion, etc. then you know there is some limitation, some fear that you may see or hear something that is greater, more advanced or elevated. Religions that say such things are usually not religions but spiritual sandbars on the ocean of life that get people stuck in the quicksand of dogma, orthodoxy and fundamentalism so that they will remain dependent on the church as well as emotionally infantile and weak-willed. Those are not good places to grow in spiritually. So select your religion wisely; purifies yourself, learn what religion is supposed to be, a spiritual culture that can lead a

Conversation with God

person to discovering the higher essence of being beyond mortality, ignorance and sorrow. Then you will be able to find the best religion that will meet your emotional needs as well as your intellectual and spiritual ones as well.

Peace and Blessings!
Sebai MAA

Mystical Answers to the Important Questions of Life

Question: Did Jesus really exist?

Dear Sebai Maa,

Did you mean in your book Mystical Journey From Jesus to Christ that Jesus was a historical human being?

Thank you

Answer

Greetings,

The historical evidences point to many mythical personalities from different traditions that were consolidated into a single character called "Jesus" by followers of what later became Christianity. However, the idea of that "Jesus" was seen differently by the two major sects of Christianity, the Gnostics and the Orthodox. The Gnostics saw Jesus as a human ideal to be attained by everyone while the Orthodox concentrated on the idea of a historical Jesus. Thus, I would like you to know that it is not my contention that Jesus Christ was a human being, but that the message contained in the myth is most important for every human being. Further, people who take the myth as reality need to be led to a higher form of thinking which necessarily needs to begin at their level. They cannot be reached with a sledgehammer, but through peace and understanding, as we were all ignorant until someone enlightened us through his/her words, deeds or writings so that we might reach a higher level of understanding. Those who throw the Christian myth out due to their understanding of it based on the church or on Western society, without understanding its mystical implications, are also throwing out the African cultural and spiritual history and philosophy upon which it is based. They are actually doing an injustice to the teachings, just like those who misuse it for their own personal, political or religious ends. If you take the time to examine our book *Mystical Journey From Jesus to Christ,* you will see what I mean. There is a deeper aspect to Christianity beyond the tradition popularized by the Roman Church and the Protestant Churches; it is a Gnostic message that traces its origins in the Asarian Resurrection tradition of Ancient Egypt. In the Asarian Resurrection tradition of Ancient Egypt, you will find the deeper philosophy and mysticism behind Christianity that was lost to the West when the Orthodox followers sought to eradicate all other views about Christianity except their own narrow and new interpretation.

Peace and Blessings!

Sebai MAA

Question: Is the Kingdom of Heaven within as it says in the Christian Bible?

Greetings,

In light of Kemetic (Ancient Egyptian) Philosophy, what is the true meaning of the Christian scripture in Luke: 17:20-21 "The Kingdom of Heaven is Within."

Answer

Greetings,

The scripture in Luke signifies that same teaching which is found in Kemetic and other philosophies, that spiritual enlightenment (the Kingdom of Heaven), is not a place, but a state of consciousness that is to be discovered within. In Christian terms, this is referred to as Christhood, or the divine anointing. In Kemetic Philosophy, this is symbolized by the resurrection of the divinity Asar, becoming aware of the higher glory of existence, which lies not in the physical plane, but in the mental plane; thus, the kingdom is within.

However, the aforesaid should not be taken to mean that Christianity, as is generally practiced in the Western countries or in the countries where Western missionaries have caused other people to practice their form of Christianity, is a viable means to attain Christhood or spiritual enlightenment. In the Western or Orthodox Christian traditions, this statement in Luke is not viewed as an injunction towards inner discovery. In fact, it is not treated as a mystical statement when it is dealt with by the Christian priests or pastors. It is perhaps seen as an ideal for individual faith in God or Jesus as a means to achieve being accepted into the Kingdom of Heaven, with the belief that heaven is a physical location where Christians will go to live with God after death. Consequently, one cannot achieve that goal of discovering and becoming one with God within through the practice of Western or Orthodox Christianity. For that discovery to occur, a mystical path that can open the mind to the mysteries of life and the metaphysical realities of higher consciousness is required. Read our book "The Mystical journey from Jesus to Christ" for more details on this teaching.

Peace and Blessings!

Sebai MAA

Mystical Answers to the Important Questions of Life

Question: Is the Trinitarian philosophy included in the Neterian Creed? What is true religion? What is Faith-based Religion?

Greetings,

Sebai Maa, why isn't the Trinitarian philosophy included in the Neterian Creed (affirmation of Neterian tenets for Neterian aspirants {followers of the Kamitan [Ancient Egyptian] Shetaut Neter Mystical Teachings generally known as the "Egyptian Mysteries"}) whereby neophytes or the masses can easily recognize the correlation with the widely known offspring religions (Christianity, Judaism, Islam) as you pointed out in your book, "The Mystical Journey From Jesus To Christ"?

Peace

Answer

Greetings,

The answer to your question is simple. It has indeed been demonstrated that the Trinity concept that is contained in the Neterian theology was indeed the template of not only the Christian, but the Hindu tradition as well. However, in Neterian religion, it is not displayed nor is it followed in the same way as in the Christian religion. The Neterian teaching encompasses the Father-Mother-Child while the orthodox Catholic (not Gnostic) Christian version attempts to extirpate the female element.

Originally, the Gnostic Christian teaching held that the Holy Ghost (Father-Holy Ghost-Son) was an aberration from the original Christian teaching (which was derived from the Neterian tradition): Father-Mother-Child (God-Mary-Jesus). The original Christian teaching comes from the Ancient Egyptian Asarian tradition (Asar {Osiris}-Aset {Isis}-Heru {Horus}) but was also informed by the Ancient Egyptian Amunian tradition (Amun-Mut-Khons). Thousands of years before the advent of Christianity, the Ancient Egyptian Sage-Pharaoh Hatshepsut proclaimed that she was the child offspring of an Ancient Egyptian woman, and Amun (God) was her father. This teaching of the virgin conception and birth was presented complete with an annunciation, just as was done in the later Christian version. This is only one example. Early Christianity adopted this philosophy, but the later orthodox catholic form changed the teaching to suit the patriarchal imperative of the Roman and gentile western cultures, and the religious theology of the Trinity was also changed. So the Neterian teaching is actually different from the Christian.

As the Neterian is not a fundamentalist tradition, it does not concentrate on simple dogmas such as the concept of one Trinity. In Neterianism, the Trinity concept is only one of the focal points of the religion; in fact there are many Trinities in Shetaut Neter religion: Asar-Aset-Heru, Ptah-Sekhmit-Nefertem, Amun-Mut-Khons, and those are just the main ones! They emanate from the original Trinity: Amun-Ra-Ptah. In the first

Conversation with God

section of the Neterian Creed, these are included where it says that all Neteru, (gods and goddesses, including the trinity systems), proceed from Neberdjer as Neberdjer is the originator of the first and great Trinity of "Amun-Ra-Ptah":

As a *Neterian*, I follow the Ancient African-Kamitan religious path of *Shetaut Neter*, which teaches about the mysteries of the Supreme Being, <u>*Neberdjer*</u>, the All Encompassing Divinity. I believe that from *Neberdjer* proceed all the *Neteru* **(gods and goddesses)**, and all the worlds, and the entire universe.

Actually, when the early orthodox Christians adopted the Trinity system, it was seen as an aberration by the Jews, and later the Muslims, since they believed in strict monotheism, which itself was also a departure from the original Neterian (Trinitarian) teaching. Like many other things that the Christians co-opted, it was done to accomplish the goal of ingratiating themselves to gentiles[12] and pagans (many of whom followed the Isiac {Ancient Egyptian Goddess Aset [Isis]} tradition, first so that the pagan Romans would accept them and leave them alone, and also so that the pagans would follow Christianity by seeing similarities to their pagan religions in Christianity. However, the Christians used something else to insure the pagan conversion: the Roman army. Once the Roman emperor converted to Christianity, to enforce the conversion and prevent the practice of other religions, the Roman forces, now under the control of Christian orthodox leaders, set out to stop the practice of any other religion and any other form of Christianity. Neterians, as non-western practitioners of religion, will fail in impressing Christians, Muslims and Jews with our religion, even though it is the foundation of theirs, because we have no army to prevent the practice of Christianity and enforce Neterianism on them! But imagine that if we did, within one generation they would forget about Christianity and Islam and Judaism and adopt Neterianism, just as Africans brought to the west and Native Americans conquered in the Western hemisphere were forced to change their religions- that thought should give everyone pause. It means that religion is not intrinsic to a person's makeup, rather, it is cultural and often also folkloric, depending on where a person is born and the culture they grow up in. Please note that the comment on having an army to prevent the practice of Christianity, Islam, and Judaism and to enforce Neterianism on them is presented not to advocate violence or in any way sanction the actions of the Roman army, but only to make the point above, that religion is not intrinsic to a person's makeup but is a cultural and folkloric factor of society.

In any case, if the Neterian Creed were to focus prominently on one "Trinity," which one would it be? And would that practice compromise the true Neterian theology? If we were to say it's ok to do that so as to show Christians that we have a similar Trinity, many might say "well this Neterianism is the same as Christianity so why should I stop following Christianity? More likely, as they look further into Shetaut Neter they would become "horrified" to see the plethora of gods and goddesses, what they would consider "idols" and "devils," that we worship. And how long would it take them to curse Neterians and bid them a speedy send-off on their journey to hell because they do not

---

[12] <u>*Archaic.*</u> A pagan or heathen., One who is not of the Jewish faith or is of a non-Jewish nation.

Mystical Answers to the Important Questions of Life

accept Jesus as their personal savior, since that is supposedly the only way to be "saved"? So, within a short time of trying to appeal to the orthodox faith-based followers of religion, the "pagans" and "heathen infidels" have been cursed and sent to hell for all their troubles! It is incorrect to bother with fanatic followers of orthodox dogmatic religions; those who are ready will take the care and time to look at Neterianism without prejudice, or fear, and they will see the highly evolved and exquisite nature of Shetaut Neter philosophy.

In Neterian Religion, Neberdjer and Neteru constitute the main teaching from the religio-iconographical perspective. This is why the Trinities are not focused upon in the same way as in Christianity. In Neterianism, each one has a special teaching, and to focus on one in the way of being supreme and making others irrelevant in a way as is done in the Western religious format would damage the teaching. In orthodox religions, the tendency is to focus on apparently simple dogmatic teachings; this way is designed for simple minds or minds that have been kept in a state of lesser development. Saying that there is only one Trinity is a simplification for simple minds, minds that cannot cognize the deeper meaning of life- minds that have been downtrodden by years of "dumbing down" and indoctrination with ignorant and obsessive notions of guilt and fear related to religion. Orthodox and dogmatic religion is for the ignorant masses that are herded like sheep to the slaughter. That does not work for Shetaut Neter because that would negate the mystical philosophy, and the Neterian teaching requires more mature personalities who accept the teaching freely. Mystical religion is for maturing spiritual seekers and not for ignorant sycophants.

The book **_"The Mystical Journey From Jesus To Christ"_** was written, in part, for those who are looking for a bridge between Orthodox Christianity and Shetaut Neter or mystical religion. For those open (mature) to that extent, it will serve them. However, that book is not written for those who want to follow Shetaut Neter in its own right, but for those who want an opening to discover the true meaning and source of the original Christian teachings. There is also another direct path, that is, for those who want to follow Shetaut Neter without apologies or kowtowing to other religions or cultures. True Neterians do not go about bootlicking other traditions or sniveling, or begging for converts, nor do they seek to enforce their way on others or prevent others from practicing their religion to the extent it does not hurt others. Neterians also do not proselytize. Generally, those who come to the Neterian tradition while holding on to orthodox beliefs after they have been urged to explore Neterianism have proven to be weak aspirants, not qualified for mystical teachings. How many times have we seen people who, as you say: "can easily recognize the correlation with the widely known offspring religions" but who nevertheless reject rationality and revert to their comforting nescience? Presenting someone the truth is not a guarantee of their following that truth because there are psychological obstructions due to what we refer to as _ariu_ (karma of the past that shapes the present feelings, thoughts and desires). Overcoming the obstructions requires maturity or force. A sufficient level of maturity to follow the teachings sincerely means one must come to Shetaut Neter on one's own, using one's reason to realize that there is a higher perspective of life to be sought after.

Conversation with God

Neterians should not try to equate Shetaut Neter with the orthodox religions and their practices or to ingratiate themselves to the orthodox followers of other religions and Neterians should not emulate their practices. An example is the tendency to repeat slogans like "praise Jesus" or "God bless America," "God willing," or "ishallah," (Arabic: God Willing). This practice may be advisable for ignorant followers of religion so that they may acknowledge that there is a greater power controlling the world beyond their egoistic designs- essentially to develop humility. But notice that the western religious cultures, supported by the masses (who repeat those slogans), seek constantly to control the world and force others to convert to their religions; what happened to God willing? If it were up to God all would be free. In reality that slogan means they will have *their* way GOD WILLING! – and to hell with everyone else's needs or rights. For proof of this, study the Christian missionary movement in the Americas and Africa and study the Arab-Muslim conquest of north and west Africa and west India.

Neterians need to abandon those practices and ignorant beliefs, while remaining indifferent to those who hold them, understanding they must grow at their own pace. Our fate is determined by our actions. God merely prepares the field of action. People themselves control their destinies and that understanding requires maturity to responsibly accept one's errors and sufferings and the courage to change one's own self, not just the world. This Neterian philosophy leads to true mastery and not slavery to God or the church or to clever politicians or dogmatic religious leaders who whip up religious fervor to justify wars and slavery of entire cultures through promotion of blind faith and demagoguery.

True Neterians should seek to discover what Shetaut Neter is all about on its own terms and leave behind their notions of other religious traditions. That is difficult for those who adopt Shetaut Neter when they are older as opposed to those who inherit it as children. This takes time, but at some point an aspirant must turn into an initiate - at some point it is time to be full fledged Neterians instead of hybrid western religion practitioners or salad-bar new age religionists (mixing and matching different pagan or mystical religious teachings as it suits one).

Orthodox and dogmatic religions cannot be repaired by adding mystical teachings to them, repeating ecumenical platitudes or showing their followers the true history of religion, because those religions incorporate a process that closes minds and atrophies intellects, and harbor seeds of religious supremacy and spiritual hubris (see the books, *Limits of Faith"* and *"African Origins"*) that lend themselves to segregation and discrimination, that translate to political and economic tyranny on other societies that practice other religions or have people of other "races." Those faults of western religions come from the patriarchal and violent cultures that gave rise to these religions and from the *seeds of conflict* (some included below) which are embedded in their holy books which they consider to be the "infallible word of God"; so those texts will not be given up easily. Many people are fascinated by the western "holy books" since they have been indoctrinated into believing that they represent "factual" "historical" events and that God directly inspired every single word in them, regardless of the obvious contradictions, errors and outright ignorance. And beware of those who consider themselves as

Mystical Answers to the Important Questions of Life

ecumenical Christians, Jews or Muslims, because as they espouse a live and let live ideal, they do not want to abandon their inherited religions and are therefore inevitably supporting the orthodox and imperialist leaders of their own cultures AND the seeds of religious supremacy and spiritual hubris (that their religion is the only true religion)- even if they say they are against that- the only way to be against that is to renounce the religion itself or extirpate those offensive scriptures from the "holy" texts, and who among them will do that? If this were not true, why is western culture the leader of economic and political-military subjugation of the world? How could the western leaders do that if they were not supported by their own people? Realize that for all the protests in the west, those same people pay taxes that support the government which is composed of almost all Christians or Jews. Where are the ecumenical Christians, Jews or Muslims when it comes to living with people of other faiths and living in harmony with people of other countries and people of other "races"? Protests alone are not enough. Protests are institutionalized forms of pseudo-democracy. The democratic system of government accommodates protests, but not serious challenges, and people are conditioned to protest but not challenge the system. Why? –because they are indoctrinated into the idea that it is the best system that ever was, even with all its faults, and it must continue no matter what wrongdoings proceed from it. What many non-western spiritualists people do not understand is that the ecumenism touted by many western religious practitioners (especially in the United States of America) is not for living with other peoples and other religions in peace, but rather for living with other Christians, Muslims or Jews only; everyone else is out. This means that other peoples must be converted or subjugated or destroyed.

Where is the turning of the other cheek of Christianity or the peace of Judaism or Islam supposedly touted by the western religions when westerners are attacked by other societies in retribution for wrongs the western countries themselves committed originally which have never been redressed? Individuals may express regrets, but as a government there is usually no acknowledgement, and regardless there is no restitution. There is no introspection, no repentance, but rather self-righteousness and immediate retaliation and condemnation of others, followed by demonizing of others and flag waving to justify the violence of war on other peoples. Those who do not accept what has been just said should read what the Bible has to say about other religions:

The Bible 2 Kings 5.15
"Now I know that <u>there is no God in all earth except in Israel</u>..."

The statement above implies that there is no other legitimate religion except the Jewish and by association, the Christian one as well. Likewise, those who do not accept what has been just said should read what the Koran has to say about Christians and Jews who come to them apparently as friends:

> 2:120 <u>Never will the Jews or the Christians be satisfied with thee unless thou follow their form of religion.</u>

> 5:54 Section 8. O ye who believe! <u>Take not the Jews and the Christians for your friends and protectors</u>: <u>They are but friends and protectors to each other</u>. And he amongst you that turns to them (for friendship) is of them. Verily Allah guideth not a people unjust.
>
> 2:113 Section 14 (Koran). <u>The Jews say: "The Christians have naught (to stand) upon"; and the Christians say: "The Jews have naught (to stand) upon."</u> Yet they (profess to) study the (same) Book. Like unto their word is what those say who know not; but Allah will judge between them in their quarrel on the Day of Judgment.

The religious texts do not necessarily determine the disposition of a people but the religious tenets are guidelines for a people's beliefs, thoughts, desires and actions, which can facilitate certain negative or positive tendencies. The true judgment comes from their own actions through history. History has shown that as a group, the practitioners of western religion act in the way described in the scriptures herein presented. Indeed the Muslims acted towards those whom they conquered in the same way as they accused the Christians. The point is that if Christians cannot even tolerate Muslims or Jews without trying to convert them, what is there to say about others which are not part of or derived from the Judaic tradition? Those who follow Neterianism (polytheists) or other religions and mystical traditions other than Christianity, Judaism or Islam are repudiated by Muslims basing their repudiation on words from the Koran itself:

> 48:6 (Koran) And that He may punish the Hypocrites, men and women, and the <u>Polytheists</u>, men and women, <u>who imagine an evil opinion of Allah</u>. On them is a round of Evil: The Wrath of Allah is on them: <u>He has cursed them and got Hell ready for them: and evil is it for a destination.</u>
>
> 98:5 (Koran) And they have been commanded no more than this: To worship Allah, offering Him sincere devotion, <u>being True (in faith);</u> to establish regular Prayer; and to practice regular Charity; and that is the Religion Right and Straight.
>
> 98:6 (Koran) <u>Those who reject (Truth),</u> among the People of the Book and among the <u>Polytheists,</u> will be in Hellfire, to dwell therein (for aye). <u>They are the worst of creatures.</u>

Sustaining the idea that the orthodox or faith-based Western religions are "benign" religions that can be at peace with non-western religions and their practitioners is a delusion because those who support western religions fanatically, <u>as well as</u> those who *acquiesce* to the desires of the orthodox or fundamentalist groups and support them, including those who consider themselves as ecumenical or peacemakers, have as the ultimate goal to establish their own religion as the supreme and "only true" religion,

Mystical Answers to the Important Questions of Life

supplanting all others; the proof of that is that they believe in the Bible or Koran and everything it says literally. Those who say they are orthodox Christians or Muslims but do not believe in the religious imperialism and hubris aspects of those religions are therefore deluding themselves about the nature of the deeper tenets of their own religions.

Mind you, the people are not the problem; rather, it is the upbringing and indoctrination with the ignorant and violent notions. The masses sustain the ignorance, but it is the deficient scripture and the dogmatic and demagogic leadership that controls them through promoting the superstition and blind faith way of following religion. In time, the western religions will change and the negative aspects will be minimized, but that will not occur in this era. For now Shemsu (Neterian aspirants) need to disengage from those traditions; that is the answer. Only when Shetaut Neter is followed from this detached perspective will the true nature and power of Shetaut Neter be revealed. Let the *ari* (karma) of the followers of other religions lead them and let the world teach them the lessons they need to learn. It is not your concern or duty or within your capacity to save them; they must save themselves. Better yet, be a model Neterian to show them something indeed different and pure so they can really see the difference- perhaps in a future lifetime they will pursue a better way.

The choice to be initiated as a Shems (Neterian aspirant) is supposed to mean that a person wants to follow Shetaut Neter and not something else. However, we know there are many who take the Shems initiation and still do not realize what it means, as they are much involved with the greater culture and its trappings. Partially, this is why the Shems level of initiation is open to all as a first stage. Certainly, those who take the next level of initiation, the Temple initiation, should know in no uncertain terms they are following Neterianism, and not Christianity, Islam, Hinduism, etc. This is why the next level of initiation is more restricted-- aspirants must prove their character and devotion to Shetaut Neter to be accepted as Temple initiates. Thus, it makes more sense that if a person wants to learn about religion in the same way as they learned it in their inherited religion, they should stay in their inherited religion.

I have said many times that just because Christianity, Hinduism and Buddhism are direct descendants of Neterianism does not mean that these traditions, or every sect within these traditions, are following the same exact teachings as were given originally in Neterianism. Nor does it mean that following Christianity, Hinduism or Buddhism such as they are today is the same as following Neterianism, just as a child is not necessarily the same as the parent; the child may go a different way and yet still retain part of the same DNA, the same appearance, etc. The child may even forget from whence they came and not give credit to the parent, and may still practice some teachings given by the parent, yet they are not the same; <u>for that to be they would need to journey home, acknowledge their parentage, their original heritage and adjust their current tradition accordingly. Until that happens, they should be regarded as distant relatives, and lovingly so. Even if the love is not returned in kind, they should be loved at a distance, in a detached manner, and not by assimilation or amalgamation of teachings in the direction from parent to child.</u> The true parent loves the child even when it strays but that does not mean that the wayward child is to be sanctioned or approved of, nor does it mean that the

Conversation with God

parent should act like the child when it strays. It should be chastised and disciplined, and if it chooses not to listen, then again, there is the world (Geb) who will do the disciplining! If one chooses not to listen to the law of gravity (Maat), the world will be the teacher when one jumps off the cliff! So too, those who choose to believe there is no reincarnation or process of *ariu* (karma) or that only western religion is true and that the end of the world will come according to the Bible or the Koran will be taught by death and time and rebirth. One day the same orthodox people who want to be buried in segregated cemeteries as Christians, Muslims or Jews will reincarnate as Neterians, Buddhists, Hindus, Native Americans, etc., and they will have to learn a different perspective. In any case, will you maintain yourself in a state of ignorance so you will reincarnate again and again with them so you can be their teacher and attain spiritual enlightenment with them some day in the future, say 10 million years from now?

If not, leave them and their ignorance alone. Enlighten them if they come to you and only to the extent of their sincerity. Stop reading the books of ignorant musings and kindergarten religion and immerse yourself in the book of life which is in your heart, your mind and the chine of the soul. Let go of the platitudes of spirituality and latch on to the philosophy of the true mystery… of Mystical Spirituality. Release yourself from the banality of human life. Embrace the heroic culture of the mysteries (mysticism). Your ariu (karmic disposition) has drawn you to the Ancient Egyptian Mystical Tradition, as opposed to other authentic mystical traditions. Therefore, look to the light of the sun, as Hrumakhet. Turn away from the ignorant darkness of fanaticism and the pseudo religion of salvation that is in reality a neurotic infection of the mind caused by ignorance and fear that have turned ego into egoism, mystery into dogma, myth into historicity, ritual into ritualism and religion into disunion.

Listen to the words of great masters like the Ancient Egyptian Sage-pharaoh Akhnaton who embraced all humanity, regardless of skin color, language or religion as kindred souls and kindred bodies. That is true ecumenism and any sage who speaks thus is pouring out before you treasures that are like unto trees of gold arranged in beds of silver. But as humans are capable of delusion, some may see a treasure while others may see poison, in accordance with their maturity or their conditioning and delusion. Yet even those who see treasure may not be able to fully grasp it; that is why these words cannot be realized by just reading or listening to them. They must be studied and practiced by a personality that has been cleansed from the infection of ignorance, the delusion of conditioning, the commingling of philosophies and the pressure of egoistic desires. Then the silver becomes sparkles and the gold begins to shine and the tree grows up from the earth to the limitless reaches of the sky wherein there is the light of enlightenment.

Peace and Blessings!

Sebai MAA

Mystical Answers to the Important Questions of Life

Questions: Did the Ancient Egyptians and Atlantians Self-destruct and did the Serpent Power teaching come from Asia to Egypt?

Hotep and Sat Nam Muata,

I thought I'd forward you a couple of responses already posted. Thanks for pointing me to the book The Serpent Power. I have the "Postures of the Gods and Goddesses" book and there is some good info there. A bunch of folks have already responded and I have copied a couple of comments below. If you're to respond, I'll gladly forward to the list. Take Care…

"wow! that was really valuable information for the seeker…and it really makes sense because it complements the theory that Kundalini was the spiritual practice of the Atlantians and after Atlantis was destroyed, the people who survived migrated and passed their sacred knowledge to Egypt, South America (Mayas) and Asia (India-Tibet). love and light"

and

"Don't forget that both the Egyptian and Atlantean cultures destroyed themselves as an outcome of their mastery over the life force. As well, they turned what was once a lush paradise into a virtually lifeless desert. Personally, I think we should study what went wrong in their consciousness before we even think of emulating them - something every serious kundalini yogi should think deeply on."

Answer

Greetings,

I truly appreciate your interest.

As you are beginning to discover, from our book *Serpent Power,* and from other sources, what is today known as Kundalini Yoga or the Serpent Power was discovered and practiced in Ancient Egypt. It was thrilling for me when I first discovered this so many years ago. As a scholar of African culture and spirituality as well as world religion and mysticism, I discovered correlations between Ancient Egyptian (African) and Indian culture, so many in fact that these became the subject of two books. As my main discipline of personal practice (*Arat Sekhem* {Kemetic Serpent Power Yoga}), I was surprised to discover so much documentation and scriptural discourse on the subject from the Ancient Egyptian priests and priestesses themselves. This is perhaps because the evidences, which were plain for all traditional Egyptologists to see, had been misunderstood or dismissed by them. In any case, I set out to document and espouse the science, at least that part which is safe and effective, for those interested in this form of

Conversation with God

spiritual practice. As stated in our book *The Serpent Power,* the first documented evidences in Ancient Egypt appear in 10,000 B.C.E., thousands of years earlier than in India (India did not exist at that time) or anywhere else. Thus, it is more likely that the teaching of the Serpent Power was transferred to India later when there was contact between Ancient Egypt and India, which is supported by the almost exact correlations in the iconographies and teachings of the two cultures (see our book *Egypt and India*). The teaching of Arat Sekhem in Ancient Egypt was advanced and formed the basis of the spiritual and material culture of Kamitan society. This is all documented in the book "The Serpent Power."

In reference to the legend of Atlantis, in fact, to this date, a lost or destroyed culture, kingdom or continent called Atlantis has never been discovered either on land or under the sea, and the same is true for the legend of Lemuria. Much embellishment has been made through the years on the few words provided by Plato. He is the only documentary source for any knowledge about Atlantis so one must be careful in accepting additions to the legend by those who imagine additional scenarios about the existence and downfall of Atlantis and its supposed associations with other cultures, additions that were not part of the original communication by Plato. As Plato himself states, the story of Atlantis was given to him by Solon who got it from an Ancient Egyptian priest who was talking about the Proto-Greek civilization today known as the Minoan-Theran who developed a thriving and prosperous culture that was related to Ancient Egypt (there was trade and cultural exchange) at about 2000 B.C.E. (see our book *African Origins of Civilization*) The Ancient Egyptian priest never said that Atlantis came before Egypt, but rather that it came before the Classical Greek era of that time (time of Thales, Pythagoras, Plato, etc., about 700-500 B.C.E.). Thera was an island home of the proto-Classical Greek civilization in the Mediterranean that was destroyed by an earthquake. These statements by Solon fit the archeological evidences discovered about the Minoan-Theran culture in all respects.

At about 1,400 B.C.E. Thera exploded due to a volcano and the Minoan people on Crete were also destroyed. Classical Greek culture then emerged from the ashes hundreds of years later. Keep in mind that there is archeological evidence of the existence of Ancient Egyptian civilization and the knowledge of the "Serpent Power"[13] as far back as 10,000 B.C.E. ALL of the books and other works of fiction writings related to the legend of Atlantis are rooted in the writings of Plato, so the mystery about Atlantis was embellished based on the simple history given by Plato which runs only a few pages and there is no substantiation for the later additional writings whatsoever. The teaching of Plato is a prehistory of Classical Greece and the archeological evidence in Ancient Egypt and Crete as well as Thera do substantiate that what modern day archeologists call Minoans and the civilization that Plato referred to as the Atlantians are one and the same.

As for the idea that the Ancient Egyptians destroyed themselves and their ecology, this idea is contradicted by 10,000 years of successful history of their renewable culture in which the use of the Serpent Power was known since the earliest times. During that time

---

[13] see the book *Serpent Power* by Muata Ashby

Mystical Answers to the Important Questions of Life

there was prosperity and order. In fact, the archeological evidence shows that North Africa started to become a desert thousands of years before the Ancient Nubians colonized North-East Africa to create Kamit (Ancient Egypt). It was not until the last 1500 years of Ancient Egyptian history that we notice a sharp decline in culture and this coincides with the invading hoards of Asiatics (Hyksos, Persians, Assyrians) and the Europeans (Greeks and Romans) who exploited Egypt as a "breadbasket" for their empires, leading to the time when the Ancient Egyptian culture finally fell in 450 A.C.E., after its land was ravaged by the Roman empire, which used its fertile land to feed the Roman armies and insatiable population. This was followed by the Christian zealots and later the Muslim conquering armies. The Christians, and later the Muslims, destroyed and forcibly closed the Neterian (Ancient Egyptian Religion) temples and forcibly converted people whom they referred to as pagans, polytheists or nonbelievers. Therefore, the role of Asiatic and European invading barbarian forces in the downfall of Ancient Egypt should be studied carefully as opposed to an unsupported theory that *"Egyptian and Atlantean cultures destroyed themselves,"* so that we may know history correctly, and also know where the world has gone wrong in order to bring humanity to the brink of ecological and social destruction, and to discover what was going right for over 10,000 years that allowed the Ancient Egyptian civilization to thrive in a way that has been unequalled by any other civilization. Further, we should perhaps study what there is in modern day religions that owe not only their existence to Neterian (Ancient Egyptian) religion, but also several of their most important tenets. Then we may discover great insights into the world faiths that will augment them and allow us all to see a more ecumenical vision of spirituality that would lead to greater peace and understanding.

As for the ecology of North Africa, the climactic changes have been shown to coincide with natural changes around the world over a period of thousands of years. The spiritual culture of Ancient Kamit was the first to affirm the protection of the environment and this is demonstrated in the "Precepts of Maat" and the "Wisdom Texts."

All of the proof and documentation for the points discussed above have been carefully documented, substantiated and catalogued in the book *"African Origins of Civilization, Religion, Yoga Spirituality and Ethics Philosophy."*

I hope this has been helpful in some way. If I can be of further assistance, I would be most willing to answer any questions from your organization.

Peace and Blessings!

Sebai MAA

Conversation with God

Question: Are the miracles discussed in the book Autobiography of a Yogi true?

Dr. Muata Abhaya, I have a few questions:

Are the miracles discussed in the book, *Autobiography of a Yogi* true?

Thank you

Answer

Greetings!

Many of the miracles discussed in the book *Autobiography of a Yogi* have been known to happen throughout history to "Yogis" (those who practice certain disciplines to promote advanced spiritual evolution) of all spiritual traditions. This is true of all cultures, not just in India. It all depends on the level of development of a human being. Yet, while walking on water, flying through the air and other such miracles are exciting, how do they help you on your spiritual journey? Does seeing someone fly automatically make you advance spiritually? No – it may promote faith, but beyond that you still have to do the work of enlightening yourself. The renowned spiritual teacher Sai Baba has been known to produce ashes from his hands and rings which he gives to pilgrims. Once he was known to say that he wished he never had the capacity to do those miracles, or at least that he had not revealed them, because those who come to him are mostly not proper mature aspirants, but rather thrill seeking followers looking for someone to follow blindly.

Of course, the word "miracles" implies a spiritual basis to an unexplained occurrence. While psychic events can occur to an individual, they may or may not be related to a "mystical" (i.e. attainment of higher consciousness) process; they may only contain lower "spiritual" value. Sometimes when human beings do not understand something they call it a miracle, but the digestion of food, how a cut heals, a bird in the sky, the shining sun, the birth of a human being, the growth of a seed into a tree are miracles too are they not? Scientists and doctors can describe what is happening, but they cannot tell you how or why. However, human beings have developed a notion that these mysteries can be explained by science and so they do not refer to these as miracles (any more). Many things that were considered miracles in the past became ordinary or even mundane once the occurrences were understood better or they became commonplace. Consider how airplanes of today would appear to people of 200 years ago.

Many times spiritual scriptures will give fantastic descriptions of things that are possible to get aspirants interested and exited about the teaching. Indeed, the capacity to intellectualize is a miracle that animals do not possess. Beyond that, intuition is the purview of the few advanced initiates which can lead to enlightenment, which is the highest miracle. However, upon attaining enlightenment any and all miracles are seen as part of the dream of human existence in which everything is viewed as being relative,

Mystical Answers to the Important Questions of Life

illusory and transient expressions of the Self. In other words, miracles are as ordinary to a Sage as any other event, or more accurately put, miracles are lumped together with everything else in creation which is indeed a manifestation of the Supreme Spirit. Is that not the greatest miracle of all? Indeed all is Divine, i.e. a miracle. Perhaps the greatest miracle is the realization of that very truth, attaining enlightenment in and of itself!

Peace and Blessings!

Sebai MAA

Conversation with God

Question: What is Avatarism?

Greetings,

Why do we speak of avatars (incarnation of god) like Asar (Osiris), Jesus and Buddha if, as you have said, we are all avatars in our own right?

Answer

Greetings!

The teaching of Avatarism is important in spiritual study because it gives the aspirant a focus for understanding the Divine and the process of coming into life and it's purpose. Indeed the Self has incarnated in a big way, as great spiritual leaders (Asar, Aset, Buddha, Krishna, etc.), but also as ordinary human beings, and furthermore, all creation is an incarnation (plants, animals, planets, stars, etc.). However, until there is enlightenment, this view is objective and the teaching allows you to understand the process of coming into existence. At some point the teacher tells you that this is not just a story about some great personalities, but is about the greatness within you as well. Indeed, you have a task to perform as a spiritual avatar. It may appear to be great or ordinary but in the eyes of God, if you live a life, which allows the spirit to flow and express through you, you are living the greatest life possible, no different than the life of Asar, Jesus, Heru or Krishna! Therefore, allow the glory of spiritual realization and righteousness to fill your life with vigor, beauty, peace and harmony and you will discover the power, bliss and peace of the Spirit and your life will be a tribute to God and a blessing to humanity.

Peace and Blessings!

Sebai MAA

Mystical Answers to the Important Questions of Life

Question: Should Saints and Sages Charge for their services?

Hello Dr. Muata. I have a question. I was having a discussion with my mother about the celebration of another spiritual teacher's birthday party and she doubts his authenticity as a saint because she claims that a true saint would not have a Birthday party where the participants must pay a $40 fee. I do not agree with her, but I would like to give her a better explanation then the one I gave. Why does this other spiritual teacher charge so large a sum? My broader question is this one: In the book, "The Path of the Masters," Julian Johnson says that objective indices of mastership are "First and most noticeable is the important fact the real Masters never charge for their services, nor do they accept payment in any form or any sort of material benefits for their instructions. This is a universal law among Masters, and yet it is an amazing fact that thousands of eager seekers in America and elsewhere go on paying large sums of money for 'spiritual instruction'. Masters are always self-sustaining. They are never supported by their students or by public charity." Julian Johnson's teacher is Maharaj Sawan Singh Ji. Please help me understand the true meaning of the above statement so that my mind may see the truth.

Thank you

Answer

Greetings,

In the Ancient Egyptian Story of "The Seven Year Famine"[14] the teaching related how, a time long ago, people in Ancient Egypt became forgetful of the need to make regular offerings to the temple and to the Divine. The Supreme Being in the form of Khnum stopped the flow of water through the Nile because the 10% tithe had been forgotten. When the King found out that the tithes had been forgotten, he immediately reinstituted it and even gave more to make up for what had been neglected. Reciprocating in kind, God allowed the waters to flow and fertility returned to the land. The Temples flourished and the people turned away from arrogance and worldly delusion and towards the Temples and the teaching and became spiritually enlightened.

---

[14] Audio lecture by Sebai Maa is available lecture through the Sema Institute of Yoga (see order form in the back of this book)

Conversation with God

"The Famine Stele", Old Kingdom (4,000 BCE).

It is amazing that so many people have the illusion that spiritual teachers should not charge for their services. Why? People make up so many illusions in their minds about what spirituality is supposed to be that many times those same illusions lead them away from getting close to that very person who is the embodiment of spiritual wisdom. Yes, unless they are sustained by their followers, spiritual teachers need to and always have charged for their services and as long as they live in the world of time and space with a physical body, which needs shelter and sustenance, they will have needs that have to be taken care of. Temples need to be sustained also.

In modern times, people especially in the USA and the western countries, have been deluded by their misunderstanding, having observed some spiritual teachers that have migrated to the Western countries and seem to need no sustenance in the form of donations. It is because those teachers are usually sustained by donors back home or enterprises that are income producing businesses, or they may be sustained by their main disciples. In ancient times, the town's people would bring food offerings, firewood, and donate their professional expertise to build the Temples. In spiritual traditions all around the world, it has been the DUTY of the aspirant to take care of those needs, with a very "selfish" desire in mind, to discover what that Saint or Sage knows! This is a good selfishness of course, and the Sages and Saints support it. If the Sage is not kept warm and with his or her belly satisfied, how can they teach anything if they are concerned with practical issues like food and shelter?

Mystical Answers to the Important Questions of Life

How could a teacher teach without food, shelter, etc.? How could the Ancient Egyptian Temples survive without support from the government and the people? How could Jesus survive without the alms from Jewish country folk? How can any legitimate church survive without contributions? How could Buddha survive without the goodness of householders to fill his begging bowl? In ancient times, the tribute to the spiritual teacher was fruits and firewood. Food for them to eat and wood to keep them warm. And you should want to keep them warm and comfortable indeed so that they can transmit to you the even hotter fire of spiritual wisdom and divine grace, for if their personality, their body are not there, where will an aspirant look for these things? In thin air? In the forest? In the ocean? In the illusions of their minds, thinking they can discover the mysteries of life on their own? In books? Even books cannot transmit the teaching, only information. In order for that information to be relevant there needs to be a living preceptor who can explain it and make it relevant and useful so that it may be understood and practiced properly by an aspirant. That kind of preceptor is worth more than any donation that could be made.

Thus, how can anyone survive in today's economy, which is based on money, where the unprecedented inflation and cost of living, due to capitalism and greed, is such that it is virtually impossible to live inexpensively unless you go far away into the country where the land values are lower, and then perhaps only have enough to purchase a mobile home? Where then would the teaching be disseminated? There is another particular problem still; building a house is still expensive, and then the Sage will be so far and how will you find him/her or let alone even know he/she exists? In our modern system of real estate, there are mortgages, utilities etc., like any other enterprise. The difference here in contributing to an authentic spiritual center/teacher is that every dollar goes to support the spiritual efforts, disseminating the teaching or other projects of the preceptor. While it is the good *ari* (karmic) fortune of anyone to donate to a Sage, there are few people of means who adhere to this ancient tradition and who understand the wisdom behind it. Even if you never attend spiritual programs but contribute, you are still promoting positive *ariu* (karma), which will help you one day. However, direct service to a Spiritual Preceptor is the highest service and contribution of all. Every mature aspirant sees the beauty and glory of working towards a righteous project, which uplifts humanity. The Sages show the way, otherwise who can? But Sages cannot do it alone, nor is money alone the need. Service and devotion purify the heart, and these open up the possibility of spiritual awakening, which is the greatest treasure.

The production of books, tapes and promulgating the teachings has its costs as well; ask any book publisher. What is of concern should be is the money needed for legitimate purposes or will it be used for Rolls Royces, Mercedes, Cadillac cars, mansions and other non-necessities, as some pseudo-gurus have done in the past. The ancient Kemetic proverb holds the key - *"God decreed that Love and Necessity should be the lords of life."* - and if you see a preceptor who lives like a movie star, purchases big expensive houses, squanders money, gives it to cronies or commits fraud, you must ask if this is an authentic preceptor or a charlatan - then you must act accordingly and not be taken in by smooth talking or exuberant preaching. Many times people are duped into believing that preachers or gurus that come from another country, like India, are not sustained by anyone. They do not consider that those people have a base of support in their home country where donations are accepted as a tradition. Since they are trying to attract adherents in new countries, they do not ask for donations, there but yet they receive donations anyway. A difficult problem in the United States is that those who are interested in the Kemetic faith are often torn between making ends meet and donating to the new faith they are trying to follow. But is this so much different from the collections in a Christian church? Perhaps the quandary comes in because they are not fully committed. They are caught between the secular culture, the religion of their upbringing and personal issues. The practice of the teaching will fail as long as this conflict continues, and the Temple will not flourish either as long as these conditions persist.

Having said all of this, think of the following. How much does it cost a soul to live on and on, reincarnating and suffering the pains of life over and over again? Throughout history, aspirants have paid the greatest and true price, their undying devotion to the spiritual preceptor- and the preceptors donate their lives to service of the Divine. That is why Kemetic priests and priestesses are called *Hm Neter* - servant (slave) or prophet (SEER) of God - Priest, *Hmt Neter*- servant (slave) or prophet (SEER) of God – Priestess; the term also means "majestic." This is why the teaching has survived to this day. Indeed, a qualified aspirant, someone who recognizes the value of an authentic spiritual teacher would go anywhere and do anything (in accordance with the scriptures) for that person because they know that person is God consciousness incarnate.

Further, the illusion persists that spiritual people should not be in business or politics. This is because people are so tainted by corrupt business people that they associate money and business people with corruption, the devil, or demoniac, sinful living. This is the immature or ignorant way of understanding. In Kemetic culture, spirituality, religion, politics, economics, etc, are all related. The problem in modern times is that politics are not conducted from a basis of righteousness and truth. In reality, egoistic and greedy people are the source of unrighteousness, and it is a blessing when authentic spiritual people can show the proper way that business and commerce should be conducted. This is the mature way of understanding.

The world of time and space works by the laws of cause and effect (Karma in India or Maat in Kemet-Ancient Egypt). Thus, one should not expect to receive something without giving something. This is the law of giving and receiving, related in Hermetic-Egyptian philosophy. An aspirant should never go empty-handed, either to the teacher or to God. They should bring an offering in some form, food, money, love, devotion, service, goodwill, faith, etc., whatever they can afford. This act of giving and humility opens the gates of the mind and breaks down the arrogance of the ego so as to understand and receive the teaching. This process is known as Divine grace. Giving to the Temple is not like giving to any other organization. Giving to the Temple is like an investment that never diminishes. It is not like the stock market- here today, gone tomorrow! There is another saying in the spiritual arena: "Money goes, wisdom stays." If the student has understood anything, it is because the teacher's grace has fallen on him or her to illuminate what they have experienced in this and previous lives. Thus, the aspirant

Mystical Answers to the Important Questions of Life

naturally should want to do everything to make sure that the relationship with that person is always harmonious and that nothing ever comes between them, no strife, misunderstanding, egoism, etc. Naturally, it is the student, the seeker, who must take care here to do all that is required in order to derive the benefits of the glory of initiation, because no one can be forced to practice or understand the teaching. The impetus must come from within, and then the teaching can be effective.

Until people are ready to understand the initiatic way, they are not qualified to receive the higher teaching. This is because the egoistic concepts and misunderstandings will always stand in their way and they thus make their own way through life without the benefit of spiritual preceptorship. This is a fate that anyone who has discovered God, or even had a glimpse of God, would cringe at and run away from. Many are called and few are chosen. The teaching is not for everyone, but for those who are ready. When they are ready they will see that any amount of money a person can pay to attain enlightenment is worth it, so what can we say of $5 per class or $40 for a dinner to support a place where one can hear God speak and to be in His/Her company? Who would not trade all the money in the world, which is ultimately perishable, for that treasure which brings joy now and is eternal? Just the thought of this possibility should carry a true aspirant into an ecstasy!

Those who do not see the logic in the initiatic way must experience more of life until they are ready to understand. Until then they deserve our compassion, patience and caring as well as guidance whenever possible, as we were cared for in unseen ways by God through unknown people who helped us along the way. At least, keeping the teaching alive until they are ready to receive it performs this service. Again, as one gives, one receives, and when God gives, it is a shower of glory and this is why Sages give so much, for they receive an unbounded bliss and this overflows to all. Just by a glance, a word, a passage in a book, this divine stream can be transmitted to a person who is ready. This is also why Sages are always there, and when a student is ready they seem to appear, but they were always there. This is the golden chain that binds spiritual teachers and their students in a karmic union of mutual love, compassion and goodwill. This is God's compassion, to be there when those who have turned away from Her for countless lifetimes suddenly, one day, are ready to listen. There will always be someone there, so there is no need to worry for the lost because they will find their way. God, operating through nature or in the form of a preceptor in person, will show them the way at the right time and in the right place. Be concerned with your life, your enlightenment, and what you need to do to succeed in the journey to supreme peace, supreme transcendence and immortality!

FROM THE STEALE OF DJEHUTI-NEFER:

"Consume pure foods and pure thoughts with pure hands, adore celestial beings, become associated with wise ones: sages, saints and prophets; make offerings to GOD."

Peace and Blessings!
Sebai MAA

Conversation with God

Question: Is Neterian religion and its priesthood only for black/African people?

Greetings,

I have a question about your priest/ priestesshood. Is the priest/ priestesshood in your organization Ancestrally inherited, meaning strictly for those who are Black/African, or can whites be initiated as priest/ priestesshood as well?

Thank you...

Answer

Greetings,

The Kemetic (Ancient Egyptian) priesthood is for those who follow the culture of Kemet (Ancient Egypt). For instance if you wanted to be a Buddhist priest, you do not follow Western culture and religion (Christianity, Judaism or Islam) and be a Buddhist priest. You must follow the culture associated with Buddhism to be a Buddhist priest. As Buddhism is primarily either Indian, Tibetan, Chinese or Japanese, you would follow one of those cultures. There is no Western independent development in Buddhist culture. Other examples, to practice Islam you follow Arab culture, to follow Taoism you follow Chinese culture. If you fully follow Chinese culture (language, customs, rituals, etc.) and Taoism tradition, you are effectively Chinese. Further, while Buddhism began in India (with association to Ancient Egypt) one could conclude that the primary source of Buddhism should be in India and not in Japan, Tibet or China. However, while it is true that the Japanese, Tibetans and Chinese brought forth positive developments in Buddhism, they were following a culture that it came with (primarily Indian) to them. If we might be able to say that Zen Buddhism from Japan is a distinct form of Buddhism, can we say that it is "different," that is, a different religion altogether? Further, could we say they are practicing something in contravention with the original Buddhism of India? It is all Buddhism, but with its distinct cultural nuances that have developed over centuries. If Buddhism were to come to the West (as it has), can we say that a distinct western form of Buddhism has developed there? No, what is practiced are the styles brought there from the East, the cultures of the East.

Likewise, if Kemetic religion is practiced in the West, it comes there with its associated culture. There is no independent development of Neterianism (Kemetic religion) in the West; it developed in Africa, therefore the specific African culture should be practiced with it. Even if over time the Kemetic religion or the Buddhist religion were to develop in the West, could they ever say they are originally Western developments? No, they would always have to say they are looking to their sources just as Zen Buddhism in Japan and Tibetan Buddhism in Tibet would ultimately have to say they are looking to India. The same may be true for the so-called Western religions (Judaism, Christianity, Islam) since

Mystical Answers to the Important Questions of Life

these originated in Asia Minor. However, those religions have been altered from their original forms and the adulterated and co-opted forms have been associated with Western culture by the Western rulers and masses.

As Kemetic religion is based in African culture, the practitioner must follow an African perspective. Since African culture, and especially the Kemetic tradition, do not recognize the concept of "race" and its degraded sociopolitical application (racism), Kemetic culture does not recognize or condone segregationist or racist policies. In fact, the teaching is the opposite, that all human beings have the same source and same kinship as well as the same Divine heritage. Therefore, whether or not the person is of recent ("black people") or distant ("white people") genetic African descent [all human beings are Africans either recently or anciently], the person should follow Kemetic-African culture. The great teachings of Sage Akhenaton as well as that of other Kemetic sages, enlightens us to the fact that all human beings, regardless of their skin color, originate from the same Spirit and the same physical creation. So we, as Neterians, cannot and do not recognize the human fabricated concept of "race" or the practice of racism. We do however recognize the cultural basis of religions and the need to follow and practice the philosophy as well as the culture of a tradition in order to experience the fullness of a religious process. Therefore, as long as the practitioner wants to adopt Kemetic/African culture, they may be accepted freely, regardless of the ethnicity (not race) or culture from which they come.

However, while the efforts of many people in different cultures to adopt Kemetic religion are appreciated and to be encouraged, the process of cooptation and delusion that they may keep Western culture and practice an African religion needs to be challenged because that process of adopting the religion without the culture facilitates cooptation and the adulteration of the Kemetic principles with alien cultural values that are incompatible with Kemetic tenets, as well as African values. One example is the Kemetic injunction against pollution of the land and water (found in the 42 precepts of Maat). The question would be how can a person who follows the practices of Europe, Japan or Australia of polluting and co-opting the cultural elements of other peoples, adopt Kemetic teachings but also support the right of Western countries to pollute the world with greenhouse gasses and other pollutants? If a non-African person in a Western country should adopt the Kemetic principles and not support the pollution agenda of the West, that would mean they are rejecting the pollution principle of Western culture and adopting the Kemetic/African, and thus, can be accepted into the Kemetic culture. Another example, Neterian/African religion/culture holds that religion is *Henotheistic*-There is a Supreme Being and lesser gods and goddesses. If a Western person should adopt that tenet, they are putting aside the monotheism of the West and adopting the African paradigm, and can be accepted into the Kemetic culture. Most importantly, if a person adopts a religion/culture fully they would also adopt its concept of "Holy Land." Can we imagine a Jewish person looking to South Africa as their "Holy Land"? Why not? Those who practice Christianity, Judaism, Islam, Baha'i, Sikhism, Buddhism, etc., look to either Palestine, India, etc., as their "Holy Land." In addition, they look at these places as special, as the source of their tradition, the place of their spiritual pilgrimage, and even where they want to be buried. A person who adopts Yoruba religion, for example, but

Conversation with God

wants to continue believing in Jesus as their savior and Jerusalem as the "Holy Land" and or be buried with their family in the hills of Tennessee or the family mausoleum in Scotland or Jamaica because they see that as their special place, etc., is not fully following the Yoruba religious culture and its traditions. Likewise, those who want to be considered "Kamitans" and never want to go to Egypt and want to stay with their families in Georgia or be buried back home in Barbados are not following Kamitan culture, but rather a self-styled hodgepodge of religious practices and name-only vows based on their own desires and not on history or the reality of the practice of the culture; in other words, what they have done is a self-created religion that facilitates their remaining part of their present culture while giving them psychological cover so they may continue making themselves believe they are something else.

But also, there are many levels of following. People follow in accordance with their capacities. Nevertheless, if you are an avid follower of a tradition, that is the culture that should inform every aspect of your life, including the place where you would want to make the final journey of life. That is of course something to work on; but the principle is to be understood. Much failure in following religion occurs due to the misunderstanding of this principle of culture of religion, especially when there is a dominant religion in the environment of human society affecting most aspects of a society and the economy.

Peace and Blessings!

Sebai MAA

Mystical Answers to the Important Questions of Life

Question: is it possible to have a meeting with all Kemetic teachers?

Greetings

Would it be possible to have a meeting between you, and the other Kemetic teachers, a sort of like a Counsel of Nicaea. What are your feelings on this idea?

Answer

Greetings

As for a meeting- realize that Nicaea was a conference of orthodox Catholic bishops selected by the Roman emperor to create a Christian religious cannon excluding the Christian Gnostics and other mystics. In our case, as the culture of Africanism, and specifically Kemeticism, is being reconstructed, there are many who have made good faith efforts to reconstruct it to the extent of their abilities and that is commendable. However, with our current state of seemingly having started from different angles, there would appear to be differences in our expositions. Nevertheless, there may be real differences and errors, but since there is no apparent uniformity and no conviction generally to meet with the goal of uniting the paths in a way that would require possibly being confronted with documentations pointing to errors that would require revisions, that kind of meeting will be difficult to accomplish in our time.

So perhaps we should give the Counsel of Nicaea credit to the extent that they met to forge a unified front against the Gnostics; however, they made compromises as they fabricated the Christian tradition. But we have no need of fabrication since the scriptures of Kemet are ample to verify virtually any detail of the spiritual tradition. If a meeting could be arranged where attendants submit their researches to that standard, it would perhaps lead to a genuine conference of Kemetic leaders, a synod, as in the ancient times before Christianity. Nevertheless, I have met with some Kemetic teachers and support them to the extent that they are trying to uplift humanity. However, realize that the work of some of them is composite, bringing in the teachings of non-African traditions. Another Kemetic teacher has publicly, despite the evidence, announced that there is no such thing as yoga in Kamit and refuted any association with the Sema Institute-wishing to distance his organization from the Sema Institute. Note that we have put forth ample evidences of the practice in Ancient Egypt, of what the modern Indians would call "Yoga" which is why we use the term for English translation; yet, those proofs are rejected by that person. Our tradition has put forth the most extensive evidences and original translations of original Kamitan hieroglyphic texts showing the origins of our understanding of the tradition. If there is to be any meeting, perhaps it will be between advancing members of the Sema Institute temple of Shetaut Neter when you graduate from the associate degree and advancing ministerial studies. Do not look outside - look to yourself as a member of that vanguard of true keepers of the faith. You must look to this and this alone as your path, and those who are unwilling or unable to understand should not be allowed to stand in the way of our/your progress - in other words- settle these matters and in no uncertain terms are speculation, dissent or purposeful ignorance to be allowed. Those who choose other paths should seek out those teachers and follow those paths until they are ready to apply themselves fully to this path. Only then will they have success in this (our) path.

Peace and Blessings!
Sebai MAA

Mystical Answers to the Important Questions of Life

Question: How to use the Tutelary divinity?

Udja Sbai Maa,

1. Does the Tutelary Divinity have to be part of a trinity, like Asar-Aset-Heru or Khepri-Ra-Tem?

I am not sure who to select as my Tutelary Divinity. I have read the guidelines that the choice is more of a personal affinity towards a particular Divinity. However, I am stretched over two choices, the first is Goddess Maat - that I have chosen for the "Om Maati Maakheru" as my hekau (Indian term: mantra), because she represents balance and that relates to my zodiac symbol, Libra.

2. When I chant the *dua Asar unefer neteraah* I feel at peace (and sometimes feel my head spinning) and sometimes also with the Dua Ra Khepera chant also.

Peace

Answer

Greetings,

Just as a person may love either their mother or maybe the father a little more because there is perhaps more closeness there, so too an aspirant can adore one special divinity, and also adore others as well that are compatible with the tradition –its all good because they are all connected, but each represents certain nuances that serve particular needs in the spiritual development of an aspirant at different times. It sounds like your first choice is Maat and the second Asar. That is fine. One divinity's symbol/iconography may not contain all an aspirant needs to focus on the Divine -especially in the early stages, that is one reason why there are many divinities, because sometimes the mind and soul need some special energy that is superbly represented in one divinity, and at other times another.

But at some point all the needs will be sublimated into one, and at that time the one will do, but even then the others need not be left behind. One does not leave the uncle behind because one has outgrown the childish pleasure of visiting the uncle and receiving gifts and an allowance. So too the spiritual evolution leads to maturity and fulfillment and all divinities become one in you, so nothing is lost. In the spiritual field there is no need to be torn between two or more lovers; all are loved in many ways and forms so that all love is fulfilled and completed in the Higher Self – which all the lesser divinities ultimately lead one to. The divinities are forms to help focus the mind for devotion practices. The tutelary divinity is the divinity used by an aspirant or a congregation for their main thematic spiritual association and spiritual practices.

Peace and Blessings!
Sebai MAA

Conversation with God

Question: who was Imhotep?

Hi, I would like to get a brief synopsis of Imhotep, who he is and what are his beliefs? Thank you..

Answer

Greetings,

The name "Imhotep" means "He who comes in peace." Imhotep was perhaps the greatest Sage of Ancient Egypt who lived in the Old Kingdom Period (5,000-2500 B.C.E.). He was a legendary figure in his own time because he was a master healer (medical doctor), royal architect, vizier, scribe, and Spiritual Philosopher. His writings have not been discovered yet, but he was revered by Ancient Egyptians and foreigners alike, who wrote about him and his works. He did however leave behind several monuments, like the Step Pyramid in Sakkara, which is a wonder of the ancient world. He was deified (canonized) and revered by all Ancient Egyptians. In the time when Hippocrates and other ancient Greeks went to study medical science in Ancient Egypt, they revered and worshiped Imhotep under the Greek name Asclepius. It must be understood that the recent Hollywood movie called "the mummy" is nothing but a gross misrepresentation of the truth, a distortion of what history records, for the purpose of greed.

Peace and Blessings!

Sebai MAA

Mystical Answers to the Important Questions of Life

Question: Is the year 2012 the end of the world?

Greetings,

I hope this mail reaches you in the best of health.

I have a couple questions that I would like the esteemed elder to enlighten me on.

Is December 21 2012 a date that Neterians should be preparing for since I am hearing lot of talk about this date?

If yes, what's the story behind this and how do we prepare?

Are there any kemetic text or books by contemporary authors that you recommend on the subject?

Peace

Answer

The date "December 21 2012" has been the object of much speculation in some circles because the Mayan calendar ends on that date (give or take a year). In that year also there will be some astronomical conjunctions of heavenly bodies. Some people have speculated that the world will end. Mind you, the Christians have been saying that the world will end for the last 1900 years, most recently in 1970 and we see what happened with that! Some New Age spiritualists have said that the world would end on the date 5/5/2000 and we see what happened with that! Some others have made wild speculations about what will happen such as:

- Hyperspatial Breakthrough
- Planetesimal Impact
- Alien Contact
- Historical Metamorphosis
- Metamorphosis of Natural Law
- Solar Explosion
- Quasar Ignition at the Galactic Core
- Resurrection of Osiris

Surviving Maya elders are upset because ignorant people have been prophesying and speculating in their name. The elders say the world will not end but will be transformed. It is more likely that the world will end or rather that human civilization will end due to

Conversation with God

nuclear war or the destruction of the environment, economic crisis or health disasters[15] rather than the conjunction of astronomical objects or the end of calendars, which are only descriptions of segments of eternity. The world is always transformed every day; things always change. If the current level of war politics, destruction of the environment, misuse of medicines and malfeasance in world economics continues we may expect serious repercussions and serious changes in the capacity to live life as we have. Things will get hard and survival will be difficult. Yet life will go on but in what form?

In our own tradition, in the writings called "Virgin of the World" our own Lord Djehuti spoke of a time when the holiness of Egyptian religion would come to be repudiated and later the world would not sustain life and that eventually the world would be cleansed and life would start anew. Eventually the faithful would gather in Egypt. There is no doubt that the world will come to an end at some point but that would ordinarily take thousands if not millions of years or a great catastrophe. The despoiling of the earth by human activity, which is occurring now, "AS WE SPEAK," is more likely to hasten such destruction than the natural process whereby the universe is created and then dissolved by God, only to create it again later on.

So, the question is not when the world will end or even if, but why and what does it mean to you as a spiritual aspirant? In order to be prepared for the best or the worst all aspirants should continue their disciplines with diligence so as to be most detached from the changes of the world. As spiritual awareness grows the changes of the world hold less power over a human being and consequently less importance. Know also that even if the world were destroyed, life would continue, on other worlds and in other dimensions. The body can be changed from living to dead and then to living again but the soul cannot be changed or destroyed. Discover the soul and you discover the immortal, transcendental and immutable Self that is beyond all calendars, transcending all astronomies, excelling all prophesies, and surpassing all worldly dramas. Therefore, the best way to prepare for the future, wherein death is assured for all, is to attain Nehast, spiritual enlightenment.

Peace and Blessings!

Sebai MAA

---

[15] See the book *Death of American Empire*

Mystical Answers to the Important Questions of Life

Question: Where there any "fighting yogis"?

Were there any "fighting yogis"? If so, how was the yoga applied to combat? If it was, what was the name of the combat system used by any fighting yogis?

How could I find out if anyone is still practicing a combat yogi form?

Answer

Greetings,

There is no evidence that there were "fighting yogis" in the sense of Buddhist Kung Fu Priests or similar in ancient Egypt, that I am aware of. However, there were police and professional soldiers who followed the path of Maat Philosophy as to their guidance in handling civil matters as well as in spiritual matters. Yogis prefer to apply the higher instruments of mental force and spiritual influence to guide and direct the course of human evolution. If Enlightened yogis are allowed to govern society in this manner there is no need for violence of any kind. Thus, society is led to peaceful resolution of conflicts and they are led to spiritual enlightenment. This was the goal of such great ancient Egyptian Sages as Sage Ptahotep, Sage Ani. Sage Amenemope, and others.

In later societies, such as the Indian Hindu and Buddhist Chinese Kung Fu, a martial philosophy was needed so as to promote the survival of society in an increasingly hostile world. Thus, in India the philosophy of the Upanishadic teaching was introduced to the Kshatrya warrior ethic. In China, the army was introduced to Taoist and Confucian philosophies. In China also, the Buddhist monks adopted Kung Fu as a means to protect themselves, but in a way that is in keeping with the proprieties of ethics, as well as spiritual philosophy and metaphysics.

From a higher perspective, yogis (mystics, spiritual aspirants, etc.) have a different foe to struggle with. It is explained to us in the legend of Asar Aset and Heru that Heru has a rival, Set. Heru is the Higher self and Set is the lower self. So we must fight with Set, our egoism, the ignorance, the pain and suffering of life and the desires that lead to self-destruction again and again through *ariu* (karma) and *uhm ankh* (reincarnation). This is the inner fight that also manifests in the world around us as frustration, suffering, loss, and death.

Peace and Blessings!
Sebai MAA

Handling Family and Relationship Issues

Mystical Answers to the Important Questions of Life

Question: I feel bad I cannot help my family, what should I do?

Sebai,

In the last few months I have come to experience relief in the teachings. I wish my family members could have this peace. I have tried to get them to read some of the books or listen to lectures and tapes but it does not work. I feel bad about it. What should I do?

Answer

Udja-Greetings,

I know how you feel in reference to being able to find solace in the teachings, and your desire to want to share that with others is commendable. It shows your caring and desire to perform selfless service to others. As people grow spiritually their natural capacity for empathy and compassion also grows, as you have experienced; it is a natural tendency to want to heal others and relieve their pain. Yet, that tendency, which is a natural development of positive spiritual evolution, needs to be tempered with wisdom; it should not be given full freedom. Otherwise, you will lose your own peace, by feeling bad as you just stated!

Why does this good feeling need to be tempered? What good does it do for your family to be miserable and then you become miserable with them? In that case, what is the purpose of your practicing the teachings, to become peaceful only to get miserable again? Misery may love company, but the mystic discovers love for detachment and dispassion.

> "To suffer, is a necessity entailed upon your nature, would you prefer that miracles
> should protect you from its lessons or shall you repine,
> because it happened unto you, when lo it happened unto all?
> Suffering is the golden cross upon which the rose of the Soul unfolds."
>
> -Ancient Egyptian proverb

Others can only be helped to the extent that they will allow themselves to be helped, due to their own *ariu* (karmic basis). You cannot force them and even if you could, they would resent it. If we help others to the extent that we are doing the work for them, we are not really helping them but preventing them from growing. Sometimes people need to go through the process of suffering so they will turn towards a different way of looking at life and how their desires have led them to where they are.

> "Those who have learned to know themselves, have reached that Good which doth
> transcend abundance; but they who through a love that leads astray,
> expend their love upon their body; they stay in Darkness wandering,
> and suffering through their senses things of Death."
>
> -Ancient Egyptian proverb

Instead, just try to be an example for them of the fruits of the teaching. Invite them to practice with you or give them a gift of a book, but do not make demands or harbor expectations about their adopting what you do. Let them be free and you then remain free. If they have any questions, answer them to the best of your ability. If they are in trouble, offer them assistance. In any case, it is incumbent upon those who want to help to find ways that can work under the current circumstances, and then it is important to do so with detachment and dispassion. Detachment and dispassion are important because if you take on the burden of other peoples sufferings, you are actually taking on a burden that does not belong to you intrinsically; you accept it via psychological transference[16] due to the illusion of individuality, egoism and sentimental family attachments. In the end, it is up to them to accept what is being offered and to discover whether or not it will work for them.

Peace and Blessings!

Sebai MAA

---

[16] *Psychoanalysis.* -the shift of emotions, esp. those experienced in childhood, from one person or object to another.

Mystical Answers to the Important Questions of Life

Question: How to handle family entanglements?

Greetings!

Although my *ari* (karma) kept me from being at the recent seminar physically, my mind was there. That brings me to the question dealing with one's karmic entanglement with family members. Another spiritual preceptor once said that one of the obstacles in the way of attaining liberation is one's family and friends.

My question is, how can an aspirant do what he truly wants (be with his spiritual family and attend seminars, lectures, etc) without negatively affecting his close associations?

Thanks.

Peace

Answer

Greetings,

This is a very good question. There is a Biblical story that is told about Jesus, It is said that Jesus was holding a meeting with his disciples, when someone interrupts him and says "your mother and brothers are here to see you." It is said that Jesus replied "who is my family? My family are those who follow the teaching," referring the disciples. While the teachings of mystical philosophy do not advocate upsetting others, they do teach that a spiritual aspirant must rise above egoistic sentimental attachments. This is often not easy for the aspirant or for family members. Family members seldom understand the spiritual journey of the mystic and invariably feel left out and abandoned. They feel: *Here is this person I love and I am losing them. If this is not bad enough, I am loosing them to a cult and they might kill themselves. They will end up in hell if they don't follow my religion, which is the only true religion, etc.* In addition, they feel they are being exposed to ideas about life that challenge their comfortable understanding about life; this can be disturbing, if not frightening. They may feel their life and faith are being invalidated or even debunked, so they feel the need to lash out in denial or attack that which they see as a challenge or as dispelling their cherished illusions of life.

As a spiritual aspirant moves away from family attachments, this moving away is of the order of removing egoistic sentimentality from one's personality, and is not necessarily a physical separation. Consider that we are not removing love, but rather sentimentalities based on egoistic notions of love and desires based on spiritual ignorance. However, consider also that there are some things in practical life that an individual needs to do that require a physical separation from family, and these are regarded as positive and even encouraged. For example, when one moves away for a new job or to go to school, there is pain at the separation and yet people still separate because a greater good is understood as the purpose; this is no different. Authentic spirituality should be considered no different. It should also be understood that family members also learn when a family member separates from them. They feel the pain of life, which is of their own making through their own sentimental attachments, and they slowly learn the karmic lesson of detachment.

In the end, the journey through life is an individual movement and one cannot stay in any family attachment forever, regardless of if they are pursuing spiritual teachings or not. Death is the ultimate separator for all…a potent lesson of detachment. Therefore, why go through the effort of becoming attached (emotionally dependent on someone for one's happiness) to someone who cannot, even if they wanted to, stay with you forever?). One is just setting oneself up to experience suffering. Imagine if someone, knowing that the sun rises and sets, develops an attachment to rising sun and suffers when it departs from their vision as it sets each night. They would be seen as insane for desiring something that is not possible, such as the sun not setting. So too human beings becoming attached to other human beings who must one day (often unpredictably) die, is insane from a spiritual-mystical point of view.

Detachment from family does not necessarily mean ignoring them, leaving them, or being cold to them; it only means that one is not depending on them for one's abiding happiness and fulfillment. One may experience elation, which is a transient experience of happiness, during associations with them, but one can never experience abiding happiness because of them. Abiding happiness can only come from your awakening to your Higher Self through attaining enlightenment.

Just as a bird can sit on a branch, be supported by the branch and enjoy resting on the branch, so too an aspirant can associate with family members and the world, and even be supported by them. However, just as that bird is not ultimately dependent on that branch because it has the capacity to spread its wings and fly off, so too an aspirant, even though seemingly dependent on and interacting with the world, should strive to be internally detached and emotionally independent from the ongoing situations of the world and family (i.e., not dependent on them for abiding fulfillment and happiness). This idea of detachment is one of the meanings of the wings that is depicted on some of the Ancient Egyptian gods and goddesses such as Aset, Maat and Heru…the capacity to spread one's spiritual wings of Self-knowledge and rise above the world of relationships and other objects of attachment. But also understand that if family associations are not a source of your abiding happiness, they are also not the source of your unhappiness. This is why it is ultimately not necessary for one to run away from family and other associations to attain enlightenment[17]. It is not the relationship itself that is the source of pain and discomfort, but rather, it is one's wrong understanding about relationships, and about life and its purpose, that is the source of pain and suffering.

---

[17] However, in a practical manner this may be necessary to promote good association if family members and other associates are unrighteous and unethical personalities.

Mystical Answers to the Important Questions of Life

Therefore, a keen spiritual aspirant learns to see clearly through the illusion of attachment, as a misinterpretation of family relations, and takes care of their own spiritual health first, which will in turn benefit everyone in the long run. As with any new situation of growth, there is fear, pain, anxiety, etc., but as time passes, the aspirant and the family members come to grips with the changes and thereby both grow spiritually. Giving birth is a painful experience for the mother and the child. An aspirant feels pain while giving birth to higher consciousness because it is painful to let go of what is familiar and comfortable; yet, there is an even higher yearning.

Likewise, family members must feel some pain in order to grow; it is part of the process of life, and no one, not even you, can protect them from it. So, you must understand that their pain about your becoming detached or being involved in a different religion, etc., is not something you are causing them. Rather, they are causing themselves to experience it due to their ignorance of Self, and this part of the process of spiritual growth which everyone has to experience until detachment is achieved. What do they say, "no pain, no gain!" There is a spiritual Kemetic teaching about this: "To suffer, is a necessity entailed upon your nature, would you prefer that miracles should protect you from its lessons or shalt you repine, because it happened unto you, when lo it happened unto all? Suffering is the golden cross upon which the rose of the Soul unfolds."

Therefore, without pain, there is no growth and no enlightenment, because the family members are holding the aspirant back, and the aspirant's inability to move on holds the family back from experiencing the pain they need as an impetus to grow out of their own prejudices, fears and sentimental attachments. On the brighter side, once an aspirant is well established in the teaching, there is no pain, but only gain, for there is a higher vision dawning in which the divine purpose is seen unfolding through the divine plan, and a person's pain is in reality the gateway to glory and eternal happiness! After all, we are speaking of one choice which offers you a limited pleasure (all family interactions are not wholly pleasurable, and the pleasurable interactions that may occur are transient as well as addictive, and in the end family members eventually die, which will cause inevitable pain) versus another choice which brings unencumbered, eternal bliss!

Blessings
Peace and Blessings!

Sebai MAA

Conversation with God

Question: How to handle family gatherings?

Greetings,

Please tell me how should I handle family gatherings? Aren't we as aspirants supposed to be staying away from worldly people? Also my family does not understand my feelings and spiritual aspirations with the teaching. Sometimes they even try to convert me. Also, they do not understand why I want to be a vegetarian and sometimes they even try to slip meat in my food? My grandmother says she prays for me so I don't go to hell. What should I do?

Answer

Greetings,

Yes indeed, as a *shems* (follower of Shetaut Neter religion, and mystical religions/traditions in general) you are admonished to stay away from worldly people. However, that injunction is meant in two ways. Firstly, you are to stay away to the extent that is physically possible, as you discharge the necessary duties of life to sustain yourself; and then also mentally. You should curtail your interactions to the minimum, but in the world you will often meet worldly people, unless you are in a temple environment. However, there too also you will meet some worldly aspirants (people who are struggling but who have not become perfected yet, who still have some worldly flaws)!

In our world today, you will inevitably come in contact with worldly people. Therefore, you should limit that contact, and when the contact is unavoidable, you should learn to handle those situations by observing the following disciplines and practices. Be patient, the contact will not last forever. Be watchful; be aware that you are in a worldly situation so observe the people and interact, but do not allow yourself to get caught up in what they are doing, saying or feeling from an egoistic or sentimental perspective. You can sing happy birthday, but internally remain aware that you are just spending time with them and you have other beliefs: in reality there are no birthdays or deathdays, but for their sake you are keeping company as part of your family duties to promote harmony –but there ends your involvement. You are celebrating with them to help them by providing elevating company (yourself) for them; you may not detect their benefit right away, but in the long run this subtle influence will develop into confidence and trust in you, and even respect; they may seek your advice and guidance in times of illness or other difficulties. Do not partake in damaging inebriants or foods. You may celebrate with them as long as the celebration does not conflict with your Neterian principles and values (the precepts of Maat). If they try to proselytize to you, simply listen and acknowledge what they are saying; there is no need to agree or disagree. If they are disposed and willing to have a real discussion about spiritual issues, you may interject some of the philosophy of your own religion. If not simply listen until they are finished or until your

Mystical Answers to the Important Questions of Life

other duties are in need of your attention, and then go your own way. Do not proselytize to them; just accept them as they are. Answer questions if they ask (but only to their level of understanding) and offer suggestions if they ask or if they are in some trouble or ethical dilemma. But let them make their decision and remain detached, even if you disagree. If they get into some trouble later, do not say "I told you so" later on. Be compassionate and understanding as your spiritual preceptor is with you. Try to love, respect and affirm the Higher Self within them, for even if they are caught up in ignorance they are after all, deep down, the Self, as you are. When you are in a short term gathering like going home for holidays or for a short visit, there is no need to get into heavy discussions with people who ultimately do not want to listen to other points of view, but only want to convert others to their own beliefs, based on blind faith or willful ignorance, like those people who purposely refuse to listen to any information that contradicts the dogma they learned about their religion. If you are staying with them long-term, then at some point you will both have to come to terms with your religious differences. That requires more diplomacy and patience.

Let them eat their meat and you eat your vegetarian meal. Check whatever they give you before you eat it or prepare your own food and bring it to the function.

Understand that they are reacting this way because they are fearful of losing you, because in losing you they are losing their illusions of life and that is painful for them. If they cannot have you the way they have known you, they are losing their life as a factor of how they grew up knowing you. You are not the same person anymore, and if they accept that you have changed, the experiences you had together would seem to become invalid and therefore their sentimental memories of early life would also be shattered. If they have to give up eating meat think about how much pleasure they are losing (from their egoistic/worldly perspective –of course the pain comes later in diseases like cancer and arthrosclerosis, etc.). Therefore, they may try to sabotage your efforts, purposely or unconsciously, to the extent of trying to trick, tempt, or entice you back to their side! Most often aspirants in your situation find that in the end most people who are like this do not really want to have a thoughtful open discussion, and they will not accept whatever you say regardless of your evidence to back it up. In reality, they wanted to engage you to try to change you and not themselves, and they will eventually become disgusted with you. If their love is stronger than their faith, they will accept you even if they cannot change you. In this manner, the power of love and attachment can have a positive effect on a person's beliefs and faith, but sometimes their lower nature (egoism, weak will, ignorance, fears, desires, etc.) is stronger and they cannot accept you even if you are their offspring. Even lower forms of love (sentimental, filial, romantic, etc.) can help a person rise above ignorant belief systems, prejudices and religious dogmas. How many times have we seen people of different religions who hated each other have family members who joined in marriage, forcing the haters to change the perspective they had on the other people; the same is true of class differences and so-called racial differences. Ordinary caring love between human beings in the world is a higher truth than prejudices, dogmas, greed and politics. Yet that love is still worldly, still sentimental and therefore, still flawed and imperfect. But Divine love is higher than sentimental love. So an aspirant should work to sublimate their sentimental (worldly) love into Divine Love, so as to rise

Conversation with God

above the barriers of worldly attachments and illusory relations. In doing so, one does not love family members less, but rather, more deeply, because one loves what is true about them, their Divine essence, which allows one to overlook and not be offended by their egoistic tendencies.

From your perspective, their efforts to change you are tests of your convictions and your establishment in the higher perspective. What good would your principles be if you lived on a mountain somewhere and were never challenged? You could develop pride and arrogance, thinking you have made a high attainment, only to find you are easily compromised when you come down to the city and deal with ordinary worldly folk! Therefore, in a sense you should say thanks, but no thanks! Thanks for the test for you have helped me attain enlightenment, and no thanks because you do not want to partake in their illusory pleasures that lead to pain, frustration, disease and suffering later on.

As a human being you came into the world with the help of others, your family. As such you have a duty to them, to provide assistance and company to the extent of fulfilling basic family necessities. Even sages have or had families and they fulfilled their duties to their families. Realize the contact will not last forever, so be patient, fulfill your duty and thereby you are fulfilling and getting rid of past *ari*. Every time you find yourself in that environment, it is a test for you on many levels; so that is an opportunity to face the challenge of worldliness. When you are confronted with alcoholic beverages or meat or elations and exuberant behavior, you have the opportunity to practice remaining detached, objective and balanced, controlling your feelings and emotions. With each test you grow stronger to overcome the egoism within yourself. This is how the world can be a help to you on your spiritual path.

So do not repudiate your family, but do not embrace what they do or want from you either. However, remember that if there is a choice between spending time with your spiritual family versus the worldly one, except perhaps in some extreme or critical/emergency situation, the choice is always the spiritual family; the other (worldly family) comes second. For example, if there is a Neterian temple function on December 25 (birthday of Ancient Egyptian divinity Heru), but your family wants you to celebrate Christmas with them, the choice to promote your spiritual evolution would be to attend the Neterian function! You can visit them before or after the Neterian function; this is giving them what they need, not what they want. Also, you need not be at their beck and call. If you need to go on a retreat and not see them for some time, then do so; but don't physically abandon them forever. That is not necessary. What is necessary is to abandon the egoistic and sentimental way of family interactions. In a higher sense, they are not family because the world is an illusion. In a higher sense, they are family because the essence of who they are is one with the essence of who you are. Therefore, love them in the higher sense and then you will discover the joy of Divine love. Again, this is how proper interaction with the world can help the spiritual evolution of an aspirant and not hinder it.

Your family will benefit when they see you growing in emotional balance, and physical health. They may not respect your beliefs and customs, but they will not be able to deny

Mystical Answers to the Important Questions of Life

your peacefulness. And they will appreciate that subconsciously and consciously, even though they may not admit it; and they will seek your assistance in matters of health and also in times of crisis. Eventually, they will be influenced to advance on their own spiritual path, perhaps not in this lifetime, but the next or the one after that. That service you have performed for them brings them and you merit in the Hall of Maat. In any case, as you become more proficient in this discipline, you will be more mentally detached and the physical interaction will not matter so much because the mind is where interaction really occurs; when there is mental establishment in the higher consciousness, nothing that happens on the physical plane really matters. But even sages, who are above the physical world (in consciousness) still care about the world to the extent of promoting righteousness, order and truth so other evolving souls can develop to discover higher consciousness and become sages too. Even present day sages were once worldly people as your family now seem to be. So they are potential sages as you are aspiring to be and will all be one day! Isn't that beautiful? In short, give them what they need, the best part of yourself, they will be benefited and you will be benefited also.

Peace and Blessings!

Sebai MAA

Conversation with God

Question: Why do I like to be in love and then fight with my lovers?

Greetings,

I have some serious questions. Why is it that we feel we must be in love or be with someone and then end up so many times wishing we had not done it? Why do people say they will never do it again and then go right back for more? Why do we feel that desire and can we be free from it, and if we were free would that not be a loss from all that loving someone can offer?

Thank you

Answer

Greetings,

Human love is a mysterious feature of human existence to most people. Many people want to be with someone so as to have someone to love and or have someone to love them back. Some believe it is a biochemical reaction, while others believe it has to do with soul mates, and others believe it is for pleasure and happiness, while still others believe the mating process is for propagating the species. Some people grow up without the type of caring and support that allows them to feel self-sufficient or at least well integrated. Therefore, they grow up feeling a void and try to fill it early on with peer groups and boy or girlfriends, sometimes even to the extent of purposely getting pregnant so that someone, the child, who has no choice but to be with them and cant run away, may be there to love them, since they did not experience that from their parents or environment. This often causes teenage pregnancies.

In terms of the spiritual philosophy, a human being desires to engage in the mating process ultimately to discover peace through a feeling of completeness that was lost when the soul assumed the role of an individual through its illusory separation from the Spirit (God), and forgot its connection to the universal and unlimited Spirit. That feeling of incompleteness arises because the soul, after its illusory separation from Spirit, having come to believe it is an individual, and having associated itself with a gender through the "dualizing" effect of incarnation into time and space, loses sight of its completeness as a soul. In reality, the soul is one with the vast, universal and transcendental Spirit of the Divine, as a drop is one with the ocean. In that state of illusory separation and identification with either a male or female body, the soul seeks to complete itself in the only way it knows how, by mating with another body; this is a movement that is assisted by the urges of the body itself.

Since this is a process engaged in the realm of time and space (there are no bodies and no gender in the transcendental realm – all is one) which is imperfect, limited and finite,

Mystical Answers to the Important Questions of Life

relationships will always be imperfect, limited and finite, no matter how transcendental they may seem to be at a particular moment. So no matter how good the sex may be, or how much people may seem to love each other, or how many children they have together, or how much money they have, there will always be imperfection, separateness, limitation and finiteness in their relations.

Furthermore, each individual person has specific psychological issues, beliefs and desires particular to their own experiences through their own history in this life and from previous ones. Those experiences or *ariu* (karmas) cause different needs within each person, and no one can truly satisfy the needs of another except through temporary illusion. The illusion is strained when the one person does not want to do what the other wants, or when the illusion that one held about the other is shaken. The mind harbors desires and repudiations in different levels of consciousness. In some levels, there are desires and loving thoughts and feelings. In other areas, repudiations are found. Further, the mind can harbor both feelings of desire and repudiation about the same objects (including persons). So a person can love something they desire in another person, and also hate things about that same person. Many times a person glosses over the things they hate so they can pursue the things they think they love or want; only later is their folly revealed as that same object evokes anger and hatred, like a fruit that seems ripe and sweet, but when cut open also has some parts that are spoiled and disgusting.

Even though people are made aware of the incapacity of others to make them happy, by the times when the other person fails to make them happy, they are only disappointed temporarily and they excuse the frustration, making themselves believe abiding happiness is possible "if only" the right circumstances are provided. Thus they are not disillusioned but only temporarily disappointed; so they put disappointment out of their minds and pursue the same actions that inevitably lead to more disappointments. Of course this process is assisted by hormones and peer pressure, and society, that continuously reinforce the ideas of the pursuit of relationships in order to be happy. Thus, most people try to fool themselves and their partner into believing that they are being fulfilled, and that they want to please the other so as to maintain the relationship. Using makeup, putting on dresses and suits, deodorants, bathing, demonstrating physical or sexual prowess, amassing power, bullying others, etc., are ways of trying to fool oneself into believing that one is desirable, worthy, or good looking. It masks one's true looks as an undesirable, or even a hateful person, from the other until the illusion has caused a "spell" on the other which is commonly referred to as "sexual attraction" and or "falling in love." Since the fooling process cannot go on forever, when the person wakes up and finds the other is not so good looking, they pass gas, have diseases or do not please them because they themselves have their own desires to be pleased, the illusion falters eventually and that causes strife. If falling in love were a real and abiding feature of humanity, how is it possible for a person to fall in love and then fall out of it later on? How is it possible to love someone and then later hate them and divorce them with great bitterness and animosity?

Falling in love cannot be real and abiding because it had a beginning and will have an end. If it were real, it would have been real always, and there would be no need for "falling" into it. From this perspective, there can only be one real form of love, the love that was there originally. That is the love that exists in eternity, the love of the Spirit. So souls can only truly love each other as souls who are transcendental, immortal and eternal and not as limited, mortal and excremental bodies. Furthermore, this transcendental form of love is not "fallen into," but rather it is discovered as the essential nature of existence.

People do not want to face the reality that life is an illusion and ordinary egoistic sentimental human relationships are illusory. They prefer to entertain fanciful notions about "eternal love" or "walking hand in hand into the sunset" and being "together forever and ever..." How many times have even the best lovers descended into merciless combatants at each other's throats over money issues, family issues, or even over putting the toothbrush in the wrong place! Ordinary human interactions are in the realm of the body, and according to the Pert m Hru text, the body is the excrement and who should want to live with excrements? If we can put aside the aspect of the body which is a miracle, a supreme work of the genius of Goddess that allows the soul to have experiences in the realm of time and space, let us examine it from another perspective, as an excremental aggregate of putrefying elements!

In Chapter 4[18] of the PMH entitled *"The Wisdom of the Secret Identity of the Gods and goddesses"* it is stated that,

> 10. It is Asar. Another way to understand this is: It is the corpse. Another way to understand this is: As to the excrements his, what will be, it is the body.

This means that the body is a corpse and a corpse is a form of excrement. When the body is enlivened by the soul, it is appearing to be alive and maintained in a constant state of renewal, but actually, it is an aggregate of elements maintained through chemical reactions; otherwise, it would disintegrate and putrefy. In other words, it is actually putrefying constantly, but maintained by renewing itself but not indefinitely. Therefore, in actuality, it is excrement but maintained appearing as something beautiful and clean; yet everyone who is alive has some excrement in them all the time, but not just the one you may think!

There are three forms of excrement that people have, that excrement of the body, excrement of the mind and excrement of the speech. There is the body excrement, which includes emanations of the body from feculent matter, urine, mucus and other refuse excreted from the body. In addition, there are excrements or corruptions of the mind, negative thoughts, that find expression through the mouth. So speech can be a form of excretion, and also thoughts and emotions which are based on negative feelings caused by ignorance of one true Divine essence and living life in accordance with an illusion.

Again, in Chapter 4 of the Pert M Hru verse 18, it is stated that "Set put excrement in the face of Heru." Set is the ego part of the personality, the illusory nature, the part that lives

---

[18] Generally referred to as Chapter 17.

Mystical Answers to the Important Questions of Life

by illusion, deceit and ignorance. That part throws excrement in the face of Heru, the Higher Self, the lucid intellect and true nature of the soul.

A wise aspirant should be like the awakened initiate that is described in Chapter 25[19] of the Pert m Hru, *"Making the transformation into Ptah,"* who says,

> 2. "Evil doubly it is, detestable, I do not eat excrement; I do not eat it! It is abominable to my Ka. It does not go into my body. I live in accordance with the knowledge of the gods and goddesses and the glorious spirit beings. I live and am empowered through their bread.[20] Powerful am I by eating it..."

The "bread" of the gods and goddesses is the *arit*, the Divine Offering, which represents the Eye of Heru, the insight (Sâaa) into the nature of Self, and the truth (Maat) which makes one true of Speech (MaaKheru) and spiritually awakened (Nehast). That offering is received through pursuing Shedy, the teachings (*knowledge of the gods and goddesses and the glorious spirit beings*) of the religious mysteries (Shetaut Neter). In Chapter 34[21] of the PMH *"Entering into the Divine Boat and Sailing For Eternity"* it is stated,

> 4. Putrefied stuff, excrement, I detest these things and will not eat that, not shall I eat it! Filth and muck, that I shall not consume.

This verse continues an important symbol in Kemetic Philosophy which was introduced in Chapter 4, Verse 10 relating to "excrement." Excrement is used to symbolize everything that is detestable in life. Most people, due to their own ignorance, are forced to eat excrement in life in various ways. Whenever a person has to do something they would rather not do, this is eating excrement. Whenever a person cannot achieve their desires, this is eating excrement. Whenever a person is disappointed or frustrated in any way, this is eating excrement. Since ordinary human beings live their lives based on egoistic notions, desires and expectations, they are constantly stressed because they are constantly frustrated about something they desire, getting away from something they dislike, or in fear over something they achieved that they do not want to lose. Life is always unpredictable. Therefore, whatever one achieves is bound to be lost, if not due to theft or damage, then due to deterioration from normal wear and tear. Also, there is no guarantee that whatever one desires will be attained, and ultimately all is left behind at the time of death. This is because the world is illusory and changeable. Thus, it is illogical to expect anything from the world, and yet people run after the world pursuing objects and illusory goals with great zeal, even though there can never be any true abiding fulfillment from such pursuits.

---

[19] Generally referred to as Chapter 82.
[20] This is an allusion to divine sustenance, in some ways similar to the Christian eucharist bread. It is a metaphor referring to the divine light upon which spirit beings are sustained. When a human being consumes this divine food, they too become Akhu (glorious spirit beings). This food is devotion to God, righteous living and wisdom about one's divine nature (i.e. to Know oneself) through practice of the disciplines of Sema (Egyptian Yoga) and Shetaut Neter (Divine mysteries).
[21] Generally referred to as Chapter 102.

Conversation with God

"Searching for one's self in the world is the pursuit of an illusion."
-Ancient Egyptian Proverb

There is another aspect of excrement that is seldom discussed or understood. The real purpose of excrement in life is to remind us that the world is not all comfort and pleasure, like a beautiful stone which when picked up reveals underneath it, maggots, roaches and all matter of putrefaction and filth. From the perspective of the ego, there are some things that are liked and others which are disliked, but those things that occur against the ego's desires are in reality the chipping away processes of goddess Maat. She sends adversity and frustration to everyone in accordance with their previous actions. It is not meant to evoke frustration, anxiety or fear, but to cut the ego down to size, for it is impossible to have everything the way the ego wants it in the world. If the disappointments and frustrations are accepted and understood as reminders of the illusory nature of the world, then the disappointments will turn into real dis-illusionment. However, most people are disappointed but not disillusioned, and so they keep on pursuing the illusory relationships of life again and again, like a dog that eats his own vomit. If this process of disillusionment were to be allowed to move on further, nurtured by sustained spiritual instruction, then the dis-illusionment turns into spiritual enlightenment. Disappointment is when you fail at acquiring your ego's desire, but still continue trying, thinking that if you could succeed you would be truly happy, even though the effort is a struggle and leads to further entanglements and suffering and even though no one in human history has ever found happiness in the illusory world of time and space. This is the predicament of the masses that are uninitiated into the teachings. They are caught up in ignorance and illusion. Dis-illusionment is when you understand that even if you were to achieve the object of desire, it will not bring you the abiding happiness you are looking for, so you give up your futile desires and place your energies in more worthy areas, such as the spiritual researches and practices. This is the path leading towards spiritual enlightenment.

From a higher spiritual perspective, sexuality and the process of relationships through death and reincarnation is for the purpose of allowing the soul to experience all of the forms of relating so as to grow to discover all the ways of knowing (this is for those souls that need this form of knowledge). When a person incarnates the relationship changes. One time you can be the son, and the next lifetime you may be the father, and still the next time you can be the daughter or wife of the other person. Discovering all of the ways to manifest love allows one to discover ever expanding dimensions of love, leading to the ultimate discovery of universal (Divine) love, and that allows the heart to expand to encompass all that is to be loved and not just your own family or neighborhood or country, but all of it and beyond; this is the way that God feels. So too universal love allows an aspirant to feel and therefore be like God or rather to discover that God essence within that is already there but clouded over by egoism, a sense of individuality, self-centeredness and spiritual ignorance.

Thus, those who want to grow in wisdom and who feel they want to have relationships with other human beings, as a means to "complete themselves" through mating,

Mystical Answers to the Important Questions of Life

friendship, companionship, reproduction, romance, etc., need to begin to face the illusoriness of life and the innate faults of human relations. But many people don't. Rather, they just move from relationship to relationship, blaming the other person for their continued unhappiness. In the end, if you want to avoid the excremental aspects of relationships, you must avoid relationships altogether, which includes relating to yourself as a real and abiding individual mortal being, who is supposedly a "clean," "good looking," "desirable," person, and facing up to what you are essentially, not that, but something higher and transcendental. You can see how "good looking" or famous, rich or otherwise "desirable" people can actually be cursed by their "good looks" and why they are perhaps even more fooled and have greater capacity to fool others in life, that is, until they get old or someone sees them in the morning before they get a chance to put on makeup (this is what happened to Marilyn Monroe when one of her husbands saw her real appearance after they slept together and he woke up and saw her in the morning). On the other hand, since some relationships are unavoidable, it behooves one to seek out the highest quality relationships, that is, relationships of truth and not of illusion, with people who are not seeking to fool each other but to enlighten each other. Then the excrements will be kept to a minimum and the relationship will bear the offspring of enlightenment instead of grief and bouts of love and hate.

Peace and Blessings!

Sebai MAA

Questions: Why does my relationship seem to be failing?

Greetings,

Why is it that everything that I thought I knew (that was so strong) about myself and wife now appears to be so frail. The more I dedicate myself to the exercises and prayer rituals the more thing appear to be weaking. Is this "normal"?

Answer

Yes, you have discovered what most encounter which is that there is an illusion factor in relationships and indeed in every area of life for that matter. Being that our economic conditions are precarious this forces the underlying personality issues to come to the surface

The teaching is designed to lead to understanding even if the problems persist. But as you spend more time with the teaching and apparently less at home or with the "relationship" the partner feels they get less of "you" - and thereby the relationship seems to be falling apart or less qualitative.

The action needed is to make sure there is balance between family duties and personal spiritual aspiration. This is why many aspirants choose not to have spouses or children. For those who did get into that before discovering a spiritual aspiration they need to fulfill their duties until those duties are no longer necessary. Yet relationships are useful for all involved if they are evolving to less egoistic stages through spiritual evolution and psychological maturity wherein neither relies on the other for personal or other fulfillment but for support and assistance when needed so that both may pursue fulfilling their missions in life and discovering the meaning of life.

It is also important to understand that just because people may love each other that does not necessarily mean that they should be together. Even sages, who love all, do not live with anyone, even if they appear to be part of a community. Their love is deeper than any physical proximity and they do good for people even though they will never meet them personally. There are some people who love in a sentimental way and the rest of their personality is immature and that will poison the positive tendencies of their capacity for love. Consider even the example of gangsters, who "love" their families but could kill anyone who crosses them! There are many people who kill the feelings, the thoughts or desires of others in the same way, just not by killing their body but their mind or heart; and that is a miserable way to live. Other people engage in frequent fighting, disagreement, passionate desires, intense sexual relations and making up after fighting and are also incapable of having inner peace or balance in the relationship. So the relationship will have as much or more misery as it seems to have bright moments and happy or pleasurable times. What form of spiritual evolution will be derived by living with these kinds of relationships? The result is usually very spotty progress if there is any at all and evolution will be delayed, stunted or may even digress, the person may devolve; and what is the use of that? From a higher perspective this could happen because the *ariu* (karma) of the people involved has led them to a negative situation and living in this way will expend that negativity so that one day they may be able to live in a better way but that may only happen after old age has set in or may not happen until death, when the personality will reincarnate in a new family and a new life in order to have a new opportunity to live in a better way that affords a healthier environment with a improved chance to grow spiritually.

In your case your relationship is merely adjusting to the new reality that you are awakening to as you leave the illusions you had created or accepted. If you both are open to the possibilities and you follow the instructions of the maatian ethical culture and the spiritual teaching you will find a new balance in a higher place, a better and more fulfilling place than where you were and are now.

Peace and Blessings!

Sebai MAA

Conversation with God

Question: Why is it that many people get bitter, ornery or depressed as they get old?

Answer

Greetings.

Since most people live their lives based on ignorance when they are young, pursuing worldly goals and worldly forms of pleasure and also believing that happiness is something you can find by doing, acquiring, experiencing or finding something in the world of time and space they live lives always looking to the future and regretting the past. The present is lost and therefore they cannot have peace in the present. Since they cannot have peace in the present they cannot cultivate a relaxed peaceful mind but rather an agitated mind. When they get older the agitations of the mind over many years come to the surface as the inhibitions are lost. Also, the bad eating habits, caused by seeking food for pleasure instead of nutrition, cause chronic diseases to become the mainstay of an older person's life and that is constantly aggravating as you see many old persons going to doctors every other day. That is a stressful and unfortunate way of life; but it did not just happen. It was a life created by living life based on the ignorance of a lifestyle of worldly pursuits and egoistic desires that could never be fulfilled so they led to frustrations and regrets. Add to this the normal disappointments of life, like ungrateful children, deaths in the family, business losses, depts., etc. and you can get an idea of how pathetic life can be. Even for those who are wealthy they cannot escape the ravages of age nor the fact that their wealth does not shield them from family misfortune or personal disappointments, it just gives them the capacity to make them better and distract themselves from the real miseries of life, by being able to at least take comfort in thinking they are above it or that they are better than others.

Many people who grow old in a negative way become angry easily, and combative and resentful or emotionally volatile. Some must pursue constant activity and never be alone with their inner thoughts because they cannot cope with all the agitated mind stuff they have accumulated. Others become depressed and regretful about life and also unable to reconcile why they feel that way in the face of constant messages in the media about how wonderful life is and how having more possessions, family and wealth are what truly give life meaning. Of course when death comes all that is meaningless, yet the propaganda continues. Many people grow into old age realizing the folly of their ways but unable to admit to them and so they actively seek to repeat ideas and thoughts that reinforce their notion of the worthwhile nature of their life because they would not be able to handle the truth, that they have wasted their life pursuing ignorant or misleading ideals. In reality, facing the truth is the first step towards finding true meaning in life and the real purpose of life, otherwise life is an illusion and one becomes the fodder for the bidding of others and one suffers the consequences of impotency and social as well as spiritual suffering.

Mystical Answers to the Important Questions of Life

The best way to avoid this state is to develop a philosophical insight into life and the nature of aging as well as the nature of life after death. Then a person can create positive mental impressions that will later blossom into peaceful and enlightening wisdom in old age and peaceful passage into senior life as well as peaceful and joyous transition into the life after death. This is truly aging gracefully! Such a person is a boon to society and should be revered as a wise elder. Then society is benefited by their wisdom. But in a society that reverences youth and wealth instead of wise elders, the priorities are mixed up and that too exacerbates the problem for the older generation.

Peace and Blessings!

Sebai MAA

Question: Why am I losing my friends since we started following the Kemetic path?

Greetings Sebai,

Hope ALL is well with you, perfect peace. Today I have two considerations to which your guidance will be very valuable.

My spiritual partner and I had an interesting discussion last night. We discovered that since we have become more involved in the Kemetic teachings and legacy, that it seems we are losing all of our friends. People who used to talk to us in a nice friendly way are now passing by; it does not really bother us, but it's there. We don't pay it much mind because good association is hard to find I guess any where in the world. I know we have caused this to ourselves by honestly walking the path towards higher consciousness, and detachment must be enjoined. What are your reflections?

ANSWER

Greetings

There is an ancient Egyptian proverb that says: "speak to those who understand you" – You need to realize that sometimes the immature (not spiritually developed yet; does not refer to inferior or superior) mind does not want to hear the words of truth because it is so degraded that it cannot accept those words - so it must shut them out and those who adhere to them. If this is the path you have chosen you must contend with that reality. Realize that those who are worldly friends are as changeable as the wind - they are not true friends because they do not live in truth and so can turn on you at any time in accordance with their desires and egoistic limitations (as you have seen) – it is better to seek communion with those who are seekers of truth, associate (shedy) with them; they are your true family - in Neter. They are your support, with some limitations, but in a better way, in honesty and peace.

Peace and Blessings!

Sebai MAA

Question: how does romantic love fit with the spiritual teachings?

Peace

I'm reading your book, *Initiation to Egyptian Yoga* and I'm following and doing well. I'm writing to ask you how does romantic love fit? I will truthfully say that I am happy with my life and am on the journey to the knowledge of Self, however, there is one problem. I care very deeply for a very wonderful young man. He is also on a journey and because of it, we are not together. Yes, I am very happy for him, however, the pain from not seeing him etc., is where my problem lies. I am not having sexual withdrawal and all that. I really miss seeing him and just being with him. We felt that we should kind of go on a 40 day quasi-fast. We speak on the phone, but I miss him and he misses me too-he told me today (smile).

Back to the reason I'm writing where does romantic love and marriage fit in the journey to enlightenment?

Peace,

Answer

Greetings,

Your question is very common. The role of sexuality and relationships in the spiritual path must be understood carefully and with maturity. Sexuality is an aspect of life, which is engendered in all by nature. However, its purpose is not indiscriminate pleasure, but to perpetuate life, and also to lead human beings to spiritual enlightenment. Nature, through the physical urges, wants to perpetuate life, but when the individual soul is ready to move beyond physical existence, it needs to control the sexual urge and romantic love and sentimentality, and take these to a higher level, that of cosmic love, which transcends all physicality. This is called Tantrism.[22]

Therefore, control of the sex urge as well as egoistic desires, are integral disciplines on the spiritual path, which are to be practiced to the level of the capacity of the aspirant. Even in householder (marital) life there must be control, otherwise the relationship will be based on sex, and since the sex urge cannot always be fulfilled, there will be constant mental or physical infidelity, mental agitation and loss of spiritual energy, as well as loss of the mental capacity to practice the teachings and disciplines that lead a person to enlightenment, and self-discovery. Throughout history, there have been married saints and sages as well as unmarried ones (of both sexes). Relationships are there as a means to help you grow spiritually, but if you do not know how they should be engaged in, they will lead to bondage, strife and anguish. If you love correctly and incorporate the teachings of mystical spirituality into your relationships, you will glorify those

---

[22] see the book *Sacred Sexuality* by Sebai Muata Ashby

Conversation with God

relationships and lead yourself and your partner to the heights of spiritual evolution. However, it should be noted that householder life is more difficult than single life, and ultimately, in the end all relations must be left behind when we go to enter the pearly, gold gilded gates to the palace of enlightenment.

What you have stated, about missing each other, etc., is understandable from the perspective of ordinary sentimental human relations. However, you need to also understand that you are both more than physical bodies, and that the sentimental closeness you feel is illusory. Consider that two people in the same room can feel like strangers (isolated and distant), and two people separated by great physical distance can feel close together. In fact, you are as close to him now as when you are hugging, even though he may be on the other side of the world! You must learn to love his essence and not just his body, then there will never be separation, and also you will discover you are both one in the Divine!

How to achieve this glorious vision of higher relationship? The issue is, do you promote wisdom or sentimentality in your relations? Do you control, cultivate and sublimate sex desire so as to lead you to a spiritual realization or do you use it only for indiscriminate self-gratification of the body and the promotion of illusory feelings of closeness? One path leads to worldliness, while the other leads to blessedness and glory. Further, you must realize that in due time you must leave your partner, through death; when they are gone (have died), what will you do then? Therefore, do your relationship fasting, but substitute it with developing awareness of devotion towards the Divine. Learn about the Divine and learn how to love the Divine in your partner, and when your partner is gone you will always have the Divine and your partner, who is an expression of tat Divine, and if you discover the Divine there will never be a feeling of loss, separation or anguish ever again, for in its place there will be Peace-inner Peace and transcendence of lower things.

Read my book *Sacred Sexuality* – it gives more details on this vast philosophy of sexuality, relationships and Self-discovery.

Peace and Blessings!

Sebai MAA

Mystical Answers to the Important Questions of Life

Question: Why did God create Creation? What is the use of Sexuality?

Udja Sebai Maa,

I am trying to get a deeper understanding of the procreation process and life in general. I know, according to Kamitan mysticism and mythology, Ra created humans; but why? He/She (Ra) was perfect. If you are perfect, why do you need the illusion or human life? Is it that Ra did not know himself, because he was perfect and needed to create humans to get to grow into himself (Chaos and Order)? What is meant by the fall? How did the fall occur and should one totally stop having sexual relations (No Sex {family relations, responsibilities, and entanglements}) until Nehast is reached or is there a higher purpose to the procreation process? It seems to me that without procreation, there would be no reincarnation or life. As you can see, I am engulfed in ignorance once again. Yes, I am in need of guidance. I have a few miles to go.

Respectfully

Answer

Udja-Greetings,

The motive for Creation is a question that aspirants lead themselves to at some point or another. There are various levels to this question, depending on the level of understanding of the aspirant, and therefore there are various levels of answering the question as well. So this answer is multifaceted, and aspirants at different levels will get different levels of meaning. Even those who read it at a lower level will get a certain answer, but after reading it in the future they will get another answer that they will be ready for then.

In the beginning, the question is asked from the perspective of a growing aspirant who relates to God in terms of human relations. That means that because humans have children to procreate, love others and see their names extended into the future for "immortality," then God may have similar motives. Or, because God is supposed to be immortal and perfect, maybe He/She wants to create people so as to have others to look at Him/Her with awe and admiration! Or maybe the God/Goddess just wants to have someone to knock around! So God is then an egoistic personality with needs and desires like humans. But if the idea of God evolves to envision God as a perfect being, then there would seem to be a contradiction, because in human terms perfection should mean completeness and detachment. And this is rightly so, however, not in the way those humans understand the concepts, for perfection to humans and to God is not the same thing. Consider that the sun is a perfect shining ball. Is it wrong for the sun to shine on the world or should it run away into deep space and forget about the planets surrounding

Conversation with God

it? After all, they have no meaning to the sun. What does the sun know or care about the people on earth, or on Mars! Consider sages and saints; they have attained God consciousness, perfection in spiritual realization and self-knowledge. However, they do not cease their activities in the world after they attain higher consciousness. What does a sage need with human interaction, the trappings of possessions, teaching, and temple building projects, etc.? Answer: they have no need! Yet they do it out of service and love! However, it is universal love and not sentimental love, so that others may have a chance to experience the glory that they experience, the splendor of their own true nature. Yet, sages do not seek to procreate themselves with the idea that they are facilitating more souls to come into the world to become enlightened. Nature takes care of that by providing a place where ignorant or less evolved personalities can live and procreate themselves. That provides a sufficient venue for any number of reincarnations! So spiritual aspirants and initiates need not worry that if they refrain from having physical children that somehow the world will become depopulated! There is enough ignorance to keep this going for thousands (if not millions) of years into the future! That is, if humanity does not destroy itself sooner than that! But even so, there are other dimensions and worlds on which souls could incarnate themselves if this world should become uninhabitable. An aspirant will automatically seek a level of celibacy commensurate with their level of spiritual evolution and their level of spiritual aspiration. But you cannot let go of something that is lower until you grab onto something that is higher.

> "One's acts on earth are like a dream."
> -from the Ancient Egyptian 'Harper's Song'

In the same way, God supports the Creation (the universe) out of love, but not sentimental love. True love is impersonal and universal, and detached, like the sun that shines on all, good or bad. God, the Sbaiu (Sages) and the Sun have no ulterior motives; they shine because that is who they are and what they do. Out of compassion, they help those who desire to remember, to see the light. So, as for your question of why did God Create humans, consider that yes, in a way humans were created by God. In the Kemetic Creation myth it is said that God Created souls from his essence. But those souls chose to become human, to take on "watery" encasements (bodies), and so became bound to human existence for a time by forgetting their true identity- this is the so-called "fall." However, as the Kamitan text, the *Pert m Heru* explains, humans are in reality Gods and Goddesses, and when they realize their true nature that they have only forgotten, they remember the true essence of their existence which transcends time and space, and ignorance and history. At that point they are referred to as "Awakened" (*Nehast*) beings or noble, elevated, enlightened (*Sheps*) beings. At that point they have discovered that they were never "created" as individual beings, and that they are and always were parts of the Supreme Spirit, but had only forgotten that and fallen into a delusion of separation, individuality, limitation and mortality. Having discovered their true nature, they have no more need of sentimental relationships, running after other individuals to love and be loved, for all are ONE!

So while we may say to an ignorant person, a neophyte, that God created things, actually there is no Creator and no Created, for all are one. But from the point of view of

Mystical Answers to the Important Questions of Life

ignorance, there needs to be a working explanation, and that explanation should lead to an ultimate transcendental realization. It should not be a rigid absolute statement such as is given in dogmatic messianic or orthodox religions, because as you may now see, the world is relative and illusory. So there can be no absolute dogmas in a relative existence; because it is the realm of ignorance and fantasy. Those who bandy such notions are like mindless subjects who have been captivated by the prestidigitation of an expert magician. Chaos and order in life arise from the confusion of self-identity. For the wise there is no fall and no rising, and there is no error in the world, and therefore no quandary about the meaning and purpose of life. Those notions arise from the ignorant mind and the desiring heart of egoistic human conception. So the apparent sojourn of separation from God is to be recognized as a dream which never happened, and therefore the question no longer will have meaning at that point; it is just a dream one needs to wake up from. Aspirants should strive to reach the level of making these fundamental questions moot, and then they will have realized the end of all goals, the purpose of existence. This is achieved by gradually mastering higher levels of understanding through study and practice of the teachings under proper guidance.

Sexuality is an aspect of human existence, within the realm of illusion. From the standpoint of ignorance, a human can procreate, but from the standpoint of wisdom, there is no human existence, and therefore procreation is an illusion. Yet during the period of ignorance, sexuality has its purpose both for humans and even sages and saints. For sages and saints, it is a means to enter the Creation, to finish growing and studying the teaching and regain their self-mastery. Having attained that enlightened state, sexuality (sexual energy) becomes a means to harness incredible energies to create great projects, thoughts and the capacity for great service to humanity, for those are forms of procreation as well. If a sage does not have physical children, a sage's books, the souls which they help, the projects they leave behind, etc., are their children. However, they may also have physical children as well, still all for the glory of self-discovery, for even if sages have physical children they do so to sustain the practical reality, the order of society when needed, and to transfer the teaching, since those children who are born into advanced families are in training for sagehood and service to humanity.

For the philosophy of Creation, see the book and audio lecture series *Anunian Theology*. For more on these teachings get the *Maat audio series* teachings on Sex-sublimation. Read my book *Sacred Sexuality* – it gives more details on this vast philosophy of sexuality, relationships and Self-discovery.

Peace and Blessings!

Sebai MAA

Conversation with God

Question: Is it necessary to have children in order to attain spiritual awakening?

Greetings,

Do I have to have children in order to get rid of my desires for fatherhood or should I become celibate and stay away from women if I practice the teachings?

Thank you

Answer

Many people feel the urge to procreate at some point in their existence. Here we are not just talking about the urge to have sex for physical pleasure. We are speaking of the deeper desire that is partly biologically induced, but also psychologically mandated, due to the *ariu* (karma) that a person has lived and the indoctrination they have received for many lifetimes. Some people have come to believe that they must have progeny because their parents did, and other people do, so they should do it too. Some people seek progeny because they are alone and feel they want someone to love and to love them back, not realizing that any love experience will bring with it pain and sorrow, and that most experiences in life are painful instead of pleasurable.

So some people seek to use sex pleasure and or procreation as a means to compensate for internal voids due to lack of completeness and or love and self-worth. The need is there because they have not matured to realize their own capacity to be self-sufficient, or they feel pain or suffering in life and or loneliness, so they need someone or something to "complete" themselves due to the void that is experienced because of their insubstantial lives based on worldly possessions and egoistic notions of life and the material pursuits to achieve happiness, which can never be fulfilling but only temporarily distracting. That feeling of incompleteness is there because they have no understanding of their deeper Self, and their personality is deficient because they did not receive sufficient love or caring in their lives, so they feel a void, a painful emptiness. Having grown up being told that life is for the "pursuit of happiness" they have come to believe that happiness comes from acquiring possessions or entering into worldly relations with others; something that ultimately can never work, since the world is changeable and ephemeral and no abiding happiness can ever be found under such conditions. So they are also ignorant, not knowing they do not need to seek for objects to "complete" themselves and that completeness comes from discovering the truth about life and the true nature of their own deeper reality. That upbringing leaves an intensity of their identification with their limited physical reality, their ego concept of themselves, drowning out any notion of a deeper spiritual Self, and so they are left with no alternative but to seek to satisfy their physical and emotional desires as a way to attempt to seek completeness and fulfillment of their needs. Some may seek fanatically to fulfill that love with fanaticisms or obsessions such as sports, religion, politics, fame or the entertainment business.

Mystical Answers to the Important Questions of Life

Some people think they must procreate so that their lineage or that of their ethnicity or race will go one in perpetuity. They do not stop to think that when the earth is destroyed at some point in the future, when the sun dies, that all the progeny of all generations will come to a halt! So that purpose would seem to be misguided. There is no way to attain physical immortality by having children, even if we examine it biologically. The biology of everyone's body completely changes once every 1-9 years (depending on how it is calculated). Therefore, you are not even the same person (physically) that you were when you were born. Every cell in your body has changed. If you had a child, the child would be physically different from you in a short time. Genetically, we may say that there is a relationship, but that relationship is not identical, and if we were to say that there is a relationship on that basis, then we should say that you are related to everyone in the world because the relationship to your own children is similar to your relationship to someone living on the other side of the world who may not even be of your ethnic group. Indeed, when we trace the genetics of everyone, everyone comes from the same genetic source. So we are all family on that basis; therefore, while recognition of family, community and country are useful in carrying on and surviving in life, in a higher sense it would be incorrect to single out individuals of ones own family, community, ethnic group or country. One should love all human beings as part of the human family.

The true relationship is of the nature of a psychological one. You are related to the extent you believe you are related. The biological relationship as the basis of a filial relationship is an illusion. Thus, if one were to realize that one is in reality related to everyone else, and indeed the universe, and therefore to everything else, why would one need to limit ones relationships to a few family members and miss out on the experiences of the entire human family and the wonders of Creation? Would that higher perspective not fulfill every possible need a human being could have? Nevertheless, in the beginning, having a physical family can be necessary to learn certain lessons of relationship, love, and sacrifice for something other than the little self, until the personality is ready to evolve.

As a human being grows, they no longer need physical relationships, and they can be sustained through psychological ones. So you may see your life through the entire humanity as part of your family. Greater still is the ability to experience oneness with all humanity and creation itself. This last is of course the experience of sages and *Shepsu* (enlightened beings).

So those who feel the desire to have a physical family should proceed to do so in a righteous manner (see our book, *Sacred Sexuality*) and those who seek a more advanced relationship should pursue that as well. Realize however, that through the process of *uhm ankh* (reincarnation) you have had countless families through out history. You have learned much in that time, and yet if you still feel the desire for physical procreation you may not be learning the lessons nature seeks to teach you through that medium. This means that you will continue to be caught in a perpetual cycle of recurring incarnations and experiences of the trials and challenges of raising children, while not learning the wisdom required to graduate to the higher levels of childbearing that occur on higher planes of existence.

Conversation with God

In order to truly grow out of lower desires, it is necessary to discover and experience higher ones. This means that along with the physical actions, there should be higher spiritual principles being applied to one's life so that the physical experience may lead to a fulfillment of the physical desire. That will lead to the aspiration and pursuit of the higher desires. Then one may give birth to higher progeny in the form of works that are remembered and live on well beyond one's physical death, and which act as living guides for all humanity. That is the work of sages and saints, they have given birth to ideas and philosophies, and insights into the nature of life that are so powerful that they in turn give birth to more and more spiritual children as their works are consumed by succeeding generations, and from those generations emerge new sages and saints that pass it on to their progeny.

Therefore, realize that you must have progeny in order to attain spiritual enlightenment but what kind and what quality depends on your level of spiritual evolution and your particular needs as a spiritual seeker. The important thing is that whichever path you follow, you should take into account your capacity to take care of the children you will produce and to infuse the spiritual teaching and spiritual disciplines into your life so that you (and your children) will gain the true benefits of procreation, and not get stuck in a lower plane of existence like most of the rest of humanity is caught, in the cycle of ignorance.

Peace and Blessings!

Sebai MAA

Mystical Answers to the Important Questions of Life

Question: How much sex is enough?

Greetings,

My question is if Western society is the most sexually liberated and the people in it are having more sex than at any other time in history, why is there more dissatisfaction and dysfunction than ever in the majority of those engaging in sexual intercourse?

Answer

Greetings,

Many people are deluded by the idea that sex must be part of every aspect of their lives due to the messages from family, television, advertising, friends, self-indulgence with sex partners, etc. Also, the stresses of life push people to seek easy modes of pleasure and relief from the stress of life. So they cannot bear the idea of life without sex, and yet the more they reach for true sexual satisfaction, the more it eludes their grasp.

It must be clearly understood that the main purpose of sexuality is procreation and not just recreation. In the ancient Egyptian precepts of Maat, it is stated: *"an dada-a"*, "I have not committed excessive ejaculating." Sex can be a sacred act to engender life and is not designed for the purpose of constant usage (overindulgence). This may seem hard to understand, but no matter how hard a person may go against this ideal they will not be able to disprove it. We are not saying that people should not engage in sex but that that activity needs to be controlled. Anyone who does not control the sexual urge cannot expect to evolve spiritually because the sexual activity itself disrupts the hormones of the body and the mind's ability to see clearly. When sexuality is uncontrolled, it acts as an addiction that can never be fully satisfied, and it drains the physical and mental energy of a person. This is why serious practitioners of the mystic sciences practice celibacy and sex-sublimation.

Those who want to discover true fulfillment, contentment and peace in life must learn to control the sex urge. Control does not necessarily imply abstinence, but management whereby the sex urge is controlled, cultivated and sublimated rather than it dominating the personality. What will be discovered is something greater than the fleeting sex experience, the glory of divine experience and inner peace.

The practice of celibacy involves not only abstaining from sexual intercourse, but from all associations which lead to impurity of the body and mental delusion. Purity of the body simply means that when a person is frequently touching, fantasizing about, longing for or otherwise desiring physical sensual pleasures, their thoughts and feelings are colored by their desires, and this coloring renders their intellect incapable of correct reasoning. Thus, delusion may be defined as the inability to act, think or feel according to

Conversation with God

correctness and truth because the desires have clouded the capacity for reasoning. So with this understanding, it should be clear that the inability to comprehend and live by the spiritual teachings is a direct result of being deluded by the ignorance and egoistic desires of the mind and body. The project of a spiritual aspirant is to first understand and accept this and then to work towards enlightening the mind and rising above the quagmire of ignorance and delusion through the various disciplines of *Sema Tawi* "Egyptian yoga" (righteous action, study of the teachings and the practice of devotion towards the Divine and the practice of meditation).

Many times novice aspirants, rather than practicing moderation in sexual intercourse, force themselves and their partners into the practice of celibacy/abstinence in an attempt "to be spiritual," to an extreme that the relationship is not ready for to the point it puts a strain on the relationship. However, due to their level of spiritual evolution, they still continue to harbor and pursue desires for other objects and experiences to feel fulfilled. This is not the correct practice of celibacy/abstinence in its higher and broader meaning. Celibacy/abstinence, as discussed above, relates to more than just sexual intercourse. It relates to an advanced level of personality integration on the part of the aspirant, through the practice of the *Sema Tawi* disciplines, to the point where the aspirant no longer desires or seeks fulfillment from ANY experience or object in the world of time and space, sexual intercourse just being one experience. Therefore, an aspirant could continue to have sexual relations/intercourse with their partner to fulfill their marital duties, but if they no longer desire to have sexual intercourse to fulfill themselves emotionally, they are actually practicing celibacy/abstinence in a greater measure than someone who fully abstains from sexual intercourse, but is constantly thinking/fantasizing about the pleasures of sexual intercourse and or other experiences and objects. Therefore, the practice of celibacy/abstinence will eventually become a natural expression of a person's spiritual advancement, just as the waning of other desires for worldly pleasures is also part of that advancement. Therefore, its practice is not something that should be forced, but rather, that should be normalized to a moderate expression, and then be allowed to wane through consistent practice of the *shedy* (*Sema Tawi*) disciplines that will sublimate one's desires for external pleasures, including sexual pleasure.

The *ariu* (karmic) bonds between people in a relationship are very intense. For this reason the ups and downs in a relationship can be intense as well. However, it would be erroneous to assume that two people have come together only in this life. They have been associated in the past and not necessarily in the same gender arrangement as the present. The male partner could have been a female in the past and the female could have been a male, or one could have been the parent and the other the son or daughter, and so on. Nature creates the situations, relationships and desires so that the soul may have the opportunity to work out the mystery of its own nature by working through the situations, relationships (forms of love) and desires. Divorce is not a viable solution for a relationship wherein two people are seriously striving to grow spiritually. It is however advisable for ignorant people who would make their lives miserable or who might possibly hurt each other psychologically or physically without reasonable hope for improvement.

Mystical Answers to the Important Questions of Life

You must realize that you have been committing the same errors from life to life, the search for a relationship to experience abiding happiness, the attempt to please that person, the desire to achieve harmony, the pursuit of pleasure from the relationship, the desire for progeny, etc. Up to now you have not realized fulfillment of your desires, only transient experiences of pleasure followed by experiences of emptiness, pain and sorrow. You are like a hamster running endlessly on a treadmill and going absolutely nowhere. True fulfillment is when your experience of happiness is abiding…that is, it does not go away or wane, regardless of your outer situations or circumstances. This fulfillment is only possible in the state of *Nehast* (spiritual enlightenment). The world can only provide transient experiences of pleasure alternating with transient experiences of pain and sorrow. For many lives you have expended your energies in the pursuit of pleasure and fulfillment and you have not found it. There is only one path for you, that is to sublimate your ego to the higher purpose of your relationships. If this is not accomplished, the soul will be wandering endlessly from one life to the next and its karmic entanglements will never be worked out. This can be accomplished by living according to a higher ideal instead of the ideal of the ego and of culture.

Peace and Blessings!

Sebai MAA

Conversation with God

Question: Is Homosexuality bad?

Greetings,

Is homosexuality a bad thing? What about people who are homosexuals, can they attain higher consciousness?

Answer

Greetings,

In the Pert m Hru text of ancient Kamit there are some injunctions related to sexuality that include the homosexual act, adultery, and excessive ejaculation. A brief study of Ancient Egyptian grammar offers some insights into the question of sexuality and specifically the behaviors that are promoted to promote an ordered society. We want to engage in this grammatical study because Ancient Egyptian society was balanced and was sustained for thousands of years. Thus we should want to look into any society that maintained that longevity in order to inform our present day culture about the course of life that is fruitful and beneficial.

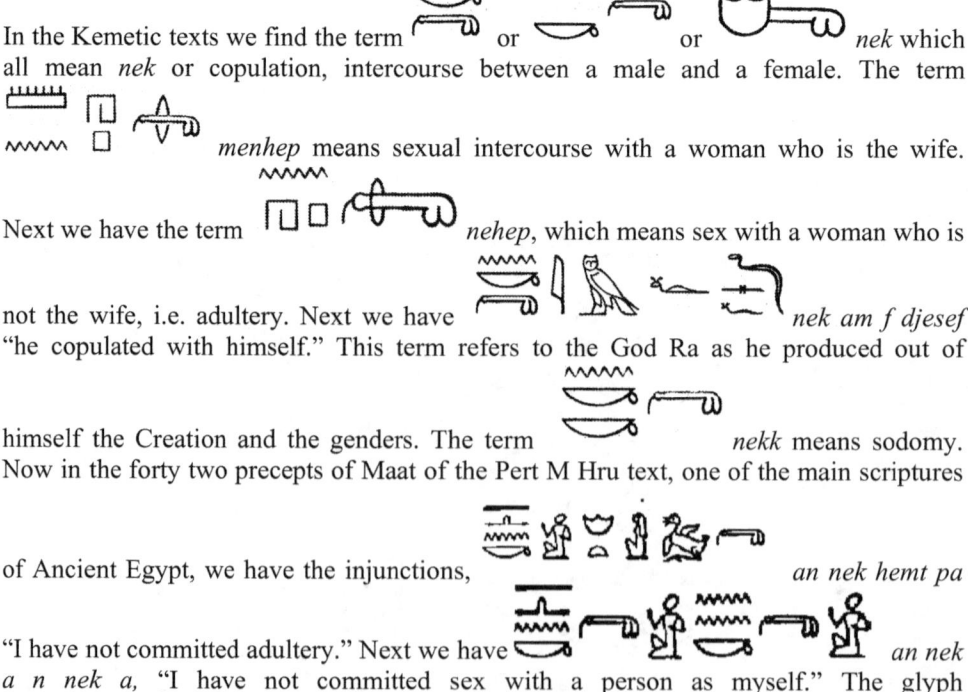

In the Kemetic texts we find the term ⟨⟩ or ⟨⟩ or ⟨⟩ *nek* which all mean *nek* or copulation, intercourse between a male and a female. The term ⟨⟩ *menhep* means sexual intercourse with a woman who is the wife. Next we have the term ⟨⟩ *nehep*, which means sex with a woman who is not the wife, i.e. adultery. Next we have ⟨⟩ *nek am f djesef* "he copulated with himself." This term refers to the God Ra as he produced out of himself the Creation and the genders. The term ⟨⟩ *nekk* means sodomy. Now in the forty two precepts of Maat of the Pert M Hru text, one of the main scriptures of Ancient Egypt, we have the injunctions, ⟨⟩ *an nek hemt pa* "I have not committed adultery." Next we have ⟨⟩ *an nek a n nek a,* "I have not committed sex with a person as myself." The glyph

Mystical Answers to the Important Questions of Life

represents a person sitting. It signifies the word "I" or "me". Another injunction explains, *an dada* "I have not committed excessive ejaculating." This last can be taken as promiscuity and or excessive masturbation. We will examine these terms within a context of Maat philosophy which is the basis of Ancient Egyptian social philosophy that promotes order and balance. All of the injunctions above can exist within or outside of a context of social order; specifically, they are acts that can be performed by a human being simply because they can be done. However, doing something in a context of social order requires certain regulations since some acts can produce disorder in a society. For example, adultery can cause disorder by causing families to fall apart. Similarly, in this view, homosexuality can cause disorder by creating an imbalance between the sexuality of males and females.

So the injunctions to not engage in these acts do not imply that the actors are less than human but that the acts are disruptions to society and should not be performed for that reason. Whether or not a human being has a tendency towards homosexuality or adultery they are still human beings and are to be accorded every right and should not be dehumanized or denigrated. Yet the acts that can disrupt society need to be discouraged for the continued maintenance of balance and order in a society. Homosexuality is contradictory to the norm of order between men and women in a society that is based on male and female balance just as adultery and promiscuity are as well since they can cause people to pursue actions that are not in keeping with family order. Also, promiscuity can lead to disease, imbalance and disorder. In an open society such a distinction of sexuality is less critical; the emphasis should be on order and truth and not so much on the form of sexuality. Nevertheless, whether a person is a homosexual or a heterosexual they should both maintain order that does not disrupt the lives of others. Also, both the homosexual as well as the heterosexual need to practice control of the sex urge and transcendence of gender in order to discover higher consciousness beyond the ego self-identity. In other words, whether or not a person considers themselves homo or hetero they are both engaging in spiritual ignorance since neither can be true from a transcendental point of view. From a relative point of view, yes there are varieties of sexuality and gender. But from a higher point of view those are illusory forms of ego manifestation that need to be managed and eventually transcended. This does not mean that for example, a male person who saw himself as a male personality, enjoyed sex with women and then became a sage, will now turn to homosexuality; it means he will discover his androgynous nature and transcend the need for sex altogether. Likewise, a person who is on the spiritual path, who sees him/her self as homosexual, just as the heterosexual, needs to work on overcoming that form of illusion, by controlling the sex urge, living within the limitations of a monogamous relationship and learning to discover the futility of gender, the illusoriness of sex and the transcendental nature of the soul.

Peace and Blessings!
Sebai MAA

Conversation with God

Question: How to control sex desire?

Dr. Ashby:

I am currently reading your book, *Sacred Sexuality and The Art of Sex Sublimation and Universal Consciousness*. Let me say that it indeed has been an enlightenment to read. It confirms some of my many notions about sexuality and the concept of Oneness. Prior to reading this book, these visions were given to me by the Creator and I feel your book was part of a Divine plan for me to learn more.

However, I have one question. You stated that sexual desire is strictly mental and that it is regulated by nature. And if we are to seek enlightenment, then we have the authority to control such urges in order to produce our greatness. I agree wholeheartedly with this. Since sexuality is given to us by nature and used for procreation, that means it is natural and unavoidable, correct?

Now if this is so, when does the spiritual aspirant know when they have acquired their oneness with the Creator (higher purpose) and now must move forward and create another life? If you are basking in the light of knowledge and truth, in order to produce a relationship that is a reflection of the magnificence of God, then your mate would need to have that same enlightenment, correct? How would a spiritual aspirant, given all the conditions and falsehoods we presently live under, re-condition and lead their mate to the same spiritual consciousness as themselves, in order to love and produce another life? I ask these questions in an attempt to enhance my understanding of the Tantric philosophy and also to apply these teachings to my everyday life. Because as we enter into the next century of existence, we will definitely need to be on a higher spiritual plateau than we are now. It begins with me. And I want to also bring as many into the light as possible.

So, if you would, please respond to me and answer my questions. Unfortunately, I reside out of state, so I am unable to attend your institute. Any help that you provide is greatly appreciated!

I look forward to your response! Thank you!

Answer

Greetings,

First of all, the idea that sexuality in its gross form (physical intercourse between a man and woman) is unavoidable is a great fallacy. Just because you have a capacity does not necessarily mean you should use it. For example, just because you can make a fist does not mean you should go around punching people. In the same manner, sexuality should be seen as an aspect of the physical body, like all others, that is to be under the control of the mind, i.e. reason.

Mystical Answers to the Important Questions of Life

Secondly, sexuality is unavoidable, but not in the context you might expect. Sex energy is not only the source of creation for new life, but the source which sustains existing life as well. Sex energy sustains people and keeps them alive. It urges them with desire for pleasure and this impetus "makes the world go around." But desire is different for different people. Some people like physical sex, others like drinking, others like power, others get pleasure from hurting others and others get pleasure from helping others. These forms of pleasure are expressions of sex energy also. A human being must use the energy one way or another; this is unavoidable. What it is used for is a different question. It can be used to lead one downward into gross matter and physicality, or it can be directed at sublime goals that will lead to spiritual enlightenment.

Therefore, a spiritual aspirant seeks to move away from gross physical relationships and entanglements and cultivates that sex energy until it copulates (unites) with cosmic consciousness, thereby leading him/her to spiritual enlightenment. So sex is unavoidable, but whether it is gross sex, or subtle, elevating sex, is up to the individual. Marital relations are to be seen as any other family relation. They are to be outgrown and transcended, just like a child grows up and moves away to make their own family. So too a spiritual aspirant must someday outgrow the physical desires of the world and join the spiritual family. Otherwise, how would it be for a 60-year-old man to stay at home living with the parents and never move on in life? Likewise, how would it be for a spiritual aspirant to adhere to illusions of being a spiritual aspirant while holding on to egoistic desires and cravings? Realize that if you attain spiritual enlightenment, which is the fulfillment of all sex desires, you need not procreate physically and you would not feel compelled by that lower sexual urge anymore. If you did so, it would be for the benefit of others; but beware that what you do for others should be for their ultimate benefit and not just to satisfy their immediate desires, which would be a shortsighted and limited perspective. To elevate others the best way is by your example and your understanding and not just by your facilitation of their ignorant desires. Spiritual enlightenment and worldly desires are like fire and water, acid and alkaline, etc. This is the underlying teaching of Tantrism. Those who see Tantrism solely as a means to enhance physical sex pleasure are highly mistaken and obviously devoid of authentic spiritual leadership.

For more on these teachings get the Maat audio series teachings on Sex-sublimation and the book *Sacred Sexuality*.

Peace and Blessings!

Sebai MAA

Conversation with God

Question: Is Polygamy allowed in Egyptian religion?

I thought that Ancient Egyptian Religion allowed polygamy, is that true?

Answer

Ancient Egyptian society was based on monogamous social order. Neither polygamy nor polyandry was allowed in ancient Egyptian culture. This factor has been extensively researched by Western and African scholars. Only in some instances relating to the Pharaoh was polygamy allowed for political alliance reasons with other countries. While polygamy would seem to be supported by the myth of Asar, in the social order it was not followed in that way. The proof is that there are no records of polygamy as a common practice in ordinary marital records of the general populace. This proves that the mythic teaching is to be understood metaphorically and philosophically instead of literally. Those who seek to synthesize other traditions that practiced polygamy into the Ancient Egyptian (Kamitan) culture are incorrect. Now that you have received a definitive answer to this question, you must accept it as final. Many people seek religions that explicitly promote polygamy because they think they will have more sexual pleasures or be served by many women. If that is their goal, they will remain far from real spiritual evolution and closer to confusion and strife, for if one wife or husband is hard enough to handle what can we say of two or more? Those who seek to engage in that practice should find another tradition since Shetaut Neter does not allow it.

Peace and Blessings!

Sebai MAA

Mystical Answers to the Important Questions of Life

Question: How to maintain family relations with closed-minded Christian relatives?

Greetings Sebai Maa,

The thing that I am struggling with is that I was raised in a Christian home with family members who have very closed minds to any other means of connection with God other than through Jesus Christ. Through my readings, I am finding that this is just not true. How can I continue my studies and still maintain a relationship with my family? I'm just looking for suggestions; also send me your address for donation purposes and by the way right now I am reading "The Wisdom of Isis."
Maat Peace

Answer

Greetings,

The best rule is: live and let live. Do not expect others to turn towards what you are doing, especially when they have learned, although erroneously, that their way is the true or only path. Instead strive to understand yourself and in so doing you will handle situations with others in a more qualitative way. Love them because they are expressions of God, just as you would still love a child, who due to immaturity, believed that the moon is made of cheese. Therefore, do not get into religious discussions that will lead to arguments or debates.

Those who are fanatical in religion many times try to convert others because that makes them feel they are securing their own faith. Those who believe in faith-based religions and follow those religions blindly must constantly affirm their faith by perpetually affirming religious slogans and platitudes based on dogmas and working to convert others because their faith is not secured by critical thinking and inner spiritual discovery. Therefore, the outer reality must conform to the shape of the internal illusion of what they have come to "believe" religion is supposed to be. If there are others who express doubt or manifest other forms of faith, the fanatical faith-based religious believer will always be uneasy and working to convert others, and the only way they feel they could rest is if everyone was converted to their faith. Since that is not going to happen, they will never have peace. And while their conversations with you may seem to be open, in reality they are trying to find a way to convert you and not to explore your religion or understand your philosophy – since it conflicts with their own, which, again must be upheld by illusion. Because reasoning breaks the illusions, reasoning and critical thinking must be prevented, so exploring other faiths is prohibited by their own inhibitions, instilled or reinforced by the orthodox religious culture they are following.

Mystical spirituality is a personal movement for those who are serious on the path, and they do not try to convince others or force others to convert to anything because the truth of the teaching is self-evident and a person can only continue to follow a path that is untrue if they close their minds to the correctness of another path. A person will do that if

Conversation with God

they have come to believe that following religion is about faith and not about truth, so they can cut off any reality that conflicts with their faith-based convictions. Those convictions are usually backed up (reinforced) with guilt and/or fear of going to hell, an idea implanted within them from their youth. The ideas implanted from youth are most powerful because they become embedded in the mind easily without their own capacity for discernment; also they are embedded along with childish fears and lack of will (which comes in adolescence).

Further, until someone is ready to grow spiritually, one cannot force them to understand the mystical teachings, no more so than one can force a fruit on a tree to ripen before it's ready. Thus the saying, when the student is ready, the teacher appears. Nonetheless, your contact with your family members serves a purpose. They have a choice…they can abandon you because of your religious/spiritual beliefs, or they can continue to love and support you, even though they do not agree with your beliefs. Thus, through their love for you, they must open their hearts to you even though from their perspective, your beliefs are contrary to theirs. This allows them to evolve spiritually; though in a small measure, it is in the right direction. Some families cannot even tolerate being associated with someone who holds different religious beliefs, and will disown the person. Therefore, the tolerance that your family is showing, to the degree they are showing that, is a positive step in their spiritual evolution. And your lesson is one of practicing detached and dispassionate love. Thereby, you will not develop any ill will towards your family, and also no expectation from them, no more than you would feel ill will towards a child who holds beliefs contrary to yours, or develop expectation that the child will accept and understand some advanced science that you may be studying, because you understand the child to be immature. Similarly, accept that your family members are in a state of spiritual immaturity, whereby they cannot understand the advanced mystical sciences…yet; it may take many more life times for them to mature to a level where they can do so. Treat them with the same acceptance, patience, kindness, tolerance and caring that you would show your young niece or nephew who disagreed with you because of their immaturity. In spite of your niece's or nephew's immaturity, you would still assist them and show them affection, and would not hold a grudge against them for their immature beliefs. You would know when they are older, they will likely develop the capacity to understand what you are trying to teach/tell them as being true…but for now you can accept them and their erroneous beliefs, and still have a relationship with them. Apply this concept to your family relative to their immature spiritual beliefs. See them as spiritual children; it may take many more lifetimes for them to develop "mystical" maturity. Therefore, study with those who are on your same path and keep council with them on spiritual matters. Aspirants learn by following a teaching and practicing it under the guidance of a preceptor. Do not be concerned with the naysayers, fundamentalists, fanatics, dogmatists or demagogues who espouse and practice limited spirituality. Focus on your experiences and insights. Be an example of the teaching you are learning. The truth is evident in the expression and not in words. Be at peace and be an example of tolerance and understanding.

Peace and Blessings!
Sebai MAA

Mystical Answers to the Important Questions of Life

Question: How to rejuvenate my passion for this marriage?

Greetings!

At 32 years of age, I have been feeling my worst. I have not had 12 years of marital bliss. I have not accomplished anything I set out to do in life. My core family includes my husband, myself and my two sons. On the outside we appear "perfect". That is, we are vegan, have African names, are "conscious". However, deep inside something is missing. I had been hearing a lot about yoga. Spirituality and meditation are high on my list, but I had not been able to make a connection with anything out there. Naturally, I am not drawn to any westernized religion or pseudo African one. I have been in search of truth - spirituality not religion. Further, that truth has to originate from Africa. Well, I researched Kemetic yoga on the internet and that is how I found you. After speaking with one of your followers, he advised that "*Egyptian Yoga: Philosophy of Enlightenment*" is a great starting point. You have many materials. In what order do we approach the information?

Would you please advise me on how I can rejuvenate my passion for this marriage and heal our relationship through yoga? The relationship as well as our progress in life has been stagnating. We have begun marriage counseling but that is somewhat on hold due to finances.

Thank you for your time.

Answer

Greetings,

First of all, be assured that your situation is not unique. Many in our culture are discovering that the superficial trappings of Africentrism, while positive are only a first step towards a meaningful movement towards self-discovery and happiness in life. You are beginning to understand that names and clothing or even attending some lectures on Africanness does not make one African nor do these things guarantee even Africans in Africa that they will discover true peace and happiness in life.

So what is missing? I believe you already know the answer to that question. Spirituality becomes ineffective when its meaning and teachings are lost in the myriad of worldly desires and ignorance about the teaching. What is missing from your life is substance, which comes from a profound understanding and experience of the teaching. But this cannot come from superficialities. When the temporary satisfaction of superficialities wears off one is left where one started and then the search is on again for some other means to fill the void. Traditional counseling will ultimately not help because the

Conversation with God

problem is a spiritual one and not a worldly one. You will discover a true solution only when you resolve to earnestly seek to discover the answers to the important questions of life. When two people in a relationship resolve in this way they inevitably discover that they have led themselves to their misery by misunderstanding and wrong ways of living. Then you and your partner will discover the true purpose of your relationship, which you are only now prepared to explore. Your disappointments are natural. Life is not bliss and ordinary marriages do not succeed. Look at the statistics. Only those marriages with a spiritual consciousness grow and glorify the spirit and thereby achieve the highest good. How is this done? By becoming an avid student and practitioner of the teaching. After "*Egyptian Yoga: Philosophy of Enlightenment*" read the book *Egyptian Sacred Sexuality* (Egyptian Tantra Yoga) which contains teachings for relationships and marriage; from there decide if you want to pursue this path further.

You say that you do not want religion but know that what you have been exposed to up to now is not religion, but myth and ritual only. These are only the beginning of religion and not its end, but they are necessary steps. This is why you are stagnant as is most of the population. But make no mistake. In order to receive a real benefit you must adopt the teaching in a serious and real way, as a religion, since that is what it is, but a religion with a full program leading to the high disciplines of meditation and transcendence. Those who embark on this path are relieved of all toils and tribulations and they discover the true meaning and purpose of their relationships. This leads to true happiness and bliss. This will rejuvenate your marriage, not just for now but in ever increasing and glorious ways. I suggest that you get the new initiation series tapes and attend the Sunday lectures. The upcoming series of talks will be best for you since they will go into the teaching from scratch and provide an overall view of the path[23].

In the meantime take heart and also realize that there is something more to life, your relationships and your spiritual journey. For now, allow these words to give you faith and strength to forge ahead towards attaining this goal. Look at our web site and read about the disciplines and the new publications and prepare yourself to embark on a new phase in your journey of life. This is the reason for your frustration. Your soul is yearning to grow and where there is no growth there is stagnation and death. All your years were not for nothing though. If you follow this path you will discover the meaning of all that has transpired as well as what you learned from those experiences. For now just realize that you are simply tired and frustrated but this is not the only possibility in life; there is much more. Your life has not been a waste nor has it been purposeless. But sorrow and frustration need not be in your future if you resolve earnestly to explore the path which I have laid out. You may study on your own but more effective is the live class, so be patient and take the actions I have suggested.[24]

Peace and Blessings!
Sebai MAA

---

[23] Audiotapes are available through the Sema Institute of Yoga. Visit: www.egyptianyoga.com.
[24] In addition to the study of marriage in Ancient Egypt and modern culture Sebai Maa has undergone PREP relationship counselor training.

Mystical Answers to the Important Questions of Life

How to Become a Healthy person and purify mind, body and soul in order to be ready to Attain Higher Consciousness?

Conversation with God

Question: on methods concerning mental and physical purification.

Greetings Sebai Muata Ashby:

I pray that you and your family are blessed with eternal bliss! I have been wondering about my practice methods concerning mental and physical purification. I have been putting forth the effort but do not know if what I am doing is correct. Mentally, I regularly meditate and study something from one of your books consistently. The thing I have not been regular in is my time for reflecting on the teachings. Are these things (practices) what is meant by "mental purification"? If not, what is it that should be done to help with this process?

As far as physical purification is concerned, I have eliminated meat from my diet every other day. I plan on beginning a Tai Chi class next month. Again I ask, is the practice of doing these things what is meant by "physical purification?" If not what should I be doing in this regard?

Your advice in this matter would be greatly appreciated.

Peace

Answer

Greetings,

All of the things you mentioned above will act to purify you to some degree. What is necessary is for you to develop an understanding of how to promote the purification process in a consistent and effective manner. The preferred way to do this is to adopt a constant program involving the basic areas of spiritual evolution (study of the teaching, devotional practices, physical exercise and selfless service as well as vegetarianism and meditation). These areas will best promote the spiritual evolution. To assist in this you should acquire the books and tapes (Shedy program) to do in depth studies and if possible follow along with the online classes. Contact us for more details if you are interested. You should try to join a local group if possible to help promote the practice and better understanding of the teaching through discussions and activities that promote higher purification of the heart in order to lead you to greater understanding and experience of the deeper meaning of the teachings. Also, participate in seminars we conduct in person.

Peace and Blessings!
Sebai MAA

Mystical Answers to the Important Questions of Life

Question: How to promote brain enhancement?

Greetings,

What would you recommend as a natural brain enhancement?   Please advise.

htp

Answer

Greetings,

Firstly, we must point out that the brain and the mind are two different things. The brain is the physical nervous system through which the subtle energy of the mind operates, just as electricity powers and operates an electrical appliance. In order to have good memory, it is necessary to practice good mental disciplines such as righteous thinking, relaxation and meditation, ethics and study of the philosophy of life that allow one to maintain balance and peace and reduce anxiety and stress. For the physical constitution there are also many herbs and practices to maintain health and memory sharpness. The creation of good memory is a multifaceted issue. Firstly there must be sanity (of course) and then good nutrition, getting all vitamins and minerals needed for good brain chemistry - original Egyptian lotus oil (which is obtainable today) has the effect of creating good memory and overall mental function, so this is why we see many ancient Kamitans being depicted smelling lotuses-even in the Pert m Heru; Ginko has a similar effect. Next also it is necessary to reduce stress in order to concentrate on the subject. Next, it is necessary to use two techniques: repetition and association. Repetition reinforces the item to be remembered (use it or loose it), and association helps the mind connect items: Ex. remember the Ra Hymn: Learn the music of the hymn and the words follow (association of music with lyric).

Practical technique - do not overtax the memory capacity. Start from scratch and take it one step at a time. Do not jump from A to Z without going through B, C, D, E, F, G, etc. Also, when attempting to learn anything, you must be relaxed and give yourself to the subject; be a sponge. When using a sponge for cleaning, you must squeeze out the

Conversation with God

contents first and then you can absorb more. Some things can and should be memorized by rote, but the best kind of memory is through understanding and connecting with the constituent parts of the item being remembered. To learn something well, you must deconstruct it and then put it back together again, so you can know it inside and out. Learning from scratch and building on that foundation serves this purpose. Sometimes you can bring learning from previous lives, and if so, you do not need to start from scratch- however if the subject is not easy then you may need to start from scratch. Every time you learn something you must make that learning part of permanent memory by using it frequently; then it comes back automatically when needed and there is no need to hold it in mind all the time. Then you can be free for the next class to learn the new material and add it to your storehouse of knowledge.

Creativity comes when you are one with the knowledge but the knowing makes the knowledge more than the sum of the information in it; then you can independently add to the storehouse and thereby you can contribute to the storehouse of knowledge of humanity. This is called intuition.

Note you do not want to oxidize the brain by consuming meat, many cooked foods and non-organic processed foods laden with artificial chemicals that produce poisons in the body. Rather anti-oxidize it with fruits and vegetables and if necessary, antioxidant supplements such as Co-Q10, Vitamin C, A, etc. Exercise helps keep the *mettu* (vessels) clear and if the teaching is practiced, the flow of life force will be clear and those are propitious conditions for learning - so practitioners of the mysteries have more capacity for intellect and higher learning, yet they must obey certain physical laws when they are learning things of the physical world.

Peace and Blessings!

Sebai MAA

Mystical Answers to the Important Questions of Life

Question: How to handle my diet?

Greetings,

Sebai Maa I have a question concerning my diet. How can I improve it and where do I start?

Answer

Greetings,

Begin by getting the book *Kemetic Diet* (available through our website: www.egyptianyoga.com). It has a step-by-step program for understanding and adopting the proper diet, not just for the body, but also for the mind and soul as well. You can immediately start by adopting a vegetarian-vegan diet, which means eliminating all animal products from your diet, including dairy, eggs, fish, and chicken. The natural plant based sweetener "agave" is a good alternative for honey. Eat no more than 50% cooked food. Also, eat fruits and vegetables daily. Select organic produce and products whenever possible. Look in the book for specific considerations for your current state, and consult a health care practitioner, nutritionist and or dietitian for specific guidelines, especially if you have any health conditions.

Peace and Blessings!

Sebai MAA

Conversation with God

Question: How to handle my diet after achieving success in the teachings and growing older?

Greetings,

I have studied the teachings and have achieved depth in meditation and balance but I have become very complacent and what I describe as lazy as compared to my type "A" personality. I have also picked up a lot of weight because all I do is work, sleep and eat. I am more relaxed but not motivated to do much of anything. Degraded movement or progress?

Udja,

Indeed, the integration process can be difficult as the practice intellectually tends to lead to greater indifference about the world and one's own personality is part of that world. While some positive changes may happen like not being so uptight, others may also occur like disinterested nature, and apathy. As time passes the initial high can become dull. Also, as the years wear on the body needs less sustenance and deteriorates so needs more maintenance. Then it is necessary to apply the will to take more care through exercise and reduction in the diet as well as taking greater care in the quality of the diet. This effort is of the nature of will, to logically adjust the activity and intake of the body even if it does not feel necessary. Many things feel OK and yet are detrimental to the body. Notice that as a personality advanced on the path there is less control of the feelings over the desires and pursuits of the personality; so the soul can exert it's will more freely. If you have trained yourself to live by truth then it will not be tedious to do exercise or eat the correct amount of food because your physical body must accept commands from the mind and not the other way around. But also you will not overdo it because you are also trained in keeping a balance. The intellect must keep close watch and dictate in these matters. Then the feelings may be allowed to reinforce those efforts.

Logically it is important to have proper maintenance of the body, not just to extend life, but also for the sake of promoting efficiency and greater qualitative service to humanity as well as garnering greater insights into the Self. A deteriorated body is a burden to oneself and to one's efforts. The task is not to revert to a type "A" personality but to adjust to a more balanced state that is neither type A nor sedentary and dull. So you simply need to make adjustments to your personality, like recalibrating the settings on a machine. So sit, meditate, do your tune-up, move on to your duty and live a full, healthy and productive life. Read the book: *The Kemetic Diet*.

Peace and Blessings!
Sebai MAA

Mystical Answers to the Important Questions of Life

Question: What should I eat?

Good Morning,

I am enjoying your books *Kemetic Diet* and *Journey from Jesus to Christ*. I was doing quite well on my diet for one week but slipped the last two days, but I will not give up. I am fighting for my life. I am addicted to this world, and I need help. I have a dull and agitated personality that I want to bring into the light so that I can be free, but my emotions are so screwed up. I need support, because I am weak. I do not want to have to take blood pressure medicine the rest of my life. I have been able to take only one pill per day instead of two since I have been staying off of meat.

I still am having a problem with constipation. Every morning I have been drinking water with lime/lemon, eating a cucumber for breakfast, taking the nutritional supplements you suggested, and eating salads and juicing every other day, but my bowels are still hard. Could you recommend some other foods I need to be ingesting?

I have for many years tried to meditate. I can't seem to keep my mind quiet. Plus this is my first time trying to study Ancient Egyptian Spirituality. I do not even know how to pronounce the words. When I am unable to pronounce words they haven't any meaning to me. I would like for you to please recommend some tapes and books that would assist me with getting into the habit of praying, breathing and doing exercises.

Thank you so much for being a light.

Sincerely,

Answer

Greetings,

I am pleased to hear of your efforts in the direction of promoting your health not just of body but also of mind and soul. Please realize that you have spent many years with the incorrect diet so it will take some time to purify and normalize yourself- usually 2-3 years. As recommended in the Kemetic Diet book, you should consult a health care practitioner to facilitate your dietary changes to be sure you are eating a well-balanced diet, and to screen (examine) you for any health issues that may be causing or contributing to the constipation. I will provide general guidelines and information below, based on the information in the book.

It is wonderful to see that the healthy changes you have so far made to your diet, including not eating meat, have already benefited you by allowing you to decrease your blood pressure medication. Be patient as you continue to apply the guidelines presented in the book. Do not go overboard with fruits. Rather stay with a balanced diet of fruits and vegetables and implement the transition procedures as outlined, including consulting a nutritionist/dietitian or other health care practitioner.

Also, pay attention to the sections of the book *Kemetic Diet* on aids to digestion. Apples, ginger and papaya can be helpful when one is constipated. They contain natural ingredients to promote good digestion. In addition, papaya enzymes as well as other products to help breaks up impacted feces in the colon are available in health food stores. You may also wish to consult a health care practitioner who does colon cleansing to help clean out the impacted colon. In addition to these considerations, understand that it will take time for your body to adapt to the changes you are making and normalize its functions once again.

Meditation is food for the soul. As far as meditation goes, the instruction is the same. You have spent many years agitating the mind, feeding it the wrong food. So now it will take some time to correct. The key is perseverance. Also, take action to feed your mind proper food - elevated spiritual teachings, keeping company with people of elevated-spiritual minds, and fast from agitating elements, violent TV shows, loud and worldly people, etc. Practice deep rhythmic breathing, sitting quietly for 20 minutes per day. Practice virtue day by day, and you will calm the restless mind. At the same time continue practicing concentration-meditation techniques, and eventually you will succeed.

Join the distance learning program or the internet classes for fellowship, inspiration and support.

Peace and Blessings!

Sebai MAA

Mystical Answers to the Important Questions of Life

Question: How to take care of the Skin without poisonous chemicals?

Hetep Sebai Maa,

    I am writing you with a question from the tape series. You were speaking about keeping the body clean and not putting poisonous chemicals on it or in it. I wanted to know if you had any suggestions about a natural oil or lotion that could be used for the skin, or is my outlook on what's deemed "ashy skin" based on an ignorant view supported by the masses.

sincerely,

Answer

Greetings,

The problem of dry skin affects many people but especially those who are light skinned. There can be some hereditary issues but mostly it is a problem that can arise from not having enough natural oil in the body or not enough moisture. Also, nutrition is a factor. But another important issue is extremes of weather. In too hot or too cold weather the problem can be severe. All of this can cause dry, scaly, ashy, brittle skin and other problems. Skin is an important organ, the largest organ, and should be taken care of properly in order to have optimal health.

It is enjoined to take primrose oil, ground flax or flax oil, olives or olive oil to promote healthy skin. Also it is recommended to take multi-vitamin supplement containing vitamin A especially. Take care with the rest of the diet that it should be more alkaline that acidic. Also be sure to consume sufficient quantities of water each day.

Follow the general guidelines outlined in our book, Kemetic Diet: do not drink coffee, sodas or alcohol, do not eat meat products, do not smoke, etc.

You may use a loofah sponge when bathing to wash off the dead skin cells.

As a rule of thumb we may say that if you cannot eat it you should not put it on your skin either since skin can absorb dangerous chemicals and one can be poisoned by them; poisons absorbed by the skin can manifest as cancer of the skin or other kinds. What we mean by this is just as when eating foods, you should be able read and pronounce all the ingredients, and also know they are healthy and from natural sources, the same should go for skin and hair products you apply to your body. Use a mild soap. Find one at the health food store that has natural and if possible, organic moisturizers and vitamins. If necessary also use a natural moisturizer from health food/natural food stores.

Conversation with God

Cocoa butter and aloe are good for the skin.

You may need to use a humidifier.

As a person who aspires for spiritual enlightenment try to understand that your purpose in treating a disease condition is to promote health for the purpose of creating propitious conditions for spiritual evolution. Health is a very attractive quality in a human being. It is not necessary to augment this with artificial makeup, etc. Therefore proceed with confidence and balance. Do what is necessary to maintain the body in health so that it may be a fit instrument for the study of the teaching. Leave other considerations aside to the extent that is possible for you and do not be overstressed. Follow the path with sincerity and you will find success.

Peace and Blessings!

Sebai MAA

Mystical Answers to the Important Questions of Life

Question: why do you recommend taking vitamins?

Greetings,
If sages and saints of the past lived a natural life in accord with the four seasons and Mother Nature, I do not think they took any vitamins or supplements, all their nutrients came from natural foods. As such, why do you recommend taking vitamins? And which vitamins or supplements would you recommend for me?
Thank you

Answer

Greetings,

On the spiritual path sometimes aspirants get the notion that they must do everything the way it was done in ancient times so as to recreate a proper situation for spiritual enlightenment. That is a misconception since all things change and even in Ancient Egypt, the culture of 5,000 B.C.E. was not the same as that of 1,800 B.C.E. However, the principles were/are always the same. The ancients did not need to take vitamin supplements because they got the vitamins and minerals from their foods which were grown in nutrient rich (fertile) soil. Additionally, they did not have to deal with the ecological conditions we have today. So some adjustments are needed to update the teaching of natural health for our times.

In the past, the earth was not polluted as it is today, the land had not been over farmed, and the soil was not depleted. For this reason, even organic foods are not as rich in many nutrients as they might have been just 100 years ago. Therefore, it is recommended that not only vegetarians, but non-vegetarians also, should take vitamins, supplements, digestive enzymes, etc. The world is an ever-changing stage in which life exists. As such, the reality that people lived with thousands of years ago is not the same as ours today. They did not contend with the loss of the Ozone layer, the unprecedented dumping of pollutants/toxins into the oceans and air pollution, etc. Therefore, it is necessary to make certain adjustments in the teachings to cope with modern situations. This present situation is the truth of the present and cannot be dealt with using solutions of the past because these particular problems did not exist in the past. Yet, the adjustment is made so that the end results of the past, getting proper amount of vitamins and minerals, may be achieved in the present. So we are not changing the teaching; we are just making it possible to achieve by coping with modern problems. Thus, the same principle of the past is still being upheld today. However, do not confuse this with the principles of the mystical philosophy. These were the same 10,000 years ago as they are today, and as they will be forever.

Therefore, in summary, a general guideline is that a yogic aspirant should have a vegetarian diet and should take vegetarian vitamins/supplements. Also, he or she should explore alternative sources of protein such as soy and almonds (nuts). Everyone's constitution is slightly different, so some adjustments are always necessary to suit every personality but these are the general guidelines which are detailed in our *Kemetic Diet* book.

Peace and Blessings!
Sebai MAA

Mystical Answers to the Important Questions of Life

How to develop Ethical Conscience and Purity of Heart?

Conversation with God

Question: Should I focus on the Maat Path?

Sebai Dr. Muata Ashby,

I want to tap into the wisdom of my ancestors--the builders of the greatest civilization ever known.

I am particularly interested in making MAAT the emphasis of my spiritual studies. I have already read *Egyptian Yoga 1 & 2*, and *Egyptian Proverbs*.

As a full time worker and part-time college student, I must be efficient in how I use my time; thus I want to be systematic in my study of the wisdom teachings. On pages 19-20 of the study guide, the class sequence places Maat fifth in an eight-step process. However, on page ten, spiritual aspirants like myself are told to study Maat "If you are interested in the path of righteous action."

In which direction should I go to begin my studies?

Answer

Greetings,

The Home Study program, for Kemetic studies, enjoins a general program of study for those who do not have a particular interest or who are new to the teaching. If you have a specific affinity with a particular aspect of the teaching such as Maat Philosophy, then that should be the basis or foundation of your studies even though you will also study the other aspects as well. The special path, which you choose for your main spiritual practices, is selected by your personality's predilections since it is much easier to adopt what one already has an interest in or good feeling about. Therefore, you should concentrate on the books that discuss the Maat path: *Introduction to Maat Philosophy*, *The 42 Precepts of Maat* and the *Wisdom Texts*, The *Book of the Dead*. Also there are audio series that should be listened to and also videos. If you are further, interested you should attend the upcoming seminar.

May the goddess Maat bless you with all Righteousness.

Peace and Blessings!

Sebai MAA

Mystical Answers to the Important Questions of Life

Question: How does the concept of Judgment work in Neterian spirituality?

Greetings,

In the book "Egyptian Yoga, The Philosophy of Enlightenment" you state that "at the time of your death, one will tell the 42 judges (your mental capacity) the 42 utterances (negative confessions)." In other words, you are saying that we will judge ourselves as opposed to the Christian perspective of being judged by another being. My question is what is your point of reference for this or how can I confirm this?

Thanks!

Answer

Greetings,

The proof of this teaching is embedded in the philosophy of the scriptures of the Pert m Heru texts as well as the iconographies related to it and other Kemetic scriptures itself. The Pyramid Texts Kemetic scripture states that the initiate is to consume the gods and goddesses and thereby assimilate their power. This same teaching is to be found in Chapter 42 of the Pert m Hru (Book of the Dead), the later version of the Pyramid Texts, which states that the gods and goddesses are actually parts or aspects of the initiate (human being). Further, the "I am" formula is used throughout all Kemetic scriptures, relating the identity of the initiate with the divinity in question (I am Aset, I am Djehuti, I am Heru, etc.). The epitome of this culture can be plainly seen in Chapter 33 (more commonly referred to as Chapter 125) of the Pert m Hru where the initiate proclaims his/her identity with Asar, the Supreme Being. Therefore, it is said that the divinities are in reality aspects of the Divine, and since we are that Divine essence, the divinities are in reality aspects of our own personality.

An individual conducts his/her own destiny because he/she is the power behind all creation. The problem is ignorance of this great truth. Ignorance keeps a human being oblivious to the inner glory and thus renders that person impotent and susceptible to the adversities of life. While the outer teaching seems to depict various deities judging the initiate, this is the esoteric teaching behind the iconography and philosophy which is gained from an in depth study and reflection on the philosophy and its mystical implications. For personal and direct experience of this teaching, you are to practice it and experience it for yourself, not only at the time of death, but really all the time, even now, as we speak. By accessing your own higher conscience you can discover the true judge of self, and that is the ultimate proof and confirmation of the teachings.

Peace and Blessings!

Sebai MAA

Conversation with God

Question: What is the difference between Ari (Karma) and the Divine Plan, also what is the relation of the soul with Life Force energy?

Greetings,

I have a few questions.

If I win the lottery this weekend, is it due to my karmic fortune or is it the Divine plan that made this possible? In short, how can one know whether something occurs due to one's karma or due to God's will? (Note: in your reply please try to include a specific example in human affairs.) I don't know it just seems a bit contradictory to say its Divine will when, in essence, we are one with that will---we are that will.

What is the relationship between the embodied soul and the Life Force energy? I believe in the Hindu tradition it is the jiva and prana, respectively. My impression is that the Life Force energy is what sustains the soul in its embodiment. Is the Life Force energy what keeps the soul in our body, and when this energy is gone, the soul leaves the body? How does the soul and Life Force energy relate and interact with one another?

HETEP!

Answer

Greetings!

The answer is both. While we as expressions of the Divine are part of cosmic will, we have deviated from that to pursue our own will if we are living at the level of ego consciousness. Egoism has its own egoistic will based on ignorance and desires. In the Kemetic field that is called *ariu* - the Hindus refer to that as Karma. A person's ariu (karmic fate) is due to their previous actions, thoughts, feelings and desires, and it is God's will that they should be able to experience the effect of their own desires so they are free to reap the rewards (consequences) of their pursuits. And that process of pursuing leads to experiences that yield knowledge which can turn into wisdom and enlightenment that produce contentment and cessation of the cycle of producing more *ariu*, reincarnation, and the seemingly endless cycle of death and reincarnation. Otherwise, they can impel future pursuit of desires in search of fulfillment, but which will only lead to temporary satisfaction followed by frustration and pain. God sustains Creation and the law of cause and effect. People experience life in accordance with the manner in which they act within that field of law (All creation is permeated by this law, so there is no escaping it –except through spiritual enlightenment – self-knowledge and transcendence of ego consciousness). It is instituted so that souls can grow by experiencing the consequences of their actions (desires, thoughts, words and deeds of the past and present).

Mystical Answers to the Important Questions of Life

One can know when one is experiencing God's will (Higher Self) when the heart is at peace and free from egoistic feeling. You may for example say that you want to see a movie for educational reasons because it has some spiritual content, but also it may have a lot of singing and dancing which is unrelated. Your ego self may have this in view deep down but on the surface of your mind you are convincing yourself that you are being virtuous when you in reality want to have sense pleasures as well. Another example is building a Temple. Let us say that you want to build a Temple to glorify God, but an obstacle comes up, and you run out of money and then you get upset because you can't complete the project. Whose project is it anyway? Your's or God's? If it is God's and you are a servant of God's will, you should not be disturbed by setbacks because it is in God's hands, God's will. If there is egoistic feeling you say, "I want this to happen," probably because it is for your own glory and prestige, and the thought of losing that causes anger and upset.

When you live in accordance with Divine will your ariu (karma) comes into harmony with that. What happens in your life is in harmony with what God wants and there can never be disappointment of frustration; hence there is always peace and inner fulfillment.

In reference to actions, an aspirant's only duty and reward is work and not the fruits of work, not the results. An aspirant is responsible for honest effort. After honest effort has been made, then we can say that whatever happens was supposed to happen. If there is no righteous effort, if a person says, "Well there is no use, just let it happen," then that situation also becomes fate (what was to happen), but it is not a righteous experience for the individual who approached it that way. *Ari* (karmic deed) is the action and the "Divine Plan" is the fated outcome. However, if right effort is made by an aspirant, the action bears the fruit of wisdom and enlightenment, regardless of the fate. So in spite of the fate, an aspirant can direct their own destiny. If an aspirant does not direct the actions in this way, they can become controlled by the force of previous *ariu* (karmic deeds) that compels them to certain actions they may not have wanted otherwise, which would lead to more entanglements and perpetuate worldly situations, sufferings, joys and more reincarnations. So if a person does not direct their life their unconscious impressions of the past and their new feelings and desires based on present forms of ignorance and egoism will direct them either to calamities and predicaments of life, or prosperities and joys; but both of these will be in never ending cycles until the other perspective, the perspective of wisdom, is adopted.

So, it is a misunderstanding to think that *surrender to the Divine* means being passive, not acting, and allowing God/the Divine Plan to determine your life. *Surrender to the Divine* means surrendering your egoism as you act, thereby acting in ways that serve your higher spiritual nature, the Self. It means surrendering hatred, frustration, anger, greed, envy, jealousy, insecurity, fear, anxiety, worry and instead practicing detached-universal love (loving the Self in all creation, in all persons), patience, perseverance, faith, selflessness, compassion, fearlessness, etc., backed up by your daily practice of the shedy (yoga-mystical) disciplines, as you initiate and perform actions. Thus, it means striving to perform righteous actions in a non-egoistic manner. Therefore, as one performs righteous actions, if one practices putting down one's egoism as one acts, and seeing oneself as a vehicle for the Divine Will to flow through, then one will feel communion with the higher Self as the work is being performed...and this feeling further erodes egoism that normally expresses as "*I* did this work." The work is performed with detachment, and the Self is given the credit for performing the action. In acknowledging that the Self performed the action, and not your ego-personality, then you are eroding that egoistic sense that develops from thinking of yourself as an individual, separate from the Self, and instead you are promoting your enlightenment, even as you perform dynamic actions in the world of time and space.

So, you can decide, do you want to receive egoistic glory and praise or censure from having performed righteous actions (I did it!), or do you want those righteous actions to lead you to attain Enlightenment (the Self did it!). The idea of the Self performing the action is an inner experience and awareness which you can have even as you accept praises or censure from others in a practical manner. So, if your boss tells you that you did a great job on a project, you would not want to tell your boss, "thanks, but I did not do it, the Self did it, so thank the Self," because unless your boss is a practitioner of mystical religion and you are in a mystical religious environment, your boss and co-workers may think you are crazy. In such circumstances, you can graciously accept the praise, but internally be aware that "you" did not perform the action, because "you" as the ego-personality do not even exist...it's all the Self. So, actions can lead one to increased or decreased egoism; the effect of the action is determined by your attitude as you perform it. Righteous actions can lead to pleasurable experiences in this life and also after death, but you will still have to reincarnate and go through this again, or they can lead to enlightenment, the cessation of reincarnation and experience of abiding joy and peace. It is incumbent upon an aspirant to promote the latter.

Hence, an aspirant who adopts this philosophical discipline of actions and deeds lives a glorious life because there is constant fulfillment and peace in every step, with every action, with every thought, with every feeling. Such an aspirant has regained the power over her/his own life instead of giving the power of their happiness to unpredictable and unsustainable outcomes in the world of time and space. This is the path of Maat Philosophy.

First, the term "embodied soul" needs to be understood correctly. As an advanced aspirant you need to realize that the soul is never in the body. The "soul in the body" idea is an elementary concept used to help the beginning aspirant. The soul is actually the Self, which has come to see itself (through ignorance-forgetfulness-dullness of mind), as a separate individual being. In order to sustain that illusory reality the individualized soul uses energy, more specifically called Life Force Energy (Sekhem {KMT}, Prana {Indian}, Chi {Chinese}, etc.). It is actually the same kind of energy that is used to sustain a dream when you sleep at night. But as you know, you must at some time wake up from the dream. All thought has energy associated with it. You think and will yourself to exist as an individual human being; therefore the energy of that thought (Life Force Energy) sustains that reality for a while, be it in the waking reality when you are "awake" or in the dream reality when you sleep. When the soul no longer wishes to continue with that thought, the energy is withdrawn from that particular individualized existence, and the soul focuses on another idea, another personality and thus experiences a new dream (lifetime). This is called reincarnation. Actually, the soul never entered the body so it can never leave what it never entered. Incarnation is only a mental experience, an attunement of the soul (Self caught up in ignorance and limitation) to a physical individualized reality and not an absolute reality. Therefore, the soul never goes into any body, it is always transcendental and free but caught by its own idea of individuality; so thereby it has made itself subject to the laws that affect individualized existence (*ariu*-karma). When a person discovers their true identity, they are free from all limitation (*ariu*-karma), and thus the energy that comes with the idea or reality of freedom is vast and they can do wondrous things on the physical plane, but also beyond.

Peace and Blessings!

Sebai MAA

Conversation with God

Questions: Can Hip Hop be a Righteous Path as I study the Teachings?

Greetings Sebai Muata Ashby,

I have several important questions that I need your counseling on. The first question is I am in a hip hop group. We promote so called "positive music." We deal with current issues, religion, and our culture. On the flip side of this there are a lot of influences that have not been positive. Another thing about this is that if we do get signed by a major record label and we have to go on tours, that will really disrupt my spiritual practice and I won't be able to raise my daughter and ground her in the spiritual principles if I am away four to six months out of the year. I read in the book *Sacred Sexuality* that we entered into the relationships that we are in now because of ignorance and that we need to let karma work its way out and that we need to learn the lessons or we will repeat the same entanglements again. I always had questions about this being in line with my spiritual discipline in the past and when I read your book *Sacred Sexuality* it brought it to the surface of my mind very quickly. I really need some counseling on what decision to make. I'm not attached to the music and I am prepared to let it go but I don't want to make a decision based on ignorance of the higher wisdom of why we find ourselves in certain relationships.

The second question is that my girlfriend and I have been together for five years. She is lazy when it comes to reading the wisdom so I share with her everything I learn via experience and the books I read. I wonder, do I need to stop telling her everything because I feel that I'm stunting her growth constantly giving her second hand knowledge, really third hand because the intellectual is only half. I don't want my ego to get in the way when I'm talking to her and I also want her to read the information for herself so that it can affect her in the special way wisdom does. Can you help with this as this is a very confusing issue for me.

The third question is that with the alternate breathing exercise. I don't understand how to breathe in the rhythm 2:8:4. I understand one cycle of alternate breathing, but not how to do it according to the other longer cycles that you give.

The fourth and final question is that I wanted to know how long am I supposed to go on my purification of mind and body before I can start practicing the serpent power meditation techniques. I read the book once, but I can definitely read it more to get a better understanding before beginning. I've been reading the book *Kemetic Diet* for about a year and I have been integrating a vegetarian diet. I was planning on buying the three video set on the serpent power and begin practicing it. I'm a little confused as meditation is a part of the beginning practices and I don't want to try and raise the energy in the wrong way. I have been chanting in these stages of my practice and I want to wait until the mind was calmed more before I got into the regular meditations (not the serpent

Mystical Answers to the Important Questions of Life

power), then once I had my diet stabilized I wanted to start the serpent power meditations twice a day. Thank you again for your time in corresponding with me and all of the things I've learned and will learn. hetep

Answers

Greetings,

Your questions are very important because as you have recognized, the issues you are facing will have a profound effect not only on your life but on that of your family's. Firstly, the actions (Ari - karma) that you are currently involved in- you have placed much investment of time and energy pursuing these and you have been led down a particular path. Also, you have been doing some readings about the philosophy as well. You should ask what is it that is causing you this quandary now? Why are you questioning the "so called 'positive music'" you are involved in? Could it be that it is not as positive as you would like? In every action as followers of the teaching, we are challenged to bring Maat (righteousness and truth) to our lives and the more that we put this off, the further away we move from self-discovery, peace and true prosperity in life – even if we earn millions. Sage Amenemope teaches us: *"better a crust of bread and the love of God, than wealth with vexation and strife."*

You are responsible for your actions and your daughter is an important one of these because you are charged with her upbringing and she is the future of the society and culture. You have by now seen what happens when children are neglected, so where is the quandary? The task is to next seek balance between legitimate worldly obligations and spiritual work. If your worldly actions disturb that balance, then you can see the result. Just survey those in the entertainment field, how they get caught up and lose themselves – no need to say more on this point. If you are beginning to seriously question your actions and their integrity, it means that higher wisdom is dawning in your mind; the higher Self in you is beaconing for an adjustment. Will you heed the word or ignore it as others do? At this point, there is no need to repeat errors or suffer needlessly going through lessons already learned. Would you place your hand on a stove a second time after you have done it once simply because your hand is moving in the direction of the stove a second time? Move forward.

However, if you choose to go forwards in this manner, the path of the householder, you will need to be more serious about the teaching as currently you are neither wholly serious about music nor the teaching, for otherwise there would be no quandary. If you truly have the strength to give up your music, do you have the strength to transform it and purify it? What does the Divine truly want to say through you and through hip-hop? Have not the gangsters and sucker MC and drug dealers, rapists and sex fiends had the microphone for long enough? Hasn't our youth been duped long enough by the ignorant, capitalist, racist, sexist culture which promises apple pie and the million dollar lotto and also by the angry, ignorant, greedy and pleasure seeking, debaucheries in the hip-hop music industry and its followers? Therefore, abandon the quandary and seek to perform your music uncompromisingly virtuously – no need to give it up. Rather give up the idea of following the path laid out by the recording industry. When will all the "so called" "hard edged," "bold" and uncompromising hip-hop turn to powerfully enlightening and empowering people instead of weakening them by feeding sensual illusions and short circuiting their mental powers? When will it lead to answers about how to raise people from the ghetto instead of reflecting the anger and hatred of the ghetto or amplifying egoistic desires and lustful sexual impulses that immerse them more in their own mess and distracts them from the way to really elevate themselves from their morass? As a musician study these questions. As a parent study how to impart these values to all children. As a friend to other human beings study how to promote peace, wisdom and elevated thought through actions, and words that will elevate them. As a follower of the teaching study how to discover the truth of the teaching and realize it within yourself and thereby discover the secrets of the universe.

Secondly, EVERYONE in the world is engaged in relationships, even sages. The question is what will be the nature and quality of those relationships; will they be based on sentimentality and egoism as with the masses, or on wisdom and enlightenment as the sages? The ancient Egyptian proverb tells us: *"When the student is ready, the master will appear."* It is natural to want to share things one feels are useful and beneficial to others but sometimes people are not ready to receive things even if they are beneficial, due to their level of spiritual evolution. This does not mean that you cannot share what you are learning to your level of understanding. However, you cannot make others interested in the teaching, though you can encourage them as opportunity allows, but only to a point – the point that they accept or reject – for they set the limits. If you trespass beyond that point you risk alienating others. Share in peace and joy, by being a model, an exemplar of the teaching in practice.

Beware that if you seriously seek to tread the path you will be highly challenged if you associate with those who are less interested – further burden is adding responsibilities that will curtail your freedom to follow the teaching. Your quandary stems from your desire to hold on to that to which you have developed attachment. Abandon the illusion of girlfriends and daughters. This does not mean go and live alone. Adopt the tantric wisdom of loving them as expressions of the Divine-read the book again. Worry more about transforming yourself and then your relations will be most impressed. Realize that teaching occurs in three ways, by example, word and subtle influence. The example is the action with dependable integrity, the word is the verbal instruction that explains and reasons, the influence is the higher vibration engendered by your soul when it is in tune with the Spirit; this is a radiation that affects all your relations and is infused in all your actions and creations (including artistic ones). How can this kind of higher vibration be engendered in an atmosphere of discord, imbalance and ignorance or in an atmosphere of vice: worldly desire, and pleasure-seeking?

Thirdly, until you resolve the bigger issues in your life refrain from any advanced breathing exercises. Simply practice simple alternate nostril breathing without counting – then practice normal inhalation and exhalation during regular meditation practice.

Mystical Answers to the Important Questions of Life

Fourthly, refrain from Serpent Power practices until the greater issues are resolved and you have achieved a greater degree of inner purification. In the mean time fully integrate the vegetarian diet and purification system laid out in the *Kemetic Diet* Book – realize that the *wadj* or green diet is not limited to food for the body – there is a vegetarian diet for the mind and the soul too – all three (health of body, health of mind and health of soul) must be taken into account before entering into the Serpent Power. Further, music and lyric intent are extremely powerful forces that affect the mind deeply in subtle ways– in accordance with the Neterian tradition you should study the principles of music and spirit in order to engender the tonal and vibrational qualities that will be conducive to the development of proper mental and spiritual evolution – get the *Ancient Egyptian Devotional Manual and Songbook*.

Finally, many people such as you are honestly seeking to make their way in the world and it is tough since there are so many choices and distractions, passions, desires, complexes and ignorance. This is why those who recognize the magnitude of the problem seek the guidance of authentic advanced personalities. The ignorant speed headlong into the fires of worldly pleasure and pain, thinking they will somehow discern the path through books or drugs or "the inner guide" or "the spirit guide." The inner light once kindled must be cultivated and purified; otherwise its insight will be colored by the egoistic feelings of the unconscious mind, effectively rendering even the best intentions defective, and the tainted actions inevitably lead to frustration and suffering. This process is arduous and requires time spent in learning and then practicing the teaching. How much time have you spent?

Realize that if you want counseling on how to carry on in the world with a higher perspective, you have received it and you would be well advised to follow it for it will eventually lead you on the path. If you want to advance in a profound and powerful way and be free of the world, to attain mastery over your life, you must do more than letters and reading books. Can one become a doctor, lawyer, or engineer by such methods? And what can be said of the wisdom teaching that is subtler. No! Rather, it is done by immersion and intense study and reflection and then application of the teaching in your day-to-day life and also in your work by infusing it into your music. What does all this mean for you?

If you are intent on this path you will reflect deeply on the message of this letter and you will realize the deeper answers to your questions in a short time.

Peace and Blessings!

Sebai MAA

Conversation with God

Question: How to Change my Life?

Greetings Dr Ashby

I am in desperate need of guidance, with regard to my diet and thoughts. If there is such a thing as rock bottom then I am currently experiencing it. I seem to always be drawn to the kind of knowledge you and others have, relating to diet and way of life, and have just bought the book, *Kemetic Diet*. The trouble I have is the difficulty in making the changes and sticking with them. I am very troubled unconsciously and am extremely overweight. I start off with good intentions, but then fail. My question is where to begin, and how I can put the wisdom of the ancients into practice. I have a vision of what I want, but find it hard to achieve. In simple terms, can you suggest a course of action?
   Kind Regards

Answer

Udja-Greetings,

Your problem is not unusual. Firstly, understand that even though you are distressed you are in a better position than most because you are interested in the spiritual-mystical teachings. So, it could be worse; you could be an ordinary person suffering without the benefit of right guidance. Realize that changing your habits for the positive is dependent on a deeper set of circumstances than just wishing. You have for many years trained yourself in one way, and now you must retrain yourself. This will take time and much patience. Next, realize that the diet is not just a matter of physical food, but also a matter of mental and spiritual food as well. This means that you must also imbibe the wisdom of the teachings for your mind and gradually discover the benefits of meditation for the soul. You need to practice fasting from the negative mental and spiritual foods, just as you abstain from physical foods that are detrimental. All this is to be done gradually, increasing your quality of food and eventually adopting a new lifestyle for body, mind and soul. All of this is explained in more detail in the book *Kemetic Diet*.

Take it step-by-step; do not try to make these changes too fast. What is important is having faith in the Divine, but also you need to establish new habits based on the teaching. This also means keeping company with those who are on the same path as you, those who are also trying to improve themselves. Lessen your worldly interactions and involvements with people of agitated minds and worldly outlooks to the extent possible. Communicate with those on the path. Again, have faith and have patience, but practice the spiritual disciplines, as detailed in the books Kemetic Diet and Initiation into Egyptian Yoga and Neterian Spirituality day by day and do not be discouraged if there are temporary lapses. Just as an infant falls several times before learning to walk, so too you will fall as you learn to truly live and not just be a robotic consumer-victim. If you truly desire to transform your life, the Divine will help you as you invoke the Divine within yourself- the greatest power in life!

Mystical Answers to the Important Questions of Life

You may contact me as often as you like for advice and support. Read the book carefully and follow the instructions exactly and you will have success eventually.

Peace and Blessings!

Sebai MAA

Conversation with God

Question: If I kill insects am I a killer and will my spiritual evolution suffer?

Udja Sebai Maa

An Ancient Egyptian Virtuous (Maatian) Cosmic Principle articulates: Do no violence (to any one or anything). The law of Ari (Karma)/law of cause and effect- a cosmic principle articulates: What you do comes back to you! In other words: "If you kill what you eat, what you eat will kill you.

Considering the above statements are true, what about eating vegetables and plants, and the accidental killing of microscopic insects life by way of the washing of the hands and body. Aren't these living organisms or life? How do they fit in to the above proverbs or saying?

Answer

Perhaps the most important area of study for beginning and advancing aspirants is ethical spiritual culture, such as Ancient Egyptian Maat Philosophy. Maat is an ethical spiritual culture, based on truth, righteousness, and balance (harmony). Maat (truth, righteousness, and balance) is symbolized by a goddess of the same name (i.e., Maat). It is a discipline of social and spiritual ethics that guides an aspirant's behavior/actions on the spiritual path. Understanding violence and non-violence is an important aspect of spiritual life that needs to be well understood in order to pursue the spiritual path in a dynamic and effective manner.

While there is relative value in life forms in accordance with their level of sentience, nevertheless an aspirant should refrain from killing any being in accordance with Maat philosophy as will be explained next. In fact, from a relative perspective, there is no way to escape violence of some kind or other in life as killing and creating is part of Creation, as you have stated (i.e., killing microbes, consuming vegetables). What the teaching refers to is malice of forethought, and egoistic involvement in violence. Killing something or someone by accident or in accordance with the laws of the universe has consequences, but does not count in terms of malice of forethought or premeditated violation of ethical values based on greed, anger, hatred, etc. The former is in accordance with the law of the universe (Maat), and the latter is in accordance with the egoism of the individual. Actions in line with Maat can allow the mind to be calm, because they are relinquishable, while actions based on egoism are not relinquishable, and therefore their impressions remain in the mind, causing agitation and preventing spiritual insight, even after death.

Mystical Answers to the Important Questions of Life

(5) *"I have not murdered man or woman."* <u>*Variant: Or ordered someone else to commit murder.*</u>

-From the 42 Precepts of Maat

Violence as it is performed by the universe is merely an egoistic judgment by a human being, for what destroys actually also creates. So Goddess creates and destroys for the greater purpose of existence and that is without malice or preference. So from her perspective she neither destroys nor creates but establishes order, balance and harmony. What are prohibited therefore are actions with malice, which are egoistic actions of passion or desire. If you kill with passion, anger, hatred, greed, etc. it is murder (evil[25]); furthermore it is futile, for it will not lead to the desired outcome (happiness-attaining one's desire). Rather it will cause remorse deep down that will lead to future torments and it will eventually elicit retaliation from the soul that was harmed.

> *Beware of punishing unjustly,*
> *Do not kill anyone, it does not serve you or bring what you desire…*

-Teaching of Meri-ka-ra
(Ancient Egyptian Wisdom Texts)

Beings possessing equal levels of sentience have equal rights to exist; therefore, just because one person wants to survive that does not give them the right to kill people in order to survive. Realize though that hoarding is a form of violence that elicits violence in reciprocation.

"…Good manners will influence her better than force. Do not contend with her in the courts. Keep her from the need to resort to outside powers. Her eye is her storm when she gazes. It is by such treatment that she will be compelled to stay in your house."

-Ani
(Ancient Egyptian Wisdom Texts)

Force is used by the meek and ego-minded. In order to promote good feeling and cooperation, one should extend oneself by sharing and caring for others, and then also others will feel open to do the same. If one person says he/she owns things that are needed by others to survive, it is their obligation to share them, otherwise those who need those things to survive may resort to violence in order to force the sharing. Nobody can own anything on earth because nobody abides forever on earth; all are transitory caretakers of their possessions while they live on earth. Following the principle of reciprocity, one should share so that one will be shared with when one's time of need arises.

---

[25] Egoistic act in contradiction with the principle of ethics to promote life.

Conversation with God

It is the food to be shared which is coveted,
One whose belly is empty is an accuser;
One deprived becomes an opponent,
Don't have him for a neighbor.
Kindness is a man's memorial

- Sage Ptahotep
(Ancient Egyptian Wisdom Texts)

Killing out of necessity to survive (not preemptively, as in "preemptive" or "preventative" war) is not killing, but following the law of Maat actually, for it is righteous that life is to be preserved and order and balance and truth protected. In the hierarchy of life, lower sentient forms have less priority than the higher, and so are accorded less prominence, especially when overstepping their boundaries of Maatian-Cosmic order. For example, microbes live in the body, but if they overrun the body they will cause disease; they are violating the Maatian-Cosmic order (of truth, righteousness and balance) and must be controlled and brought to their balance. Taking vitamins, herbs, etc, kills some of them to bring them back to order, to balance. An occasional roach can live in a house with people, but if too many abound then it is a person's right, nay, even a duty to kill them off before they cause disease, to restore order and balance. Philosophically (which is the main important aspect for aspirants to consider), eating plants, which may kill the plant, is not violence because it is the process for human survival established by Maat (through Neteru {nature}). Even if we eat "live" food, we are "killing" it, as well as the microbes that are living on it as our digestive juices break the material down to be processed by the body.

Killing animals for human food is not only unjust because it hurts them, but because it is unnecessary and non-Maatian (unjust, unrighteous, unbalancing), because the human body is not designed for eating and processing animal products. One important consequence of the act of eating animals is to suffer the diseases associated with eating meat, such as cancer and arthrosclerosis. Killing animals is violence because human beings do not need to kill them to survive, and indeed, all evidence shows that it is detrimental to the human body to eat animals. Therefore, eating meat is done for the sake of egoistic pleasure.

Ignorant human beings believing that they are creating or killing is a violation of Maat, for only she (goddess Maat) established that order. Such a belief is based on spiritual ignorance that gives rise to ego and egoism. This is the first error. If a human being takes on the burden of thinking they are killing or creating they are assuming the responsibility and consequences of those beliefs and will suffer accordingly. While creating (making a baby, building an object, making music, painting a picture, etc.) seems to be a joyous process, actually, if done egoistically, it is a precursor for pain and suffering. Only The Divine[26] creates through you; you do nothing and so should not take on the egoistic

---

[26] In Kamitan religion the term Neter does not necessarily signify male or female but The Divine transcending but including gender. So the term Pa Neter is properly translated as "The Divine".

burden. God has done it, so let God bear the consequence. However, a very important point to understand is that this capacity to transcend "doership" (taking the responsibility for creating or killing) can only arise when one has attained a high level of spiritual purity through the practice of Maat. So, someone who is engaged in an-Maat (evil actions, against Maat) cannot detach from "doership" of their wrong action, because the very fact that they are performing an evil/wrong act points to their high level of egoism and impurity, which renders them susceptible to the laws of cause and effect (ari/karma). Therefore, only persons performing works with spiritually pure intent and internal dedication to The Divine have the opportunity to detach from "doership" of those deeds, and thus ariu. This is because their actions, being based on spiritual purity, gives them the choice of seeing themselves as the doer (and generate ariu/karma, albeit good karma) or seeing the Divine Self as the doer of the actions, and themselves merely as a tool in the divine hands carrying out the Divine's work, the latter allowing them the opportunity to transcend karma and attain enlightenment.

Killing people, except for reasons of self-defense or survival (as discussed above), is a higher violation. Preemptive war or war of aggression and conquest is completely prohibited by Maat, but self-defense is allowed, again, for the same reasons. This is why an aspirant must learn to adopt and implement the Maat culture, to live by truth and not egoistic notions. An aspirant must learn to act with peace and neutrality. An aspirant's actions must be based on truth and not egoistic desire, for egoism is the way to hellish[27] experiences after death and future reincarnation. The path of Maat is the way of peace and freedom and immortality. When an aspirant has reached perfection in action, there will be peace, harmony and balance, no matter if there is killing going on or if there is creating. Then such a one has become one with the goddess and in so doing, has attained *Maakheru* or truth of speech, the ultimate truth (Enlightenment); one has transcended the relative perspective, the lower existence in time and space, as well as the egoistic identification with killer or killed.

For those who are enlightened, there is no death, and no birth; they have transcended the opposites of Creation and cease to exist in the past or future, but have attained the eternal present. Glory be to Maat! Isn't she just wonderful?

Peace and Blessings!

Sebai MAA

---

[27] The term hell in Kemetic religious philosophy is not to be confused with the Western orthodox religious concept. In Kemetic religious philosophy hell is a temporary condition wherein a person experiences suffering due to their actions while they were alive. After some time of suffering they return to the earth to b born again.

Conversation with God

Question: How can meditation cleanse Karmic seeds if all deeds must be judged by Maat?

Greetings.

You have said that a way of removing impurities from our unconscious (karmic seeds) is through meditation. Is this true? But isn't the justice of Maat (goddess or Cosmic principle symbolizing truth, righteousness, balance) so perfect that no thought or deed can go without judgment, so that we must face the fruit (reaction) of all karmas (action) (even the karmic seeds in the unconscious)?

The reason I ask is because I just learned that one of the three impossibilities of the Buddha is that not even he, the Enlightened One, can do away with his own karma.

Thanks. Peace.

Answer

Greetings,

The question you have asked requires a detailed understanding of what in Shetaut Neter is called *ariu* (what the Indians call "karma"), what it is and how it operates in relation to a human being. As you know, the "Karmic Seeds" are actually impressions lodged in the unconscious mind, which arise from a person's previous actions, thoughts, feelings, etc. As such, they are infallible in their effect on the life of a human being because they sprout in the form of desires, which in turn lead to thoughts, and these in turn lead to more actions, and those actions lead to more impressions, etc. The cycle feeds on itself as long as there is ignorance in the mind as to one's true nature (The Self). This ignorance is not just intellectual, but psychological and spiritual as well. These impressions have control over the thoughts, actions and fate of an un-enlightened human being. Even Heru, Krishna, Jesus, and Buddha could not escape this karmic law.

However, there is another rule of *ariu* that the mystics from ancient times discovered. With the dawning of self-knowledge, the karmic seeds, which would have sprouted as future thoughts and desires, become burnt up like popcorn. Ariu or impressions in the unconscious are generated and sustained by one's ignorant egoistic notions of oneself and the world (egoism). Therefore, once egoism has been removed by the dawning of Enlightenment, which bestows knowledge of one's true essence as well as the world, ariu or impressions are destroyed (burnt up). Just as corn that is popped as popcorn cannot sprout any more, so too these burnt up mental impressions of an enlightened sage cannot sprout and lead to more ari. An enlightened sage will not fall prey to being caught up in the illusion of relative reality and will not develop desires of seeking fulfillment in the world, which drives the development of ariu/karma. And yet, just as popped corn can be

Mystical Answers to the Important Questions of Life

eaten and enjoyed (experienced), so too an enlightened sage can engage in actions in the world and even enjoy them, but not build up ariu/karma (bondage) due to ignorance. Keep in mind that the mental impressions are based on ignorance of one's true essence. So, once self-knowledge or enlightenment is attained, there is no more ignorance, no more egoism, and therefore, no more ariu/mental impressions. So, while an ordinary human being is constantly sowing seeds of *ariu* (karmic entanglement), an enlightened sage lives life experiencing the events of their lives like popped corn. All the karmic seeds of a living enlightened sage have been cleansed and removed (burnt up), except for one, that which remains and sustains his/her life from the time span of her/his enlightenment to the death of his/her physical body. At the end of his/her life, the last popped kernel is eaten…that is, the last remaining ari (karma) which is sustaining her/his current life is exhausted; there are no more karmic seeds to propel future desires and the embodiments that would have come in the future. If this were not true, then there would be no escape from *ariu* and there would be no purpose to practice yoga, meditation or religion, etc., because as you would be getting rid of some *ariu,* you would be creating more *ariu* at the same time!

Learning the philosophy of the mysteries (Shetaut Neter {Ancient Egyptian Mysteries}), reflecting upon it and practicing Maat (ethical culture) cleanses the mind from gross *ariu.* Gross *ariu* is like the darkness of the dark room that prevents you from seeing where the light switch is. Practicing meditation eradicates subtler *ariu*; it is when you find the light switch and turn on a light in a dark room. Think of a dark room full of junk. If the light is off you enter there and stumble. When the light is turned on, you can see your way, avoid trouble and even clean the room out. Meditation is a light, which shines on the unconscious mind, illumining your true deeper Self, which is the reality behind the desires, cravings and ignorance which is blocking your awareness of your own higher spirit. Impressions of fear, limitation, mortality, hatreds, pleasures, etc., are eradicated through this process, because they cannot exist in the light of your true nature, which transcends them. Therefore, *ariu* is burnt up like the popcorn. The enlightenment process (*nehast*) is the perfection of Maat, and thus the highest judgment about ordinary egoistic life is that the ignorance, which was the basis of degraded life, was illusory, and is therefore invalid and ineffectual, since it was surpassed and transcended by ethical wisdom. Judgment by Maat does not necessarily mean punishment, for if ignorance is eradicated there is nothing there to punish, just as if you turn on the light in the room there is no more darkness left to be illuminated. For the person who has become "enlightened," his/her present embodiment continues and he/she exists as an ordinary human being, but his/her mind does not produce or harbor illusions (*ariu* -Karmic seeds). You live out the rest of your life as "popped popcorn" and do not produce new seeds of ariu (karma). Therefore, when you leave this earth you have nothing to hold you; you simply divest of your last drop of *ariu* (the body).

Therefore, Enlightenment is above and beyond *ariu*. After enlightenment is attained, the life of an enlightened person continues in accordance with his or her purified *ariu.* However, the soul and mind are no longer affected by whatever does or does not happen thereafter. A Sage may become ill, have financial ups and downs and experience many ordinary situations for the rest of his/her life due to previous *ariu*. However, the practice

Conversation with God

of the teachings mitigates the negativity of those events, and in any case, enlightenment prevents suffering and karmic entanglement. Going back to the analogy of the room, if the light is turned on there may still be some stuff in there, such as furniture, boxes or even junk, but you would not stumble around; you would see where everything is and nothing would bother you or obstruct you from finding something in the room if you needed to or resting there if you needed to.

Thus, in the state of ignorance, *ariu* and their fructification are infallible, and there is no escape because this state is controlled by ignorance and its attendant egoism. Conversely, the spiritual teachings, which lead to enlightenment, are also infallible in that they eradicate the cause of karmic fructification, i.e. ignorance of the Self. This is why the practice of the spiritual disciplines is so important. God's justice is not designed to produce suffering for every single mistake a person makes due to spiritual ignorance. God's compassion and mercy is embedded in the law of *ariu*. Truth is more powerful than ignorance because truth has the virtue of being a reality while ignorance is an illusion. Thus, one instant of truth has the power to overcome centuries or even millennia of ignorance, just as one may have many dreams during the night but only has to wake up once in the morning. The dawning of enlightenment in the human mind sweeps away millions of years of ignorance and reincarnation and desires, etc. It is God's mercy and love that is transmitted to humanity through the work of sages and their students, to spare people from the untold misery they would otherwise have to experience in the future. The wisdom of enlightenment, gained through meditation, Maat, and wisdom, dispels millions of years of ignorance just as a light can illumine a room even if it has been dark for millions of years. The light of self-knowledge is the truth, the power and the glory which dispels the ignorance of egoism and the illusions which a person is trapped in over countless reincarnations of the past.

May the glory of understanding this great teaching be yours to live and to share!

Peace and Blessings!

Sebai MAA

Mystical Answers to the Important Questions of Life

Question: Does Neterian religion & philosophy promote forgiveness of enemies – Part 1?

Greetings,

This question is based on a lecture I recently attended. Overall I think your presentation was positive. We would certainly be better off, if we practiced much of what you are saying.

Dr. Ashby, you spoke about forgiveness and peace. Of course, I have to put everything in a political context, and what I heard made me think of Malcolm X's wake up, clean up, and stand up program, minus the stand up, at least a clear call for standing up.

Wake up to your divinity.
Clean up--practice Maat, eat right, etc.

But as I see Kemetic history, they stood up and fought (physically and spiritually) to maintain Maat, against internal and external enemies--the dynamics of *Isfet*[28]. Had the Maatian dynamics not been able to dominate the dynamics of Isfet, Kemet would not have lasted so long.

We live in a world dominated by the dynamics of Isfet--primarily the European power structure/White Supremacy Dynamic and their cronies of color.

How do we restore Maat without challenging the dynamics of Isfet--within and without? Surely, reciprocity is one of the cardinal virtues of Maat.

I also think their concept of forgiveness is more Euro-Christian than it is Maatian. South Africa is going to hell, largely because Mandela forgave the Europeans before demanding repentance. Repentance always precedes forgiveness, but most Christians want to go straight from the commission of a sin/ crime to forgiveness, bypassing repentance. Hey, you have to repair the damage first. In the Maatian context, Khun-Anup says the following:

"Punish the robber and save those who suffer."
*"Punish those who deserve punishment and none will
equal your righteousness."*
"If you turn your face from violence, who will punish wrongdoing?"

But, by no means is he saying be like the Europeans-- "answer not good with evil and put not one thing in the place of another." I would say, answer evil with righteous (Maatian) justice. That assumes that we are a Maatian people.

---

[28] unrightousness

Conversation with God

I also heard a bit of abstract humanism in your lecture that I would challenge.

Most often I don't like to confront positive people in public forums. All too often, when there is a serious challenge, we lose focus of the positives.

Your message was too valuable to do that.

Answer

Greetings,

Your comments are very much appreciated.

The question of meting out punishment and retribution and how it relates to Maat Philosophy has been asked previously. This is an extremely important question which deserves much discussion and reflection.

I would also like you to know that you are not the first person to make such comments in private or otherwise. I do not see these comments from serious people as impediments to the upliftment of the community since they bring out important issues which need to be dealt with and understood. Further, I do not see these comments as challenges but as honest attempts to understand the teachings. Since Kemetic Philosophy also promotes humility and selflessness, I do not cultivate egoism and therefore do not have an ego to bruise. Listeners are free to agree or disagree. Freedom of speech is a hallmark of Maat Philosophy as long as it is honest and true speech. Rhetoric and confusion are Western principles and they should not be allowed to get in the way of authentic discussion of philosophical principles. Sometimes people hold back on their comments because they know the answers to the questions but do not want to hear them due to fear of having to listen and adhere to these. Therefore, it is unfortunate that you chose not to bring these up at the meeting.

Sometimes listeners of any spiritual tradition tend to highlight certain teachings that agree with their own predilections as opposed to others that challenge their world views. Perhaps you did not attend the entire three days of the seminar since we dealt with the issues you are inquiring about within the framework of Maat Kemetic Philosophy. Certainly the Kemetic teaching advocates punishment from a social political point of view in order to maintain order in society. But it does not advocate grudges or revenge, neither against individuals or other countries. It does however advocate justice and not just punishment.

> "Be always more ready to forgive, than to return an injury; they who watch for an opportunity for revenge, lieth in waste against themselves, and draweth down mischief on their own head."
>
> -Ancient Egyptian Proverb

Mystical Answers to the Important Questions of Life

While promoting truth and righteousness, Maat Philosophy also advocates forgiveness and understanding. Read the writings of Sage Ptahotep, Sage Ani, etc. (excerpts below). Sometimes honest seekers on the path fall into the error of focusing on certain teachings to the exclusion of others because some teachings support their egoistic sensibilities at a particular time or another. This often happens to those who follow secular cultural values and or orthodox religions like Islam or Christianity. They end up meting out punishment to everyone who does not believe as they do. The teachings of Maat must be viewed in a context as a whole and they are to be applied to all equally. However, one cannot practice any philosophy entirely intellectually. One must practice and live the philosophy in order to discover its inner wisdom. The Ancient Egyptian "Story of the Eloquent Peasant" that you have cited deals with a peasant, Khun-Anup, who is seeking redress for a wrongdoing. He is seeking justice and not revenge. If punishment is necessary to teach a lesson, that punishment can be justified. But if a lesson is learned, the punishment is not necessary since the goal of learning and growing that will prevent future injustice has been achieved. If an injustice has not been acknowledged or redressed and no justice has been served, does that mean that the person who was wronged should maintain a grudge indefinitely? Would that not make the victim a perpetual captive to the original injustice? And would that not impair the capacity of the victim to heal and grow by learning from the injustice and promoting her/his own strength to prevent that injustice in the future, instead of focusing energies on the perpetrators and not employing them towards elevating their own conditions?

Those in the African-American community who choose not to forgive the European community for past and or present and future wrongdoing will continue to doom themselves to a life of limitation and unrest because their recrimination and resentment will draw them into the same fire of delusion, weakness and hatred which leads not to heaven but to hell. It is curious that those who say they are Africentrists and or students of Kemetic philosophy conveniently overlook the precepts which deal with these issues and hold up those proverbs which speak of upholding laws or exacting punishments. Why is that? This is indeed a hard pill to swallow. but it is our own wisdom which says this, not Muata Ashby.

If there is any question about this, perhaps it should be directed at the ancient Egyptian Sages who established Maat Philosophy, the same basic concepts of ethics which are also the basis of every authentic (mystical) world religion of modern times? If there is any abstract humanism in the philosophy which resembles European philosophy, it is perhaps a remnant of Kemetic philosophy embedded in European philosophies which some Europeans have tried to uphold, recognizing its intrinsic practical and spiritual values.

In Kemetic Culture, it was the Per-aah's (i.e., Pharaoh's, King's) first duty to protect the land from Isfet (Unrighteousness). However, this unrighteousness was not just referring to attacks from outside the country, but also corruption from within. While most people like to assign blame on other groups or cultures, they seldom apply the principle internally; they do not like to chastise themselves for eating meat, doing drugs, overindulgence in sex, smoking, spending too much money, etc. Those are isfet also.

Conversation with God

In Ancient Egypt, all actions, including wars, police actions and the discharge of law and order in the court system were to be based on Maat Philosophy, and judges were priests of Maat. This means that the carrying out of justice is to be done without resentment or passion, since these cloud the intellect and lead to favoritism, nepotism, sexism, etc., which lead to the disintegration of individual morals, spiritual strength, family cohesiveness, community harmony and cultural decay. The following proverb *"Punish firmly and chastise soundly, then repression of crime becomes an example. But punishment except for crime will turn the complainer into an enemy,"* does not say "punish with resentment, recrimination, vengeance, etc.," but only for crime committed.

Therefore, what is needed to practice Maat to its perfection is mental peace and purity, freedom from passion and resentment, wisdom, integrity, non-violence, forgiveness, etc., even while upholding the laws and discharging justice. Maat does not play favorites, nor does she allow wrongdoers to escape the universal laws of life which all human beings must observe. This means that even those who seem to "get away with murder" cannot. That is one of the main teachings of the "Story of Hetheru and Djehuti" also known as the "Story of the Golden Cow." It is not necessary for any human being to take on the burden of being "God's instrument of retribution as if God could not handle her affairs! This is a sign of lack of faith in the Divine and it is rewarded with anguish, strife and adversity.

However, she also does not advocate hatred and resentment towards evildoers or their descendants. This is the culture that leads to more misunderstanding and violence. Is this not the same culture that led us to where we are today? How can this kind of culture lead to prosperity and success?

The road to greatness is hard since it requires the giving up of long held notions which comfort the passions and are hard to relinquish. Even Malcolm X, towards the end of his life, realized that the philosophy of hatred towards "white" people was misdirected. In reality there is a political and economic force, sustained by a plutocracy composed of a small group that may be referred to as a "power elite," controlling the masses of "white" and "black" people through dogmas and ignorance, such as the notion of "race" and faith-based religion, and that is where the true problem is to be found and that is what needs to be combated. To hold ignorant people responsible for actions they do not understand misses the more important point of stopping those politicians, captains of industry and religious leaders that use dogma, fear and ignorance to perpetuate unending pain and suffering and conflict between the masses, making them think they are rivals, when in reality it is the politicians who are vying amongst each other (using the masses as cannon fodder) for control of the world economy, which requires the confusion and subjugation of the world populations.[29]

However, the rewards of success on such a journey are inner peace, contentment and success, both personally and as a community and humanity as a whole. This is the lofty

---

[29] For more detailed analysis see the book *Death of American Empire* by Sebai Muata Ashby (2006)

Mystical Answers to the Important Questions of Life

vision which lifted up Kemetic society and allowed the culture to persist for over 5,000 years.

Below are some teachings that directly relate to your question of how to handle wrongdoing. I believe they speak for themselves and clearly advocate justice, but not unrestrained or uncompassionate punishment, and certainly not unnecessary punishment. If a person is hurting others, then justice is required and punishment may be warranted. If a person has learned their lesson or ceases the wrongdoing, there is no further need for the punishment; then understanding and forgiveness are in order. The objective is to reach peace and understanding and not just to administer punishment. When would we ever punish a child without explaining why and trying to reach understanding? If the child realized the mistake, what is the point of punishment except revenge? Realizing the mistake here means understanding the error and pain caused as well as the fault in the thought process that led to it, and a sincere personal desire to avoid that error ever again in order to prevent that suffering to self and other. And even if we fail in our duty to punish when punishment is due, is there escape from the great judgment administered by God?

GOD PUNISHES THE EVILDOERS

> "MAAT is great and its effectiveness lasting; it has not been disturbed since the time of Osiris. There is punishment for those who pass over it's laws, but this is unfamiliar to the covetous one....When the end is nigh, *MAAT* lasts."

> "Indeed they who are yonder (those who live righteously will join GOD after death), will be living Gods, punishing anyone who commits a sin. Indeed they who are yonder will stand in the boat (boat of RA) causing the choicest offerings in it to be given to the temples. Indeed he who is yonder will become a sage who will not be hindered from appealing to GOD whenever they speak."

> "O think not, bold man, because thy punishment is delayed, that the arm of God is weakened; neither flatter thyself with hopes that the Supreme winketh at thy doings; Its eye pierces the secrets of every heart, and remembered are they for ever..."

ON FORGIVENESS

Sage Ptahotep:

> "If you meet a disputant who is not your equal or match, do not attack, they are weak. They will confound themselves. ***Do not answer the evil speech and give in to your animal passion for combat by venting your self against them.*** You will beat them through the reproof of the witnesses who will agree with you."

Conversation with God

"If you are angered by a misdeed, then lean toward a man on account of his rightness. Pass over the misdeed and don't remember it, since GOD was silent to you on the first day of your misdeed."

"Why seeketh thou revenge, O man! With what purpose is it that thou pursuest it? Thinkest thou to pain thine adversary by it? Know that thou thyself feelest its greatest torments."

"Be always more ready to forgive, than to return an injury; they who watch for an opportunity for revenge, lieth in waste against themselves, and draweth down mischief on their own head."

"The root of revenge is in the weakness of the Soul; the most abject and timorous are the most addicted to it."

"One cannot force another to grow beyond their capacity."

ON NON-VIOLENCE

"If you meet a disputant who is more powerful than you, fold your arms and bend your back. Confrontation will not make them agree with you. Disregard their evil speech. Your self control will match their evil utterances and people will call them ignoramuses."

ON THE BEHAVIOR OF INITIATES

(7) "Be free from resentment under the experience of persecution" (Bear insult)

(8) "Be free from resentment under experience of wrong," (Bear injury)

FROM THE PRECEPTS OF MAAT

(3) "DO NO VIOLENCE (TO ANY ONE OR ANYTHING)."

(30) "DO NOT ACT INSOLENTLY OR WITH VIOLENCE."

Peace and Blessings!

Sebai MAA

Mystical Answers to the Important Questions of Life

Question: Does Neterian religion promote forgiveness of enemies – Part 2?

Hotep Dr. Ashby,

I welcome the opportunity to respond to your email. The Friday lecture was the only one that I attended.

I did not raise these issues Friday night, because the Q&A session on that evening was not conducive to dialogue.

While I recognize that Maat is the foundation for cosmic and social order, when I use the term I'm primarily referring to a philosophy of social ethics based on the Seven Cardinal Virtues--Truth, Justice, Harmony, Propriety, Reciprocity, Balance, and Order. Maatian Ethics, like any other philosophy with various contributors over long periods of time has apparent contradictions, and different interpretations, as you well know.

No one can say that Ptahotep is more correct that Khun Anup, and vice versa. Dr. Kwame Nkrumah says that "each historical situation produces its own dynamics." Their writings and the writings of the Sebait in general, reflect the history at a particular juncture.

Ptahotep was writing during what was probably the pinnacle of African freedom, power, and productivity. Tranquility and peace were the dominant aspects of his day. Had he been writing during a time of either internally driven Isfet, or a time of foreign invasion and domination (Hyksos period) his views may have been different. We see this in the writings of later Seba.

Sometimes we make the mistake of trying to apply our traditions wholesale to our current conditions without critical analysis of those conditions. Ptahotep was not dealing with a people who have suffered a Maafa[30] at the hands of the white supremacy dynamic. A people who Diop says needs their personalities reconstructed. He didn't live in a world dominated by the Yurugu syndrome--spiritual retardation which infects life-sustaining institutions. Dr. Karenga's Kawaida Theory helps us understand why tradition must be informed by reason, and tested by practice.

My objective is to synthesize knowledge from a variety of sources. This is necessary because the problems that African people face today are so complex that no one source can provide all of the answers. Synthesizers have no room for exclusion based on egoistic sensibilities. Critical thinking does not allow for such. That which is not currently applicable is filed for later, relevant usage.

---

[30] calamity

Conversation with God

You've written an epistle on forgiveness without dealing with my fundamental point--repentance precedes forgiveness. The Sebait write extensively about justice, and balance--right measure. X-amount of damage, requires x-amount of repair. For African people, European repentance for their crimes against humanity requires reparations for us. You expect us to forgive them before they repent. Brother, they haven't even apologized. That's why I say your concept of forgiveness is more Euro-Christian than Maatian. African life is just as valuable as the others who have received reparations.

If you got hatred, resentment, and revenge out of what I wrote, you've misread me. That's why I added the quote from Khun Anup. Surely, we must pursue justice without revenge and hatred.

Certainly, the Niswt (King) was the living embodiment of Maat. But Ahmose and Nefertari did not wait for God to send a strong wind to drive the Hyksos from Lower KMT. They were divinely inspired to physically liberate their land and restore Maat—righteousness and order. Within the context of our historical situation we need Maatian consciousness and similar Heka (effective action).

Abstract humanism is most often used by liberals who want to avoid using race as the basis for dealing with issues. I should mention that I believe race to be a pseudo-scientific concept, but it has become such a powerful force and farce that discussion of it cannot be avoided. I don't quite understand what you are saying about abstract humanism being in Kemetic philosophy, but if it's there it's hard to imagine that it's pertinent to the psychodynamics of the current historical situation.

I see the fundamental problem of African people as one of powerlessness. Without power-the ability to either control or significantly influence life-sustaining institutions, people cannot hope to live in peace. We must strive to develop a moral people, and a moral community, and that community must be ready to stand up and fight on every level to make Maat a reality.

Answer

Greetings,

I appreciate your interest and comments.

First, I would like to point out once more, that there is a deficiency with this exchange because as you have said, you did not participate fully in the program that we presented last weekend. This places us all at a disadvantage because the depth of the philosophical issues involved in this discussion were dealt with at some length during the presentation as well as afterwards in separate conversations with the attendants and should have been dealt with at that time. Sometimes honest seekers of knowledge err in not delving deeply into a subject before coming to a judgment. Many times people seek to hold on to their concepts and do not approach the teaching with the openness required to benefit from the teachings. Here we mean by approaching the teaching to include the practice of the

Mystical Answers to the Important Questions of Life

disciplines such as worship, meditation, diet change, etc., and not just reading the philosophy since understanding the depth of the philosophy cannot be achieved simply by reading the writings of the philosophers or doing historical researches into political events or legal precedents. Having partial knowledge, these seekers believe they have understood a teaching while in reality they have colored it with their own interpretation based on their background, history, desires or concepts. Sometimes seekers make excuses as to why they cannot attend lectures and seminars. If the struggle of liberation (physical, mental and spiritual) is supposed to be paramount, what should come in the way of receiving the nectar of spiritual wisdom? If a man was told he will win a lottery if he only goes to a certain place to receive the ticket, what other appointments would be more pressing? Those who arrogantly dabble in this philosophy are like the unsuccessful well diggers. They dig here and there but never in one place and deeply to discover the depths, because in their minds they think they already know what will be said and in the process, they belittle the teaching and maintain themselves and the community in an ignorant state.

Those who are truly concerned with good speech should consider that the manner or intent behind a question is the determiner of its righteousness or unrighteousness. Should not the ignorant ask ignorant questions, or should they remain ignorant for fear of not adhering to some notion of propriety based on ignorance? All questions are valid if they are honest attempts to learn and reach understanding. A true seeker of truth will not allow impropriety or embarrassment to stand between them and truth. However, true seekers humble themselves to those who merit respect and do not challenge them with concepts based on passion and ignorance of the teaching only to cause argument and confusion so that they themselves to not have to make the important changes they know, deep down, that are necessary in their own lives.

Mystical Philosophy is not like academic study of an ordinary nature. It requires more than intellectual knowledge to be comprehended. It requires that the person reflect upon and practice it in order for it to bear its real fruits. Otherwise, there is no real frame of reference for the higher aspects of a teaching to be given or understood. Not until that point is reached wherein a student is well versed in the intellectual as well as the practice of a philosophy, should that person venture to enter into judgments either condemning or affirming it. How can a calculus teacher explain calculus concepts to an arithmetic student and how can the arithmetic student judge the value or lack of value of calculus without undergoing the rigorous discipline of study and practice algebra, geometry and then of calculus? For someone like this, no amount of proofs or arguments will suffice because their mind is made up to the way they want to feel, think and act based on their closely held concepts about the world. They would then say that calculus is too hard or the teacher is too idealistic or in error, or perhaps calculus is useful for others maybe but not for me. How can a teaching be imparted if there is lack of regard for the teacher or the teaching as a whole? You indeed added the quote from Khun Anup but you neglected to add the other teachings, presumably because as you stated they seem to be contradictory. However, perhaps you did not consider that the teachings are not absolute instruments to be applied in every situation indiscriminately but meant for certain situations and not others; for example, the injunction for not telling lies does not imply one should not lie in every situation; what if lying would save someone's life, certainly saving a life is a higher truth than telling the truth in that situation is it not? Yet that does not mean that the injunctions are invalid. Furthermore, the principles of the Maatian teaching are valid whether or not they are able to be applied. In other words, just because a maatian injunction cannot be followed does not mean that it should not be followed.

> "MAAT is great and its effectiveness lasting; it has not been disturbed since the time of Asar. There is punishment for those who pass over it's laws, but this is unfamiliar to the covetous one....When the end is nigh, *MAAT* lasts."

In your letter you said that "No one can say that Ptahotep is more correct than Khun Anup…" that statement implies that the philosophy expressed in either parable is mutually exclusive. Ptahotep's writings extolled injunctions for wisdom and good conduct; the Story of the Eloquent Peasant expressed, through parable form, the need and importance of seeking justice and standing up for oneself in that process. Seeking justice and achieving justice actually have the same effect in terms of elevating the personality whether or not justice (however that is defined in terms of an outcome) is achieved. Furthermore, justice may involve punishment of a wrongdoer, but what if the injustice occurred due to an accident or an error or misunderstanding? If you killed someone by accident for example, if you were driving a car and did not see someone and hit them, or by misunderstanding instructions for setting up a machine that later blew up and killed someone, should you be killed? That is blind justice and not wise justice. Justice should be blind to egoism, coercion, bias, etc., but not to mitigating circumstances or to the true goal that the legal system should have, to maintain balance in society so that the needs of all will be met and not to maintain perpetual enmity, conflict and hatred amongst peoples.

Secondly, many seekers make the mistake of formulating the idea that somehow, their plight is different from all people who have come before. You stated: "Tranquility and peace were the dominant aspects of his (Ptahotep) day. Had he been writing during a time of either internally driven Isfet, or a time of foreign invasion and domination (Hyksos period) his views may have been different." This statement seems to imply historical relativism, if not moral relativism, meant to absolve our responsibility to follow the instructions of our ancestors with the idea that if we have different challenges then we can ignore their own teaching and do what we want, etc. People have been known to utter comments such as "Jesus did not suffer as much as I suffered" or "things were easy in the times when Buddha was born but I am too oppressed by the world to think about philosophy right now." They believe that certain wisdom teachings are for past ages when things were supposedly different, easier, and not as complicated or rough. This is one of the most misguided notions on the spiritual path and it is recognized as a great obstacle to attaining spiritual enlightenment. During one of the several struggles throughout Kemetic history, Kemetic culture was threatened with extinction. This is pointed out in the writings of *IPUWER* wherein the extent of civil disruption rivaled the condition of any modern country ravaged by war, disease, rampant corruption and civil unrest as well as the complete breakdown of social and government institutions, i.e. total chaos:

Mystical Answers to the Important Questions of Life

Lo, the face is pale, the bowman ready,
Crime is everywhere, there is no man of yesterday.
Lo, the robber --- everywhere,
The servant takes what he finds.
Lo, Hapy inundates and none plow for him,
All say, "We don't know what has happened in the land."
Lo, women are barren, none conceive,
Khnum does not fashion because of the state of the land.
Lo, poor men have become men of wealth,
He who could not afford (S) sandals owns riches.
Lo, men's slaves, their hearts are greedy,
The great do not mingle with their people [when they rejoice-].
Lo, hearts are violent, storm sweeps the land,
There's blood everywhere, no shortage of dead,
The shroud calls out before one comes near it.
Lo, many dead are buried in the river,
The stream is the grave, the tomb became stream.
Lo, nobles lament, the poor rejoice,
Every town says, "Let us expel our rulers."
Lo, people are like ibises, there's dirt everywhere,
None have white garments in this time.
Lo, the land turns like a potter's wheel,
The robber owns riches, [the noble] is a thief.
Lo, the trusted are like ------
The citizen [says], "Woe, what shall I do!"

Lo, the river is blood,
As one drinks of it one shrinks from people
And thirsts for water.
Lo, doors, columns, cofferS2 are burning,
While the hall of the palace stands firm.
Lo, the ship of the South founders,
Towns are ravaged, Upper Egypt became wasteland.
Lo, crocodiles gorge on their catch,
People go to them of their own will.
'-The land is injured",
One says, "Don't walk here, there's a net,"
People flap like fish,
The scared does not discern it in his fright.
Lo, people are diminished,

In those times of strife the sages recognized one central problem, the lack of Maat in society. With the restoration of Maat (implying, order, punishment of wrongdoers, reconciliation, forgiveness and justice for all equally) there was a return to harmony and balance in society which allowed it to resume the greatness that was temporarily lost.

Conversation with God

Therefore, the argument that those who created Maat Philosophy did not have to cope with hard times, social strife, respond to violence or that they were living in an idealistic abstract humanist dream world must be rejected as a misunderstanding of history and a consequent misinterpretation of the theory and purpose as well as the manner in which Maat Philosophy is to be applied to modern times; nowhere in any Ancient Egyptian text do we find it written that Maat is to be suspended when Egypt is under attack. It is a wonder that after 50 years of independence in many African states, the conditions for many African peoples have worsened. Therefore, it is the application of modern philosophies, theories and theories of government that should be suspect and scrutinized. For example, you mentioned Dr. Kwame Nkrumah and his philosophy. What happened to him and his country (Ghana)? While he was well meaning and suffered to liberate his country, he fell victim to mismanagement and internal corruption, dissent and social disorder. Granted, much unrest was fomented in Ghana by western forces, but still Ghana succumbed politically due to internal weakness and lack of an ethical basis due to loss of cultural cohesion through the slavery and colonialism periods.

While the statement by Mr. Nkrumah may be correct, that "each historical situation produces its own dynamics," it is also true that there are some universal constants in human social order, just as there are constants in the physics of the universe. In fact, truth (Maat) is always the same in the past, present and future. Otherwise, how would we know it to be true? That which changes cannot be true because it is inconsistent; it can only have relative value, conditional significance and therefore relative usefulness in terms of determining correct social principles as a basis for authentic social order and prosperity. Therefore, this argument must be rejected in light of Maatian injunctions. It is exactly this principle which needs to be applied in our times. Is there any wonder that there is unrighteousness in the society generally and there is a lack of Maat? Why not try speaking of the "outdatedness" of Maatian principles once they have been tried, implemented and failed as opposed to judging these without understanding, or practicing them?

"The closer you get to the truth, the simpler it is"

One of the problems of Africentrism is its close affiliation with Western paradigms of thinking, theorizing, conceptualization and philosophizing.

> "The Greek tongue (Western language and thought process) is a noise of words, a language of argument and confusion."

In this error, some Africentrists often use Western paradigms for determining what the African culture is and the best answers are for themselves, instead of looking to themselves and discovering their own rich heritage of philosophy, principles and standards. I ask here is that not the way of western culture? Ideas such as making war by claiming that war is necessary in order to have peace is a typical example of a Western paradigm that many people around the world have adopted, which has led to the perpetuation of wars. It seems akin to "we must have an apology before we can forgive" and this also means before one can be free from the another who has done wrong which keeps one tied to and disturbed by the object of hatred or resentment and that also ties up

Mystical Answers to the Important Questions of Life

the capacity to grow beyond the unrighteous occurrence that led to the disturbance. Due to confusion in the agitated mind, there is always an impetus to discover some complex formula to deal with the problem which is in reality a self-created and self-imposed web of concepts based on ignorance. You stated that some teachings should be "filed for later, relevant usage." That perspective also seems Western, just as Christians or Muslims worried about conquest first, and then promoting "civilization" and Biblical values later, like destroying Native Americans or the atrocities of the African slave trade and then worrying about the ethics, justice and the moral implications later. This view is incorrect.

Ethics are relevant always, especially when one is under attack or persecution, otherwise one becomes as cruel and lawless as the attacker, and both the attacker and the victim go to hell together. You also stated "X-amount of damage requires x-amount of repair." Here again, that sounds like "an eye for an eye and a tooth for a tooth" which is again, a Western paradigm and not an African-Kemetic one. This follows the idea of fighting fire with fire instead of fighting fire with water. But fire burns everything. Thus, hatred is countered most successfully with understanding and not with more hatred. Justice cannot be an end onto itself in the absence of understanding, because without understanding more unrighteousness and injustice will always arise.

These ways of thinking often lend themselves to a "picking and choosing" (like at a salad bar – salad bar spirituality) of those aspects of the philosophy which go along with the subjective sensibilities, and thereby promote degradation in the teaching and its understanding, and consequently its practice. You have brought up the teachings of Khnun-Anup, but not those of the other Sages because you believe that this supports your argument, but in reality your selective application of the teachings is deficient due to the aforementioned reasons. Therefore, the theory of the uselessness of Maatian principles for modern times must be rejected in light of history. Maat philosophy withstood the onslaught of invasions, breakdowns in Kemetic society, etc., for over 5000 years. Therefore, we should look to a breakdown in the practice of Maat in its complete form, and the development of ignorance as the source and cause as well as the solution for the problem of not only racism, but also, sexism, hunger, disease, hatred, violence, and all other imbalances in society.

The very idea that the human plight is complicated, requiring a plethora of ingredients to forge some new solution because we are dealing with a new situation that no one ever had to deal with is a very modern concept indeed. Why not the logic that if it is confusing, then it is an incorrect form of reasoning? Mind you, simple does not necessarily mean easy. The sages of old recognized that time moves on, but human nature stays the same, and no matter how much new technology may emerge, the faults and virtues of human nature remain the same, and therefore require the same treatment from age to age. Therefore, the mystical psychology of the Ancient Kemetic teachings is especially able to cope with the "psychodynamics" of the human being, especially the psychosis of those who identify with the African experience. In fact, the philosophy of righteous living, Maat, is simple when a person resolves to give up the egoistic and sentimental attachments as well as the negative aspects of the personality which are Setian (demoniac) in nature (anger, hatred, greed, lust, envy, jealousy, etc.), but most of all ignorance of the true nature, the higher Self. Until this lofty but attainable goal becomes the main objective of life, the unenlightened mind will always find a way to convince one that one must struggle or blame others or punish others first, and then worry about higher spiritual issues when the times are calmer or easier. The easier times never come, and a person wastes their opportunities all due to ignorance and egoism (Setian behavior). Therefore, indulging in the disease of hate cannot lead to the cure of peace and harmony, but will lead to more strife and disharmony and a doomsday mentality of impotence and slavery. How can such a person, beset with a deficit of self-awareness and virtue, succeed righteously in any struggle?

Continuing to push for punishment of evildoers and or their descendants at the exclusion of opening the door to forgiveness and reconciliation is in effect the perpetuation of hatred and resentment. While outwardly those efforts (push for punishment of evildoers) appear to be righteous or justified, at a subtle psychological level they are based on the goal of revenge, and this is referred to in the scriptures as physical, mental and spiritual bondage. However, reconciliation without the recognition of what is a just outcome will be incomplete. Forgiveness does not require reconciliation and can occur in the absence of reconciliation and it does mean that the one forgiving has moved on from the emotional and psychological obstruction of hatred and resentment so they can become whole and be powerful in their life again.

In closing, I will repeat once more that Maat does not preclude self-defense or other actions when necessary to respond to certain kinds of injustices, and at the same time the promotion of non-violence and humanism (which is defined here as concern with the interests, needs, and welfare of human beings) is not negated by the need to practice self-defense or the struggle to liberate oneself from injustices.

Therefore, the teachings of Khun-Anup ("Punish the robber and save those who suffer") do not conflict with those of Ptahotep (from the Ancient Egyptian Wisdom Texts), but Ptahotep modifies and refines the concepts:

> 36. Punish firmly, chastise soundly,
> Then repression of crime becomes an example;
> Punishment except for crime
> Turns the complainer into an enemy.

The teaching from the Instructions of Merikara (also from the Ancient Egyptian Wisdom Texts) is also instructional:

> (3) May you be justified before The God,
> That a man may say of you even when you are absent,
> That you punish in accordance [with what is just for the crime].

The practice of self-defense without a philosophy of righteous action (ethics) is like driving a car at night without headlights. It is very difficult to see the way and the journey is perilous and full of anxiety as well as confusion. Any social philosophy devoid of

Mystical Answers to the Important Questions of Life

humanism will degrade to the level of the base egoistic tendencies of the human character with its worst manifestations, hatred, selfishness, and greed, which are based on ignorance of the higher unity of humanity and constitute the sources for all social maladies. However, the use of violent action is to be entered into only on the last resort, and not under the urging of passion for revenge, but out of necessity of duty in self-defense. Revenge is not a divine principle nor is hatred a virtue. Reconciliation and understanding are better than revenge and recrimination. Does anyone knock out their teeth when the teeth bite the tongue? Then why harbor resentment and recrimination, which only serve to prevent positive action and promote self-pity, self-doubt and dependency?

Those who hate, regardless of the reason, whether one was wronged by the other and regardless of who is right or wrong, all go to the hellish condition of miserable existence, while alive, and then also after death, because the vibration of hatred has shaped the mind and that is a form of torment that atrophies the intellect and prevents spiritual evolution. Should a battered woman wait until her husband, the batterer, apologizes or makes restitution, before she picks herself up and gets on with her life? Should she spend the rest of her time blaming him for her miserable state and sit around complaining about how bad life is? Or should she move on and make her way, strengthening herself so as not to allow the battery to occur again, commanding respect instead of begging for it like a panhandler who is lost in the wilderness of life with no direction except the illusory dreams of a corrupt culture based on greed, sexuality, drugs, poisonous diets and pleasure seeking? How can this person be expected to understand her plight if she does not purify herself from the negative thoughts, foods and lifestyles of the corrupt culture? So she stays and continues to accept the battery, and this is her own doing for she chooses not to allow herself to change because it is comfortable where she is. The future away from her hellish condition seems even more fearful because she has no inner fortitude due to a life of unrighteousness, and so the cycle continues.

If people are to be lifted up it cannot be with the rhetoric of hatred and false pride. These are the failings of the unrighteous leaders that become social diseases affecting the masses. Rather, Maat is what endures and while it is hard to practice Maat in the midst of temptations and injustices, the answer is not to excuse the wrongdoing on our own part by blaming its cause on others. When those perpetrating injustice are gone those practicing Maat will remain. Otherwise, the oppressors and the oppressed, both practicing unrighteousness, will perish in the cauldron of mutually assured destruction due to the evil of vice.

If it is true as you have said you saw: "the fundamental problem of African people as one of powerlessness," then we need to know where true power is to be found. With paradigms and customs of the conquerors that lead us to live and think in ways that dis-empower us spiritually, mentally and consequently materially, or by discovering the true essence of our own traditions that made our ancestors great and have made any people great throughout history, and which are universal principles applicable to all historical periods? Perhaps the next time I visit your area you will be able to attend a full session in order to draw a fuller understanding of the teachings as they constitute a science of life and cannot be disseminated entirely through books or letters. In order for an individual or a group to learn an advanced discipline, they must spend the time and develop sensitivity to the subtle meaning of the teachings. This is true in ordinary disciplines of life (medical science, engineering, law, etc.), and it is more important in the study of mystical philosophy. In the meantime I hope this letter may assist you in your quest.

May the Blessings of Maat be with you.
Peace and Blessings!
Sebai MAA

Mystical Answers to the Important Questions of Life

Question: What is Meskhent and Where does the term: "Know Thyself" come from?

Hetepu (Peaceful Greetings),

I have this week a copy of your book *The Ausarian Resurrection* (new title *African Religion Volume 4: Asarian Theology*) which I will read with great interest.

The last week here in England we lost the National football manager due to his view on reincarnation and the type of body we get based upon our Karma. I have several quotes from your books on the subject matter and have used them hopefully to good effects. Here in London I have spoken on community radio station on karma and reincarnation before. I do believe you use the Ancient Egyptian term Meskhent in the same way as the Indian word Karma. I am now collecting my notes for my next radio show, I would like to know from you the Etymology of the word Meskhent. I would also like to hear the full inscription found on the temple of KMT (Ancient Egypt) about the Ancient Egyptian term *Rech-Ib which means to* "Know thyself." Would it be possible to hear this from your lotus lips?

Thank you for the word

All glories to you and The Sema Institute.
Yours in good faith

Answer

Greetings,

The answers to your questions can be found in the Ancient Egyptian *Ru Pert Em Heru* text or "Book of Enlightenment" (also known as the *Book of Coming Forth by Day* and incorrectly known as the *Book of the Dead,*). The Ancient Egyptian goddess *Meskhent* presides over the future birth of an individual, but she represents only the culmination of the process, which is known as *uhm-ankh* or "reincarnation." In reality, it is the individual who determines his or her own destiny by the actions they perform in life. However, the wisdom of the Ancient Egyptian Sages dictated that the process should be explained in mythological terms to help people better understand the philosophy. The process works as follows:

The Ancient Egyptian deities *Shai* and *Renunut* govern an individual's fate and their fortune. These deities are the hands of the great god Djehuti (he symbolizes the intellectual development of a human being) and he inscribes a

Conversation with God

person's fate once they have faced the scales of Maat, that is, they are judged in reference to their past ability to uphold Maat (virtue and righteousness) in life. A person's intellectual capacity reflects in their actions. Thus, it is fitting for the intellect to judge its own actions. Further, it is oneself who judges oneself; God does not judge anyone because we are all essentially gods and goddesses, sparks of the same divinity, so God within us, our higher self, judges us. This is an objective judgment of the subjective personality which only the self-same individual is responsible for, and it occurs at the unconscious level of the mind, beyond any interference from a person's personality or ego consciousness which is on the surface level of the mind. Therefore, one's conscious desire to go to heaven at the time of death or one's conscious repentance at the time of death for misdeeds in life cannot overcome the weight of the *ari* – (action, thing done, make something, deed - equivalent to the term Karma) one has set up during a lifetime. So it is important to begin now to purify the heart and cleanse the soul so as to become ☰ or ☰ *Maakheru* (true of speech-pure of heart) at the time of the judgment. The gods and goddesses are cosmic forces which only facilitate the process, but from a mythological and philosophical standpoint, they are concepts for understanding the mystical philosophy of the teaching.

Once the judgment has been rendered, goddess *Meskhent* takes over and appoints the person's future family, place of birth, social status, etc. This is not meant as a punishment, but as a process of leading the soul to the appropriate place where it can grow spiritually. If before you died you desired to be a musician, and you have accumulated the proper amount of merit for that posting, the goddess will send you to a country, family and circumstances where this desire can be pursued. If you were a mugger in a past life, you may end up in a place and situation where you will experience pain and suffering such as you caused to others, and this experience will teach you to act otherwise in the future, thus improving your future birth and future capacity to grow spiritually. It is more difficult to grow spiritually in a negative environment of violence, denigration, lack of basic necessities, strife, surrounded by ignorant people, etc. What you do after the next birth becomes effective (after being born) is dependent in part on the basis formed by the previous actions in past lives, but more significantly, upon your own free will and your actions in this new lifetime. Your actions in this lifetime will thus engender and determine the next lifetime, and on and on. This process is *Meskhent*- "destiny of birth." Meskhent is the manifestation of one's *shai-nefer*, positive destiny, or one's *shai-mit*, negative destiny. This is one's harvest or what one reaps from one's actions.

This is the process leading to *Uhm Ankh* (reincarnation). The objective is to lead oneself on a process of increasingly better births until it is possible to have spiritual inclination and the company of Sages and Saints who can lead a person to self-discovery (*Rech-ab*). When a person achieves this self-discovery, he/she is

Mystical Answers to the Important Questions of Life

referred to as *Akh* (enlightened, or being of light) or *Sheps* (noble enlightened person who has passed on).

First, a person must become virtuous because this purifies the person's actions and thus, their Ari (karmic) basis. Negative Ari leads to bad situations, but also to mental dullness, and it is hard to understand the teachings when the mind is in a dull state, full of base thoughts, desires and feelings- this is the opposite of *Rech-ab*. It may be referred to as *inj-Set* (mind afflicted by fetters of Set). The afflictions that the soul is afflicted with cause *an-maat* non-truth (wrong actions, disorder), and error leads to *asftu*, unrighteousness, as the result. There is much mental agitation and suffering. The positive karmic basis allows harmonious surroundings and birth into the family of spiritually minded people as well as the company of Sages, but most importantly the clarity of mind to understand the wisdom teachings. If the soul is judged pure in reference to Maat, it will not be led to reincarnation (Kemetic term *uhem ankh*), but to the inner shrine where it meets its own Higher Self, i.e. the soul meets the Supreme Being (God, Asar) . This meeting ends any future possibility of reincarnation. It means becoming one with the Divine Self. It is termed Enlightenment or *Nehast* (Resurrection), i.e. the Ausarian Resurrection. This is the only way to break the cycle of reincarnation.

Philosophically, life in the absence of karma and reincarnation is worthless and futile. Consider that if there is no *ariu* (karma) or reincarnation (*Uhem Ankh*), then life is meaningless and disjointed. That would mean that things happen for no reason or due to blind luck; some people are rich and others are poor by luck; some others are living in a peaceful area while others live in a war zone by blind luck; others are gifted while others have no skills, etc. If there is no afterlife and life is only for the purpose of pursuit of pleasure, then what has been accomplished by that life, even if you are able to have unlimited pleasures? If you only live once and life is for the pursuit of pleasure and wealth, a pursuit without end or fulfillment, it is a form of doomed existence at the end of which is only death and oblivion. Or for orthodox Christians, they may say that after death there is a heaven for those who were good while alive, or for those who, after a life of evildoing, repented before death, whereby all the negative actions are automatically forgiven. So, in this orthodox Christian paradigm, the actions had no meaning – if one can be good or evil and go to heaven anyway as the orthodox Christians propose, just by believing in Jesus, then actions (good or bad) have no intrinsic value; so why not therefore allow chaos and let everyone do whatever they want to do, since it has no meaning under those criteria?

While forgiveness is possible, escape from the mess that one has made of one's mind and its unconscious impressions is not so easily overcome. So karma is not fate, but rather a destiny that a person has created through the actions they have engaged in which have led

Conversation with God

to the accumulated unconscious impressions in the unconscious level of mind from desires, thoughts and feelings of the past (in the present and previous lives). A person can change their karma by their present actions. Great patience with oneself is needed for such an undertaking, because affecting change and transformation in the personality is a gradual process that takes persistent self-effort and diligence, and occurs over a period of time. There is a parable of an aspirant that felt overwhelmed because of the negative ari he/she had engendered…the people in the town where he lived had ostracized him/her because of his/her negative deeds. The aspirant felt hopeless to change himself/herself. Sitting by a well, the aspirant noticed that the concrete where the rope used to pull the water up from the well was rubbing on it was worn down…there was a depression in the concrete. The aspirant thought, if it is possible for this concrete which is so hard to be affected by this soft rope, it is also possible for me to work on myself and change my hardened ways…with persistence, no matter how long it takes.

Thus, the individual is always responsible for their present conditions by the actions they performed previously which led them to the place they are today, etc. However, one's current condition is not set. Otherwise, people could not change and they would be fated to suffer or be happy based on some perverse cosmic joke. It is not like that. God has provided free will, and with that free will a person can have a glorious life full of wisdom and prosperity, or a life of strife, suffering and frustration based on egoism and egoistic desires.

Also, just because life without karma and reincarnation is empty and meaningless, we cannot say that karma and reincarnation are realities. They are realities because those who have practiced certain spiritual disciplines have discovered them to be realities. Also, parapsychologists have made experiments demonstrating them as realities.[31]

The Ancient Egyptian word "Meskhent" is based on the word "*Mesken*." *Mesken* means birthing place. Thus, *Meskhent* is the goddess (cosmic force) which presides over the *Mesken* of newborn souls. She makes effective, a person's desires and unconscious inclinations.

I have detailed this information in the following books:

Egyptian Yoga Vol. 1
Egyptian Yoga Vol. 2 (African Religion Vol. 2: Amun Theology)
Introduction to Maat Philosophy

The original Ancient Egyptian Hieroglyphic texts containing this teaching are:

Ru Pert Em Heru (especially Chap. 125 and 125A)
Wisdom Texts of Ani
Wisdom Texts of Merikara

---

[31] One example of a parapsychological study is from Brian Weiss in the book *Many Lives, Many Masters*.

Mystical Answers to the Important Questions of Life

Temple of Aset in Agylkia Island (formally and Philae)
Temple of Asar in Abydos
And many other texts.

I hope this was helpful.

Peace and Blessings!

Sebai MAA

Conversation with God

Question: What should I do about my insatiable desire for winning?

Dear Sebai Maa,

What should I do about my desire for winning? I am a baseball coach for little league kids and I can't relax when the kids are not winning their games. I know I should have a higher perspective in life but I still have this desire to win and last time I even yelled at the kids for losing. I want to be a good follower of the teachings but I feel internal conflict inside. I feel terrible, like I haven't learned anything from your books.

Sincerely

Answer

Greetings,

I would like to open this reply with a Kemetic proverb:

> "If you wish to be as a master you must love impersonally, caring for all equally; wants must yield to self control, live as though you have achieved and acquired everything you need and also as if you have lost everything; even the thing or person you might love most; for material things are transitory."

Firstly, in order to progress in transforming your personality you must first have your thoughts straight and then you must have a strategy to implement your righteous thinking in day-to-day life. Then your feelings and emotions will eventually come into line with your aspirations to practice the teachings in a more elevated manner.

You know you should not act that way but do you know why? Philosophically isn't it ridiculous to always be bent on winning at all cost even though it is not always possible to win? When two teams pray to God before play so they can win, which team does God favor? It is a ridiculous notion that winning is everything since winning cannot exist without losing. Therefore, doesn't losing have some value as well? Is the purpose behind losing to yell at the children and attack their self worth and self-esteem? Does this make them better children, or better players? Is this how you would like to be treated by your spiritual preceptor for not practicing the teachings in a "winning" (perfect) manner?
And doesn't winning also have to have some value besides just winning? Also, shouldn't the focus of the game be something that is achievable, and therefore something other than on winning (100% of the time), such as the practice of detachment, mastering the

Mystical Answers to the Important Questions of Life

passions, equanimity (in painful and pleasurable circumstances), etc.? Otherwise, one is setting oneself up for an upset...such as you are experiencing.

What will happen one day when you can no longer play baseball, when your body is old? What will you do, drink beers waiting for your liver to give out as you yell at the players so you can live through them vicariously? Will you be one of those ignorant people who can quote the best teams of the last century, but regrets not doing something better with their life and know nothing about the best philosophical teaching, the best myth or the best meditative experience that opens the doors to eternity? Will you be one of those who can list the names of the players on the teams but cannot list one divinity and their kin and what they represent, or cannot name the important sages of the mystery teachings? It's funny how people say studying the Ancient Egyptian myths and philosophy is hard, supposedly because there are many divinities and too much to remember, yet they can remember all the World Series of the last decade and what each player did and who lost the game and who was the most valuable player, etc. -all useless information since it has no abiding meaning, no transcendental import, no insight into the nature of life and death and will be forgotten by posterity once you and your friends, its standard bearers, are all dead! Who cares about the players and winners of the first World Series? All the people who played in it, saw it, heard it or bet on it are all dead and gone! So what difference did it make? It may have made a difference in their lives because they had an excuse to go out and have a pastime where they could carouse, drink, and make fools of themselves by rooting for one team or another and acting like animals who act on instinct instead of intellect, getting caught up in a crowd mentality and losing individual self-control. However, their actions had no meaning when they engaged in them, so they certainly have no meaning now, just as ignorant participation in and fanaticism about sports have no substantive meaning today either, if the sport is taken as a pastime or an egoistic contest whose prize is the capacity to boast about one's prowess over another just so that next year the other may do the same. That is the way of the worldly-minded person, the way to disappointment in life, distress after death and reincarnation to do it all over again.

After all, unless you are a player or coach getting paid, what concern should it be of yours if one team or the other wins? Even if you were getting paid as a coach, you are paid to provide a positive environment and a learning experience, to do your best by elevating your skills, not stressing, not just to win always – which is impossible, but to gain a higher benefit from the sports, like building character, cooperation and developing other skills like planning, healthy exercise, hand-eye coordination, etc. All of this occurs in the moment and not in the past or the future; so the benefit and higher enjoyment can occur in the now but that would be lost in the concern for winning or losing. If you are being paid just to win, get ready for the heart attacks, such as happens to many coaches; better to relax; it's not worth it! There is no benefit when yet you get caught up in the frenzy of play time. Like ignorant parents who punish their children for losing a game because the parent's ego was not fulfilled or because the parent missed their chance to get rich playing for the big league, so they want to use their children to do what they could not, the parents are missing out on what could have been a rewarding experience of raising their children. That is the ignorance of life, a miserable way of life, for all concerned; most people are caught up in something or the other. Think of the difference

Conversation with God

if you go to an airport to pick someone up versus going to the airport with no body to pick up. If you have someone to pick up you would be anxious, looking all around to find them. If not, you would look at everything and everyone there as being same, and you would have peace of mind. The idea is to have peace of mind regardless of the objective you are pursuing.

So you must learn that you should develop indifference about winning or losing and then you will have equanimity and peace. This does not mean not trying to win. It means being OK whether you win or lose since losing has certain benefits also. In losing you still get to enjoy the rush of playing and the joy of feeling your skills being used and the personal challenge of bettering yourself. Losing can lead to new knowledge that teaches you what to do to win. If you are so upset about losing, all of that is *lost* to you. You will not enjoy the moment nor will you learn from it, and neither will the children you are coaching. You will teach them, by your actions, the wrong way to live and the wrong way to enjoy life, and also, how to humiliate themselves and others when they win or lose. That is a pathetic way of life and yet that is accepted as the norm in modern western culture. It leads to developing more desires to find others to humiliate so one can feel good about oneself. This happens because people have nothing better to live for and they do not have inner discovery, so they try to give their lives meaning through worldly experiences. Since worldly experiences can never be consistent or permanent, they are setting themselves up for future disappointments, yet they never learn, so they continue to cause themselves pain, sorrow and aggravation.

If you have understood this philosophy, then the next step is to implement it. Before each practice or play time, reflect within yourself and remember this teaching and think about the things you will say, how you want to feel, whether you win or lose. You should be gracious in loss and conciliatory in gain. But regardless of which one happens, you should respect yourself and your team for they are expressions of the Divine, little gods and goddesses, potential sages, and they are your charges. As any head of a family, you set the tone for what is right or wrong. They will follow your lead in behavior, if not in belief, but right behavior is the first objective, then right feeling follows. When there is right thinking and right feeling, that personality will have peace and joy regardless of gain or loss in the external world, since the true gain of life is internal, not external. Therefore, show them the way to become wise human beings, and as you show them by your example, you will reach the heights of enlightenment and become a beacon for them.

As you practice this discipline, never mind that you will not always be able to live up to its lofty ideal all the time. Realize that they, and you, are working to relearn years or lifetimes of wrong belief and behavior. If you can keep company with those who are striving as you are, and with sages, that will be a great help in keeping your thoughts on track towards the truth and away from illusion and nonsense. However, you will become more aware and sensitive to your own egoistic feelings and expressions earlier, and you will be able to counter them sooner and sooner, until you will be able to catch them when they are sparks before they turn into forest fires that take over the personality and ruin your experience, causing you to have regrets later ("I wish I had not done that, I wish I

Mystical Answers to the Important Questions of Life

had not said that", etc.). With patience and diligence you will eventually succeed in overcoming the negative and irrational qualities of the personality, and you will become a purified human being and an asset to all with whom you may come into contact. This is an example of how you can use your job or profession as a vehicle to bring forth your spiritual purity. This is a way to spiritualize your life, to infuse the teaching in your day-to-day professional activities, so that you will be practicing the teachings even when you are not in the formal temple and not meditating or reading scriptures, chanting or listening to a lecture. If you succeed you will make your very activities the prayer, your every step a chant, and that is what it means to practice Maat philosophy, to purify your actions and make them divine, thereby making yourself divine. Then you will win the prize of all prizes, the glory of all glories, that is truly worthwhile, is abiding and memorable forever and beyond.

For those who participate in sports, the real experience of life is *playing*, that is always there. Winning and losing fluctuates all the time but "being there," that is, experiencing playtime, whether there is winning or losing, is always the same and that is the higher reality, the abiding truth within the context of our concern here. If a person were to hone the skills, practicing becoming one with their action, being less concerned with the outcomes (winning or losing) and reflecting on the miracle of their existence and their capacities, they would be able to gain a deeper experience that goes beyond the sport, for the body, mind, ball, bat, glove, etc. are all manifestations of spirit which is changeless.

Winning or losing is based on *ariu* (karma) which is changeable, variable. One can do everything right and still lose; what does that say? This other way to view sports is an idea of concentrating on perfecting skill in the moment so as to discover the mystery of life through the pursuit of the perfection,[32] which is a form of concentration effort that makes the mind one-pointed and opens the door to experiencing oneness with the source of life itself through the joy of physical activity and the meditative state of being in the "zone." This higher perspective on sports, which amounts to a kind of meditation in action, experiencing the moment which stretches into eternity, could allow that player to experience joy beyond winning and losing and would promote the empathic quality to help everyone enjoy the games through ethical play, rather than cheating, drug abuse and trying to win at all cost.

Many athletes have discovered a special level of consciousness that can be reached through sports called "the zone." It is a level wherein they are one with the game, their body and their capacity to play; everything falls into place and it is enjoyable. If that experience were treated as a window into insights about the nature of the universe, it could be a great boon; however, most athletes develop hubris and conceit instead, thinking they are the producers of their capacities, not taking into account that ones body and mind are sustained by food, life force and the universe, without which there would be no life at all. So the conceit is misguided and that misguidance is evident when old age sets in and the skills are lost and the conceited ego must stumble and fall as an old person

---

[32] It is important to note here that I am speaking about using the *pursuit of perfection*, not achieving perfection in the sport.

Conversation with God

slipping and falling. So, without reflection deeper aspects of life and consequently without humility, they feel they are worth more to the team, and they then ask for more money, which in turn inflates their ego more. Of course, the irrational adulation of their fans help to whip up the flames of egoism and self-deluded self-importance. So the experience was reduced to a monetary value and the personality was cheapened thereby.

Another form of experience is the "runner's high." It is a special place that a runner's consciousness reaches after some time where they feel separate from the body. It is close to an out of body experience, but the body awareness remains even though it is through delayed reaction to the commands of the mind due to the tiring of the muscles and the overuse of the chemicals used by the nerves to control them. Nevertheless, the loosening of the connection between the mind and body points to the existence of the mind without body which could be another form of insight into the nature of Self as a being transcending the body as well as time and space, and of course also transcending winning and losing. The experience can be enjoyable, however, if treated only in that way, for pleasure, or as a curiosity, it will not lead to greater insights, but rather to intensification of the ego and body consciousness. In any case, what would a person do when they get old and cannot reach the "zone" or get the "high" anymore? Those methods have some value, as outlined above, but are only possible for those who are at a sufficient level of health.

Additionally, sports like baseball, basketball, football, etc., that promote outer activities produce external strength. Physical activities like Yoga, Aikido, Kung Fu, Tai Chi and Tjef Neteru (Egyptian Yoga) produce inner strength because they develop the inner Life Force. That Life Force can be accessed at any age and at any time; no special equipment or paraphernalia are required. If the inner sports were melded with the mystical philosophy, the result would be power to explore the inner world and attain enlightenment. If the power of the outer sports were employed towards this same end, in addition to the inner practice, the capacity to practice and experience higher consciousness would be enhanced further.

There is an ancient Egyptian game that was played by the Pharaoh; it was the ritual of hitting Set. In Kemetic mythology, Set is the divinity that symbolizes egoism and unrighteousness. The player was to take a special stick and was to hit the ball as far as possible. Think of this in the context of track and field, but within the context of a spiritual ritual and you will get the picture. Imagine if the goal was not just to hit the ball out of the park to get a homerun and receive accolades and fans as well as people throwing themselves at you, but to get unrighteousness far away so as to experience the purity of Spirit and attain enlightenment, which after all is like winning every game in the world that has ever been played and ever will be played. This is the real prize, the hall of fame that sages have been inducted into from time immemorial! Do not succumb to the egoistic worldly perspective of winning at all cost; that is the thrashing about of ignorant souls on the surface as they fight each other for supremacy only to be endlessly knocked about by the waves and ultimately blown away by the winds of time. Learn to discover the depths of the ocean of life by using your profession as a vehicle to explore the depths of your being.[33]

Peace and Blessings!

Sebai MAA

Question: Is violence ever justified in the name of righteousness?

Greetings,

I have some comments and some questions. What are Sufi dervishes and what deity(s) preside(s) over the internal life force energy?

Is violence ever justified in the name of righteousness? I understand that Jesus and Gandhi were proponents of nonviolence but I am under the impression that any sage would defend themselves through violent means if Someone (wild animal, criminal, etc) were attacking them. Is this so? My question stems from reading the Indian book Bhagavad-Gita. When Krishna urges Arjuna to fight for the sake of righteousness, even though he will violently kill many humans, is this just? I understand that the Gita should be understood as a metaphor for resolving an inner battle, but if we take the events in the Gita as factual, can the Pandavas kill the unjust Kauravas and be justified? Please help me understand this, for I am having difficulty with it.

Answer

Greetings,

In reference to the first question, the Sufis are supposed to be the mystical sect of Islamic religion. The Dervishes are a sect of Sufis who practice a famous dance as a meditation and communion with God in the form of Allah. Some Sufis, like Rumi, have recorded highly mystical philosophies. However, there have been some instances of Sufis who have engaged in spiritual terrorism, like the destruction of Ancient Egyptian religious monuments throughout history.

The Kamitan Divinities who preside over the Life Force energy are Aset, Nebethet and Maat. Looking at the caduceus with the shaft intertwined with two serpents, the central shaft is Maat and the two serpents are Aset and Nebethet. (See the book *The Serpent Power*)

There are two perspectives on the question of the justification of violence, one is worldly and relative and the other is transcendental and enlightened. Violence can be justified in the name of righteousness in reference to the world but not in reference to an enlightened

---

[33] Sebai Maa has a Bachelor degree in Recreation Administration

Conversation with God

Sage. If a car is going to run a person down another has to violently push them out of the way. If a person is beating another to death another has to violently restrain him or her. If a person is insane and wants to make war on another they should be restrained by force if necessary. However, if one country exploits another, thereby fostering anger, injustice, hatred and resentment it is their own *ariu* (karma) that will bring retribution. However, war alone will never resolve the issues of injustice and unrighteousness that provoked the conflict since the true source of the problem is egoism, desire and greed. This is why understanding, righteousness, fairness, sharing and caring for others are the sure ways to prevent violence and disharmony. Also, that is the way to heal wounds caused by previous unrighteousness.

A sage is not concerned for his or her personal survival and therefore will not do violence to preserve his or her life for the sake of living as a human being who clings to life for life's sake. If a Sage sanctions violence it is for the good of the world as described above. For this reason, the Bhagavad Gita enjoins war, but there is also another war, to protect the order of society and war against the lower nature (unrighteousness) within oneself.

So there is another war; in Ancient Egyptian religion the conflict is the war of Heru and Set, the war between the lower and Higher self. In the inner spiritual struggle, we are also not to kill our enemy, the ego, but we are to subjugate it and transcend it. In society as well as between societies and countries, we are not to promote killing, but reconciliation and understanding. However, if understanding is not possible and the society is attacked, then it is within the right of the culture to repel that attack. In the same way Ancient Egypt had to go to war, and we find no writings from the sages against war for the protection of Ancient Egyptian society, but they do enjoin not killing and of course not making war, meaning, no murder for personal gain and no wars of conquest, but only for self-defense.

The sagely logic for war and social self-defense is that while sages have transcended physical life and its purpose, to attain enlightenment, the unenlightened still remain in need of physicality. Therefore, they need a proper place to live in peace and practice the spiritual disciplines. Therefore, such a place is to be created and protected to the extent it does not cause violence to the environment (pollution) or hurt other people and their societies. This also means that one society does not have the right (as in might makes right) to conquer or exterminate another society for the sake of their own survival -that is the law of animals, which exist on instinct. Humans have the capacity for intellect and should therefore comport themselves with greater ethical conscience. When intellectual capacity is employed to justify wars of conquest or capturing the natural resources of others for one's own benefit or enrichment at the expense of others or the environment, that is a sign of a degraded culture and of a degraded ethical conscience in the leaders and followers of such leaders within a society. So to the extent that a people can promote peace and prosperity without injuring others or attacking others, they have a need and therefore practicing higher social culture and have a right to seek the necessary conditions for living a fruitful life (a life that includes the necessities of life and can lead to spiritual enlightenment).

Mystical Answers to the Important Questions of Life

On the other hand, at the same time, even though the perpetrators are indeed wrong for their unrighteous actions, the people who are enslaved or otherwise abused, are abused to the extend their *ariu* has led them to that condition and they have a right to seek better conditions, but that will only be possible to the extent that they are able to improve their *ariu*. The way to improve *ariu* is through righteousness, ethics, devotion of purpose, right worship (practicing the three steps of religion) which all promote powerful culture, strong cultural identity and clarity of social justice, leading to physical social liberation and inner spiritual enlightenment. It is natural to defend yourself, this is a God given ability, and also attacking is a God given ability. A Sage's actions to protect himself or herself are for the good of the world and not for personal gain. However, what makes people different from animals is the ability to choose forgiveness and understanding as opposed to hatred and revenge.

In the Hindu story of the Mahabharata as well as in the Ancient Egyptian story of the Asarian Resurrection, violence is promoted when there is no other solution. The stories have an inner reference as well as an outer. The inner is that there is a battle between the Higher self and the lower self within a human being. The outer is the battle of righteousness versus unrighteousness between human beings. In Ancient Egypt, there was an army and police force. And in ancient times, they were used as a force to preserve the country from danger. This is a noble cause (the purpose of armies and police), but only if it is based on righteousness and truth. Likewise in ancient India, the Kshatrya caste (warriors) were given the duty of preserving righteousness in society by following the path of the warrior (Dharma). The problem comes in when the noble goal changes to greed and egoism, which lead to corruption of the ethics and the conquest and destruction of others as well as one's own conscience. Armies and police can be used as enforcers of dictatorships and slavery and that is most unrighteous. This is the corruption of law enforcement and the degradation of society due to a deviation from the path of righteousness. That deviation occurs when the leadership and the populace are ignorant of the true nature of all human beings, seeing them as separate entities and as lower beings than themselves. Evil political leaders (lack of ethics {due to spiritual ignorance} causing the personality to be controlled by desires) use that ignorance to goad people through fear and anger to commit unspeakable acts of cruelty and violence. All of that leads the soul to hell while on earth, and then also after death. In Indian legend, that is the path of the Kauravas. In the Ancient Egyptian heritage, that is the path of Set and his fiends. In Indian culture, righteousness, order, truth and peace are the path of the Pandavas. In Ancient Egyptian culture, righteousness, order, truth and peace are the path of Heru and the followers of Heru. The path of Heru is the goal of all spiritual aspirants; it is called 𓅃 𓏞 𓆓 𓂻 𓊖 *Shemsu Heru* - Followers of Heru Shemsu Heru.

Peace and Blessings!
Sebai MAA

How to Control and Cultivate the Mind in order to Achieve Sanity, Wisdom, Prosperity and Positive Spiritual Evolution?

Mystical Answers to the Important Questions of Life

Question: how to positively affect behavior modification?

Greetings,

Which book would you recommend that outlines how to positively affect behavior modification in terms of the spirit as opposed to the regular meditation techniques or prayer that many practice and teach, but yet are still unable to prevent or heal themselves from being mentally (cannot stop their own negative traits) and physically (cannot stop overeating or eating incorrectly) sick? I ask because of the interest to discover and practice the technique from a Yoga perspective, written by someone with an understanding of the plight and condition of the so-called black male in America that was stripped of all vestiges of culture. Many of the practitioners of Yoga or preachers that I have seen are overweight and unable to control their own passions and emotions or have no clue on the psychology and spirit of the Afrikan in America.

Thanks!

Answer

Greetings,

Your question is well taken. If there is a qualified aspirant (student) then a qualified teacher and an authentic teaching is needed for a proper learning situation. There are many people espousing the teachings of yoga and mystic spirituality, but when you look at their lives, there are serious contradictions. Further, one must distinguish between a "perfected being" meaning an enlightened personality (sage) who teaches yoga, and an aspirant or advancing student who is teaching yoga as a means to further develop himself/herself in the teachings; in the advancing aspirant, one may expect to find contradictions, however these should be dwindling over time (weeks, months, years, lifetimes). Contradictions is something that should not be expected in an authentic spiritual teacher, but certain physiological traits that are out of the control of the teacher should not be taken as failures of the teacher to follow the teaching for him/her self. For example, a person's physiology may cause them to be overweight, but that is not caused by overeating and should not be blamed on egoistic misconduct. Another consideration is that at times, an aspect of an authentic teacher's life or action may appear to be a contradiction to a neophyte aspirant due to her/his spirituality immaturity and misunderstanding of the teachings; it is not uncommon for aspirants to disagree with the action/advice/recommendation of an authentic spiritual teacher and leave the organization.

An authentic teacher must live the teaching and the following Kemetic proverbs will explain further.

Conversation with God

"If an example is set by him or her who leads, he or she will be beneficent forever, their wisdom lasting for all time."

"Every parent teaches as they act. They will speak to the children so that they will speak to their own children. They will set an example and not give offence."

"To teach one must know the student; to know the student one must know the student's symbolism."

Thus, an authentic teacher will tell you it takes more than prayers or mere words to transform the mind and lead one to spiritual enlightenment, much more an entire community. In order to have an effective initiatic situation, first an authentic teacher is necessary, one who has lived the teaching. Then that person who will be the teacher must be able to impart it. Being enlightened does not automatically make one an effective teacher of mysticism. Thus, not all enlightened persons can teach mysticism. An authentic teacher will have a command of the philosophy and the mythology of the teaching and the capacity to explain it to the different types of personalities taking into account their learning styles, the "student's symbolism."

Some people are visual (spatial) and they connect better through images, pictures and spatial understanding. They speak in terms like: "do you see what I mean? Answer: I see what you're saying." Even if they are on the phone they would say "see you later." They appreciate slide shows, seeing the teacher in person and assimilating the visual queues that are part of non-verbal communication. So to reach them it is important to be able to provide images in graphic form or verbal form through speech that allows their mind to see the setting of parables that contain spiritual wisdom. Some people are verbal (linguistic). They connect better through words and their precise meanings and the nuances of linguistics, both in speech and writing and may speak in terms like "do you hear what I'm saying" answer: "I hear where you're coming from!" So to reach them the teacher should be able to discuss the teaching by expressing in a pleasing and interesting voice that expresses personal insight and complete knowledge as well as reason. Related to the verbal is the Aural (auditory-musical) type of person. They connect better through music and sound, devotional music and chanting. Some people feel their way to wisdom (Tactile/Kinesthetic). Along with "feeling" the essence of a conversation and the person they are speaking with they appreciate rituals, articles they can touch and spiritual activities they can partake in. They might say things like: "I understand how you feel, what you said really touched me," so to reach them the teacher needs to be able to present feelings and emotions that the learner can connect with including empathy, humor, sorrow, exaltation, fearlessness, caring, love, righteous indignation, joy and contentment, among others. Some people are logical (mathematical-scientific) and may speak in terms of "wow that really makes sense," or "that figures." They appreciate the exploration of and intellectual mastery over intricacies of the philosophical and metaphysical inner workings of the universe and how the pieces fit together like a puzzle.

Mystical Answers to the Important Questions of Life

The personalities described above may prefer to learn in two broad formats. The first is in groups (social, interpersonal). They connect better and prefer to learn in group situations or together in an environment with other people, while others are solitary (intra-personal), preferring to work alone and use self-study methods. These are important languages (visual, aural, kinesthetic, etc.) that are needed to communicate with students, i.e., their symbolisms. Of course, several styles may manifest in the same person even though there may be a dominant learning style in their personality which will be their main pathway to understanding. It is important to note that the solitary type cannot work alone until they have something to work with, a foundation in understanding the teaching and a competent capacity to reflect upon the teaching which they may read, listen to or visualize in private (using books, tapes, graphics prepared by the teacher), so that instruction must still come from the same source as all the other types of learners.

Then the correct culture is needed. People have to understand that culture is more than wearing special clothing or uttering a few words from the "Motherland."

Next there must be authentic aspiration in the student; only then will there be the proper ingredients for promoting spiritual enlightenment.

Aspirants, depending on their experiences in this and past lifetimes, may find that they are drawn to a particular mystical tradition due to their ethnicity in this lifetime and/or an inexplicable affinity because of their ariu (unconscious mental impressions) from past lifetimes. Here at the Sema Institute, our main goals are dissemination of the teachings, but also the Kamitan mystical culture. Let other mystical traditions teach their own cultures in their own way; this is also good.

Culture is an important aspect of imparting the mystical teachings, as it provides a means of further relating to aspirants. How can you teach a person if you cannot reach them at their level, their history and experiences? So the teacher must be an example, knowledgeable and able to teach and know the student's culture and how to lead themselves to perfection and then how to lead others. Anything less than this is just that, a struggling human being doing the best they can, and that is good, but that is not a spiritual master. Spiritual practice involves subtle teachings and practices, and they require one who is an expert, not just in quoting scriptures, but their subtle spiritual meaning, and how to discover God by transforming every aspect of the personality while handling the world at the same time. Therefore, with these guidelines, may you find a true teacher to lead you to the Supreme.

Peace and Blessings!

Sebai MAA

Conversation with God

Question: How can one best handle anger?

Greetings!

I have had a problem with anger. I am quick to get upset and I really want to change. I know I hurt myself and my family when I blow up. What can I do?

Thank you

Answer

Greetings,

Anger can be a normal aspect of human response to certain situations of stress or unrighteousness. For example, anger may be an appropriate response if someone tries to hurt you or if an injustice is being perpetrated (righteous indignation[34]). Even sages may show anger in an attempt to impress others of the seriousness of a problem. But sages can control their anger while most people lose control during anger and say or do things they regret later. However, the stresses of life such as meat eating, the wrong pursuit of fulfillment of desires, which leads to inevitable frustrations, have created a situation of misuse of the anger response. Anger is not supposed to be a perennial emotion or mode of expression; rather it should be a distant and rare expression of displeasure or discomfort when other means of communication fail. However, in an overly stressed society or when leading life in an incorrect manner that leads to stresses and suffering, anger can become the mainstay of a person's life.

Anger at a base level can be a coping mechanism to deal with fear: fear of being attacked by others, fear of losing possessions, fear of losing position or prestige, fear of facing loneliness, fear of facing one's fears, etc. Anger can be a way to assert self-worth by fighting with others in order to dominate them, because one has no better (mature) way to prove oneself. Anger can be a response to anguish and anxiety about life's problems. For those who are driven by feelings and emotions instead of intellect and ethics, anger is a trance state of consciousness that is most often destructive to the physical constitution of the person getting angry and to the environment or people around them. Along with damage to the physiology of the individual, anger impairs the intellect and thereby people act in a trancelike state based on their ignorant notions and base feelings and emotions. Many times that creates a "high" that those people become addicted to, and so they develop a habit of picking fights often; sometimes they fight over little things just so they can feel "alive," because they cannot deal with silence or peace since that peace or

---

[34] anger and contempt combined with a feeling that it is one's right to feel that way because others have clearly and perhaps intentionally violated someone's rights or a situation has arisen that correctly elicits such a reaction.

silence would allow them to experience the anguish, anxiety or fear they dread. In this manner, anger can develop into a pathological[35] mental illness that leads to the ruin of the personality and the deterioration of their capacity to evolve spiritually. Thus, a person who is susceptible to the problem of anger cannot progress well on the spiritual path.

STOP - BREATHE - REFLECT - VISUALIZE - PHILOSOPHIZE

The way to control and overcome anger is to apply the following techniques. STOP: First, when you have become angry or when you start to feel anger, stop what you are doing and separate yourself from the area. Go to a quiet room. BREATHE: When anger comes, the breath becomes erratic, and with that erratic breath, the mind loses its balance. Rhythmic breathing is the fastest technique to regain physiological balance, mental balance and balance of the psychic energies of the mind. Breathe in and out rhythmically for several minutes until the body regains its physical composure. REFLECT: just because you can get angry does not make anger correct. If you feel you have been wronged, the first step should be to speak to the person and try to resolve the issue. If you have not been wronged and this is just part of a pattern where you "push other people's buttons" and they push yours, and you easily make each other angry and fight, realize that it is not necessary to live that way. Losing your calm can be a greater loss than losing a fight, even if you are right, so one should reflect carefully before allowing oneself to engage in angry behavior. So is it really worth losing your calm, damaging your body, agitating your mind, as well as hurting yourself and your loved ones? VISUALIZE: How would you like your responses to life's challenges to be? If you want to respond with peace, then close your eyes and visualize a typical anger situation. This time, in your mind, change your response to it; take a deep breath, do not lash out but calmly explain to others how you feel and what you think about what is wrong in the situation. Visualize that your explanation has been heard and people now understand your feelings and you will work out the situation. Practice this visualization several times every day. The next time you are faced with an anger situation, try to respond as you did in your visualization. Remember that the first few times may be awkward but your responses will improve. The important thing in the beginning is to catch the anger response and regain control of the personality, not necessarily working out the situation or problem with others or the world.

PHILOSOPHIZE: Remember that you do not control others; however, you can learn to control yourself. If others do not respond to your new way of handling anger, you still succeed if you control your anger and change to the proper response. If you succeed, you will remain in control of your intellect and feelings as well as emotions. You will be able to handle the world better, creating more peace instead of strife, and you will be better able to study and practice the spiritual teachings. Along with the above instructions, cleanse your diet from negative ingredients. Diets containing processed foods, too much cooked foods and meat (beef, poultry, fish) cause anger in the personality by causing certain physiological imbalances. From a philosophical perspective, realize that your display of anger is an intensification of your egoistic nature which has no validity. Your ego's attempt to control all the situations of the world and the lives of others to make

---

[35] Of, relating to, or manifesting behavior that is habitual, maladaptive, and compulsive.

Conversation with God

things to your liking is futile and will only create more situations of frustration. Anger is related to hatred. What is directed with anger soon becomes hated as a supposed obstruction to your happiness and source of unhappiness. This is incorrect logic. Actually, the things you have come to believe are sources of happiness, like offspring, wealth, fame and fortune, as well as sex, properties, parties, etc., are actually the objects on which you have learned to project your need for happiness. You have learned from family, society and your own internal ignorance that the pursuit of those things lead to happiness; but how can they if they do not last and if they cannot be held onto? You may spend your whole life looking to create a good family, get money, get fame, etc., but never experience true peace and happiness because all situations change, and gaining possessions (beyond the necessities of life) is always accompanied by the stress of maintaining and protecting them. True happiness is not something to be acquired like buying a new car or something that occurs when you engage in an activity like going to a party, because those things are not abidingly fulfilling and can be lost at any time. Rather, abiding happiness is something to discover as the essence of your very nature, and in order for that discovery to take place, there needs to be peace and introspection so that one may discover that one already has all that one needs to be content. That knowledge comes when there is self-discovery. So practice these techniques for control of anger, and then also the disciplines for self-discovery, and you will overcome the negative aspects of the personality: anger, hatred, greed, lust, envy, jealousy, etc. You will discover happiness that does not depend on external conditions, the whims of others, or the ignorant pursuit of pleasure as defined by worldly, ignorant people. You will discover virtue, peace, and the joy of giving and the glory of selfless service.

Peace and Blessings!

Sebai MAA

Mystical Answers to the Important Questions of Life

Question: how can I break out of the sense of psychological slavery?

Dear Mr. Ashby,

I want to thank you for keeping in contact with me. I am now in possession of many of your books. They are so informative, that it is helping me to do what I always needed to do. That is, I need to deal with the sense of inferiority. You have let me know that we were a great people. And that we still are a great people.

I realize that I do not have to be ashamed of being classified as black. One of these days I would like to meet you. At this time, I am working on developing a business for myself so that I can eventually become financially independent. If I had the time, I would go to your convention in Chicago.

Anyway, I will continue to study your books and practice meditation in order to deal with my mind. I must break out of psychological slavery once and for all!

Hotep

Answer

Greetings,

Thank you for your kind words.

Always remember that where there is true aspiration and sincere work to study and practice the teachings, there will be ultimate success.

Therefore, continue to purify yourself, continue to better yourself financially so that you can practice the teaching in a more qualitative way, and avail yourself of the means at your disposal to advance where you are, and one day your higher aspirations will be fulfilled.

By now you already know, at least intellectually, that you are not an inferior being, that your life has been shaped by internal and external forces that have produced ignorance in your mind that shapes your outlook. You now know that the teaching demonstrates an alternative outlook that has the virtue of being a reality as opposed to the illusions you have lived by due to your upbringing, society, your own illusions, etc.

However, knowing something intellectually does not guarantee that you have realized its meaning and that the knowledge has become effective in transforming your life. What is needed now is for you to clear the way so that you may increasingly discover more of the teaching, and yourself to verify and validate your true essence. Then there must be

Conversation with God

dynamic and diligent practice of the disciplines for self-discovery (sema-yoga disciplines). As you engage in the process of self-discovery you will find solace and wisdom as well as great power that are your true nature. That is our heritage and our true legacy. There are many "black" people who have been led to ignorance about themselves, but there are "white," "yellow," "red," etc., people who have also been led astray. The problem of ignorance is the real scourge on the body of humanity that has caused untold strife and suffering. Therefore, it is incumbent upon you and all aspirants of all cultures to promote their own upliftment and that will in turn uplift humanity as a whole as well.

May the wisdom of Neterian Philosophy elevate you to the heights of self-knowledge.

Peace and Blessings!

Sebai MAA

Mystical Answers to the Important Questions of Life

Question: how to destroy this ego-based mind that likes to rationalize "wrong thinking"?

Greetings,

The subtle forms of egoism that I am battling that I must "pull out by the root" are the following. I find that my mind likes to rationalize its thoughts and actions so that it seems O.K., but deep down inside I know it (mind) is doing wrong. Many times it (mind) convinces me that it is O.K. to do something that is wrong. An example, if I get upset with my mother, my mind will say, well, your day is already messed up so it is O.K. to eat processed foods, watch T.V., overeat, lust, etc. In general, my mind tries to justify "wrong thinking", through faulty rationalization. Another example, my mind will say, oh you did the postures this morning so you can go to bed without doing your postures today or you did not do your postures today so tomorrow you will have an intense session (wrong thinking since it will depend on my karma for the day whether I have an intense session or not). Or the mind will say, you don't have to read the scriptures today, just make sure to read double the amount tomorrow (rationalization that usually doesn't manifest).

Besides practicing my *Shedy*[36] diligently, are there any specific things I can do to destroy this ego-based mind that likes to rationalize "wrong thinking"?

Peace.

Answer

Greetings,

The battle you are describing within yourself is the same battle which every aspirant must face. It is a factor of your ego which you have allowed to expertly fool your personality through illogical rationalizations. The rationalizations are excuses which you have learned to elicit and accept so as to allow yourself to pursue your desires. It is a way that the ego has developed to counter your soul's efforts to move towards self-discovery. So in essence, your ego has neutralized the soul's desires. In other words, Set[37] within you has won the battle against Heru[38]. However, take heart; while battles may be lost, the war is not lost. You must first realize that the recognition that you are rationalizing and cleverly fooling yourself through your egoistic justifications is a high attainment in itself. Most people fool themselves, adopting illogical notions, religious dogmas, blind admiration of flawed political or entertainment figures or sports fanaticisms without even realizing what has happened; they lead completely ignorant and deceived lives,

---

[36] Daily spiritual practices (Kemetic yoga disciplines)
[37] In Ancient Egyptian myth: lower self
[38] In Ancient Egyptian myth: higher self

Conversation with God

misguided by their desires and sucked in by the seductive appearance of worldly pleasures which masquerade as sources of happiness or fulfillment.

What is necessary is continued effort towards what is right and correct, even while forgiving yourself when you fall. You must have faith in that same little voice that is your conscience. At the same time, you must take the proper action to cleanse your mind of illogic, egoism and delusions through study of the teachings and resolving to act in accordance with Maat. Your conscience, the voice of Maat within you, will eventually lead you to right action, not just part of the time but all the time. But what if you already know what is right but can't make yourself do it? You need will power to follow through with what is right and true; just knowing it without the power to follow it is not sufficient. Therefore, you should be sure to practice meditation. You already know what is righteous but you lack the will to follow through on what you know. Meditation is the wellspring of will power to succeed in the spiritual battle. Sit for meditation for a set period even if the mind is distracted.

Further, remember your previous successes against the desires of the ego. Or before the negative behavior is about to manifest, resolve to act differently and prove to yourself that you can succeed even once against the ego. Having succeeded you will have a positive history to look back on whenever the negative feelings try to arise. Counteract them with the truth of your mastery over them and then go forth to do your duty, even if the temptation to act wrongly lingers in the mind. Do not allow the negative thoughts to fester in the idle mind. Get to work doing some positive project (chanting, exercises, chores, go to work, volunteer to help the needy, etc.). Therefore, do not wait for the negative pattern of behavior to manifest; be preemptive in your activities. Do not wait for the ego to sneak up on you or whisper ignorant ideas and rationalizations without challenging them with the teachings –you must learn how to neutralize the ignorance of the ego. Now that you know what is happening, work to change the reactions of your mind before they control you. If you do this you will be practicing advanced Shedy[39].

"Destruction of the ego" really means achieving control over it and not allowing it to dictate your fate. If you succumb to the rationalizations and desires of the egoistic thoughts, you are a slave. Therefore, with faith rely on the Divine Self, in the form of your heroic soul, who will ultimately win the battle. Do not give credence to the rationalizations even if your mind says "Now see, you failed again so why bother?" The Ego is the toughest adversary of all, greater than the greatest military power or force. Thus, it is the greatest challenge of life to achieve self-mastery (Enlightenment). Rest assured though, that if you follow the path you are on, in time you will succeed.

Peace and Blessings!
Sebai MAA

---

[39] Shedi- spiritual disciplines of Shetaut Neter (Ancient Egyptian Religion) and Sema Tawi "Egyptian Yoga"

Mystical Answers to the Important Questions of Life

Question: How to control thoughts?

Udja!

   Sebai Maa I am curious about something that I have been reflecting upon. Namely control of one's actions, words, and thoughts.

Now it seems that actions and words only come about after one has had a thought. Therefore, when one controls their actions or words they are interrupting a process in midpoint. With practice one learns how to recognize one's thoughts faster and faster and can then cutoff (control) the old process. (Think then do) This applies to both actions and words.

However, thoughts are a different matter. It doesn't seem like one can control a thought after one has already had it. One cannot control something after it has already occurred, other than previously stated new potential actions or words associated with it. Controlling thoughts by its nature must mean being present to and at the place where thoughts develop before they happen. This seems like the only way to actually control thoughts.

Query? Is this true? If so, how is this done?

The place where thoughts emanate from is in the deeper parts of the *NRUTEF* I would imagine. Getting here I think means you have reached *NEHAST*. If so, does this mean that it is only after receiving NEHAST can one truly control one's thoughts? If I am incorrect, then how do we actually control one's thoughts?

Peace

Answer

Greetings,

While it is more difficult to control a thought and its consequences after it has arisen in the mind, it is possible. How? In the following sense: thoughts are an outgrowth of *ariu* (previous deeds-karma) that cause new desires. The residue from *ariu* (actions) an unenlightened person has performed in the past lodges in the unconscious mind and when stimulated, as if sprouts forth as a new desire. That desire evokes a thought in the mind and the mind engages an action to fulfill it. One may not be able to control the thought, but one can control the physical actions and the new formation of *ariu,* that is, IF the mind has been trained and has developed enough will to counter the power of the desires generating the thoughts to be countered. If the mind is trained in the philosophy on how to watch emerging thoughts and not act on them, just be a witness to them, then the action is under control and no new negative *ariu* can form that would create other thoughts in the future because actions are now controlled. In other words, if new formulations of unwanted thoughts are not allowed, no new negative residues can form related to them. If there is sufficient will to counter (neutralize) the emerging negative thoughts, then eventually, the negative *ariu* is exhausted and the mind is rendered purified and clear. Through this discipline, the thoughts are controlled automatically when the unconscious impressions are purified- the new sprouting thoughts will be virtuous then. This shows the importance of right action - Maat Philosophy. However, even if the complete cleansing of negative *ariu* did not occur, there is a certain level of cleaning after which the remaining *ariu* will be inconsequential, not an obstruction to control of mind or attainment of higher consciousness. So the act of engaging in the practice of the spiritual disciplines actually does interrupt the process of thoughts and their consequences. Actually it allows a person to take control of their life instead of being controlled by their thoughts, desires and instincts like ordinary animals are. Practicing an authentic and effective spiritual program for life actually allows a person to become a real human being, where as before they were only animals or potential human beings. Those who live at the level of animal instinct and reaction are easy prey for those who would like to exploit them, like unscrupulous political leaders, businessmen and religious leaders who want to control and virtually enslave them.

When a human being is born there is *ariu* (a karmic) basis that comes attached to the soul with them from previous lives. That basis may have a tendency towards positive or negative, but in most people are mixed. However, their own nature, through their own *ariu*, has a strong influence on the unenlightened person's, belief, intellectual capacity, health, fortune and destiny. Firstly, through their *ariu*, they have led themselves to their particular family, country and situation of birth. If they experience prosperous or unprosperous (adverse) conditions, virtuous or vicious conditions, etc., they have led themselves to that; so two persons with similar genetic structure can have different lives depending on the circumstances they have led themselves to through their own individual soul's *ariu*. This is why it is important to have leaders who promote righteousness and order and truth in society, since most people, who are not spiritually and ethically mature, are led by their base instincts and feelings. And it is important for a human being to follow the philosophy of truth and righteousness, even while not understanding it, like a child growing up who grows up following the rules of the community, even though they do not yet know the wisdom behind them.

A soul that has been negative can develop in a positive way in a positive society but even a mixed soul or one that tends towards positive can develop negative tendencies in a negative culture. The key is choice; one must learn to choose positive over negative; that will lead to the cleansing spoken of earlier. A human being has the capacity of choice because they have a spark of the Divine intellect and only the intellect can truly make a choice, that is if it is healthy and not an atrophied intellect like most of the masses of people around the world who are led by their egoism. The choice of the ego, as it is based on ignorance, will lead the soul to illusion, error, and suffering. The choice of following

Mystical Answers to the Important Questions of Life

the wisdom teaching and the *maatian*[40] regulations leads to enlightenment because they are based on truth. However, that choice can only be made by the wise and not the ignorant, those who are wise enough to know the error of their ways even though they are not fully pure or virtuous. However, an ignorant person, a person mired in vices, degradation, anger, hatred and greed, has no choice and will be caught up in the matrix of ignorance leading to a cycle of pain, sorrow and disease until there is sufficient clarity to make the right choices. For such a one, that clarity comes when sufficient suffering has eradicated enough of the ignorance of egoism. That can take many many many many lives (thousands, millions)! When the personality has attained sufficient purity, a person can look introspectively. Even now as we speak we could not even talk about the mind as something separate from self and look at it objectively if there was not already a high level of purity. A person who is caught up in egoism sees the self and ego-mind as one. The evolving person who learns that the awareness of their individual self, with its desires and preferences, is separate from their higher nature, is already experiencing the dawning of enlightenment.

The Ancient Egyptian term *yanrutf*[41] refers to a level of consciousness beyond mental conceptions. It is a place beyond the seeds of *ariu;* it is the place where the transcendental Self is found by a spiritual aspirant. When one is seated in that throne room (*Yanrutf*), that is indeed the *Nehast* (awakening), a place from which one can dictate the feelings, thoughts and of course the actions. This place (*Yanrutf*) circumvents the ego; the power of the ego and all residues have been nullified and ignored; even if they remain they do so as if in a puppet state, now only to do the bidding of the Self – after the experience of *Yanrutf* and Nehast it is God/Goddess who dictates thoughts, feelings and actions; it is Goddess/God who controls the manifestations of the life of the enlightened beings. For enlightened beings there is no question of controlling thoughts, feelings or actions anymore. For them their Divine aspect (Heru) rules, not the ego (Set). Isn't that glorious?

Peace and Blessings!
Sebai MAA

---

[40] ethical
[41] mythical place in Neterian philosophy that is beyond thoughts and conceptions – transcending time and space-free of egoism

How to Handle the World and the Day to Day Challenges of Life and Still be a Successful Spiritual Aspirant?

Mystical Answers to the Important Questions of Life

Question: What can I do about my failing daily spiritual discipline?

What can I do about my daily spiritual discipline? I am not doing the exercises and the world seems to pull me in constantly?

Answer

Greetings

Your plight is not unusual. You may consider "starting out small and growing big." This means that you should incorporate the barest element of the program and then add on as your ability and desire increase. So begin doing one thing and do not burden yourself with more in the beginning. If you do nothing else, perform the daily worship program (30 minutes) and no matter what commit to just do this. If that is too much, just do one reading of the daily chants, which takes 5 minutes and then do 5 minutes of meditation and no matter what commit to just do this. See what will happen.

Further helps to the spiritual discipline are conducting regular study group sessions. You may wish to start a group in your area. This helps to maintain motivation, enthusiasm and interest high. Listen to the tapes and lead discussions on the topics presented to the best of your ability.

Further, attend the seminars-they are a great booster in maintaining the spiritual discipline.

Another option is setting up a seminar/workshop in your area. If you agree with this idea, you should be the person in charge and the work you will do to manage the program will help you to develop devotion towards the teaching and the teacher, and this will give you impetus to promote your own spiritual discipline.

If all else fails do the following: listen to, or read one elevating teaching per day and meditate for 5 minutes. Just make that commitment. This may not seem like much, but if you add this little spice to your daily life, it is like putting a little condiment in a soup, it changes the taste. Its effects are tasted throughout the day and your life will be gradually so affected that you will one day have the strength and will to do more and more and you will succeed.

Let us know how you do from here.
Peace and Blessings!
Sebai MAA

Conversation with God

Question: How much should I work to support myself?

Greetings.

I had a dream the other day that involved you, your mother, and I. You told me in the dream "don't work." Your mother (whom I met in class once) seemed not to understand so I told her--- "he's saying that I should always remember the purpose of life (attaining enlightenment) is more important than anything else and not work more than I should if it interferes with this goal." What can you tell me about this dream? Could you give me your interpretation?

I feel that this dream may even have a greater truth after you asked me this Sunday as I was leaving class----"do you have to go now?" My reply, "Yeah I have to go to work."

Although I know that you really cannot separate work from your spiritual discipline (like that time a reporter asked Gandhi why doesn't he take a vacation because he worked so much and he said he was on vacation everyday), is there a point where you have to limit the amount of work you do?

Especially for an aspirant. Because lately I have not had time (due to work) to do my formal practice, like meditating, postures, etc,

Sebai, thank you for your words of wisdom. I have not told you, but the night of my initiation, you came to me in my dream and I was faced with the arduous task of choosing between you or my mother. Of course, I chose you (to follow you, to be with you). I guess that dream is a symbolic representation of me renunciating the world (my mother) and accepting God (through you), from the day of my initiation forth.

Thank you. Peace.

Answer

Greetings,

When an aspirant dreams about the teacher or the gods and goddesses or mystical philosophy principles and teachings, it is a very auspicious event because it means that the teachings are penetrating the subconscious and conscious levels of the mind. This is a form of yoga that occurs in the Dream State. Further, it means that a process is ensuing in which the personality of the aspirant is integrating the teaching and thus the personality is integrating, growing in discovery of the Higher Self within. The teacher is the outer manifestation of the Higher Self, which is instructing the student. The dreams, visions and intuitions are internal means by which the student receives teachings directly from the Higher Self.

Mystical Answers to the Important Questions of Life

A serious aspirant should take care of the practical realities of life, but not do anything that impinges upon the spiritual disciplines, except by emergency, for example, if your house is burning you should not say "I will finish meditating and then I will put out the fire." An aspirant should seek out careers and jobs that are in line with the teachings and that inspire the inner gifts of the soul. These activities should be in harmony with nature and with humanity. They should be uplifting and inspiring to others. They should not be a chore. Chores are necessary in life and should be seen as part of the spiritual journey and therefore, should be performed joyously and in the spirit of service to the higher Self, for it cannot experience without the body, and the body cannot function without the chores, eating, bathing, cooking, studying, caring for others, etc. When action is seen in this way, it takes on the quality of Yogic Action, and will lead to selflessness, and thus also to enlightenment. Even Gandhi found that he needed to take one day each week to devote to the spiritual practice, not taking any calls or interviews.

The career should not be a burden, but one should feel joy and inspiration everyday, and thus it will not be a drain, but it will become part of the spiritual discipline. Still the formal practices should not be disturbed especially in the case of novice aspirants, but also even advanced aspirants. Ideally an aspirant should work part time, leaving sufficient time for the formal practices and for reflection and personal as well as family obligations. There is more to life than the job. A person should learn this early in life instead of at the end when they retire and they have no life but the job - and what happens when they can't work anymore and they have not built up a spiritual practice? In the case of highly advanced personalities, who have discovered a form of perfection in action, they can perform great works and never feel tired or disturbed by the success or failure of those works. As a person discovers greater and greater harmony, they draw on cosmic power. Otherwise an ordinary person becomes exhausted and worn out instead of regenerated and rejuvenated. This is the glory of the path of Action, what we call Maat Philosophy.

Peace and Blessings!
Sebai MAA

Conversation with God

Question: is it possible to grow spiritually attaining enlightenment by listening to tapes and reading books and meeting at conferences?

Answer

Greetings,

The books and tapes are a foundation to build on, but they are not firm. It is like making a building with bricks, but without cement. The structure will stand but would not withstand the force of wind; with the slightest tremor or even the push of a regular sized man, it would fall over. Books, tapes, and conferences are forms of "good association" methods to commune with the wise person who wrote them or spoke them, but that is limited. Those methods cannot correct you or impart to you certain wisdom or psychological and psychic energies needed to understand the teaching. Would you want to have a heart operation by someone who read about it from a book written by an experienced surgeon or would you prefer to get someone studied but also was overseen by the experienced surgeon or even get the experienced surgeon him/her self to do the surgery? Study and reflection can take you only so far.

If you want to start a fire to keep warm there are two ways: you can start a fire yourself or get close to someone who already has a fire. If you don't know how to start a fire you are in trouble. What if you did not even know what fire was? Most people do not even know that there is a fire, a fire of philosophy that is there to relieve the miseries and ignorance of human existence. Others know about it but do not know how to access it. Still others have read many things and think they have it! They are living in the house without cement to keep the bricks together and when a storm comes (adversity in life) their house crumbles and their personality suffers. In reality there is only one way to get fire, from the person who has it, and then eventually you can make your own fire and when you are tested by the world you will not fall over! But that will take time; it takes time to make a powerful self-sustaining fire of spiritual wisdom (*Udja rekh*).

Many people can make fire but it is weak because they are reciting what they have read or heard but do not understand the deeper essence. So their fire might be blown out like a candle in a strong breeze. What they need is a fire that will not be blown out even by the stormiest weather, the deepest flood, the greatest misfortune or the utmost frustration. On March 5, there is a Kemetic Spring Festival of Goddess Aset commemorating the day She lays to rest the storms that had not allowed the boats to make their journey. Aset is the presiding divinity of spiritual wisdom; as she calms the storm of the sea for the ships to come into port she also calms the sea of the mind and its divergent streams of thoughts and desires that cause a storm in a person's life, the chaos that leads to miseries, frustrations and sufferings that prevents people from coming in from the rough seas into the port of peace, contentment and abiding happiness. Keep in mind that those methods (books, tapes, conferences, etc.) are no substitutes for the even higher association that is possible in a temple community where you meet every day with other aspirants to listen

Mystical Answers to the Important Questions of Life

to the teachings of a qualified preceptor; that listening process is the highest good association as the Sage is the representative of Aset. Every aspirant should work towards that, but doing the best they can in the mean time to prepare for that eventuality.

Peace and Blessings!
Sebai MAA

Conversation with God

Question: Is College worth it?

Greetings Sebai Maa,

It is an honor to send you this e-mail. I have read your books and they have so much information in them, you can not get this info in a university. I was wondering, should a person who is in college studying religion and philosophy stay in college knowing that what they are teaching is not really true. I will sign up for your courses, but I know the prejudices schools have about Kemetic culture, and Mystical Religion in general. So in essence, what should a person who knows that what his/her school teaches is false, but needs the degree from the school to function in this world, do? Thank you

Answer

Greetings, (Greetings)

I am gratified that you appreciate the work we are doing. If you intend to work in "the system," i.e., the general society, it is almost impossible to do so unless you have their required credentials. Realize that there is a glut of PhD's now, and especially in the religious studies field. Ideally, if there were enough support within our own culture, we would not need to have the credentials from anyone else. But we are not in that situation. Therefore, you should complete your college degree, but also supplement your studies by going outside the box. Then you will have something unique to offer professionally and for yourself you will have true insight that will lead you to unlock the secrets of life and become a true beacon of light for humanity, even as you perform your work in "the system."

Peace and Blessings!

Sebai MAA

Mystical Answers to the Important Questions of Life

Question: How to become free from Globalization?

Greetings Sebai Maa,

Can you inform me on the process of which one becomes a sovereign person with economic and legal freedom per status quo?

Answer

Udja - Greetings,

If you seek economic freedom, it is difficult since we are increasingly all caught up in an interdependent web of globalization, which is supported by the extreme litigiousness and technological nature of world culture. Even in the depths of the Amazon, they cannot escape the reach of greed and those who would, because of economics, steal the land and use it for profit.

As an individual, it is very difficult to become financially free unless you have a good skill or profession, and then only if you prudently and wisely manage your income, savings and investments. As an ordinary individual, the answer also is to associate with those who seek purity, to use economics and legality to promote peace and equity for all and that is the closest one can come in the world of time and space to a situation of autonomy and freedom. As for internally, through the practice of the spiritual philosophy and the mystical disciplines, such as Sema Tawi (Kemetic yoga), one can become totally free from the world in a way that is impossible physically.

In order for that to happen the status quo of ordinary society must be used correctly and managed properly, and then it will be changed, but then also that must be eventually transcended. That is the highest human culture, the greatest achievement. And that philosophy and higher perspective of life is what illumines the world with hope. That is the legacy of elevated personalities, the sages.

Peace and Blessings!

Sebai MAA

Conversation with God

Question: How to protect oneself from evil spells?

Greetings,

I have a question.

I would like to find out what is the best way to protect oneself from attacks from others such as spells. What did the ancient Kamitans do to protect themselves from sorcery?

htp

Answer

Greetings,

Propitiation of the divinities of protection (Aset, Anpu, Maat) is efficacious in promoting psychic protection from inimical forces. I will discuss some general and then some specific aspects of the practice of psychic self-defense. There are different levels of that worship. You can make offerings of food, incense, lighting candles, chants and libations and that offering brings the merit of assistance from the divinities. That basic worship is gross and must be conducted with gross items and the gross mind. However, realize that on a subtler level, propitiation also means following the wisdom and disciplines of the mystical teachings such as meditation, and not just making ritual offerings, burning incense, lighting candles and offering libations or chants, etc. Gross offerings such as ritual offerings, burning incense, lighting candles and offering libations or chants, etc., only help you to the extent you are able to sustain those limited efforts. If those offerings are stopped then the benefits do not last long.

The higher level of propitiation occurs when the mystical/spiritual principles symbolized by those divinities of protection are perfected in the mind and heart of the propitiator. The best defense against psychic attack (negative influences from evil spirits, demons etc.) and evil eye (negative thoughts) from others or negative thoughts and feelings from one's own unconscious (due to negative actions of the past) is to become purified by Maat. That is, to study the philosophy and then follow the discipline of Maat. One must discover the deep meaning of truth, righteousness and nonviolence. Reinforce this practice by study of the scriptures, chants and songs of Maat and with ritual purification and daily worship (carry out the daily worship program - daily- without fail), meditation and practicing Maat in one's daily life. Practice non-violence- do not return evil thoughts to the evil minded- that brings you down to the level of demoniac consciousness with them. Rather, forgive them for being spiritually immature, just as you would forgive a young child who wished you harm because you did not give into the child's tantrum. Tend to your own spiritual practice and keep *Shedy*- meet and associate as much as possible with those who are like you practicing the philosophy of Maat and others who practice Maat in different forms (those who are righteous, have integrity and are nonviolent) even if they do not follow Shetaut Neter particularly. Righteousness, purity of heart, body-mind and soul is like a suit of armor against inimical forces of all kinds, and also the doorway that opens up the inner peace needed to discover the inner reaches of the Divine Self. Goddess Maat will herself, in the form of purity, protect you from inimical forces. Then you will repel those negative sentiments and thoughts and you will be free to pursue the true meaning of life. When you become one with Maat, that it to say, Maakheru (true of speech), you are free from any and all inimical forces since you have become one with the power that immunizes the personality from that which makes the personality weak and susceptible to inimical forces: ignorance and unrighteousness. Resources: read the book *Introduction to Maat Philosophy* and study the audio lecture series on the book, *42 Precepts of Maat and the Philosophy of Righteous Action*.

In order to promote the psychic self-protection one should enjoin the daily practice of the spiritual disciplines; this maintains a healthy aura that is efficacious against regular maleficent energies of the world as it promotes higher awareness of the teaching and propitiates the presence and grace of the positive psychic forces, the neteru, and their energies.

For more specific issues additional propitiations can be made to bolster certain cosmic forces so that they may come forth to provide greater protection or to disperse maleficent energies. This practice may be performed in a passive or directive mode. The passive mode is to promote self-protection and wellbeing; the directive is to direct the forces to the desired objective specifically. The intent of the performer of the ritual formulates the mode of the propitiated energies.

There are many forms of this practice and an aspirant may select in accordance with their feeling, in accordance with these guidelines, or a form may selected by a preceptor. This ritual is accomplished by making special ritual offerings which generally include incense, libation and oil as well as food (specific rituals may include other items).

The passive ritual may include the protection verses of Chapter 6 of the PMH), a protective invocation to Aset. The directive form is accompanied with specific formula hekau such as: *htp di s neter iri ndj n nshn – this offering is given to cause the divinity to protect against the evil of Set*

Or

htp di s neter iri ndj n dua-ti – this offering is given to cause the divinity to protect against the evil this person

The directive form may be strengthened by carrying the hekau in a written form, on sanctified papyrus, purified by the liquor of Maat and the waters of libation. The formula is written on the papyrus and is carried on the person to be protected as an amulet.

Conversation with God

A sample formula that is more directive is in the Pert m Heru:

17. I will not live on what is an abomination. I will eat only the bread made with white grain and my wine will be made with the red grain from Hapi.[42] I will sit in the clean place, under the date palm tree of my goddess Hetheru, who dwells gloriously in the spacious disk[43] as it travels to Anu, containing within it the sacred books of divine words which were written by the god Djehuti. (Chap. 26B[44])

These utterances are to be carried out daily or as often as needed the efficaciousness increases with the intensity frequency and purity of the ritual performance. Having uttered these hekau and prepared the amulet properly the aspirant should rest assured that the neteru are working with them to neutralize the inimical forces. Thus one should go about ones business undisturbed.

Now, the Neterian Theurgy is based on a simple but powerful premise that a human being should develop to become master of the cosmic forces. This means attaining higher consciousness so as to control the lower forces of nature. Psychic energies are subtle energies but they are part of the lower forces of nature when they are associated with egoistic or negative desires, why? Because negative desires are based on untruth and so cannot have the force of truth which is abiding and enduring. Untruth cannot abide nor can it endure. The fundamental truth is that all human beings are sparks of the Supreme divine; therefore they can potentially partake in the power of that Supreme Entity whereas a person engaging in negative thoughts or desires or directing these to others for their own personal gain or out of ignorance do so out of their own egoistic, individual capacity. Though that can have tremendous force it is infinitesimal in comparison to the overwhelming force of the Supreme. Thus one should ally oneself with that higher force in order to be free from, be unaffected by and victorious over the lower forces and those who wield them. Recall the Ancient Egyptian proverb:

> *"Salvation is the freeing of the soul from its bodily fetters; becoming a God through knowledge and wisdom; controlling the forces of the cosmos instead of being a slave to them; subduing the lower nature and through awakening the higher self, ending the cycle of rebirth and dwelling with the Neters who direct and control the Great Plan."*

Ultimately, ritual reinforces the power of the myth which is a metaphorical representation for the mind of neterian cosmic forms which are concepts based on essential energies that operate in the relative reality of Creation. There are indeed forces that can be manipulated for negative purposes and the more egoistic or less aware a person is of their universal essential nature they are susceptible to those forces. However, a sage, having transcended the illusoriness of the relative reality and having become indeed powerful over those forces by discovering them and their position as master over them, has no need for rituals

---

[42] The Nile river god.
[43] Sundisk of Ra.
[44] Generally referred to as Chapter 68 from papyrus Nu.

Mystical Answers to the Important Questions of Life

to reinforce the wisdom and power of myth. Their metaphysical attainment in mystical awakening has caused them to become like the *ur-uadjit*, or "spacious disk" which is too bright to be obscured by the "darkness of ignorance". Until such time as that attainment is completed the ritual and amulets are enjoined. Thus sages do not require such protection but may do such for their followers, the world or society and thus lead them in the ways of protective theurgy for the people's benefit.

Additionally, read the books *Egyptian Mysteries Vol. 2 Dictionary of Ancient Egyptian Gods and Goddesses* and *The Kemetic Tree of Life*

Peace and Blessings!

Sebai MAA

Conversation with God

Question: How to handle a rough journey?

Udja and djeta dua to the divinity in your eye. It's been some time for me to reflect on the projections of hidden raised steps. It was a blessing to have received your radiant rays at the conference, even though upon my dreams I visited you before. Since the gathering in Georgia, the experience remains etched in my memories. My journey home was not too pleasant. My luggage was lost and several books and calendar just received were also lost. I had to question why it happened and initially had my doubts. Although I have even more questions, I pray they will be answered.

What came before Kamit (Ancient Egypt), were there any other great civilizations?

Thank you

Answer

Greetings,

It is good to hear from you and thank you for your kind words of praise. All is due to the Divine.

As for the easy or rough journey, consider that that happening was ordained due to your *Ari* - everything is. Be thankful something harsher did not happen. However, it did not because you transcended it to that extent. That is, your level of virtue necessitates some challenge but not disaster, as other people. So just observe it and yourself. See it as an opportunity to practice Maat, being peaceful, non-resentful and patient. Then the adversity will serve you and not trouble you! All questions are answered in time!

As for Africa, if we ask what came before Kamit (Kemet, Ancient Egypt) might we not also ask what came before that and before that and before that...ad infinitum? The point is that certainly there were other civilizations, if not in this time cycle, then in the previous one and the one before. Each cycle, according to the teachings of Seti I, lasts for millions of years, and then Ra dissolves creation and later emerges again from the Primeval Ocean to create another Creation. So which one can we say is THE original? Which one came before which? In fact there is no time and no space and in reality all that is true is the essence that sustains the Creations, and that is God. We adopt the Kemetic teaching not because it is the oldest or the first or the primary. Indeed, there is no record of any high culture and civilization with extensive religion and philosophy before the advent of Kamit in our current human historical period. However, we do follow Neterian (Ancient Egyptian) Spirituality because it is authentic and because it resonates with us; it is special to *us*, just as other paths are special to others, and through it we are able to reach the heights of enlightenment, to know God and become one with Her, thereby attaining immortality and infinity! Thus in fact we eventually transcend Africa and whatever came

Mystical Answers to the Important Questions of Life

before or for that matter, what may come in the future, for all of that is transitory and we want what is abiding, what is real, what is the ultimate truth.

Your questions are thoughtful and important.

Peace and Blessings!

Sebai MAA

Conversation with God

Question: how to handle a challenge or an adverse situation and make a right decision?

Greetings,

How do I know how to handle a challenge or and adverse situation, and how do I go about making the right decision?

Answer

Greetings,

When confronted with a challenge, as a rule of thumb an aspirant should forge ahead, facing a righteous duty or trying to accomplish a worthy goal if it is noble and righteous (in accordance with the precepts of Maat). If it fails or succeeds is in the hands of Maat, and she will be the judge of whether or not it should be allowed and when it will succeed. Perhaps the time was not right, but it may be more propitious in the future, so the project should not be abandoned if it is a worthy goal, but one should learn from the experience to improve the next effort. Actions should be tempered with wisdom based on sound reason; one should not expect success to come from efforts that are unreasonable or efforts made without proper materials to accomplish the goal being striven for. Thus, some actions should not be engaged in until there is capacity (internal maturity, necessary materials, community interest, capital, etc) to achieve success of the final goal. Yet, sometimes it is good to strive for something that is out of our grasp because the success is not just in the final goal, but also in the striving itself. At those times the striving process helps us to achieve the goal of cultivating virtues and dealing with failures and egoistic desires. But in general, a task should be chosen not because it is a waste of time, but because it has the potential to do the most good for self and for all. However, "self" here means the virtuous self and not the egoistic "selfish self." That makes the choice harder because doing what the ego wants is usually easy; when ethics come in and one is faced with doing something that is against one's personal desires or comfort, then the internal conflict ensues. But that conflict is not usually over what is right or wrong, but over what is personally gained or lost. Some decisions are gray, having pros and cons; then the decision should be based on what is more correct in an objective sense.

Sometimes when confronted with a challenge or an adversity, certain feelings come up in the personality, perhaps of anxiety, repudiation, fear, etc. As a rule of thumb, one's feelings of apprehension about pursuing a project or facing a challenge should be allowed to influence rationality if they are intuitional (meaning you are having an insight of something you "know" but yet cannot explain) but not if they are egoistic. Those feelings of egoism are based on not wanting to do something because it is uncomfortable for you personally. That is not a sufficient basis to retreat from a challenge or an adversity that needs to be faced. Here is the sticky part: sometimes people conflate intuition with egoistic feeling. Just because you may feel something strongly does not make it true or intuitional wisdom. Intuitional wisdom may or may not promote personal comfort. The real test is if that wisdom allows you to recognize a higher truth of your experience or your situation. Generally, only those who have purified their feelings through study and practice of ethical culture as well as right worship and reflection on and practice of the teachings can have clear intuitional insight into their deeper self as a subject apart from their own thoughts, feelings and desires of their ego personality. Otherwise, most people who have not engaged in intensive spiritual work on themselves would easily repudiate something based on their interpretation of shallow feelings based on their own egoistic desires. Many times people turn away from making the choice they know they should make by rationalizing doing what is most comfortable by finding excuses or not facing the wisdom they know is true because deep down they did not want to follow that path anyway. Egoistic intent behind a choice invalidates the correctness and virtue of a choice.

When the personal feelings create irrational emotions that impair the rationality of a choice, those feelings and emotions are seen as masters of the personality and will lead the personality to pain, suffering and error. When a wise choice is recognized, the feelings and emotions should be allowed to add emotional content to the choice, to support the choice; then the feelings and emotions are servants, instead of masters controlling the personality. Then the choice will have not only the energy of the intellect behind it, but also the force of feelings and emotions. Many people think of that as "passion," but passion is the force of desires based on irrational desires supported by infatuation with the object of desire. When a decision has intellectual rationality and purity of feeling, the expression of the decision will have crystal clear clarity and a dynamic force associated with it in its execution. When an action is righteous (based on rationality and truth), it is called *maat ari* (righteous {pure, true} action). When a determination, a choice is righteous and contains the force of pure feeling, it has strong will behind it and it is called *maakheru* (truth of speech, true willing speech).

If a person is not capable of making a decision, if they are conflicted, after reflecting within themselves on the basis enjoined above they may consult a wise person or a spiritual preceptor for advice. They may also consult the scriptures and writings of the sages containing practical applications of their wisdom. If no wise person is available and they cannot find insights in the scriptures, they may consult an oracle, but only in important situations (not everyday mundane situations) and after they have worked to resolve the issue by accessing their internal oracle, the Divine Self, through reflection and intellectual and intuitional understanding of the issues.

Because the outcome of an action is based on several factors besides the person who is making the decision about the action, the final outcome is not guaranteed even if the correct decision was made. Sometimes the universe has a greater plan that includes teaching a person this very same lesson of the secondary importance of outcomes; perhaps also a person needs to be frustrated in order to strengthen their resolve and produce a better outcome next time. Perhaps the outcome is not desirable for others but the effort was beneficial to the actor and that was all the world needed. Perhaps the necessary elements to make an outcome positive are not available or if other people are involved, they are not ready to assist to promote a positive outcome. Thus, the world proves that external outcome is not a given nor is it necessarily the main purpose of

Conversation with God

action. From a spiritually evolutionary perspective, intent is more important than results, because the intent allows us to be free and clear of actions. Egoistic intent attaches on to actions and their results whether or not the result is positive or negative. In this case there is responsibility (blame, guilt, fault, etc.) and enjoyment or suffering in accordance with the result, which leads to regret, anguish, distress, etc. that causes the personality to be agitated and not find peace. Altruistic intent allows one to take responsibility, but not blame for the outcome of actions, to have a clear conscience about the action; thus one can avoid guilt, anguish, etc., and find peace regardless of the outcome.

> "Though having thought fornication or murder but not having committed these,
> the Mind-led man will suffer just as though he had committed fornication,
> and though he be no murderer,
> as though he had committed murder because there was will to commit these things."
> —Ancient Egyptian Proverb

Therefore, the outcome of an action, like the fruits of the planting of the tree, should not be the main factor in making a decision but rather the goal that for which one should strive. However, the greater the altruistic intent, the greater the likelihood will be of obtaining an altruistic outcome and likewise, the greater the egoistic intent, the greater the likelihood will be of obtaining an egoistic outcome. So, the more important factor in deciding about and proceeding with an action is ethics; is the decision correct or not? Correctness is determined by the higher truth of a choice. For example, all creatures want to avoid pain and promote pleasure. This is a universal truth that invalidates (makes unethical) the idea that it is OK to produce pain and suffering on people and other creatures purposely, or to allow others to suffer when one can do something to alleviate their suffering, because if one were in pain, one would want others to help alleviate it. Yet, suffering has its purpose, that does not mean that suffering should be promoted.

> "To suffer, is a necessity entailed upon your nature,
> would you prefer that miracles should protect you from its lessons or shalt you repine,
> because it happened unto you, when lo it happened unto all?
> Suffering is the golden cross upon which the rose of the Soul unfolds."
> —Ancient Egyptian Proverb

So ethics means following the path of correctness based on natural manifestations of truth and not arguments based on intellectual inventions, arguments that are manufactured (conditional) or egoistic (truths that support our desires). This is not to say that since the creatures of the world are instinctively directed towards pleasure and avoidance of pain that that is necessarily the best situation for them. Sometimes suffering is needed to learn certain lessons of life or learn to think differently about a situation that will lead to greater understanding. However, this last statement should not be taken to mean that suffering is a better thing than pleasure or that one can decide which is best for others. Therefore, one should not purposely put oneself or others in situations of adversity with the idea of "this suffering will be good for me/them." Rather, through the external mechanism of interaction with nature and with other living beings, the world teaches in accordance with what is necessary for a person to learn at any given time. A person's

Mystical Answers to the Important Questions of Life

own tendencies towards virtue or vice also play a part in leading them towards situations of pain or pleasure. In any case, the individual need not seek out pain and suffering for they are natural aspects of existence which will occur automatically. So it is wiser to promote what is positive since the world will always present opportunities for suffering. If suffering must be experienced, despite the best effort to promote a positive outcome, that suffering should be accepted as a higher lesson; in so doing the suffering is minimized and the lesson from it is better assimilated, thereby reducing the chance for experiencing that same suffering in the future, since its purpose was fulfilled and there would be no need to revisit it.

> "Though all men suffer fated things, those led by reason (guided by the intellect), do not endure suffering with the rest; but since they've freed themselves from viciousness, not being bad, they do not suffer bad."
>
> —Ancient Egyptian Proverb

Having engaged in this process and having received instruction, the questioner should follow that advice and not rationalize ways to avoid following it or modifying it to make it somehow more palatable to their own egoistic sensibilities or to avoid a stressful situation that should be within their capacity to withstand. If a person follows these instructions, they are living by truth. Otherwise, they are contributing to their own delusion about the situation and promoting their own ignorance as well as postponing a real and productive solution to the problem which would promote their spiritual evolution and eventual attainment of spiritual enlightenment.

Peace and Blessings!

Sebai MAA

Conversation with God

Question: Do you recommend the use of oracles?

Hello,

In our class an issue has come up on three separate occasions. There seems to be some confusion (among the beginner students) as to the work of Sema in contrast to the work of another Kemetic teacher and his oracular system. I know on a previous occasion you said that you do not recommend oracle readings and I believe it's because the reader is giving up his own personal development and harnessing of cosmic power to "chance" (for lack of a better word at this time). Also, when I met you at a Sema Institute conference a few years ago, you also made some comments about the system used by another Kemetic teacher to be a potpourri of differing systems. Personally I have resonated with your work because it seems to me that it is bringing forward the teachings as was thought by the ancients without the added dimensions. This is the perspective (along with illustrations) I share with the class when the issue comes up. Because of your knowledge and practice with the Yoga system of India and Christianity, the way it's being brought fort by Sema is a more archaic view, which is what we need. What are your thoughts regarding the cards of the Taro used by different spiritual groups?

Answer

Greetings,

Your assessment is mostly correct. Oracles have their place in that there are some decisions that we should allow God to make. Sometimes in life there are important questions that ordinary people cannot decide between. They may represent a choice between two equally distasteful paths or equally important ones that overwhelm the personality. Then oracles may be used in this special occasion, when the personality cannot handle it and when there is no wiser person around with whom to consult. Oracles may be used at ritual occasions to determine the will of the Divine in reference to a divine decision relating to temple affairs. So Oracles are allowed in our culture, but with limitations – the Ancient Egyptian proverb states, "do not rely on the oracle." The oracle is to be used sparingly and managed by qualified clergy, not for common use. The teaching of Shetaut Neter is pure because it is derived from the original scriptures and unlike some other systems it is not a channeled, hybrid or synthesized creation. Few other teachers can make this claim or produce the voluminous works of documentation to prove such. Those who wish to follow well spoken personalities, who have little or no works that document their researches and mastery of the history, mythology, and philosophy of Kemetic culture, may do so on their own. Those who follow (shems), our path (Kemetic), must do so firmly in the conviction that this is an authentic path and leaving others aside- otherwise there will be confusion and stagnation. Those who have doubts should explore other paths until their doubts are confirmed or dispelled, and then they may be proper followers.

Peace and Blessings!

Mystical Answers to the Important Questions of Life

Sebai MAA

Question: How are oracles to be used?

Greetings,

There are many people who believe in oracles. Doesn't the Kemetic tradition promote the use of oracles? Aren't there Kemetic groups that advocate the use of oracles? There are times when it may be difficult to not use the oracles. A case could be when a child enters the earth, how would you or the Sema Yoga Institute determine know what the objective of the child is or what direction that child should be geared toward? In one Kemetic group, this is called an "incarnation objective" or one would get an "Astrological Chart" made.

Children are often totally driven by their emotions and therefore cannot be guided by their spirit due to the screen of ignorance.

Thanks!

Answer

Greetings,

Children are indeed driven by feelings and emotions because they do not have the capacity to exercise good judgment as their brain and nervous system has not developed yet to an extent that could allow them to exercise their intellectual capacity. Yet there are many adults who have atrophied intellects because they have led their lives based on egoistic desires, allowing their feelings and emotions to guide their path and cloud their thought processes. Ignorance of the deeper essential nature of self is another factor; many adults live life based on egoistic notions which also serve to cloud the intellectual capacity. Children have not matured enough to discover their intellectual capacity. Also, both children and adults suffer from the inability to remember their previous lives. Those adults are mentally like children even though they may have physically adult bodies and they carry on living like and making choices as children do. One of those improper choices is the misuse of oracles. Further, although it can be said that in general, children are driven by feelings and emotions, each child individually expresses different levels of self-control, because of their own individual ariu, that is, the impressions in the unconscious mind from their experiences in past lifetimes that are impelling them in this lifetime. So, for example, a child who has attained a high level of spiritual advancement in a past life time, yet still has a few subtle impediments to cause him/her to be reborn to fully become enlightened, may possess a mature and dispassionate disposition from childhood, due to his/her ariu. However that is not the norm but the exception, which is why many people are interested in oracles or seeking out father figures to tell them what to do, etc.

Conversation with God

Oracles are indeed part of the Kemetic tradition but they were never meant for daily use or as a substitute for proper human intellectual will and decision making development. Enlightened sages are their own oracle. Therefore, the ideal for anyone threading the path to attain Enlightenment is to develop an oracle capacity within herself/himself through the practice of the mystical disciplines. How will one develop this internal capacity within oneself if one is always dependent on some outside oracle to direct one's life? Even in the parent-child relationships, if the child always goes to the parent and has the parent make the decision for him/her, the child will never learn to reason and think properly. What the child also needs as she/he grows is for the parent to give instruction as to how the child should go about reasoning the situation through for herself/himself. Otherwise, the child will be forever dependent on the parent, and what will the child do when the parent is no longer around? Similarly, many people have fallen into a dependency on oracles to the extent of having their decision making capacity crippled by their misuse of oracles. Some people become so dependent on oracles they have to consult the oracle before going to the grocery store or even going outside into the yard! Oracles are meant to augment and not substitute the decision making capacity of a human being and as such they are meant to be used sparingly.

The cosmos certainly has an effect on a human being. Since everything is connected, everything affects everything else to some degree. This is especially true of nature. Those animals and other beings that operate on instinct are subject to the forces of nature. However, when a human being is low in spiritual awareness, they too are susceptible, but when they grow in spiritual awareness they rise above the influences of nature. This is because when a human being discovers they are in reality one with the Divine Self they rise above nature itself, they become masters of nature. Nature draws its power from the Ultimate Source (Goddess, God, Divine, Supreme Being). If a person grows to discover their oneness with the Ultimate Source, they assume the power position over nature as one with God(dess), the Supreme. In other words, at that point nature no longer masters them; they now make the rules, not nature. As a person practices and learns the philosophy of Maat, they come into harmony with the guiding principle of nature, who is the goddess herself. Doing this, they at the same time come into harmony with all that is good and true in life, and thus have no need for oracles any longer. So expansion in consciousness and coming into harmony with the Divine will through right action, right thinking, right feeling which is given by Maat, are the pathways to becoming the architect of one's own destiny and being free from the lower nature and its influences. It is also the way to fulfill all the missions and objectives of life, which will allow the soul to move on to discover the ultimate essence of its existence.

Peace and Blessings!

Sebai MAA

Mystical Answers to the Important Questions of Life

Question: I don't know what to do, can you help me?

Udja Sbai Maa

I have a lot to say but do not know how to begin. I must admit though that this has been mentally and emotionally one of the most difficult times of my life. Right before I began reading your first book Spiritual Enlightenment, a series of events in my personal life began that have had my head spinning continuously. I had been having problems in my marriage anyway, but an event happened that was very traumatic. At the same time I was dealing with my personal issues I attempted to begin implementation of living a spiritual life. I then thought rightly or wrongly that some of the things that were happening may have been fate, based upon what I thought was the interpretation of the reading of your book. I now realize that to a large degree we create our own fate, but I have yet to realize for what spiritual reason did I create the mess that has occurred with me.

Right now in my life there is only one thing that I am sure of. That is no matter what appears to be negative situations, I am going to continue as an initiate until I find my teacher and then become ENLIGHTENED. Everything else though I am totally confused about. I really am. My personal life has been terrible. I hate my job. Even if I met my teacher today, financially I am not in a position to leave my home and be taught. Physically I am a small man anyway, and I have lost weight dealing with I think my personal issues, and some of the personal issues the other day started taking a toll on me physically. I do not know what to do nor do I know what else to say.

I need help but do not know what type.

Thank you for reading.

Peace

Answer

Greetings,

Firstly, we create our own destiny; once the destiny has been created what has come to pass, that we refer to as "fate." Now, if your situation has led you to have serious and mature desire to attain enlightenment, then it has served its purpose of causing you to become disenchanted with the world. But now you must transform that dissatisfaction with the world into proper initiatic understanding and practice. Otherwise it will turn to dullness and you will end up tormenting yourself and your family and devolve, instead of evolve spiritually. If you truly want to attain enlightenment, you must do something before you can succeed in the spiritual quest. First you must normalize before you spiritualize. Yes you are the creator of your own fate and so you must fix what you have done poorly in the past. You cannot achieve enlightenment until you achieve balance, so you must work on your marriage and work on your job and work on straightening out your life. Only those who have an orderly life can be accepted into the ranks of initiates, so you are not ready. However, this does not mean that you are not ready to attend spiritual classes or programs. Rather, attending spiritual programs led by an advanced spiritual teacher or if possible, an authentic enlightened spiritual teacher, will assist you in the process of normalizing your life.

Your marriage is not the problem nor is your job. You suffer in these through lack of understanding that God has allowed you to experience these situations due to your own misunderstanding of the past. So now you must have faith and not run away from your troubles, and if you meet them in a proper way you will succeed and overcome them. Even if you were to get a divorce or win a lottery, your mind would continue to be filled with impurities that would frustrate your progress towards enlightenment, so these are not the answer. Seek out counseling and discover what you have done to make your life the way it is. Learn to forgive yourself and your spouse for past and continuing ignorance so that your mind may not be clouded with emotion and anger; seek martial counseling to heal your relationship with your spouse, and to determine if the marriage should continue or end. Understand that you have been led to your job by your own volition, and it is yourself who you hate for leading yourself to a miserable life. Therefore, blame no one and accept responsibility.

Also, realize that "you" did it so "you" can undo it. Act responsibly and instead of crying out, pray to the Divine. Instead of blaming or feeling guilt or self-pity, start understanding and accepting responsibility. Instead of hating your job, see it as a challenge through which you can rise above pettiness, impatience and fear. Stop fighting the world and turn to the Divine as your ally in the struggle of life.

If you truly have faith, you will stick it out and you can receive immediate help if you breathe deeply when anxiety and strife appears around you. Pray and meditate every morning without fail before starting your day. In the evening pray and meditate, chant and study. Offer yourself and your troubles to the Divine and begin to see your acts as service to that Supreme Being and do not see yourself as a miserable weak being. Have you not understood you proceed from a Divine source and is that not the highest power? So what does that mean about you? You may not feel it now but it is there and you must have faith that you can and will achieve it. Then you must begin to act like that and rely on that and have faith in that. No person with true faith has ever been denied the grace of the Divine. Therefore, take heart and you will be purified and your teacher will be made known to you. So work on purifying first, and do not look for something you are not ready for since you will not be able to make use of it this time; for now your teacher is your Self within, and your trainer is your boss. They will teach you patience, forbearance, forgiveness, understanding and finally dispassion and peace (hetep). Then you will be ready to receive your teacher; as the Kamitan proverb says: "When the ears of the student are ready to hear, then come the lips to fill them with wisdom."

Mystical Answers to the Important Questions of Life

In the meantime, keep reading and doing whatever spiritual disciplines you understand to the best of your ability. Then, after a time you will begin to understand what spirituality is all about. Then you will begin to understand what it means to be an initiate and to have an authentic teacher and who that person is.

May the Divine shower you with the glories of peace and purity

Peace and Blessings!

Sebai MAA

Conversation with God

Question: Why shouldn't I kill myself?

Udja Sebai Maa,

Given what I think I know at this point in my so called life; Why can't I kill myself and escape all this madness at this point and return to my original self and home? I really appreciate all your guidance and time and there will be no more questions after this one.

Peace

Answer

Greetings,

Questions are the duty of an aspirant and answers are the duty of the preceptor. So if you refrain from questions, you close the door to learning and wisdom and trap yourself in the prison of your own ignorant thoughts. One of the biggest mistakes an aspirant can make is: believing that they *know* what it's all about or that it is inappropriate to ask questions. In a proper teacher-student relationship, the teacher determines when the student knows and not the other way around (see the book *Initiation Into Egyptian Yoga*). There are two forms of knowing. The first is intellectual and the second is intuitional. The first one is far easier than the second and easier for those who are intellectual. However, that intellect capacity is usually fraught with egoism and therefore the knowledge is based on an egoistic matrix, that is, the knowledge is related to the ego and its thoughts, feelings and desires but most of all, its paradigm. Specifically, the result of the ruminations of such a person always revert to the basic erroneous foundational idea: "I am an individual and so how do I figure out the world in accordance with my conception of it." Such a person is not easily swayed and they usually become a self-willed aspirant who ends up telling the teacher how things are instead of the other way around. In such a personality, the intellectual prowess has inflated the ego due to lack of humility and deep reflection beyond the ego nature. The question itself denotes egoism, so there is lack of higher, intuitional "knowing."

Firstly, if you "think" you know, you do not know. At noon do you wonder if the sun is shining or is it dark like midnight? No, there is no need to wonder. In intuitional knowing, wisdom is not a quandary but a certainty and is self-evident (not requiring faith).

Second, if you truly understood the philosophy, you would not entertain foolish notions such as "killing oneself" and "escaping" or "madness." Why? There is more to know, about self and spirit. That is your mission in life and the goal of all true aspirants.

It may seem hard for you to believe at this moment that your situation is not abiding, but consider that you were not always miserable all your life, and even now you are not

Mystical Answers to the Important Questions of Life

always miserable. Consider that you were not miserable when you were born or when you were asleep earlier today. Neither misery nor happiness (pleasure) are endemic conditions of mind; they must be remembered. This is why a person feels peaceful when they first wake up in the morning, for a few moments, until the memories of why they think they are miserable rush in, and the feelings related to those memories and thought processes are not far behind. A person may have lost a loved one and may be resting in peace, but if another person who knew the deceased comes in and reminds them of the dead person, then the memories rush in along with the sentimental feelings of loss which produce the thoughts of sorrow all over again. It is a form of self-torment based on ignorance about the nature of Spirit (there is no death) and sentimental attachment (feeling of closeness or separation or loss of the physical personality).

So the notion that life is completely and totally miserable is incorrect. If there are other people in the world who are not miserable, it means that misery is not abiding. So why are you experiencing it? That is the question! Could it be that the misery you are experiencing has something to do with your thoughts, actions and outlook on life? The answer is yes! Both misery and happiness are functions of ignorance or wisdom; the more ignorance, the more misery and the more wisdom the more happiness! This means that you can change your life from miserable to blissful depending on your understanding about life and your actions and feelings based on that understanding.

Therefore, stop entertaining notions about killing yourself wait and investigate, delve deeper into the philosophy, make a plan to implement the teachings and see what happens. Make it a scientific project. Experiment with your personality; practice detachment, dispassion, study of the wisdom teachings, practice devotion, do good deeds, meditate, as prescribed. Then see if you remain miserable or not. If you practice properly and make the proper changes in your life, you will find a wider world and a higher perspective that the emotions that are clouding your intellect are not currently allowing you to see. When you discover that, you will say to yourself "wow, I used to believe in that? I used to do that? I used to allow that to bother me?" And you will also say, "I am now free of that ignorant way of life that leads to misery."

Realize, from a mystical-spiritual perspective, there is no killing one can do, for what is killed reincarnates, and then what will you do? Kill the body again? And to what end? There is no escape from the madness because one has created it; it travels with you from life to life in the form of unconscious impressions left behind from previous thoughts, desires and actions (*ariu-* or karma). So suicide only postpones its end. But there is an answer to the problem: get rid of ignorance and you will be free from misery! There is no returning to the "original Self" until there is an end to ignorance of egoism and there is experience of the Absolute, which transcends all mentations (activities of mind) and quandaries. Realize that your emotions and pain are not absolute realities. So if you wait and patiently seek for the truth there will be an end then. Better to forge ahead NOW and work through the mystery of life; figure out why there is such sorrow in life and how to overcome it. When that knowing of all knowings is known, then there will be an end to sorrow and there will be no need to escape. Then you will be a true servant of the Divine, a saint roaming the earth as a beacon of light for all who ponder the way, a balm for all

Conversation with God

injuries of the heart and mind, a joy to those who cry and an answer to those who wonder why. The philosophy alone will not help you to completely make the changes enjoined here. So the sages of old have always said: *"Seekest thou God, thou seekest for the Beautiful. One is the Path that leadeth unto It - Devotion joined with Wisdom."* Allow Divine Worship to come into your spiritual practice, do the rituals and chants, utter the hymns, do good deeds in the world along with asking questions and reading. Then the mind develops humility and the ego subsides. Then the mind is capable of truly becoming enlightened. In case you wonder, wisdom is the result of knowledge applied in action, which yields wise experience. Thus, knowing in the intuitional sense is an experience that transcends mind. In such a place there is no birthing, no killing, no escaping and no bondage and that is what we call Nehast, the Great awakening. May you attain that ultimate goal! We end here with two pertinent Ancient Egyptian Proverbs:

"To suffer, is a necessity entailed upon your nature,
would you prefer that miracles should protect you from its lessons or shalt you repine,
because it happened unto you, when lo it happened unto all?
Suffering is the golden cross upon which the rose of the Soul unfolds."

"Though all men suffer fated things, those led by reason (guided by the intellect),
do not endure suffering with the rest;
but' since they've freed themselves from viciousness,
not being bad, they do not suffer bad.
Though having thought fornication or murder but not having committed these,
the Mind-led man will suffer just as though he had committed fornication,
and though he be no murderer, as though he had committed murder
because there was will to commit these things."

Peace and Blessings!

Sebai MAA

Mystical Answers to the Important Questions of Life

Question: challenged by the world in difficult ways, will this change?

Seba Maa.

Greetings, I pray that all is well with you and Seba Dja. I continually thank you and Seba Dja for being lights in the world. Those of us who want a spiritual guide are very thankful to have the both of you in the world.

I was initiated while at the Solstice Festival. I recall you indicating that we as new Asr's (initiates) would be challenged by the world in difficult ways. I am currently going through what appears to be difficult times.

It is interesting to have the world bombarded me with these difficult moments. I have made a conscious effort to detach from the world. I did not think I needed the world to beat me up anymore to let me know that looking for happiness within it is an illusion. I have believed that for quite some time. What gives? Is this a sign of progress? If so, will future progress be a reflection of future difficult times? If not, what is happening?

Any advice?

Answer

Greetings,

Take heart, the world always changes so circumstances always change. That is a problem but also an opportunity to correct errors and improve life. However, for those who are ignorant, caught in the illusion of life, they may not change or may change very slowly and suffer greatly in the mean time. In order to take advantage of the world's changeable nature there are two mechanisms that you must take care of in order to be free from the world. They are not necessarily to be handled in a sequential order but rather in a simultaneous manner. The first is the external action; the second is the internal. The external world must be understood as an illusion but this does not mean that it is to be ignored. You must apply the teachings of Maat in order to bring balance to your external life in the world. Then you will reduce the anxiety due to worldly entanglements. This frees your mind up to handle the worthwhile aspects of life in an efficient and fruitful manner.

Secondly, the internal world. You must begin to develop internal peace and spiritual strength. These come when an aspirant reduces the pressure of egoistic desires and these are reduced when ignorance about the Self is reduced. Desire leads to frustration because no worldly desire can be truly fulfilled. Therefore rely on the Spirit, wherein there is all fulfillment. Learn to handle the world but also becoming dispassionate and detached from the world, with patience and perseverance. The key is to be steady in your spiritual practices and studies even as you struggle in the world and eventually your struggle becomes a challenge and eventually you become the champion. Difficulty in dealing with

Conversation with God

the world comes from handling the world as if it could be fixed to the liking of the ego's desires. This is the ignorant path. Pain and suffering exists for the purpose of pushing us on the righteous path. So there is some good in suffering and indeed it is necessary for the evolution of the soul. Recognize that you are suffering and miserable but do not wallow in your misery; you are not misery, but are only experiencing this temporarily due to conditions you created. Thus, do not waste time complaining or blaming yourself or the world. Get to the source of the problem: ignorance-itself. The world is like a brick wall; ever tried to push against a brick wall? It goes nowhere and it requires more effort and leads to frustration. It is better to study the wall, to understand it and the futility of pushing against it. Learn to get around it, to get to the other side by sidestepping the obstacle which you have placed there yourself. The world is neither your heaven nor your hell, but as long as you treat it so it becomes so, for as long as you struggle with it. Learn and practice the teaching that allows you to circumvent the misery of life. But you will accomplish little without patience and perseverance. Perseverance means relentless practice of the teachings and disciplines. Follow all instructions. Work to replace chaos in your life with Maat. Be the best shemsu (follower) of the teaching given by the teacher. Have faith in yourself and in the teacher and in the Divine and you will surely succeed!

Peace and Blessings!

Sebai MAA

Mystical Answers to the Important Questions of Life

Question: How can I deal with my hateful boss?

Hello, I have a boss who seems to hate me for no reason. It seems I can't do anything well. He seems to argue with me every chance he gets. I try to explain to him I have done what I thought I was supposed to do but he does not listen. He does not treat my coworkers like this. Every day I go home thinking about the arguments and frustrations of the day and I can't relax. What should I do?

Answer

Greetings,

Human relationships are often complicated and unintelligible, that is until we realize that there is most often a deeper basis for them. For example, why do people fall in love with the people they do but not with others? Why do some people like vanilla and others chocolate? Why do some people like to live in certain areas with certain kinds of people versus others? Why are there some people who do not care about such things at all?

As a human being travels through time and space and many lives, certain tendencies develop into likes and dislikes in accordance with their *ariu* (karmic experiences). Sometimes they may link up with other souls that have similar interests. At other times they may repudiate other souls with dissimilar interests. In any case, souls tend to have communal experiences. For example, everyone living in the United States of America is having a similar experience based on similar desires, and therefore they will have similar results and consequences to the common pursuits. However, within that general vast context there are individual variations. Some people within the group like each other and others dislike each other, due to individual experiences with other individuals. Some people may be having internal issues that have nothing to do with the other people. Yet, in most cases, even when you may not have done anything wrong you may feel another person's wrath due to their own internal problems or because deep down at the soul level (unconscious mind) they may "remember" you did something to them in a previous life. This memory does not occur at the conscious level, but rather at the unconscious; it is more of an unexplainable feeling rather than a conscious thought. You have perhaps had that experience of walking into a room of strangers and meeting someone you instantly disliked just by looking at them?

Regardless of the reason for the strife, it is important to take steps to extricate oneself from the cycle of conflict because if you do not, whether you are right or wrong, you will end up continuing the strife in this life and the next, and the one after that, and so on.

> *"Seek to perform your duties to your highest ability,*
> *this way your actions will be blameless."*

Conversation with God

-Ancient Egyptian proverb

Firstly, consider that your boss may be right; you may not be doing your job to your best ability. If that is the case, make the improvements. Then, if he continues to be annoyed with you simply acknowledge that and rest content in the fact you have done your best and that is all that can be required of anyone. If you have made the improvements or if you think you are not at fault read on...

> *"If you want to have perfect conduct, to be free from evil, then above all guard against the vice of greed. Greed is a grievous sickness that has no cure. There is no treatment for it. It embroils fathers, mothers and the brothers of the mother. It parts the wife from the husband. Greed is a compound of all the evils; a bundle of all hateful things. That person endures whose rule is rightness, who walks a straight line, for that person will leave a legacy by such behavior. On the other hand, the greedy has no tomb."*
> -Ancient Egyptian proverb

If you have done your duty to your best ability and if you do not engage in egoistic fights with anyone, realize that your effort will be noticed in contrast with that of the person accusing you. In time, they are the ones who will be called out and seen for their error. So be patient and they will be forced to change or they will be replaced.

> *God is ever in his perfection,*
> *Man is ever in his failure.*
> *"Truth protects from fear."*
> -Ancient Egyptian proverb

Consider that as bad as things may seem to be they could be worse; you could have a more demanding person on top of you. There is no such thing as perfection and that pursuit makes many people stressed out, anxious or overly demanding. However, sometimes the job is not the issue; there may be problems at home, other anxieties affecting them that come out as demands on subordinates, you. So that seems to put undue pressure on you.

In addition to what has been said, you may also try to apply the injunction of hearing in order to create good will.

> *"They who hear are beloved of GOD. Hearing creates good will.*
> -Ancient Egyptian proverb

When a person is honestly heard, they feel more favorable towards the listener and towards the world, and if not understood at least they feel accepted and respected. That respect allows them to lower their defenses and feel more secure in the relationship so there is less need to attack. More wisdom for handling such personalities comes to us from the Ancient Egyptian sage Ptahotep:

Mystical Answers to the Important Questions of Life

"A person in distress wants to pour out their heart even more than they want their case to be won. If you stop the person who is pleading, that person will say "why does this judge reject my plea?" Of course, not all that one pleads can be granted, but a good hearing soothes the heart. The means for getting a true and clear explanation is to listen with kindness."
-Teachings of Ptahotep

Make sure those who are vexed with you know that you respect them as human beings and that you have given them a fair hearing, not that you just listen and then disregard their speech. One technique for this is paraphrasing. When your boss is telling you about your work, even if it is criticism about your work, before you respond to what he is saying, to defend yourself or otherwise, first, validate that he has been heard. To do this, paraphrase what he just said to you as impartially as you can (i.e., without tone or voice inflections to indicate resentment on your part, and without adding extra words to indicate your upsetness and disagreement). So, for example, if you boss says, "You folded these towels worse than I could imagine." You would say something to the effect of, "so, you are saying that you feel the towels are folded improperly." Your boss would then say, "Yes…" and maybe go on with more criticism, or "no, that is not what I said," and he would restate his statement again, which you can again attempt to paraphrase. Just keep paraphrasing by repeating back to him (with understanding…i.e., showing that you understand his perspective) what he is telling you, until he has finished what he has to say, and has paused for your response (after your last paraphrasing of his statement). Now, you can respond to what he has said. Your boss will have felt heard and validated, and this in and of itself will likely make him let down his defenses and be more relaxed. There are also communication techniques for responding in a manner that reduces, if not eliminates conflict; one such technique is referred to as "I" message.

"If you meet a disputant who is more powerful than you, fold your arms and bend your back. Confrontation will not make them agree with you. Disregard their evil speech. Your self control will match their evil utterances and people will call them ignoramuses."
-Teachings of Ptahotep

There is a great law of the universe, the opposites of creation; it manifests as the two genders, the opposites of direction (up, down-etc.), here-there, etc., but also hard and soft. In Kemetic myth, the archetypal opposites are Aset (wisdom) and Set (egoism). If someone is acting egoistically towards you, you should act wise instead of egoistic along with them. Wisdom here means balance, peace and silence, while the other person is unbalanced, loud, and unruly. As they say, "it takes two to tango," so if one is soft and one is hard, there will be a neutralization of the situation. If both are hard, there will be discord, strife, violence and escalation. When there is confrontation, there is also erratic shallow breathing, due to the disruption of the life force energy of the body. When it comes time for you to be "hard," this means determined, steadfast in the teachings, displaying indomitable will in standing for your rights, dignity and self-respect – but that does not require violence unless you are being physically attacked. It requires determination and steadfastness in the face of those leveling unrighteous accusations or demanding unrighteousness from you in the form of participation in an unrighteous deed or being a part of an unrighteous altercation. So if others breathe erratically and shallowly, you breathe rhythmically and deeply.

When others speak loud you speak soft; when others throw things you dodge them or catch them and set them down gently; when others speak rudely, you reply kindly. When others speak softly, and if they need your insight, then you speak firmly; when others are hurting, you be the balm, the comfort for their hurt; try to be like the initiate who is spoken about in the Pert M Hru text who says: *There are sick, very ill people. I go to them, I spit on the arms, I set the shoulder, and I cleanse them.* This teaching may also be thought of as maleness and femaleness; this is an aspect of the practice of what is called *tantra* yoga. Each individual, whether male or female, has both male and female energies, and thus, the capacity to act "male" or "female." Males tend to have more male energy (emitting, putting out), and females tend to have more female energy (receptive, receiving), but this is not absolute. An aspirant is to balance the male and female energies within themselves, thus having the capacity to both be receptive and emitting, as the situation requires; this is accomplished through the practice of disciplines of Shedy.

Thus, when others are being "male," that is, "emitting, putting out," you can be "female," that is, "receptive, receiving." When others are being female (receptive, receiving), you can be male (emitting, putting out). If there is proper male-female interaction from this tantric perspective, a "joining" can occur in which the two give birth to understanding.

"Every gesture, is a world to be mastered."
-Ancient Egyptian proverb

But also realize that whatever happens to one in one's life, it has the sanction of one's ariu. Nothing can happen to one unless it is in line with one's ariu (which is based one one's previous actions in this and previous lives). Therefore, whatever the apparent cause, you are getting payback for your previous actions of this life or a previous one. The thing to do is make use of that pressure to train your personality to not react and to be detached and dispassionate while performing your duties and taking care of your business. Then you will overcome the necessity to experience that again in the future. Things always change. At some point in the future your boss will change or will be replaced, or you will be the boss or you will move on to a better place/job. In the mean time, focus on your actions, seeking to master your work but realizing there is no absolute perfection, but seeking mastery is a mastering road that leads to sufficient purity, peace and wisdom to survive in the world and attain the goal of life, spiritual enlightenment, and emancipation. That is the perfection to be sought, the perfect knowledge of who you are beyond a miserable worker getting bothered by your boss.

However, the understanding of working off past ariu should not be taken to mean that one should stay in a position of abuse because it's one's ariu/karma. Eighty percent of the time, what needs to change is one's attitude in handling relationships, as has been described. However, 10% of the time, one needs to remove oneself from the situation, especially when it is not spiritually, mentally, or physically healthy or safe to remain there, either because the other person is abusive, or one's own capacity to handle the situation is overwhelmed to the point that one cannot even attempt to apply the techniques discussed.

Peace and Blessings!
Sebai MAA

Government, Economics, Social Order, Social Justice and the importance of ethics? Handling social and Economic Problems

Mystical Answers to the Important Questions of Life

Question: What is our responsibility in assisting others who are in need?

Udja,

Given the recent disaster of the hurricane hitting Louisiana can we do something for victims of hurricane Katrina as a group? What is our responsibility in assisting others as a Kemetic religious tradition?

Thank you

Answer

As Neterians it is incumbent upon us to serve humanity. The Pertmhru text states that Neterians should give to the poor and downtrodden in three important areas: Food and water, shelter and opportunity. Therefore, certainly it is appropriate to assist the Hurricane victims and the victims of any other disasters or misfortunes. Help should be given to the extent of one's capacity, feeling that one is acting for the Divine and not for one's ego gratification. It is ok to feel good about giving but the higher way is to also understand that Maat is working through you in the giving process. As the sun serves without asking for rewards or special mentions. In our tradition we are provided by the sages with three important injunctions about our duty to help others:

give bread to the hungry, water to the thirsty, clothes to the clotheless and a boat to those who were shipwrecked.

Chapter 33 of Papyrus Ani.

There are three fundamental human needs: food and drink, shelter and opportunity to move and progress. these may also be considered basic human rights because all require them to survive and therefore none have a right to hoard or withhold them since those who have them would not like them to be withdrawn; therefore it is the duty for those who have to share when there is a need but sharing can be also interpreted as sharing the means to gain these through knowledge, technology, etc. As they give, Neterians can also utter prayers of well being thus:

Htp di si Neter iri ankh udja senab.
"Peace offering is given so that the Divine may grant life, vitality and health."

Up to here the answer has been given for neophytes and mid-level aspirants. Below is a more advanced teaching- in addition to the above but for more advanced aspirants.

Conversation with God

As the neophyte must reflect on serving so too the advanced aspirant should reflect upon how best to serve. Advanced as well as neophyte aspirants should serve humanity. However, consider that out of the three Maatian service injunctions, the giving of opportunity is most important of all, once the basic needs are taken care of. Thus, in this sense opportunity is the will and awareness to seek what is best for oneself. Is it best to live in a place where there is danger when a well-known and expected disaster will hit? Is it right to assist those who live unrighteously so they may be facilitated? What about smokers, thrill seekers, meat eaters, etc? Who should be helped and how? What the people really need is spiritual strength, strength of will and wisdom to not live as weak personalities dependent upon the good graces of those who have a different agenda. Therefore, working to enlighten people is the highest form of giving because it will allow them to avoid misfortunes. So advancing aspirants should give in this way all the time in order to help people steer clear of disasters. The greatest disaster is living a life of misery followed by death and reincarnation and then experiencing more of the last.

Next, consider that this type of misery, that is so widely touted recently because it is close to home, is actually experienced perennially by people around the world and in our own communities. Why then is this special? What about the pain and suffering due to lack of medical treatment because the society refuses to institute universal medical care like all other "developed" nations? What about the thousands who die daily of malnutrition, the millions of women who are mistreated daily, the thousands who die of needless wars, etc.- all over the world? What about the Neterian culture- is that prospering or is it suffering and what is being given to that, to those who are trying to follow that? These disasters affect more people than the tsunami of 2004 or the hurricane of 2005.

Nevertheless, occasions such as these should give aspirants pause to consider that while most of the time life seems sustainable, workable and hopeful, the ultimate end is death and destruction of the body and its seemingly important concerns. Thus, such events should promote growing repudiation of and dispassion for the world and human culture and its hubris. Aspirants should feel the pressure of Sekhmit's paws on their heels and redouble their efforts to provide for their own safety, prosperity and enlightenment instead of living deluded lives like the ignorant masses. Aspirants should promote increasing humility and prioritize their lives according to the real goal of life, realizing that disasters can hit at any time. So even as they work to promote sustainable culture and the perpetuation of life they should recognize that life in the world is only a temporary visit to the realm of time and space and therefore it cannot be the ultimate goal of life, nor should they squander their resources to help those who persist in traveling towards the ravine or helping governments that have plenty of money for the rich and for war and should be forced to redirect that to saving its own people. Realize that the calamities of the quagmire in Iraq and the disaster in the Gulf Coast that the United States has experienced happened for that purpose and to awaken its citizens to the hollowness of its power and ingenuity and the hypocrisy of the capitalist ideal as well as the lingering disease of racism that still exists. If people give too much and assist in those disasters the government will be free to carry on its deluded though incompetent rampage around the world promoting some pseudo new world order. One way to donate is spending time to pressure the government people to do what is right for all citizens. That may actually

Mystical Answers to the Important Questions of Life

produce more benefit than any individual or group donation. Remember that football games and tennis tournaments and movies are still played and in fact never stopped throughout these crises; because we must go on? Why, so that the economy is sustained? All should drop what they are doing to help those in need and put the economy on hold, but the fact that that is not done shows the priority of the society.

Furthermore, consider that the misery people experience is of their own fashioning through *ari*. It is mitigated also through *ari*. If you are able to help someone in need it was because his or her *ari* allowed it. If you cannot reach someone who is drowning it is because their *ari* did not allow it, etc. Therefore, advancing aspirants should develop detachment and dispassion even as they extend the helping hand to relive pain and suffering. They should not get caught up in the pain or happiness of others but they should promote peace and sanity as a foundation for all to pursue true peace and prosperity which can only be discovered in that glorious place called yanrutf.

As someone who lived through the eye of Hurricane Hugo and who felt the calling of the Neterchert and who lost everything I can say that from that nothingness there is the inevitable movement to grow and in that, opportunity. So even from death and destruction there is the capacity to grow by learning that there are more important things than material possessions but more importantly, there are more important things than life. Those who have suffered, do suffer, and will suffer will learn that lesson in time. In the end none die and none are born, they only experience. So there is no need to feel sad at the death or suffering of others but rather compassion and effort to assist them are appropriate.

It is natural for evolved human beings and aspirants to desire to comfort others and heal others- it is a normal capacity of healthy human beings. The difference between that and mystics is that mystics do not attach egoistic or sentimental feelings to it, just like the sun. As the sun shines always, mystics shine always with the glory of wisdom; that is true charity, other forms being only limited forms. Also, mystics feel that all the time and for everyone and not just when a crisis hits or for those in their own neighborhood or family. As the sun they shine and they give warmth of comfort and peace because that is who they are and that is God's compassion working through them to elevate and advance souls- that is god's love expressing through them; Let it express through you thus also.

When giving, acknowledged a person's desires but look to their need and serve their needs. The need is a divine right and the desire might be an egoistic expression. Be a watcher, promote peace, have compassion but also act and give with wisdom and then the world will be set right but most of all you will remain in peace and you will reach enlightenment.

Peace and Blessings!
Sebai MAA

Conversation with God

Question: Is Ancient Egypt the source of the caste system and capitalism?

Greetings,

This question comes from a discussion with someone who was regurgitating some information they read regarding the state of the current capitalist society. It was suggested that the Ancient Egyptians hierarchical way of living and worship was the predecessor of the caste system and of current elitist capitalist exploitation.

While I believed that this is a misunderstanding I didn't really know how to respond.

Could you please help me clarify this? Thank you.

Peace

Answer

Greetings,

Such a comment as you have relayed may be similar to someone comparing the Ancient Egyptian Sage Ptahotep to a personality like President George W. Bush Jr., the former a philosopher, sage and humanitarian, and the latter an avowed "war President." These kinds of statements denote ignorance and lack of diligence in reflection and study of history and philosophy while making assertions that are at best infantile, and at worst dangerous to one's own welfare and that of one's culture. For, knowing history prevents others as well as one's own egoistic notions from "pulling the wool" over one and enslaving one. Nevertheless, such questions are to be answered if asked in the lecture hall by sincere aspirants, however, as you have brought them to our attention I will reply briefly, though I would not entertain such otherwise.

In contrast, the two cultures follow different philosophies of government. While it is true that Ancient Egypt made use of a hierarchical system of government, it is not true to say that Ancient Egypt had an absolute monarchy like Europe.[45] It is also incorrect to say that Ancient Egypt had a capitalist system.[46] The Ancient Egyptian government is often referred to as a Theocracy, but a more accurate term would be "Ethiocracy" [Ethical-Theocracy]. In fact, the pre-Late-period (Late period is when Egypt was conquered by Asians and Europeans) system of government in Ancient Egypt, going back to the Old Kingdom Period (5000 years B.C.E), may be termed "**hierocracy**" ({hiero = clergy} -

---

[45] See the book *Egyptian Mysteries Vol. 3, DVD Lecture How to Build a Spiritual (not necessarily religious) Civilization*
[46] See the book *Death of American Empire*

Mystical Answers to the Important Questions of Life

government by priests or religious ministers), since the leaders were priests and priestesses and the Per-aah (Pharaoh) was considered to be a priest(ess) as well.

In terms of economics, Ancient Egyptian Maat philosophy required a socialistic arrangement.[47] One of the reasons for their success (lasting for thousands of years) is that the Ancient Egyptian culture was founded and governed by an ethical philosophy that discouraged and prevented government excesses and economic frauds, unlike a capitalist market economy or fiat currencies that promote fraud, depletion of resources and a "winner takes all" mentality that promotes corruption and vice. Ancient Egyptian government followed Maat[48] as its foundation and the concept of "Heka-Hekat" (Shepherd-flock) –it is the concept from which the Christian usage of the appellation of "Shepherd" for Jesus came. Maat philosophy, when applied to social order, demands the Per-aah was the Shepherd (Heka) who had a fiduciary relationship to the people (Hekat). The Per-aah was responsible primarily for, but not limited to, taking care of the basic needs of the people (food, clothing, shelter/opportunity)[49] and protecting the Holy Land (Kamit-Ancient Egypt), which included safeguarding the land from pollution.

As far as has been demonstrated by USA and European history, the current capitalist globalization system of present day Europe and the USA is an evolution of the previous systems of government and economics (conquest, enslavement, colonialism, serfdom), which has the main goal of protecting the wealth of the rich and if necessary, using people as cannon fodder to accomplish that goal.[50] The current system is not concerned with protection of the land if protecting it is an obstruction to profits. The USA government began as an aristocracy (a group or class considered {by themselves} superior to others.), and developed to an oligarchy (a wealthy class that controls a government.), which is what we have today.[51]

At no time in recorded history is there any record of aristocracies or plutocracies operating in Ancient Egypt- except when dominated by Asians or Europeans. Such forms of government would have been contradictory to the foundation of Maat, the concept of *Heka-Hekat* and the code of the clergy who were after all the true power. Therefore, the notion that Ancient Egypt was the foundation of modern western capitalism, or modern western aggression and imperialism must be rejected absolutely. While there is evidence that the Ancient Egyptians recognized different ethnicities and hues of skin they did not assign those differences to a concept of race or caste. This is akin to recognizing people who are of different occupations, doctors, lawyers, carpenters, etc. There is no evidence that the well-defined social divisions of Ancient Egypt, royalty, farmers, civil servants, army, clergy, were used as rigid "castes," preventing people from moving between them or intermarrying, like the practices of the Indian or the European racist social systems. If anything, there are contrary evidences from Ancient Egyptian writings and letters demonstrating interaction between all peoples and aspiration for good positions from all

---

[47] See the book *Death of American Empire,* See the book *African Origins*
[48] See the book *Introduction to Maat Philosophy,* See the book *Egyptian Mysteries Vol. 3*
[49] See the book *Egyptian Book of the Dead*
[50] See the book *Death of American Empire*
[51] ibid

Conversation with God

segments of society. There is no evidence of apartheid and no evidence of racism in Ancient Egypt or in ancient Greece for that matter. Again, there is contrary evidence demonstrating intermarriage and absence of any notion of skin color as a criterion of human worth or as a basis for social segregation. People from Nubia as well as Asia and Europe, even when taken as slaves through war, were accepted and "naturalized" (accepted/adopted) as Ancient Egyptians unlike the modern Western and Arabic culture that forces perpetual segregation of peoples by the color of skin, favoring rule by the lighter skinned members of the population. While the caste system of India may have originated as a means to organize the population, it apparently devolved into a system of segregation by skin color. Later on in the Western countries and the United States of America it further devolved as a system of slavery and domination of one "race" over all others. Nothing like that has been observed in Ancient Egypt. After all, racism is a form of mental illness, a product of extreme egoism, fear and greed caused by spiritual ignorance, stress and unethical unfettered desires for power and pleasure-seeking. Additionally, there is no evidence that Ancient Egyptian culture, when controlled by Ancient Egyptians and their traditional governing systems, initiated or perpetrated wars of aggression or conquest, only self-defense.

While it is one of the greatest failings of human nature, the ability to develop illusory belief systems of one's own or agree with those of others who can speak well or with influential arguments without presenting any evidences is both breathtaking and damming. Such behavior is not allowed even in authentic universities – except for those places that want to perpetuate dogmas at the expense of truth, like schools that teach Creationism as an event that occurred no more than 6000 years ago even though there is ample evidence to the contrary. Thus, an aspirant should learn the difference between opinions and wisdom. Wisdom is based on knowledge gained, tempered by experiences learned. Wisdom is valuable as it is backed by the evidence of the lives of the wise and their substantiation of the facts and the authentication of their proven insights. Opinions are based on egoistic desires and partial or total ignorance which may or may not be influenced by others or misunderstanding experiences in the world. Opinions are worthless-without proof. For this reason, potential aspirants or honest seekers are admonished to come in contact with authentic teachers.

The present question we are dealing with here falls in the realm of history, but I am not aware of any history class which would make such an assertion as your acquaintance has made, and if they did I wonder what evidences they would present to back it up? Sometimes people are ignorant because they never had the opportunity to study history or were never instructed on the importance of history, and also how to discover the truth through primary sources instead of relying on books written by peoples from other cultures who have a vested interest in maintaining the ignorance of the masses or reflecting some cultures in less than admirable light, or from television documentaries designed to cause controversy, greater viewership and higher profits. Sometimes people prefer to engage in prejudice or bias or outright willful ignorance (purposely not investigating) so that they may retain their preconceptions and thereby not have to come to terms with their own ignorance and change their belief system AND their behavior. Whatever the case may be, such ignorance continues to be perpetuated and conflated with

Mystical Answers to the Important Questions of Life

history and social studies books presently used in schools. Therefore, our role in countering such lack of knowledge is a substantial task, but only those who are truly interested in wisdom will hearken to the answer when it is given and proven. Thus, we are forced to reserve our energies for such ones who display the qualities of virtuous seeking and diligent aspiration for self-discovery and self-mastery.

Peace and Blessings!
Sebai MAA

Conversation with God

Question: What Should Neterians do about Racial Violence and Suffering?

Are Neterian's to observe our ethic group being murdered "Wholesale" using many methods by the "so called" elite and do nothing or is that an illusion also? I am requesting your insight on this issue as to why the onslaught of killing is being committed on the black or darker poor uneducated people by the white "lighter" rich educated people in time and space and what can be done to stop this type of activity?

Answer

GREETINGS,

Neterians like others are sensitive to and can be affected by the realities of the world of time and space. However, just because there are realities to be acknowledged it does not necessarily follow that those realities must be accepted or confronted either physically, mentally or psychically. Consider that when you sleep you are confronted with many realities and why do you not act on them when you wake up? The answer is because though they are real they are not true. Something that is real but not true may also be referred to as an illusion. Why? Because the reality is of the nature of a transient dream. Yet, even in a dream people can suffer until they wake up. In the case mentioned here the dream is of race, there are no races, but yet people act as if there are; in reality all are the same souls encased in watery containers [bodies]. Not all Neterians are of a particular ethnic group but all do belong to the same "race", the human race, which originated in Africa, and should feel universal human compassion for the suffering, and righteous indignation towards those who cause pain, when that response is appropriate. So Neterians should work to promote the welfare of all human beings and all nature. The other illusion is that of death, there is no death, but from a relative standpoint there can be suffering and who wants to suffer or see others suffer? Perhaps sadists and the psychopaths but definitely all of the ones who have intensified their egoistic beliefs to the extent of caring only about their desires and not the welfare of others, who they see as different and repugnant. Nevertheless, to the extent it is possible to relieve pain and suffering and ignorance it is appropriate to assist whenever possible to alleviate pain and suffering-this is an expression of ethical culture and divine conscience; so we are also instructed to do by the *Pert M Heru* teachings, especially Chap 33 but also the Sages of the wisdom texts exhort us to extend a helping hand. One can help physically, mentally or psychically depending on the situation; physically through physical action, mentally though thoughts and elevating reasoning; and psychically through harnessing subtle energies that move cosmic forces and peoples hearts. But that help is to be tempered with wisdom and also we cannot completely fight other peoples battles for them since as soon as we stop they will again falter and fall under the misery of life all over again. So, what are we to do? We are to assist others to help themselves, to help us all, working to teach them, working to provide the necessities of life for all and opportunity to succeed; we are

Mystical Answers to the Important Questions of Life

to promote justice. But realize that in order to be successful in changing the world of human society our efforts need to be combined with the efforts of others and if there are insufficient numbers the change will occur very slowly and many people will suffer in the mean time. Nevertheless, to the extent that people suffer before we can relieve their pain, that suffering is dictated by their delusions about the world be it from past actions or present ones and fated by their destiny due to their actions of the past. So, it is mandated by their soul; thus we should feel compassion but not feel anger, hatred or depression over it since it is in the Divine plan; and one day it will end and all will wake up. But in the mean time we should render assistance with this philosophy in mind and we will remain free of resentment, hatred, fear and depression so our actions will be more dynamic and powerful to help those who need uplifting. Many times some people of an ethnic group, that has been wronged, understandably take to resentment, anger, hatred and violence, which perpetuates the cycle of vice, ignorance and war. While there are some situations where war may be justifiable or appropriate [even by Kemetic standards] it is also real that there are situations where war is futile or impossible or undesirable and reason and or civil disobedience are a more plausible solution, and saving that, surrender is not an option. However, in a struggle such as this, where most people are overwhelmed with and debilitated by their own ignorance, desires, resentments, etc. it would be impossible to organize them for a war, for example, such as was depicted in the movie [*The Spook Who Sat By The Door*], so one should not expect the massive torrent of ignorance in the world to respond positively to the wisdom of life but one's mission should be to radiate health, right reasoning and peace as an example; one should provide righteous speech to teach by word and one should provide pure thoughts, desires and prayers to influence the environments, hearts and minds of others about the way of peace, light and truth that leads to harmony, reconciliation and enlightenment.

Peace and Blessings!
Sebai MAA

Conversation with God

Question: Should I stay in the Military?

Peace,

I am a 17 year veteran of the U.S. military. I have been very conflicted by being in the military and the role of the military. This conflict within has increased 10 fold since the invasion and illegal occupation of Iraq. The military has been a stable source of income for my family and me over the past 17 years. I am a single parent of three, and with each reenlistment I have justified doing so to take care of my family. I can no longer use this excuse as justification for reenlisting given what I know and how I feel about what is going on. The conflict still rages because I am so close to retirement (in three years). However, I really feel spiritually obligated to act.

I understand that the U.S. military is used to oppress peoples all around the world. And that the wealth/luxuries we have here (USA) are in direct proportion to the poverty experienced in so called third world nations. I loathe the military even though it has put food on the table for my family and me, and a roof over our heads. I am unable to accurately explain all of my feelings about being in the military; suffice it to say it is burdensome, restricting and conflicting. I am writing however for guidance on the matter. What are your thoughts about the military and conscious people (those striving to cultivate their spirit) in the military? Can one be conscious (aware of the interdependence and interconnection of all things) and be in the military? I would have to say anything causing this much turmoil (inner conflict) isn't good. I thank you for your time and would greatly appreciate your feedback and advice on this matter.

Thank you

Answer

Greetings,

Your conflict is understandable and you are not alone; from the reports and histories of the U.S.A., it appears that the military has been used from the beginning of the creation of the USA as an imperial force. Many people have felt compelled to be part of the military because the economics of the society allow them no other alternatives. They thus become instruments of imperial foreign policies that are also unethical, if not immoral.

The military is not unrighteous in and of itself. However, the unrighteous use of the military is <u>corrupt</u>, if not criminal. In its correct usage the military is supposed to be an instrument of protection from unethical and dangerous forces. It is not supposed to be used for conquest and domination through brainwashing and indoctrination of its members with absolute loyalty to superiors and blind obedience to any order and insensitivity to the pain they cause to peoples of other countries. It should not be a place to learn how to denigrate others and put one's own country and peoples above others. If all societies used their military for protection, for service to all human beings, not just one's own country, there would be no wars because protecting humanity means protecting all peoples from tyranny, including one's own. So the higher purpose of the military, to protect the weak and protect the country, and humanity, are noble causes. However, they cease to be noble when they are perverted by greed, selfishness, amorality, religious fanaticism and delusions of superiority.

One can be a soldier and still realize the oneness of Creation and oneness in Spirit. Yet that realization does not erase the practicality of having to deal with the ignorant, the greedy, the sociopaths, the insane, the fanatics, the amoral peoples and others whose capacity for intelligence-reasoning, compassion, love, understanding, etc., have been incapacitated through ignorance, egoism, fanaticism, etc. Just because a burglar is deep down one with God as you are does not mean you will let him come into your house, steal your stuff, rape your family and kill you! The teachings of Maat do not preclude one from self-defense, but they do prohibit attacking, provoking, and hurting others verbally, physically or mentally! So if killing occurred only under the prescribed injunctions, the killing could be justified. After all, there is no death. Souls reincarnate or move on in their journey after the death of the body.

Yet, killing is prohibited even though a person's soul moves on after death, since life is an expression of the Divine, one's very Self. Though when that awareness has been so lost by someone that they pose a threat to others and there is no other alternative in order to protect others, then such action may be justified. Otherwise such people who are extremely dull in their conscience should be confined in order to protect society. The order of the universe is to seek balance and peace (Maat). Anything that disturbs that balance will be met with a countering force in order to restore the balance. In the myth of the Asarian Resurrection, the God Set attacked and murdered Asar. He was met with the power of Heru who defeated him and subjugated him without debasing himself, and in so doing he elevated himself to his rightful place as ruler and enlightened king. Asar went on to the Netherworld and Set was displaced, subjugated and made to serve the cause he had opposed: order and truth. This should be the model for dealing with criminals or attackers. So one who attacks should be met with a countering force (defense) in order to neutralize the attack; if this protocol were followed, one would be acting as Maat's instrument and not for personal, egoistic, greedy, power-hungry reasons. Thus, one's actions cease to be binding since they are not carried out with egoistic intent, but the intent to follow the laws of the universe.

Thus, the actions taken by one who acts will lead to his/her suffering or peace here and in the hereafter, to the extent they conform to the standards of Maat, the higher ethical code of Creation itself, which is higher than the petty rules and regulations of political and military leaders, which is tainted by greed, power-seeking, and so many other corruptions. If one were to practice this discipline to its highest capacity, one could achieve the goals of the teachings even while in the military. However, if an ethical soldier would be placed in unethical situations and asked to perform unethical or immoral acts, then that army is not conducive to the higher spiritual development of its soldiers; it will produce the opposite, atrocities, jingoism, racism, all manner of corruptions, war profiteering, raping and pillaging and murdering of innocent populations and civilians

Conversation with God

along with self-destruction of the bodies and moral fiber of the army itself as well as the society it belongs to along with it.

It seems though that as you approach your retirement you are also approaching your ethical threshold whereby you can no longer sustain the delusion you have allowed yourself to support, that you are doing a good thing by taking care of your family even though the organization you are a part of has been used in an unethical or perhaps even criminal manner. In this matter, if you follow what you already know to be the righteous course you need not ask for my advice. Simply know that the skills you have already acquired can be put to uses that do not support denials (lack of facing the truth) and delusions. Trust in the Divine to close a door so that another may open and a new life may stream in. Then perhaps the world's burden will be lighter and your next generation may not follow the path of deluded automatons that become fodder for the cannons of futile neo-colonial efforts that in the end will not succeed, except to kill many people on all sides and leave the earth devastated as well as leaving hearts heartbroken even as the war profiteers make their profit and the middle class continues buying cheap junk from China.

There is a better way; that way is the path of truth that all human beings should be taken care of, protected, healed, and loved. Deviation from this fundamental rule of humanity is the source of resentments, hatreds, greed, violence and all manner of sorrow. It has been so from the beginning and will be so in the end; why not now also? If there is to be peace and harmony in the world, how will it work if we assist the forces that prevent equality and inclusion? Join with those around you who are feeling as you are and working for a better way. You already know the answer; your conflict demonstrates that but your self-delusion is causing you to quandary. My advise is do what you know you must do, what you must do you will know clearly when you decide to make your decision on the basis of truth and correctness alone and put aside your delusions and rationalizations. Nevertheless, if you need further reflections on these issues consult my book *The Death of American Empire: Neo-conservatism, Theocracy, Economic Imperialism, Environmental Disaster and the Collapse of Civilization*

Peace and Blessings!

Sebai MAA

How to become Spiritually Enlightened by understanding the Mystical Wisdom Teachings of the Sages and the Metaphysical disciplines for attaining higher consciousness?

Conversation with God

Question: What is meant by integration of the meditative experience?

Greetings,

Sebai, you have spoken of the ease of achieving body separation in the advanced meditation state. Sebai has also mentioned that relatively speaking, the difficulty is actually in being able to integrate the meditative experience into your everyday life.

What is meant by integration of the experience?
Why is it difficult?
What can be done to foster the proper integration of the meditative experience?

Peace

Answer

Greetings,

From a mystic or metaphysical perspective integration refers to the aspects of consciousness (**The Khu or Akhu** -shining spirit, **The Ba** -soul, **The Sahu** -glorious body, **The Khaibit** -shadow, **The Ab** -heart, **The Sekhem** -power (life force), **The Ka** -mind (desire-astral body), **The Ren** -name, **The Khat** -physical body) and how to cleanse and enlighten them so as to experience higher consciousness on every level of existence. From a disciplinary and psycho-spiritual perspective integration occurs in the mind-body complex or aggregate of elements that constitute the human personality.

The term "personality integration" refers to the four main aspects of the personality that are affected by the spiritual disciplines: intellect, feeling/emotion, action and will. Intellect is worked on through philosophy, the wisdom teachings. Feelings are worked on through devotional disciplines. Action is worked upon by ethical conscience (Maat) in practice. Will is developed through formal meditation (the other disciplines constitute informal).

As the disciplines are practiced one aspect of the personality may develop while others may lag. There needs to be time to integrate the new found knowledge or feeling or action or power gained through meditation so as to rebalance the personality and operate on a higher level overall. Also, integration occurs when the personality acclimates to higher experiences. For example, as the practice of meditation gets deeper new experiences are achieved that may be shocking or awe inspiring and life changing. There needs to be time to make sense of them in the new context of life from before –ignorance, to the after- higher wisdom.

This process can be difficult to the extent that the lower personality is held onto; the inability to let go caused by subconscious impressions of individuality that give rise to desires to remain human instead of the moving towards a superhuman state. Such mental impressions can cause complexes, neuroses or psychoses if not resolved. But it is more important for aspirants to resolve those complexes before attaining certain levels of higher consciousness experiences – they must integrate first- another way to say it "normalize before you spiritualize." This is why the so called fanciful idea of instantaneous enlightenment, like being touched by a spiritual master and spontaneously experiencing higher consciousness is dangerous and unnatural. It took time to become degraded so it takes some time to become enlightened. The self (operating through the nine aspects of consciousness and the four main psychological elements of the physical personality, devolved (allowed itself to get caught up in the mire of human desires, emotions and ignorance) over many lifetimes, using many personalities through the two genders. However, while it is not necessary to spend the equal amount of lifetimes getting to enlightenment it does require some time to evolve.

Enlightenment occurs in degrees, like an airplane that moves from a stopped position to slow and eventually fast and then to fly. Unlike a helicopter which goes straight up but if the engine fails it comes straight down (artificial means, drugs, doing certain practices before being ready, etc), the integrated personality is like the airplane. If the engines fail, the plane can glide. But the master is like the rocket ship that goes up but does not need to ever come down. And that is the fullest integration, when all the aspects of the personality have been perfectly harmonized so that, like sounds vibrating at the same rate blend into one, or as many panes of glass can be seen through at the same time when clean, this personality has blended with the one of the universe, the transcendental Self, and the beyond. So for this fully integrated personality there is no discord, no up or down, here or there, trouble or peace, me or you, like or dislike. The struggle of life comes when there are two and three and four…

When the "many" dissolve (through integrating the aspects and elements of the personality), then there is one and one is THE one. This is called integral movement. It is one of the least understood and most fundamental and most overlooked aspects of the spiritual practice, perhaps because it is not so glamorous; it requires much patience and great stamina to plod along relentlessly regardless of failure, frustrations, handling the

Conversation with God

day-to-day situations, facing the world, etc. Yet it is necessary; one cannot understand calculus without algebra, or algebra without more basic mathematics. Think about your own life, did you understand two years ago what you understand now? Even the same exact teaching will have deeper meaning as there is greater integration.

That is that "magic" of personality integration. In our tradition, the term "pert" as in *"Pert m Hru"* may be considered as referencing the integrative process. Pert means going forth, "moving towards," "m" means "as" or "in, and "Hru" means "the form of light"; it does not mean being light or being enlightened in the sense of something not requiring movement or effort. There needs to be a movement towards enlightenment, an integrative process that culminates in the light or enlightenment.

Peace and Blessings!
Sebai MAA

Mystical Answers to the Important Questions of Life

Question: Is the self controlling the self or the self controlling the personality?

Sebai Maa,

Udja Peace and Blessings

Permit me please to ask this question. I believe that the self is the essence of all things, also it is the reality of all things, to me that makes it stable while the personality is a projection of that reality, it is a reflection, an illusion and is perishable, therefore it is not stable. My question is how can the self control the self when there is only one self? Is the self controlling the self or the self controlling the personality?

Answer

We must first clarify which self you are speaking of, the "self" or the "Self." The "self," with the little "s" refers to the limited personality with limited ego consciousness defining itself through illusions, individuality and ignorance while the "Self" refers to the "Higher Self," universal, unlimited, immortal and transcendental consciousness. If the Self is all, then even the illusions are the Self, the reflections are the Self, that which is perishable and abiding is also the Self and also the personality is the Self, so what is not under the purview of the Self?

Therefore, if there is control of chaos this is also the Self so who is controlling what? Only by delusion (belief in illusions and projections) is it conceivable that the Self is not the ultimate authority, for all the agreements or protestations of the ego; in the end the Self abides and the ego (personality) perishes. So who has the last laugh in the spiritual game? If you find out who that is then you find the answer to your question also.

Hint: as long as the personality is beset with ignorance, it believes it is the ego personality, the mortal and perishable part, the weak and powerless part. When enlightenment dawns, the Higher Self is recognized as the true essential being which is transcendental and immortal and yes, powerful.

Peace and Blessings!

Sebai MAA

Conversation with God

Questions: How to handle the bodiless state?

Dear Sebai Maa

Greetings,

1. What is the purpose of the bodiless state?
2. Should one be silent or pray etc. when in it?
3. How does one come out of it (i.e. return to body-state)?
4. Should there be a period of rest or reflection afterward, or prayer, etc.?

Please reply at your earliest convenience.
Peace,

Answer

Greetings,

The purpose of the bodiless state is firstly to allow the mind to experience existence without the body, that is, without dependence and consciousness of existence as a physical being. Secondly, this experience allows the personality to be convinced that there is certainly existence beyond death, and so thirdly, it encourages further spiritual development-evolution- for this is not the beatified state yet but merely the opening of the door of the beyond which has higher states of being.

The practice of meditation, chants, prayer, rectitude, purity of mind, calmness of mind, etc., are the means to purify so that it may be possible to open the door through meditation and transcendental experiences. Then upon opening the door, those means should be relaxed and the aspirant should remain open to the experience. They are like a taxi; you take it to your destination and then it drops you off. You go inside and it goes its own way.

Coming out of it is of no concern. Rest assured that your soul will bring you out of it when the purpose of the experience is completed. Realize that there is no need to fear – you enter into the state every day at sleep – the only difference is that during meditation you are entering while awake. After your session there should always be a period of reflection, and marveling at the glory of higher realms within yourself. Further, to make the best use and effectiveness out of the discipline there should be journaling of the experiences – the journal to remain completely private- sharing your innermost thoughts of the experience and the intimacy of your own growing awareness of your own depths and the prospect of discovering the Divine.

Peace and Blessings!
Sebai MAA

Mystical Answers to the Important Questions of Life

Question: What are these Meditative sensations?

I actually wanted to communicate some of my meditative experiences with you and get your feedback. I sometimes get a lot of heat energy circulating the body. In the beginning I was confused by it but now I'm ok.

This morning I had an experience where there seemed to be a jolt or shock (nothing extreme but noticeable and a little different than before) in the region of the heart energy center. It also seemed as though I was getting a terrible headache.

For the past few days I have been rather peaceful. I have been concentrating on going inward more, reducing talking and practicing detachment.

Could you please shed some light on the aforementioned?

Thank you

Answer

Greetings,

Heat and circulation of energy are possible experiences of meditative practice, especially at the beginning of the effective practice level (when the practices are actually starting to work to transform the nervous system and mind). Barring any physical ailments, jolts or shocks can occur when there are strong blockages of the inner Life Force that needs to course through the nervous system in order to promote a harmonious balance between the physical and psychic levels of consciousness, so that there may be a transition from physical to astral awareness. However, the jolts or shocks should be rare and with purity should not occur after a time.

Barring any physical ailments, including high blood pressure, body pains and or headaches can occur as part of the process of opening up blocked sections of the nervous system. Certain meditations can place more pressure on the brain or pains can be experienced in the head as the Serpent Power opens up Sekhem Life Force pathways (even if you do not practice the Serpent Power discipline as your main discipline). The pain can be intense but it is not strictly a physical pain, rather a psychic pain. Again, it is only temporary until the openings are properly established. In any case, the more you explore the inner world the outer one will have less importance, but you will naturally have less time to be attending to worldly mundane-nesses, so you will be more attuned to qualitative worldly experiences. However, you should have a complete check up by your health care practitioner just to be sure that a physical ailment is not the cause of these experiences.

Peace and Blessings!
Sebai MAA

Conversation with God

Question: Does enlightenment bring back memories from previous lives?

Greetings:

I have spent the 19 years of this incarnation searching for a very well hidden truth (be it deliberately or forgetfulness), and having just finished reading Egyptian Yoga Vol. 1 and *Egyptian Tantra Yoga*, and am just starting *Egyptian Yoga Vol. 2*. I can truly say I am on the path to finding it. Thank you!

I am writing to humbly ask if you could shed some light I have on some questions I have on the teachings:

1. When one attains cosmic consciousness, are the memories of past incarnations returned to you?
2. With each successive reincarnation, does the strength of the life force (Ra) increase? I ask because the awakening process of the direct path is a gradual one in order that one is not overwhelmed by immediate awakening, and as the attaining of cosmic consciousness requires countless rebirths, is the function of said rebirths not only to gain experience of creation, but a gradual increase of the life force?

Any help you could render on the above topics would be most appreciated, and thank you once again for shining a light into the darkness that is the modern world.

Thank you

Answer

I am gratified by your kind words.

1- In reality, life memories are like the happenings of a dream, when you wake up in the morning they may seem to have been vivid or may be forgotten even then. Upon waking you can choose to remember, but what would be the purpose in recalling a dream? Nevertheless, you can recall those memories if you choose to, but it is not necessary to do so in order to attain enlightenment. What is necessary is to resolve and neutralize the sum total effect of those memories which are remnants or residues, the distillations of past actions and experiences, feelings, etc. that relate one to ignorance, individuality and egoism and al that is of the relative reality and not of the absolute and transcendental reality.

2- Nehast, the Spiritual Awakening, is like *Ra-Nefertum* (Khepri), the new born sun, growing into Ra-Harakti (noonday sun). In the morning there is coolness and gradually the darkness gives way to the light, and yet no one can say where the day begins and the

Mystical Answers to the Important Questions of Life

night ends and yet there is increase in Ra, increase in power, of self-knowledge and will, until there is fullness of the Noonday sun, the fullness of enlightened consciousness and then ending in completeness in Ra-Tem, the setting sun. The power in Ra is subtler than the life force (Ra-Sekhem) that emanates from him. It is the nature of Ra-Akhu (Spirit). It is the power at the source of all life and creation. That power is discovered through enlightened consciousness and comes from spiritual awakening –*nehast*, expanding consciousness, the result of expansion of the mind -*awet ab*, and not from reincarnation in itself. Reincarnation is an opportunity to awaken but it can also be for devolution and the slumber of ignorance. Spiritual power comes from self-knowledge and to the extent that one has spiritual knowledge one will have that much spiritual power. Reincarnation is a venue to discover that power but some may need fewer reincarnations to realize the higher consciousness while others may need more.

Peace and Blessings!

Sebai MAA

Conversation with God

Questions: Can an enlightened person be wicked? Can an unenlightened person be righteous?

Brother Ashby,

There are many people in the world who do not believe in the Divine Consciousness or have misconceptions about the underlying reality of creation. Some are good people, some are not. Can an enlightened person be wicked? Can an unenlightened person be righteous?

Peace

Answer

Greetings,

Just as there were many people who did not believe the world is round and there were others who did not believe in hygiene in the operating room, things we take for granted today, there are indeed those who do not believe in Divine Consciousness or the existence of God for that matter. However, not believing in something that is true is a matter of ignorance. Ignorance is defined as "absence of the knowledge of truth." Yet, the ignorance is there due to lack of diligence in pursuing knowledge. Most people who say there is no God also actively prevent themselves from learning and discovering or do not take the time or practice disciplines to discover whether or not their assertions are correct. As such, there are many forms of ignorance. People have no idea what is 100 meters below the ground or what makes the heart beat, and yet the earth is here and the heart beats whether or not people believe in it. Of course, there are those who believe in hypotheses about the nature of reality as if science could answer all the questions about nature. Knowing about how something works, like knowing about gravity and its effects on planets, does not provide insight into what planets are made of, where they came from, why they exist, etc. This is ignorance, yet there is a higher reality that the ignorant will not discover unless they take steps away from their ignorance to discover what is beyond; perhaps because they are comfortable in their ignorance or fearful or lazy, whatever the reason, it is called *"preventing the ears from listening to the knowledge of right and wrong."* We can say this, from our own perspective, because those who have taken steps to research the inner world, just as those who have researched the outer world, have discovered a wider reality, which may be denied, but not negated, by those who purposely maintain themselves in a state of ignorance. So those who do not take time to purify themselves, study philosophy and practice intensive meditation over an extended period, may deny the existence of Divine Consciousness, but their denial is baseless and irrelevant.

As for wickedness and righteousness, consider that the path to enlightenment is through righteousness and not through wickedness. You cannot become enlightened through wickedness. Wickedness intensifies egoism and causes mental agitation through fear of retribution, resentments, regrets, etc., and in order to attain higher consciousness, a meditative, balanced mind must be cultivated. However, righteousness in itself does not produce enlightenment either; a righteous person can still have egoism, thus feeling themselves to be an individual personality, separate from all other persons and objects, and from Divinity. However, righteousness is a foundation of peace and order so that the spiritual disciplines may be practiced effectively. If the spiritual disciplines are properly enjoined, righteousness can lead to inner self-discovery and contentment as well as spiritual enlightenment.

Further, after becoming righteous, an enlightened person does not suddenly turn towards wickedness. Rather one remains as one was before, peaceful and satisfied, resting in the Self. As one is resting in the Self and in need of nothing else, one is devoid of disturbing desires that most people have which lead them to covetousness, greed and unrighteousness. Know that upon attaining spiritual enlightenment, a sage transcends good and evil. They attained that goal through good, and not through evil, yet their actions are now beyond such categories since those are relative notions devised by people in varied circumstances (mental concepts). But they still would not commit evil (egoistic) acts even though they are beyond them. However, non-enlightened persons would be susceptible to evil acts just as they are susceptible to good deeds; evil acts (or deeds) form *ariu* in the personality that will cause future sufferings and reincarnations.

Consider that good and evil are relative terms, or dependent on the context. For instance, if a person is stabbed in an alleyway that can be considered bad, but if a surgeon stabs a person in an operating room to cut out a tumor, that can be considered good. The stabbing act is neither good nor evil; the moral implication is derived from the circumstance and intent of the actor. As an actor playing a role for the betterment of humanity and in fulfillment of their own *ariu* (karma), the sage has purged all egoism, and egoism is the source of evil. Having transcended the notion of individuality and ego conscience, the sage is unaffected by their actions; he/she has become a non-doer, a person who does things and yet has nothing to do with the deeds or their outcomes. Thus, they are free from the *ari* (feelings, desires, enjoyment or repudiation) attached to the actions and will not suffer the consequences of those actions either in this lifetime or any other.

Therefore, while sages have transcended good and evil, their actions are not evil, for they have no ego to entertain or satisfy and allow fomenting evil desires within themselves. Nevertheless, their actions may be considered evil because some people may not understand their actions. For example, a sage may teach about the unrighteousness of meat eating to a young man. The young man may be delighted to learn to purify himself in order to come close to initiation into higher philosophy. Yet, the young man's parents may think it evil since they see the knowledge and the sage as taking their son away from sentimentality (e.g., eating cultural foods that he has eaten since childhood that they consider a family tradition) and their influence over him. The sun cannot be evil or good; it does its duty, yet those who lay out in the sun too long may get skin cancer. Should they curse the sun for being evil? No, the evil is ignorance. In fact, the source of all evil is ignorance and ignorance is the source of egoism. A person may have a car break down on the road and cause them several hours of delay and they would consider that as a "bad" thing. What if they were to find out that the delay caused them to miss driving through a street at the time when an airplane engine fell from the sky and would have crushed their car and them with it? Consider that a murder or a rape may be considered evil by society, but what if we were to discover that those crimes allowed the victims to pay a karmic (ariu) debt for a wrong they themselves had committed against the current criminals (who attacked them now), in a previous lifetime. The victims died, but were able to grow beyond the obstacle of the *ari* that was holding them back due to the unrighteousness of their past (e.g., in being a victim of the same crime they previously perpetrated, they were able to experience and understand the unrighteousness of their previous actions)? How should we therefore characterize what happened to them? Within the context of *ariu* (karma), we can say it was a good development. However, from the standpoint of society, we cannot promote raping and killing. Thus, from a philosophical standpoint, the crimes as well as the caring that occur in human society should be accepted and understood as the operation of a higher program of spiritual evolution that sometimes requires pain and suffering. Yet as leaders of society, sages always promote peace, justice, understanding and forgiveness in order to promote righteousness and the proper environment for spiritual evolution, growing beyond the ego consciousness which is after all the real way to end all sufferings in life.

We know, from our Ancient Egyptian Creation Myth, but also from modern day quantum physics experiments, that the world is not solid and matter has no real substance and it appears real because of the senses, just as a dream appears solid and real and yet is not real. So, in an even grander sense, from a transcendental viewpoint, since the world is ephemeral and illusory, created out of subtle matter that will someday dissolve into its constituent parts, which actions can we say are abiding? If everything will end one day and everything that has ever occurred in the history of the world will be swept away with the dissolution of the universe, what is real, good or evil? From this perspective what occurs on earth matters not. Yet from our standpoint here and now there is relative meaning. Even sages would not want to break a leg even though it has no meaning from a transcendental point of view! Thus, caring, healing and relief of pain are promoted so there may be peace and enlightenment through understanding this lofty philosophy. The unenlightened people can be righteous or unrighteous in accordance with their level of moral development, that is, the closer one moves towards egolessness one moves closer to righteousness and conversely, to the extent one moves towards egoism one is more unrighteous. A person who is in a dark room may grope in darkness, looking for the door. If they move away from the door that is worse ignorance. If they move towards the door while still groping in darkness they are still ignorant but moving towards knowledge. The unenlightened moving towards righteousness and truth are like the one in darkness moving in the right direction. The movement in the right direction is the practice of righteousness. Upon becoming enlightened the movement culminates in opening the door and letting the light in and the room becomes illuminated and there is no more groping, there is knowledge so no matter what direction the sage moves in the room it is all within the realm of knowledgeable- all good.

Peace and Blessings!
Sebai MAA

Mystical Answers to the Important Questions of Life

Question: If I Feel like a detached witness is this an illusion?

Greetings:

Sebai Maa, two mornings while doing my morning chanting and meditation I had an interesting experience. It seemed as if the Divine reciprocated my devotion during my meditation. Usually during my chants and prayers, I will "feel" like I am present with the Divine. This time before I could start that myself, the same feeling came over me itself. I thought that the Divine was reciprocating. Am I right or could this be a trick of the mind?

This morning me meditation seemed deeper. So much so that once I awoke, while hugging my wife, I could tell (I could feel) the touching as sensations being registered in my brain. I could feel that I was not touching anything but was experiencing stimulations. Is this also a trick of the mind? If not I want to keep moving forward. It seems like there is so much more ahead.

Any words or advice?

Peace

Answer

Greetings,

Remember the third Great Truth of Shetaut Neter: "S-Uashu s-Nafu n saiu Set." "Devotion to the Divine leads to freedom from the fetters of Set." Saiu Set relates to the fetters of the personality. As spiritual enlightenment dawns (on the way to awakening {Nehast}), there will be many new feelings that arise because a new world, heretofore unknown by the mind, has been accessed. The devotion purifies the personality by dissolving the ego. Then you begin to discover the world in which the enlightened sages live. The apparent world is indeed merely a set of impulses experienced by the brain and then the ego makes sense of them in accordance with its illusory sentimental attachments, infatuations and desires it has projected unto the world as objects for seeking satisfaction of its desires and passions. Those meanings are interpreted by the intellect and offered to the soul for its experience.

Actually, there is no true direct experience of the world. When you touch something, it is your finger that touches, your nervous system actually interprets that act – you are not having a direct experience with the object itself at that point. This is why if a person is experiencing numbness in a body part due to damage to their nervous system, even if an object is made to touch the affected body part, the person would not register that touch in that body part. Intellectually they would know they are touching the object, but there would be no sensation of touching the object. This is because, as explained above, the sense of touch, or sight, hearing, taste, and smell for that matter, does not register directly, but is relayed through the nervous system, and then the mind-intellect interprets it through the filter of ego. Thus, a person can also have an intact nervous system, but still experience "psychological" or "hysterical" blindness due to an emotional trauma; in this situation, the emotional trauma is clouding the intellect and overriding the nervous system's impulse. Thus, even if you hug someone and the mind thinks you are close, in actuality you are as close to them as you are to someone on the other side of the world. This is why in a dream, a delusion, or in imagination you can touch something and feel it as real also. It is the mind that perceives and the mind is the intermediary between the world and the soul, so the soul is separate from the world and the more you discover the soul, the more you separate yourself in your awareness from the world as being a "real" and abiding reality. You open up to a greater world and that world is a higher reality, a higher truth, beyond the confines of the little ego and its limited experiences through one body.

Therefore, continue in the present way and allow yourself to experience the expanded glory of life and the goal of life: Nehast, the spiritual awakening-enlightenment.

Peace and Blessings!

Sebai MAA

Mystical Answers to the Important Questions of Life

Question: How can a person be enlightened and not know it?

I was reading the questions and answers on your web page which formulated a question for us. In response to a question you said that a person can be enlightened and not know it; please elaborate, and if a person is enlightened and does not know it is that true enlightenment? Because as you said, realization! Your Egyptian Book of The Light is very powerful, infinite thanks.

Peace

Answer

Greetings,

Your question is well taken. You must remember that enlightenment (experience of self as universal, transcendental and immortal) is an abiding state of consciousness. In fact we are all enlightened beings because we all possess, deep down, the transcendental consciousness that sustains our existence. However, those who are not aware of this transcendental consciousness or who only experience glimpses of it, say during meditative experiences or spontaneously at any given time, are considered to be in a state of "ignorance" or "advancing" while those who are, are referred to as "Enlightened."

Ignorance may be defined as "absence of the knowledge of the truth. A person can retain certain attachments to the ego personality that do not allow them to realize full higher consciousness because of the ignorance or worldliness that remains in their ego personality; yet another person can retain some ego aspects and yet be enlightened because those attachments are not seen by that person as abiding realities or as sources or pathways to happiness or self-identity, so there is full acknowledgement of the enlightenment.

In other words, when a person becomes enlightened, their ego personality becomes purified and transparent so that it does not block their vision of the world or of the transcendent, but if certain kinds of impurities (those that relate to the concept of self identity) remain in the ego level of mind, the deeper inner experience of enlightenment may not translate as enlightenment through their ego level of mind since they are approaching it through mind and its definitions and concepts. This condition is referred to in the teaching as "diffidence." Diffidence can persist in neophytes as well as advanced initiates; the difference is in the subtlety of the ignorance that causes the diffidence. In advancing aspirants, diffidence may be thought of as "subtle doubts or misunderstandings that block or prevent the full realization of higher truth."

This condition is alleviated when the ignorance is removed and the mind realizes the transcendental consciousness that is already there but without the subtle obstruction. Thus from the perspective of ordinary human existence, a person can become virtually

Conversation with God

enlightened and not realize enlightenment fully until ALL self-identity related ignorance is completely removed or until it is explained to them, like a person who has lost their eye glasses until someone points out that the eyeglasses are in their pocket. This is the diffidence model because it is defined by subtle impurities that cause diffidence in the mind.

Conversely, those who possess (experience) the characteristics of transcendental consciousness may do so but may not interpret those in worldly terms or may not understand those in worldly terms. A person may be enlightened genuinely, having approached higher consciousness through their own language of understanding or via intuition, which bypasses mind altogether, but not know it in the terms that ignorant people or intellectual people would define it (using mental concepts and definitions). For example, if a person had a million dollars she may not know the term millionaire when other persons call her that and yet she is a millionaire nevertheless, regardless of whether or not she knows the term. In the same way an enlightened person can be enlightened and yet not know it in terms that another person would call it but yet the enlightenment is real. In the diffidence example, above the person may have a million dollars but not be aware of it, thinking they have a lot of money but not knowing how much and also not knowing how to access it. In this second example, the person is aware of transcendental consciousness they are experiencing (knowing they have the million dollars and how to access it) but not aware of the terminology. Such a person would not be well suited to be a teacher, a sage, but they nevertheless have achieved the goal of life, the coveted goal of spiritual enlightenment and are to be revered for that. Enlightenment is not a state of consciousness that is defined by mind and its concepts or definitions. Otherwise, we could not say that a Chinese person practicing Taoism was enlightened because he did not call it Enlightenment as defined in the English language. Mind can circumscribe and constrict consciousness (in an illusory and temporary but effective way) but it cannot define it. It is abiding whether or not there is mind. Yet if there is ignorance in the mind and the personality relies on mind for its definition of self, then mind controls the identity in the self-conception of the individual who is ignorant by presenting the personality with an illusory and limited concept of self. Therefore, the task of becoming enlightened is not just about learning teachings, but also how to understand their meaning within one's own experience. For a teaching sage the task is not just to become enlightened, learning teachings and understand their meaning within his/her own experience but also learn how to understand them within a universal spiritual and philosophical as well as religious context and to be able to explain all of that to an aspirant and lead them on the path to understanding their own spiritual and then mystical journey. This is why though there may be many supposedly wise people around yet there are few who are truly enlightened and even fewer who can express that enlightenment or teach about it to others. This is the perspective model since it depends on which perspective we are looking at enlightenment from, the inner conscience of the enlightened or the concepts of the external observer. Nevertheless, regardless of the perspective used, the person is enlightened regardless.

Peace and Blessings!
Sebai MAA

Mystical Answers to the Important Questions of Life

Question: How do I know when I have Enlightenment?

Greetings,

Since enlightenment is attained in degrees, is there a definitive point in a person's life when they know they have reached that state?

Answer

Greetings!

When a human being reaches a point of internal realization (experience in fact-not just intellectual reasoning) "I am not this limited personality, I am The eternal spirit" and when that person realizes that there is no going back to individuality, then this realization is called *Nehast,* "spiritual awakening" or enlightenment. A person can erroneously think they are enlightened by developing illusions and spiritual arrogance. A person can also be enlightened and not know it! It is important to study in order to understand what this "becoming enlightened" really means. That is the task of attending philosophy classes, meditation, application of ethical principles in life, devotion to the Divine, cleansing the body, mind and soul, chanting, etc. Enlightenment is something unmistakable and easy once the mind is purified, but easily mistakable and difficult when there is misunderstanding and diffidence. Therefore, an aspirant comes to a realization and "Knows" at some point, but this knowing is a realization rather than an attainment. You cannot get enlightenment as you would go to a store and buy a lamp for your house and then say "I have acquired light." Enlightenment is a realization, a discovery of that which is already there, but subsumed by ignorance, emotion, misunderstanding, anger, hatred, greed, and desire. Of paramount importance is preceptorship, because that person can make sure the aspirant stays on track with the teaching, the practice and preventing arrogance or misunderstandings; this only works if the aspirant develops humility and respect for the preceptor. Through the instruction of a qualified spiritual preceptor and through proper training and purification, an aspirant can learn to realize enlightenment. So purify, and realize!

Peace and Blessings!

Sebai MAA

Conversation with God

Question: If there is no mind can there be illusion?

Greetings!

Since the mind serves as the source of liberation or bondage, I was wondering if, on the planet earth there were no human mind, would there still be ignorance or cosmic illusion (maya) on the planet earth?

Peace!

Answer

Greetings,

This question is like: if nobody hears the sound of a tree falling in the forest, is there any sound?

Nothing can exist or happen if there is no consciousness present to be aware of it and to sustain it. There is Divine consciousness in the tree just as in all animate or inanimate objects of the universe. However, the human mind is that special reflection of the Self, the Universal Consciousness that pervades all, which is aware of bondage and liberation as an individual and the opposites of Creation, existence and non-existence, you and me and male and female, etc. Therefore, if there is no mind (in this context mind means conscious, subconscious and unconscious) there is no bondage or liberation and therefore no illusion which is a form of ignorance that produces bondage. Both bondage and liberation are forms of awareness, concepts of the mind which are dependent on the mind for their existence. Therefore, cosmic illusions also cannot exist without mind. Further, there can be no planet earth without mind, nor computers, or fingers to retrieve this message or eyes to see it either. All creation depends on the universal mind (God's mind) and the powerful enlightened mind is aware of freedom just as the weak ignorant mind is aware of bondage. It is a matter of right awareness or wrong awareness, purity of mind or egoistic mind. For an individual human being this is the difference between liberation and bondage.

On a higher perspective, when a soul has incarnated at least once (incarnation into time and space and form is necessary to create illusion) and has fallen for illusory manifestations and worldly experiences (believing them to be realities) and has come to believe itself as an individual and not as a universal Soul, one with God and the Absolute, then that soul associates itself with *ariu* (referred to in Indian culture as samskaras – part of the concept of Karma). That *ariu* which are subtle impressions, lodge in the unconscious of the personality and these carry over after death. So when the physical body of an ignorant person (a person in bondage) dies, their gross mind disintegrates, but the *ariu* are carried forward in the Astral body (-subconscious levels) causing future reincarnations. If the person were to die at the end of creation when Ra-Tem (God) dissolves the universe (physical plane of existence) at the end of time, then there would be no physical mind (conscious {waking} and subconscious {dream} levels at all because

Mystical Answers to the Important Questions of Life

there would be no elements for mind to exist with {mind is composed of subtle elements [earth, water, fire, water, ether]}. Yet the impressions (which cause illusion in the mind) would remain as seeds in dormant form (in the causal body/unconscious mind) until a new Creation emerged where they could be fructified (acted upon and experienced). Therefore, in that scenario illusion can persist beyond mind.

Peace and Blessings!

Sebai MAA

Conversation with God

Question: is Enlightenment equal to Civilization?

Greetings Sebai Maa.

I am just trying out my hand in typing. I would like to ask two questions. Being enlightened and being civilized, could these be looked at synonymously, because to me being civilized is having control over the animal nature in us, which is the lower aspect of our divinity.

2. Could the god and goddess, Nun and Nunet, respectively, be looked at as Nun, the male who carries the semen with the sperm hidden in it, which I see as "the word," and Nunet, the female aspect, the female who receives that word, that manifests through pregnancy. While Nun remains in a non-dual state, the duality comes through the female aspect? Is there any sense to my question?

Peace Peace Peace Peace

Answer

Greetings,

One can be civilized but not enlightened. Civilization comes when people reach a certain level of organization and recognition of the value of promoting the common good for the benefit of all members of society, but that does not require spiritual enlightenment, just a certain level of spiritual and cultural advancement. Nevertheless, Enlightenment may be thought of as the highest form of civilization because it allows a human being to act with the utmost caring of humanity and sensibility for nature. It is indeed a state of control of the lower nature within oneself, which allows the higher to flourish.

In Ancient Egyptian cosmology, Nun and Nunet are dual aspects of the singular essence that is the primordial ocean of Creation, once it differentiates into the opposites of Creation (male-female). In the scripture however, it is described that either Ra (Anunian Theology) or Ptah (Memphite Theology) is the creative principle that engenders the Creation (i.e. the differentiation in the undifferentiated matter into the forms of time and space). This concept of engendering or begetting is ascribed to the Spirit and not to the matter. The matter is the vehicle of the will of the spirit, which is transferred through conscious thought (Hekau-the word). Both the male and female aspect of the primeval ocean become impregnated with the non-dual will of the Divine which manifests through the appearance of duality (Nun and Nunet). Duality does not come through the female aspect, but rather the apparent separation of the homogeneous primeval ocean into seemingly distinct and separate objects itself, which created the illusion that there is one and other(s). The very existence of two aspects (male and female) is the source of duality, not the female nor the male in itself. So from this higher perspective, both male and female in time and space are parts of the female principle (Creation), which are engendered and sustained by the (male) Spirit.

Peace and Blessings!

Sebai MAA

Conversation with God

Question: What is the Path of Divine Love and How does it Lead one to Spiritual Enlightenment?

Udja,

It is written that Devotion and Wisdom will lead a person to Nehast.

Practically speaking Wisdom, or the Yoga of Wisdom, is not difficult to practice. Read something from the teachings everyday, reflect, and then meditate on those readings. The intellectual aspect of the personality will in time become purified.

Devotion is another matter, practically speaking. It is my understanding that it is simultaneously chanting, singing, and the movement of one's emotional feelings to the Divine, and more. I am going to read the book about Divine Love again, but in the mean time, practically speaking, how does one practice Devotion if it is more than what I just mentioned?

HTP

Answer

Udja,

The path of Divine Love is as you have listed above but your description may be considered a little bit dry and intellectual. This path is like falling in love with a person, which in a way is irrational, but instead falling in love with a form of the Divine, a form that allows one's feelings to open up and experience the deeper nature of that Divine with feelings. As in love with a person, one finds out about them, learning about them by spending time with them. An aspirant spends time through study of a myth and practice of the rituals related to the myth. Through ritual there is the touching, the holding of the idols and the symbols of the divine lover and caressing the images and treasuring of their words and deeds, that is, their teaching and then there are the little things that lovers do for each other, the bringing of gifts (offerings), the dressing up, the washing of the object of love, the calling of the beloved's name and the Divine responds with comforting and the unconditional acceptance of the aspirant and the opening up of inner space of peace and contentment. There is the learning about the little things that the lover does, likes and feels and thinks about and the desire to please the lover more than oneself. That, by living with that Divine, and seeing the world with her as she sees it, and going through the same struggle with him as he goes through it, a wider and magnanimous perspective arises in

Mystical Answers to the Important Questions of Life

the heart; And feeling with them, crying with them through the struggle of their ordeal, which is also our ordeal, and then finally being triumphal with them and all the things that go with supporting the loved one and being supported by them so a bond that transcends sorrows and failures and gains and losses and life and death is created. Then there is the Tantric aspect of Divine Love, the merging, the making love and the after glow of lovemaking with the Divine, that unlike lovemaking in the world, here becomes perennial. And then there is the offspring of that love making, the child of light that grows in the heart as the Divine impregnates one with the spirit of self-knowledge, this is the mysticism. The neophyte grows into the mature initiate and then the master, the victor over the forces of hate and greed that is one's ego and selfish desires. And that love, being victorious over the egoism, now also is universal and not just reserved for the Divine form, for that being is in reality a representation of all there is and one's love has expanded one's feeling capacity to encompass all that is. And so there is the ecstasy and satisfaction that no earthly way of loving or love for material things can provide; and there is the pleasure of incomparable bliss of knowing the Divine with intellect but also with heart so that understanding and feeling blend into a totality of knowing and awakening such that terms like satisfaction, contentment and peace are apt but still incomplete words to describe the experience of such a one who has succeeded on this path.

Having realized that love that is born of the realization of one's own magnanimousness, one's own glory, which is shared with all and manifests as all and having realized that one is beautiful, worthy and detached, then one can see others and the environment as images of the Divine and share that same love with them by doing good to and for them as service but really as one's advanced expression of love, which is caring, and sharing with them as one with them even if they do not understand or appreciate it.

Peace and Blessings!

Sebai MAA

Conversation with God

Question: Am I ready to study the Book of the Dead?

Greetings!

I was wondering how can you tell if an aspirant is ready to move on in his spiritual studies and unravel the mysteries in our mystical text *Pert Em Hru*. Thank you.

Answer

Greetings,

Like other studies. The student shows his or her readiness by their way of pursuing the studies (level of devotion, diligence, understanding, etc.). Thus, aspiration, the inner desire to grow spiritually, is important.

Then it is also important to understand that like the *Dhamapada, The Tao, Bhagavad Gita,* and other scriptures from the world religions, it is necessary to study under the guidance of a spiritual preceptor. Many people think they can read these scriptures and understand them with their intellects. One can read the 42 Precepts of Maat in 5 minutes. That does not guarantee understanding. We had a class that went over the 42 Laws (precepts) of Maat that took over a year to discuss seriously, and this (Maat) is the basis of the Pert Em Hru, because in order to be able to understand it there must be purity of heart and Maat does this. Practicing Maat (ethical conscience) purifies the personality (body-mind-soul) so that the proper understanding of the teaching may take place. So without proper purity, even an interested person would not fully understand and attain enlightenment if they are not properly initiated into Maat Philosophy and its practice in day to day life.

Ideally, prior to entering into the study of the Pert M Hru, the aspirant should follow the plan of proper study of religion. This means that a person should follow the three steps of religious practice: *myth, ritual and mysticism.* The myth is the Legend of Asar, Aset and Heru. Next are the rituals associated with the myth and the *Pert M Hru* text. Then the philosophy behind the myths, the mystical aspects, are to be *listened to, reflected upon and meditated upon.* This is the proper course leading to the study of the *Pert m Hru.*

Peace and Blessings!
Sebai MAA

Mystical Answers to the Important Questions of Life

Question: Have I attained the goal of the teaching? Am I ready to be a Spiritual Preceptor?

Dear Sebai Maa

I wanted to thank you for your teaching and to let you know that I think I have attained the goal of the teaching. I reach a deep level of meditation and feel the oneness and that is what you say. I also think I am ready to be a Sage, a Sebai, and teach others. That is it. Is there anything else?

Thank you

Answer

Thank you for your kind words.

Have you truly attained the teaching? The following may be used as a guide for you to gauge your standing. In meditation, have you reached that state where there is a fullness of no-thing? Has that fullness become the perennial awareness of life or does it fade when you leave the meditative state? Have you discovered that power that is deep within, that roars with the force of a million oceans? Have you discovered the vision which transcends body and mind and flies on breath to the infinite? Have you shaken off the control by time and space and the mind and senses? Have you discovered that place where you might say when I die let it be in this place? Have you discovered resoundingly and fully, that body and mind and desires and thoughts are not me, I am something else, something more, something beyond, something all? Have you discovered that ultimate darkness where all is lost and words fail and the "I" is no more, yet there is fullness and immortality? Is the idea of going back to the way things were before, to live in ignorance; is that idea abhorrent, inconceivable, and ludicrous? Does poetry easily spring from your tongue, like the words of the goddess that were never sung?

And in the world, have you lost the reason to respond to attacks? Have you set aside the ignorant judgments of others? Do you have absolute control of your personality; is it governed by the precepts of virtue? Do you dictate what it will do, how it will do it, where it will go, what it will say, how it will feel, where and when? Or do you need to coax it, to play along with its moods, its feelings and emotions? Have you shed the weakness of desire and hatred and the pursuit of pleasure? Have you forsaken anger, hatred, greed, lust, prejudice and resentment? Have you forgiven those who hurt you? Are your words sweet like honey and your care for others delicate as the butterfly's wings and gentle as the summer breeze? Have you gone beyond party affiliations, good and evil, war and peace? Have you discovered the indomitable will to stay on the path, be the path and stay above the path? Have you discovered the energy of Creation, that courses through all things, the power of stars as well as the power of a lion, the swiftness of a gazelle, the speed of a hawk or the unstoppable force of a hippopotamus? Have you

Conversation with God

discovered your true nature, wherein there is a realization that you can be anything, empathize with anyone, do anything, accomplish anything? Have you discovered that peace which is undisturbed by the villainous, the shameless or the greedy? If your personality is ruffled, can you bring back the calm instantly by mere will? Have you faced your personality's limitations, its excrements, negative thoughts, depressions and your personality's quirks and realized "that is not me!"? But have you discovered that this body, this personality is acceptable and there is no need to be someone else, to be part of another ethnic group- another family- another country-do you now say "what I am is acceptable, my age is acceptable, my existence in this world, at this time, at this point in history-this is all acceptable." Have you become the embodiment of virtue, needing no reflection to think through truth and justice? Have you discovered the glory of a single breath, a scintillating drop of morning dew or the magnanimity of the first morning ray of light as well as the unfathomable depths of the darkest night? Do you see yourself in your fellow humans, both "good" ones and "bad" ones, in animals, in plants and in planets, stars and the vastness of space as well as the depths of the ocean? Do you spontaneously send peace and blessings to all people, all creatures and all nature? Do you exude poetry spontaneously? Do you experience song in your speech and dance in your step? Have you discovered that "nobody makes me whole but I complete the universe"? Have you discovered a mission to serve and to love all? Is it acceptable to you if it rains or shines, whether it's cold or hot, whether you are rich or poor, whether they praise you or shun you? Have you grown beyond appearances; do you care how others see you, as pretty or ugly, young or old? Have you experienced the orgasmic afterglow as the underlying essence of your ordinary day to day being? Have you experienced your timeless nature; traversing the past and the future through your own eternity? Have you realized you are not a sex, nor a gender, nor a human? Have you reached that contentment and satisfaction with life beyond frustrations, where what is, is acceptable, what isn't is no loss, and what can be, will, if needed? Can you strive without expectation; can you experience success without elation or pride, and can you experience failure without disappointment? Have you discovered the ecstatic pleasure of service to humanity, the abiding happiness of being a servant of the Divine, a conduit of innumerable blessings to the world? Has reading these words led you to a spontaneous ecstasy?

Then, if you have discovered these things, if you live them and your actions are directed from them and if you live in them as resident and not as visitor, just having intermittent success sometimes, but falling prey to the beast of ego at other times, then you have an abiding attainment. Do you abide in these things, and not lose them in the face of criticism, self-doubt, adversity, in pain, or in illness? Do you fully live in the teaching and your attainment; is this your unbroken reality, from the time of waking to the time of falling asleep? Is this what you dream about? Does it permeate your thoughts, does this teaching pervade your desires? Or is it lost when you are attacked or provoked, when you feel desire, greed or anger? When in pain or sick do you say "why me" and lose the glory of the Divine and forget the teaching?

As for being a Sebai, a Spiritual Preceptor, if you answered the questions in this volume (book) in the same way or better, if you have written volumes espousing the teaching and can present it lucidly and deal with any questions that may arise, without a loss of

Mystical Answers to the Important Questions of Life

insights, without calling on your own preceptors for help, then you may be ready to work without a net, as a full fledged teacher.

If you think you have arrived at the place where nothing grows and are steadfast therein, wait for the tests, for the world will test you and try to shake you. If you find yourself abiding in steadfastness, not falling to disappointments, not succumbing to unsettledness, not buying into illusions; if you remain aware of your Divine nature even through physical pain and physical discomfort, if you remain patient even when disrespected, if you retain awareness of the divinity in others even when they act in demoniac ways, then you may be ready. If you have arrived there and have discovered the nothing and the fallacy of things and the repudiation of them and the freedom that that brings, then you may be ready. If you have not understood what has been just said or what has been said elsewhere then… read on…

If you have experienced insights; if you have experienced the true experience, but it is not abiding, then you are on the royal road, that path that is the golden highway that leads to union with the sun, that burning fire into which the souls dissolve and the heart is supremely contented; and you will eventually attain the ultimate achievement as long as you follow the path of light, with diligence and honesty. The challenges will be sources of more knowledge and fodder for examples to show others about the true nature of the world, and you will draw strength from them.

If you have attained these things in an abiding way, it is a grand achievement, a glorious attainment, found, you have, the meaning of life, know you, the reality behind the images on earth, seen you have, the mystery of Creation and become compassion's ally, you have. Now, are you, an illuminer of the world, a beacon of love, a balm for all hearts and the answer for all minds, Done all that is to be done, have you. Achieved what there was to achieve have you, Done you have as our ancestors of time past, in the temples. Upheld you have, the tradition of the sages and the discipline of the priests and priestesses. Glory to them, Glory to you and Glory to God and to all who have attained, are attaining and will attain.

Peace and Blessings!

Sebai MAA

For Q & A on the subject: Science, Faith or The Transcendental? The Debate over Creationism or Evolution and other Related Issues see the book "The Limits of Faith" by Sebai Dr. Muata Ashby

INDEX

Ab, 82, 288
Abraham, 89
Absolute, 35, 60, 61, 66, 265, 304
Actions, 190, 254
Africa, 17, 18, 98, 105, 114, 115, 163, 197, 252, 282, 328, 334, 335, 336, 337
African American, 21
African Religion, 73, 213, 216, 325, 330, 333
Africentrism, 163, 208
Akhenaton, 115
Akhnaton, 102
Allah, 100, 223
Allopathic, 325
Amenta, 329
Amentet, 331
American Heritage Dictionary, Dictionary, 77, 251, 333
American Theocracy, 336
Americas, 98
Amun, 35, 67, 82, 87, 88, 95, 216
Amun-Ra-Ptah, 95
Ancient Egypt, 3, 17, 18, 21, 22, 26, 30, 52, 55, 56, 59, 61, 68, 69, 83, 88, 89, 90, 93, 94, 95, 96, 102, 103, 104, 109, 111, 112, 114, 117, 120, 125, 126, 128, 132, 138, 148, 156, 157, 160, 164, 171, 175, 187, 190, 191, 192, 195, 198, 199, 200, 208, 210, 213, 216, 219, 223, 224, 225, 235, 236, 239, 250, 251, 252, 256, 257, 258, 266, 270, 272, 278, 279, 298, 306, 324, 325, 326, 327, 328, 329, 330, 331, 332, 333, 334, 335, 336, 337, 338, 340, 341
Ancient Egyptian Wisdom Texts, 191, 192, 210
Ancient Nubian, 105
Anger, 230, 232
Anger,, 230, 232
Ani, 123, 191, 199, 216, 275
Animals, 66
Ankh, 65, 213, 214, 215
Anpu, 248
Anu, 250, 330
Anu (Greek Heliopolis), 137, 250, 330
Anunian Theology, 149, 306, 330
Arab-Muslim, 98
Ari, 49, 180, 181, 185, 190, 215, 252
Arjuna, 223
Aryan, 326
Asar, 32, 35, 82, 94, 95, 108, 119, 123, 136, 160, 179, 206, 215, 217, 285, 310, 329, 331, 332, 340, 341
Asar and Aset, 329
Asarian Resurrection, 61, 93, 225, 285, 329, 331, 332, 333
Asclepius, 120
Aset, 35, 61, 82, 95, 96, 108, 123, 128, 179, 217, 223, 244, 248, 249, 271, 310, 327, 329, 331, 332, 340
Aset (Isis), 35, 61, 82, 95, 96, 108, 123, 128, 179, 217, 223, 244, 248, 249, 271, 310, 327, 329, 331, 332, 340
Asia, 85, 103, 115, 280, 337
Asia XE "Asia" Minor, 85, 115, 337
Asians, 278, 279
Asiatic, 89, 105, 335, 336, 337
Aspirant, 21
Assyrians, 105
Astral, 35, 74, 82, 304, 329
Astral Plane, 35, 74, 82, 304, 329
Aten, see also Aton, 341
Atlantis, 103, 104, 334
Avatarism, 108
Awakening, 64, 294, 329
awet ab, 295
Ba (also see Soul), 41, 47, 50, 51, 61, 62, 82, 83, 288
Back, 145
Balance, 203
Being, 30, 46, 55, 56, 57, 60, 66, 71, 82, 83, 88, 96, 109, 115, 140, 179, 215, 228, 262, 306, 330
Bhagavad Gita, 224, 310

Bible, 59, 89, 94, 99, 101, 102, 127, 331
Black, 37, 89, 114, 213, 337
Boat, Divine, 137
Body, 82, 293
Book of Coming Forth By Day, 329, 330
Book of Enlightenment, 213
Book of the Dead, see also Rau Nu Prt M Hru, 178, 179, 213, 279, 310, 330
Breathe, 231
Buddha, 61, 108, 111, 194, 206, 334, 335
Buddhism, 17, 18, 26, 101, 114, 115, 330, 335
Buddhist, 56, 114, 123, 328, 335
Bull, 82
Bush, George W., 278
capitalist system, 278
career counselor, career, job, 243
Catholic, 95, 117, 331
Catholic Church, 331
Causal Plane, 35
Celibacy, 154
Challenging, 76
Change, 188
Chaos, 147, 149
Chi, 166, 182, 222
Child, 95, 331
China, 61, 114, 123, 286
Christ, 89, 90, 93, 94, 95, 97, 161, 171, 329
Christhood, 90, 94
Christianity, 17, 18, 30, 59, 89, 90, 93, 94, 95, 96, 97, 99, 100, 101, 114, 115, 117, 199, 258, 324, 330, 331
Church, 93, 331
Civilization, 17, 89, 104, 105, 278, 286, 306, 327, 335, 336, 337
Collapse, 286, 335
colonialism, 77, 208, 279
Concepts, 67, 71
Conflict, 336
Congress, 2
Conscious, 33
Consciousness, 33, 64, 66, 74, 158, 296, 304, 329
Consciousness, human, 325
Coptic, 329
cosmic force, 60, 62, 214, 216, 249, 250, 282, 331, 334
Cow, 82, 200
Creation, 17, 55, 56, 57, 60, 61, 80, 82, 88, 147, 148, 149, 151, 156, 180, 190, 193, 250, 252, 285, 298, 304, 305, 306, 311, 313, 329, 330
Creationism, 280, 314
Crete, 104
Crime, 207
Culture, 199, 229, 328, 334
Cymbals, 339, 341
Death, 79, 122, 125, 128, 200, 278, 279, 286, 335
December, 121, 132, 331
Denderah, 329
Desire, 267
Detachment, 126, 128
Devil, 30
Devotional Love, 327
Dharma, 225
Diet, 5, 28, 169, 170, 171, 172, 176, 184, 187, 188, 326
Diop, Cheikh Anta, 203
Disease, 28
Divine Consciousness, 296
divine food, 137
Djehuti, 59, 122, 179, 213, 250
DNA, 101
Dream, 242
Dream, REM sleep, 242
Drum, 339, 341
Dualism, 61
Duality, 306
Duat, 32, 329
Early Christianity, 95
Eat, 169
Edfu, 329
Ego, 236
Egoism, 180
Egyptian Book of Coming Forth By Day, 329
Egyptian civilization, 89, 104, 105
Egyptian Mysteries, 17, 95, 195, 251, 278, 279, 326, 332
Egyptian Physics, 330
Egyptian proverbs, 26, 327
Egyptian religion, 18, 90, 122, 160, 224
Egyptian Yoga, 324, 326, 328, 329, 330, 338, 339, 340, 341
Egyptian Yoga see also Kamitan Yoga, 2, 5, 21, 23, 32, 36, 41, 53, 55, 73, 82, 83, 137, 145, 163, 164,

Mystical Answers to the Important Questions of Life

178, 179, 188, 216, 222, 236, 264, 294, 324, 325, 326, 328, 329, 330, 338, 339, 340, 341
Egyptologists, 103, 333
Empire culture, 336
Energy, 182
Enlightenment, 2, 17, 21, 34, 46, 55, 61, 64, 163, 164, 179, 182, 193, 194, 195, 213, 215, 236, 260, 261, 289, 302, 303, 306, 308, 325, 326, 327, 328, 329, 330, 331, 332, 334
Ethics, 17, 105, 203, 209, 326, 327, 335, 336, 337
Ethiocracy, 278
Eucharist, 90, 329
Euro, 197, 204
Europe, 115, 278, 279, 280
Evil, 100, 137, 225, 333
Evolution, theory of, 314
Exercise, 2, 168, 329
Eye, 137
eye for an eye, 209
Eye of Heru, 137
Faith, 58, 95, 98, 314, 337
faith-based, 88, 97, 100, 161, 162, 200
Fear, 80
Feelings, 288
Folklore, 87
Food, 111, 275
Forgiveness, 201, 210
Form, 343
Freemasonry, 85
fundamentalists, 162
Geb, 102, 329

Ghana, 208
global economy, 336
Globalization, 247, 336
Gnostic, 59, 93, 95
Gnostics, 93, 117
God, 16, 21, 22, 24, 26, 28, 36, 44, 55, 56, 59, 60, 61, 62, 64, 65, 77, 82, 83, 88, 89, 94, 95, 98, 99, 108, 109, 111, 112, 113, 122, 134, 136, 137, 138, 146, 147, 148, 156, 158, 161, 180, 181, 185, 193, 196, 200, 201, 204, 210, 214, 215, 216, 218, 223, 225, 229, 239, 242, 250, 252, 258, 260, 262, 266, 270, 277, 285, 296, 304, 313, 327, 329, 330, 334, 341
Goddess, 2, 32, 44, 58, 61, 62, 82, 96, 119, 136, 147, 191, 239, 244, 249, 260, 330, 331, 338, 341
Goddesses, 5, 103, 148, 251, 328, 333
Gods, 5, 24, 61, 88, 103, 136, 148, 201, 251, 328, 333
gods and goddesses, 52, 55, 56, 60, 61, 62, 87, 88, 96, 115, 128, 137, 179, 188, 214, 220, 242, 330, 333, 334
Good, 30, 125, 171, 191, 333
Good Association, 30
Gospels, 331
Great Awakening, 64

Greece, 104, 280, 326, 334
Greed, 270
Greek philosophers, 59, 89
Greek philosophy, 324
Greeks, 52, 59, 89, 105, 120
Haari, 340
Hall of Maat, 133
Hapi, 250
Harmony, 76, 203
Hatha Yoga, 336, 337
Hathor, 329, 331, 332
Hatshepsut, Queen, 95
Health, 174, 325, 330
Hearing, 270
Heart, 332
Heart (also see Ab, mind, conscience), 332
heart attack, heart, heart disease, 219
Heaven, 94, 331
Hebrew, 59
Hekau, 26, 306, 341
Hell, 100
Henotheism, 55
Hermes, 59
Hermes (see also Djehuti, Thoth), 59
Hermetic, 59, 112
Hermeticism, 59
Heru, 30, 33, 34, 35, 59, 61, 79, 81, 90, 95, 108, 119, 123, 128, 132, 136, 137, 148, 167, 179, 194, 213, 216, 224, 225, 235, 239, 250, 282, 285, 310, 329, 330, 331, 332, 333, 340, 341
Heru (see Horus), 30, 33, 34, 35, 59, 61, 79, 81, 90, 95, 108,

119, 123, 128, 132, 136, 137, 148, 167, 179, 194, 213, 216, 224, 225, 235, 239, 250, 282, 285, 310, 329, 330, 331, 332, 333, 340, 341
Hetep, 49, 173
Hetheru, 82, 200, 250, 332, 339
HetHeru (Hetheru, Hathor), 339
Hetheru (Hetheru, Hathor), 82, 200, 250, 332
Hieroglyphic, 216, 328
Hieroglyphic Writing, language, 216, 328
High God, 58
Hindu, 95, 123, 180, 225
Hinduism, 17, 18, 26, 30, 101, 330
Hindus, 102, 180, 332
Holy Ghost, 95
Holy Land, 115, 279
Horus, 95, 340
human rights, 275
Humanity, 332
Hyksos, 105, 203, 204, 206
Ignorance, 179, 259, 296, 301
Ignorance, see also Khemn, 179, 259, 296, 301
Illuminati, 18
Illusion, 80
Imhotep, 120
imperialism, 77, 101, 279
India, 50, 98, 103, 104, 106, 111, 112, 114, 115, 123, 225, 258, 279, 326, 327, 328, 335, 336, 340

Indian Yoga, 324, 326, 340
Indus, 326
Indus Valley, 326
Initiate, 325
Instructions of Merikara, 210
Intellect, 22, 288
Iraq, 276, 284
Isfet, 197, 199, 203, 206
Isis, 95, 96, 161, 327, 329, 331, 340
Isis, See also Aset, 95, 96, 161, 327, 329, 331
Islam, 17, 18, 95, 96, 99, 100, 101, 114, 115, 199, 324
Israel, 99
Jamaica, 116
Japan, 114, 115
Jerusalem, 116
Jesus, 30, 45, 89, 90, 93, 94, 95, 97, 98, 108, 111, 116, 127, 161, 171, 194, 206, 215, 223, 279, 329, 331
Jesus Christ, 93, 161, 329
Jewish, 96, 99, 111, 115
Jews, 89, 96, 99, 100, 102
John the Baptist, 90
Judaism, 18, 89, 95, 96, 99, 100, 114, 115, 324
Judeo-Christian, 89, 99
Justice, 203, 206, 209
Ka, 47, 68, 71, 82, 83, 137, 288
Kabbalah, 324

Kamit (Egypt), 105, 117, 156, 252, 279, 333
Kamitan, 55, 95, 96, 104, 116, 117, 147, 148, 160, 192, 223, 229, 262, 326, 334
Karma, 112, 180, 190, 213, 214, 304, 328
Kemetic, 5, 18, 21, 23, 28, 37, 55, 56, 59, 70, 82, 87, 94, 103, 111, 112, 114, 115, 117, 129, 137, 144, 148, 156, 163, 169, 170, 171, 172, 173, 176, 178, 179, 180, 184, 187, 188, 193, 197, 198, 199, 201, 204, 206, 209, 215, 218, 222, 227, 235, 244, 246, 247, 251, 252, 258, 259, 260, 271, 275, 283, 335, 338, 340
Khaibit, 82, 288
Khat, 82, 288
Khemn, see also ignorance, 333
Khepri, 119, 294
Khnum, 109, 207
Khu, 82, 83, 288
Kill, 265
King, 109, 199, 204, 331, 334
Kingdom, 94, 110, 120, 278, 331
Kingdom of Heaven, 94, 331
KMT (Ancient Egypt). See also Kamit, 182, 204, 213
Know Thyself, 213
Koran, 99, 100, 101, 102

Mystical Answers to the Important Questions of Life

Krishna, 30, 61, 108, 194, 223, 331
Kundalini, 50, 103
Kundalini XE "Kundalini" Yoga see also Serpent Power, 103
Kung Fu, 123, 222
Lake, 90
Latin, 56
Learning, 168, 195
Life, 5, 35, 50, 137, 164, 180, 182, 188, 222, 223, 293, 328, 334, 337
Life Force, 35, 50, 180, 182, 222, 223, 293, 328
Love, 3, 111, 131, 161, 308, 327
Maakheru, 119, 193, 214, 249
Maat, 23, 31, 44, 48, 49, 50, 81, 102, 105, 112, 115, 119, 123, 128, 130, 133, 137, 138, 142, 149, 153, 156, 157, 159, 161, 178, 182, 185, 190, 191, 192, 193, 194, 195, 196, 197, 198, 199, 200, 203, 204, 207, 208, 209, 210, 211, 212, 214, 215, 216, 221, 223, 236, 238, 243, 248, 249, 252, 254, 260, 267, 268, 275, 279, 285, 288, 310, 328, 331, 332, 334
MAAT, 327, 328
Maati, 119
MAATI, 328
Mahabharata, 225
Malcolm X, 197, 200
Mars, 148

Masters, 109, 216
Mathematics, 77
Matter, 330
Maya, 121
Mayan calendar, 121
Meditation, 26, 50, 172, 195, 236, 325, 327, 328, 341
Mediterranean, 104
Medu Neter, 333
Memphite Theology, 306, 330
Merikara, 210, 216
Meri-ka-ra, 191
Mesken, 216
Metamorphosis, 121
Metaphysics, 56, 330
Middle East, 324
Min, 329
Mind, 71, 73, 101, 121, 209, 256, 266, 302
Minoan, 104
Moses, 89
Move, relocate, 62, 185
Music, 26, 52, 167, 184, 185, 187, 192, 228, 340, 341
Muslims, 96, 99, 100, 101, 102, 105, 209
Mut, 82, 95
Mysteries, 59, 77, 85, 278, 279, 326, 332
mystical philosophy, 23, 59, 68, 82, 85, 97, 127, 175, 212, 214, 222, 242, 335
Mystical religion, 97
Mysticism, 2, 17, 57, 77, 78, 87, 326, 327, 329, 330, 332, 335, 336, 337
Mythology, 2, 56, 85, 87, 88
Native American, 56, 96, 102, 209

Native American XE "Native American" s, 96, 102, 209
Native American XE "Native American" s See also American Indians, 96, 102, 209
Nature, 38, 145, 148, 154, 175, 260
Neberdjer, 61, 87, 96, 97, 325
Nebertcher, 88
Nebethet, see also Nebthet, 223, 341
Nefer, 52, 113, 339, 341
Nefertem, See also Nefertum, 90, 95
Nefertum, 294
Nehast, 17, 34, 44, 61, 64, 69, 81, 122, 137, 147, 148, 155, 215, 239, 266, 294, 299, 300, 303, 308, 333
neo-colonial, 286
neo-con, 336
Net, goddess, 341
Neter, 17, 18, 44, 55, 56, 74, 87, 88, 95, 96, 97, 98, 101, 112, 117, 130, 137, 144, 160, 192, 195, 236, 249, 258, 275, 299, 327, 329, 332
Neterian, 18, 43, 61, 95, 96, 97, 98, 101, 105, 114, 115, 130, 132, 179, 187, 188, 197, 203, 234, 239, 250, 252, 276, 282, 333, 335
Neterian theology, 95, 96

Conversation with God

Neterianism, 17, 95, 96, 97, 100, 101, 114
Neters, 250
Neteru, 38, 47, 87, 88, 96, 97, 192, 222, 333, 339, 340, 341
Netherworld, 285
New Age, 121
non-dualism, 60
Non-violence, 202
Nrutf, 239
Nu, 250
Nubia, 280
Nubians, 105
Nun (See also Nu primeval waters-unformed matter), 87, 88, 306
Nunet (formed matter), 306
Nut, 82, 329
Ocean, 252
Old Kingdom, 110, 120, 278
Old Kingdom XE "Old Kingdom" XE "Kingdom" Period, 120, 278
Om, 35, 119, 340
One God, 89
Oneness, 158
Orion Star Constellation, 331
Orthodox, 93, 94, 95, 96, 97, 98, 99, 100, 102, 117, 149, 161, 193, 199, 215, 333
Orthodox religions, 97, 98, 149, 199
Osiris, 32, 95, 108, 121, 201, 329, 333, 340, 341
Pa Neter, 55, 192
Pain, 268
Palestine, 115

Peace, 13, 14, 16, 17, 18, 19, 21, 23, 24, 25, 27, 28, 31, 32, 34, 35, 36, 37, 38, 40, 41, 44, 45, 46, 47, 49, 50, 51, 52, 53, 55, 56, 58, 59, 60, 62, 64, 65, 69, 75, 78, 79, 80, 81, 82, 83, 86, 88, 89, 90, 92, 93, 94, 95, 102, 105, 107, 108, 113, 116, 118, 119, 120, 121, 122, 123, 126, 127, 129, 133, 139, 141, 143, 144, 145, 146, 149, 152, 155, 157, 159, 160, 161, 162, 164, 166, 168, 169, 170, 172, 174, 176, 178, 179, 183, 187, 189, 193, 194, 196, 202, 212, 217, 223, 225, 229, 232, 234, 235, 236, 237, 239, 241, 242, 243, 245, 246, 247, 251, 253, 257, 258, 260, 261, 263, 264, 266, 268, 273, 275, 277, 278, 281, 283, 284, 286, 288, 290, 291, 292, 293, 295, 296, 298, 299, 300, 301, 303, 304, 305, 306, 307, 309, 310, 313
Peace (see also Hetep), 13, 14, 16, 17, 18, 19, 21, 23, 24, 25, 27, 28, 31, 32, 34, 35, 36, 37, 38, 40, 41, 44, 45, 46, 47, 49, 50, 51, 52, 53, 55, 56, 58, 59, 60, 62, 64, 65, 69, 75,

78, 79, 80, 81, 82, 83, 86, 88, 89, 90, 92, 93, 94, 95, 102, 105, 107, 108, 113, 116, 118, 119, 120, 121, 122, 123, 126, 127, 129, 133, 139, 141, 143, 144, 145, 146, 149, 152, 155, 157, 159, 160, 161, 162, 164, 166, 168, 169, 170, 172, 174, 176, 178, 179, 183, 187, 189, 193, 194, 196, 202, 212, 217, 223, 225, 229, 232, 234, 235, 236, 237, 239, 241, 242, 243, 245, 246, 247, 251, 253, 257, 258, 260, 261, 263, 264, 266, 268, 273, 275, 277, 278, 281, 283, 284, 286, 288, 290, 291, 292, 293, 295, 296, 298, 299, 300, 301, 303, 304, 305, 306, 307, 309, 310, 313
Per-aah, 199, 279
Perseverance, 268
Persians, 105
Pert Em Heru, See also Book of the Dead, 213, 216, 329
Pharaoh, 95, 160, 199, 222, 279
Philae, 217, 329
Philosophy, 2, 3, 17, 21, 44, 55, 59, 94, 105, 123, 137, 163, 164, 178, 179, 182, 190, 198, 199, 200, 205, 208, 216, 234, 238, 243, 249, 279, 310, 325, 326, 327,

Mystical Answers to the Important Questions of Life

330, 332, 334, 335, 336, 337
Physical, 35, 205, 222, 343
physical realm, 70
physical world, 19, 22, 60, 68, 133, 168
Plato, 52, 104
police action, 200
Prana (also see Sekhem and Life Force), 182
Prayer, 60, 100
pressure, 30, 39, 46, 48, 49, 68, 102, 135, 171, 267, 270, 272, 276, 293
Priest, 112
Priestess, 112
priests and priestesses, 103, 112, 279, 313, 329, 333
Priests and Priestesses, 326, 333
Protestant, 93
Psychology, 330
Ptah, 35, 95, 137, 306, 330
Ptahotep, 123, 192, 199, 201, 206, 210, 270, 271, 278
Punishment, 210
Pyramid, 59, 120, 179
Pyramid Texts, 59, 179
Pythagoras, 52, 104
quantum physics, 298
Queen, 334
Ra, 35, 41, 50, 51, 83, 90, 96, 119, 147, 156, 167, 250, 252, 294, 304, 306, 329, 339, 341
Ra-Harakti, 294
Rama, 30
Realization, 327
Recreation, 223
Relationships, 145

Religion, 17, 57, 87, 95, 97, 100, 105, 160, 213, 216, 236, 246, 327, 329, 331, 332, 333, 334, 335, 336, 337, 340
Ren, 82, 288
Rest, 236, 292
Resurrection, 61, 93, 121, 213, 215, 225, 285, 329, 330, 331, 332
Revenge, 211
Righteous action, 182
Righteousness, 178, 249
Ritual, 332
Rituals, 56, 330
Roman, 93, 95, 96, 105, 117
Romans, 96, 105
Rome, 334
Rosicrucians, 18
Saa (spiritual understanding faculty), 137
Sages, 49, 59, 79, 88, 109, 110, 111, 113, 123, 148, 199, 209, 213, 214, 215, 282, 325, 329, 330, 332, 334
Sahu, 82, 288
Sailing, 137
Saints, 109, 110, 214, 330
Saints and Sages, 109
saiu Set, 299
Sakkara, 120
Salvation, 250
Salvation, See also resurrection, 250
School, 38
Scribe, 120

Sebai, 13, 14, 16, 17, 18, 19, 23, 25, 26, 27, 28, 31, 32, 34, 35, 36, 37, 38, 40, 41, 42, 44, 46, 49, 51, 52, 53, 55, 56, 58, 59, 62, 64, 69, 75, 78, 79, 80, 81, 82, 83, 86, 89, 90, 92, 93, 94, 95, 102, 105, 107, 108, 109, 113, 116, 118, 119, 120, 122, 123, 125, 126, 129, 133, 139, 141, 143, 144, 145, 146, 147, 149, 152, 155, 157, 159, 160, 161, 162, 164, 166, 168, 169, 170, 172, 173, 174, 176, 178, 179, 183, 184, 187, 189, 190, 193, 196, 200, 202, 212, 217, 218, 223, 225, 229, 232, 234, 236, 237, 239, 241, 242, 243, 245, 246, 247, 251, 253, 257, 259, 260, 263, 264, 266, 268, 273, 277, 281, 283, 286, 288, 290, 291, 292, 293, 295, 298, 299, 300, 303, 305, 306, 307, 309, 310, 311, 312, 313, 314, 335
secrets of the universe, 186
See also Ra-Hrakti, 35, 41, 50, 51, 83, 90, 96, 119, 147, 156, 167, 250, 252, 294, 304, 306, 329, 339, 341
See Nat, 341

Sekhem, 50, 82, 103, 182, 288, 293, 295
Self (see Ba, soul, Spirit, Universal, Ba, Neter, Heru)., 2, 19, 26, 28, 30, 31, 35, 45, 46, 48, 50, 52, 56, 60, 61, 67, 68, 73, 83, 88, 103, 107, 108, 119, 122, 128, 129, 131, 137, 145, 146, 149, 150, 170, 181, 182, 185, 193, 194, 195, 196, 210, 215, 222, 236, 239, 242, 243, 249, 255, 260, 262, 265, 267, 285, 289, 291, 297, 304, 326, 327, 328, 329, 332
Self-created lifestyle, lifestyle, 28, 188
Self-knowledge, 128
Sema, 3, 5, 17, 18, 29, 109, 117, 137, 154, 164, 213, 229, 236, 247, 258, 259, 324, 334, 343
Sema Tawi, 154, 236, 247
Semitic, 89
Serpent, 35, 50, 103, 104, 187, 223, 293
Serpent Power, 35, 50, 103, 104, 187, 223, 293
Serpent Power (see also Kundalini and Buto), 35, 50, 103, 104, 187, 223, 293
Serpent Power see also Kundalini Yoga, 35, 50, 103, 104, 187, 223, 293
Set, 30, 33, 123, 136, 215, 222, 224, 225, 235, 239, 249, 271, 285, 299, 333
Seti I, 252, 328, 341
Setian, 209
Seven, 109, 203
Seven Year Famine, 109
Sex, 147, 149, 153, 158, 159, 329
Sexuality, 145, 146, 147, 149, 151, 158, 159, 164, 184
Shai, 213
Shedy, 14, 57, 137, 166, 236, 248, 325
Shepherd, 279
Sheps, 148, 215
Shetaut Neter, 16, 17, 18, 44, 56, 95, 96, 97, 98, 101, 117, 130, 137, 160, 194, 195, 236, 249, 258, 299, 329, 332, 333, 335
Shetaut Neter See also Egyptian Religion, 16, 17, 18, 44, 56, 95, 96, 97, 98, 101, 117, 130, 137, 160, 194, 195, 236, 249, 258, 299, 329, 332, 333, 335
Sikhism, 115
Sirius, 331
Skin, 173
slavery, 98, 208, 210, 225, 233, 280, 333
social studies, 281
Society, 64
Solon, 104
Soul, 64, 67, 68, 86, 125, 129, 202, 256, 266, 304, 333
South America, 103
Spirit, 16, 41, 45, 53, 61, 64, 66, 74, 81, 86, 107, 108, 115, 134, 136, 148, 186, 222, 265, 267, 285, 295, 306
Spiritual discipline, 325
Spiritual Preceptor, 22, 23, 28, 41, 111, 311, 312
Spirituality, 2, 18, 21, 57, 87, 102, 105, 163, 171, 188, 252, 324, 326
stages of religion, 91
Step Pyramid, 120
Strabo, 52
Stress, 5
Study, 73, 162, 178, 244
Sublimation, 158, 329
Suffering, 125, 129, 256, 266, 282
Sufi, 223
Sufi, see also Sufism, 223
Sumer, 85
sun, 148
Sun, 148
Sundisk, 250
Superpower, 336
Superpower Syndrome, 336
Superpower Syndrome Mandatory Conflict XE "Conflict" Complex, 336
Supreme Being, 55, 56, 57, 58, 60, 66, 82, 83, 88, 96, 109, 115, 179, 215, 260, 262, 330
Supreme Divinity, 56, 57

Tai Chi (see also Chi Kung), 166, 222
Tantra, 164, 294, 329
Tantra Yoga, 329
Tao, 310
Taoism, 324
Tawi, 154, 236
Television, 172
Tem, 295, 304
Temple, 18, 101, 112, 181, 217, 329, 332
Temple of Aset, 217, 329
Thales, 104
The Absolute, 325
The Black, 89, 337
The God, 210, 328
The Gods, 328
The Pyramid Texts, 179
The Self, 194
The way, 56, 225, 231
Theban Theology, 82, 325
Thebes, 325, 328
Theocracy, 278, 286, 335
Theology, 56, 82, 149, 213, 216, 306, 330
Thoughts, 66, 71
Thoughts (see also Mind), 66, 71
Thrice Greatest Hermes, 59
Tibetan Buddhism, 114
time and space, 19, 41, 50, 55, 56, 57, 60, 61, 65, 67, 71, 72, 74, 76, 80, 88, 110, 112, 134, 136, 138, 148, 154, 182, 193, 222, 239, 247, 269, 276, 282, 304, 306, 311, 333
Tomb, 328, 341
Tomb of Seti I, 328, 341
Tradition, 102
transcendental reality, 22, 61, 62, 294, 333
Tree, 251
Tree of Life, 251
Triad, 325
Trinity, 95, 96, 97, 329, 341
True happiness, 232
Truth, 100, 196, 203, 270, 299
Uhm Ankh, see also reincarnation, 214
Understanding, 190, 333
United States of America, 85, 99, 269, 280, 336
Universal Ba, 62
Universal Consciousness, 66, 158, 304, 329
Unrighteousness, 199
Upanishads, 330
Upper Egypt, 207
USA, West, 43, 110, 279, 284, 343
Vedic, 326
Violence, 191, 223, 282
Virtues, 203
Visualize, 231
wars, 98, 200, 208, 224, 276, 280, 285
Waset, 325
western religions, 98, 99, 100, 101
Western religions, 100, 114
Western, West, 93, 114, 115
White, 197
Whitehead, 76
Will, 182, 185, 219, 289
Wisdom, 50, 105, 136, 161, 178, 191, 192, 210, 216, 266, 271, 280, 308, 327, 328
Wisdom (also see Djehuti), 136
Wisdom (also see Djehuti, Aset), 50, 105, 136, 161, 178, 191, 192, 210, 216, 266, 271, 280, 308, 327, 328
word of God, 98
World War II, 336
Worry, 186
Yoga, 2, 3, 5, 17, 21, 23, 29, 32, 36, 41, 49, 53, 55, 82, 83, 103, 105, 109, 117, 137, 145, 163, 164, 178, 179, 216, 222, 227, 236, 258, 259, 264, 294, 308, 324, 325, 326, 327, 328, 329, 330, 332, 334, 335, 336, 337, 338, 339, 340, 341, 343
Yoga XE "Yoga" Exercise, 2, 5
Yoga of Wisdom (see also Jnana Yoga), 308
Yogic, 243, 336
Yoruba, 115
Zen Buddhism, 114

Conversation with God

SEMA INSTITUTE

Cruzian Mystic P.O.Box 570459, Miami, Florida. 33257 (305) 378-6253, Fax. (305) 378-6253

Other Books From C M Books
P.O.Box 570459
Miami, Florida, 33257
(305) 378-6253 Fax: (305) 378-6253

This book is part of a series on the study and practice of Ancient Egyptian Yoga and Mystical Spirituality based on the writings of Dr. Muata Abhaya Ashby. They are also part of the Egyptian Yoga Course provided by the Sema Institute of Yoga. Below you will find a listing of the other books in this series. For more information send for the Egyptian Yoga Book-Audio-Video Catalog or the Egyptian Yoga Course Catalog.

Now you can study the teachings of Egyptian and Indian Yoga wisdom and Spirituality with the Egyptian Yoga Mystical Spirituality Series. The Egyptian Yoga Series takes you through the Initiation process and lead you to understand the mysteries of the soul and the Divine and to attain the highest goal of life: ENLIGHTENMENT. The *Egyptian Yoga Series*, takes you on an in depth study of Ancient Egyptian mythology and their inner mystical meaning. Each Book is prepared for the serious student of the mystical sciences and provides a study of the teachings along with exercises, assignments and projects to make the teachings understood and effective in real life. The Series is part of the Egyptian Yoga course but may be purchased even if you are not taking the course. The series is ideal for study groups.

Prices subject to change.

1. *EGYPTIAN YOGA: THE PHILOSOPHY OF ENLIGHTENMENT* An original, fully illustrated work, including hieroglyphs, detailing the meaning of the Egyptian mysteries, tantric yoga, psycho-spiritual and physical exercises. Egyptian Yoga is a guide to the practice of the highest spiritual philosophy which leads to absolute freedom from human misery and to immortality. It is well known by scholars that Egyptian philosophy is the basis of Western and Middle Eastern religious philosophies such as *Christianity, Islam, Judaism,* the *Kabala,* and Greek philosophy, but what about Indian philosophy, Yoga and Taoism? What were the original teachings? How can they be practiced today? What is the source of pain and suffering in the world and what is the solution? Discover the deepest mysteries of the mind and universe within and outside of your self. 8.5" X 11" ISBN: 1-884564-01-1 Soft $19.95

Mystical Answers to the Important Questions of Life

2. *EGYPTIAN YOGA: African Religion Volume 2-* Theban Theology U.S. In this long awaited sequel to *Egyptian Yoga: The Philosophy of Enlightenment* you will take a fascinating and enlightening journey back in time and discover the teachings which constituted the epitome of Ancient Egyptian spiritual wisdom. What are the disciplines which lead to the fulfillment of all desires? Delve into the three states of consciousness (waking, dream and deep sleep) and the fourth state which transcends them all, Neberdjer, "The Absolute." These teachings of the city of Waset (Thebes) were the crowning achievement of the Sages of Ancient Egypt. They establish the standard mystical keys for understanding the profound mystical symbolism of the Triad of human consciousness. ISBN 1-884564-39-9 $23.95

3. *THE KEMETIC DIET: GUIDE TO HEALTH, DIET AND FASTING* Health issues have always been important to human beings since the beginning of time. The earliest records of history show that the art of healing was held in high esteem since the time of Ancient Egypt. In the early 20th century, medical doctors had almost attained the status of sainthood by the promotion of the idea that they alone were "scientists" while other healing modalities and traditional healers who did not follow the "scientific method' were nothing but superstitious, ignorant charlatans who at best would take the money of their clients and at worst kill them with the unscientific "snake oils" and "irrational theories". In the late 20th century, the failure of the modern medical establishment's ability to lead the general public to good health, promoted the move by many in society towards "alternative medicine". Alternative medicine disciplines are those healing modalities which do not adhere to the philosophy of allopathic medicine. Allopathic medicine is what medical doctors practice by an large. It is the theory that disease is caused by agencies outside the body such as bacteria, viruses or physical means which affect the body. These can therefore be treated by medicines and therapies The natural healing method began in the absence of extensive technologies with the idea that all the answers for health may be found in nature or rather, the deviation from nature. Therefore, the health of the body can be restored by correcting the aberration and thereby restoring balance. This is the area that will be covered in this volume. Allopathic techniques have their place in the art of healing. However, we should not forget that the body is a grand achievement of the spirit and built into it is the capacity to maintain itself and heal itself. Ashby, Muata ISBN: 1-884564-49-6 $28.95

4. INITIATION INTO EGYPTIAN YOGA Shedy: Spiritual discipline or program, to go deeply into the mysteries, to study the mystery teachings and literature profoundly, to penetrate the mysteries. You will learn about the mysteries of initiation into the teachings and practice of Yoga and how to become an Initiate of the mystical sciences. This insightful manual is the first in a series which introduces you to the goals of daily spiritual and yoga practices: Meditation,

Conversation with God

Diet, Words of Power and the ancient wisdom teachings. 8.5" X 11" ISBN 1-884564-02-X Soft Cover $24.95 U.S.

5. *THE AFRICAN ORIGINS OF CIVILIZATION, RELIGION AND YOGA SPIRITUALITY AND ETHICS PHILOSOPHY* HARD COVER EDITION Part 1, Part 2, Part 3 in one volume 683 Pages Hard Cover First Edition Three volumes in one. Over the past several years I have been asked to put together in one volume the most important evidences showing the correlations and common teachings between Kamitan (Ancient Egyptian) culture and religion and that of India. The questions of the history of Ancient Egypt, and the latest archeological evidences showing civilization and culture in Ancient Egypt and its spread to other countries, has intrigued many scholars as well as mystics over the years. Also, the possibility that Ancient Egyptian Priests and Priestesses migrated to Greece, India and other countries to carry on the traditions of the Ancient Egyptian Mysteries, has been speculated over the years as well. In chapter 1 of the book *Egyptian Yoga The Philosophy of Enlightenment,* 1995, I first introduced the deepest comparison between Ancient Egypt and India that had been brought forth up to that time. Now, in the year 2001 this new book, *THE AFRICAN ORIGINS OF CIVILIZATION, MYSTICAL RELIGION AND YOGA PHILOSOPHY,* more fully explores the motifs, symbols and philosophical correlations between Ancient Egyptian and Indian mysticism and clearly shows not only that Ancient Egypt and India were connected culturally but also spiritually. How does this knowledge help the spiritual aspirant? This discovery has great importance for the Yogis and mystics who follow the philosophy of Ancient Egypt and the mysticism of India. It means that India has a longer history and heritage than was previously understood. It shows that the mysteries of Ancient Egypt were essentially a yoga tradition which did not die but rather developed into the modern day systems of Yoga technology of India. It further shows that African culture developed Yoga Mysticism earlier than any other civilization in history. All of this expands our understanding of the unity of culture and the deep legacy of Yoga, which stretches into the distant past, beyond the Indus Valley civilization, the earliest known high culture in India as well as the Vedic tradition of Aryan culture. Therefore, Yoga culture and mysticism is the oldest known tradition of spiritual development and Indian mysticism is an extension of the Ancient Egyptian mysticism. By understanding the legacy which Ancient Egypt gave to India the mysticism of India is better understood and by comprehending the heritage of Indian Yoga, which is rooted in Ancient Egypt the Mysticism of Ancient Egypt is also better understood. This expanded understanding allows us to prove the underlying kinship of humanity, through the common symbols, motifs and philosophies which are not disparate and confusing teachings but in reality expressions of the same study of truth through metaphysics and mystical realization of Self. (HARD COVER) ISBN: 1-884564-50-X $45.00 U.S.   8 1/2" X 11"

Mystical Answers to the Important Questions of Life

6. *AFRICAN ORIGINS BOOK 1 PART 1* African Origins of African Civilization, Religion, Yoga Mysticism and Ethics Philosophy-Soft Cover $24.95 ISBN: 1-884564-55-0

7. *AFRICAN ORIGINS BOOK 2 PART 2* African Origins of Western Civilization, Religion and Philosophy (Soft) -Soft Cover $24.95 ISBN: 1-884564-56-9

8. *EGYPT AND INDIA AFRICAN ORIGINS OF Eastern Civilization, Religion, Yoga Mysticism and Philosophy*-Soft Cover $29.95 (Soft) ISBN: 1-884564-57-7

9. *THE MYSTERIES OF ISIS: **The Ancient Egyptian Philosophy of Self-Realization*** - There are several paths to discover the Divine and the mysteries of the higher Self. This volume details the mystery teachings of the goddess Aset (Isis) from Ancient Egypt- the path of wisdom. It includes the teachings of her temple and the disciplines that are enjoined for the initiates of the temple of Aset as they were given in ancient times. Also, this book includes the teachings of the main myths of Aset that lead a human being to spiritual enlightenment and immortality. Through the study of ancient myth and the illumination of initiatic understanding the idea of God is expanded from the mythological comprehension to the metaphysical. Then this metaphysical understanding is related to you, the student, so as to begin understanding your true divine nature. ISBN 1-884564-24-0 $22.99

10. *EGYPTIAN PROVERBS:* collection of —Ancient Egyptian Proverbs and Wisdom Teachings -How to live according to MAAT Philosophy. Beginning Meditation. All proverbs are indexed for easy searches. For the first time in one volume, ——Ancient Egyptian Proverbs, wisdom teachings and meditations, fully illustrated with hieroglyphic text and symbols. EGYPTIAN PROVERBS is a unique collection of knowledge and wisdom which you can put into practice today and transform your life. $14.95 U.S   ISBN: 1-884564-00-3

11. *GOD OF LOVE: THE PATH OF DIVINE LOVE The Process of Mystical Transformation and The Path of Divine Love*   This Volume focuses on the ancient wisdom teachings of "Neter Merri" –the Ancient Egyptian philosophy of Divine Love and how to use them in a scientific process for self-transformation. Love is one of the most powerful human emotions. It is also the source of Divine feeling that unifies God and the individual human being. When love is fragmented and diminished by egoism the Divine connection is lost. The Ancient tradition of Neter Merri leads human beings back to their Divine connection, allowing them to discover their innate glorious self that is actually Divine and immortal. This volume will detail the process of transformation from ordinary consciousness to cosmic consciousness through the integrated practice of the teachings and the path of Devotional Love toward the Divine. 5.5"x 8.5" ISBN 1-884564-11-9 $22.95

Conversation with God

12. **INTRODUCTION TO MAAT PHILOSOPHY:** *Spiritual Enlightenment Through the Path of Virtue* Known as Karma Yoga in India, the teachings of MAAT for living virtuously and with orderly wisdom are explained and the student is to begin practicing the precepts of Maat in daily life so as to promote the process of purification of the heart in preparation for the judgment of the soul. This judgment will be understood not as an event that will occur at the time of death but as an event that occurs continuously, at every moment in the life of the individual. The student will learn how to become allied with the forces of the Higher Self and to thereby begin cleansing the mind (heart) of impurities so as to attain a higher vision of reality. ISBN 1-884564-20-8 $22.99

13. *MEDITATION The Ancient Egyptian Path to Enlightenment*   Many people do not know about the rich history of meditation practice in Ancient Egypt. This volume outlines the theory of meditation and presents the Ancient Egyptian Hieroglyphic text which give instruction as to the nature of the mind and its three modes of expression. It also presents the texts which give instruction on the practice of meditation for spiritual Enlightenment and unity with the Divine. This volume allows the reader to begin practicing meditation by explaining, in easy to understand terms, the simplest form of meditation and working up to the most advanced form which was practiced in ancient times and which is still practiced by yogis around the world in modern times. ISBN 1-884564-27-7 $22.99

14. *THE GLORIOUS LIGHT MEDITATION* TECHNIQUE OF ANCIENT EGYPT New for the year 2000. This volume is based on the earliest known instruction in history given for the practice of formal meditation. Discovered by Dr. Muata Ashby, it is inscribed on the walls of the Tomb of Seti I in Thebes Egypt. This volume details the philosophy and practice of this unique system of meditation originated in Ancient Egypt and the earliest practice of meditation known in the world which occurred in the most advanced African Culture. ISBN: 1-884564-15-1 $16.95 (PB)

15. *THE SERPENT POWER: The Ancient Egyptian Mystical Wisdom of the Inner Life Force.*   This Volume specifically deals with the latent life Force energy of the universe and in the human body, its control and sublimation. How to develop the Life Force energy of the subtle body. This Volume will introduce the esoteric wisdom of the science of how virtuous living acts in a subtle and mysterious way to cleanse the latent psychic energy conduits and vortices of the spiritual body. ISBN 1-884564-19-4 $22.95

16. *EGYPTIAN YOGA The Postures of The Gods and Goddesses* Discover the physical postures and exercises practiced thousands of years ago in Ancient Egypt which are today known as Yoga exercises. Discover the history of the postures and how they were transferred from Ancient Egypt in Africa to India through Buddhist Tantrism. Then practice the postures as you discover the mythic teaching that originally gave birth to the postures and was practiced by

Mystical Answers to the Important Questions of Life

the Ancient Egyptian priests and priestesses. This work is based on the pictures and teachings from the Creation story of Ra, The Asarian Resurrection Myth and the carvings and reliefs from various Temples in Ancient Egypt 8.5" X 11" ISBN 1-884564-10-0 Soft Cover $21.95   Exercise video $20

17. *SACRED SEXUALITY: EGYPTIAN TANTRA YOGA: The Art of Sex Sublimation and Universal Consciousness* This Volume will expand on the male and female principles within the human body and in the universe and further detail the sublimation of sexual energy into spiritual energy. The student will study the deities Min and Hathor, Asar and Aset, Geb and Nut and discover the mystical implications for a practical spiritual discipline. This Volume will also focus on the Tantric aspects of Ancient Egyptian and Indian mysticism, the purpose of sex and the mystical teachings of sexual sublimation which lead to self-knowledge and Enlightenment.   5.5"x 8.5"   ISBN 1-884564-03-8 $24.95

18. *AFRICAN RELIGION Volume 4: ASARIAN THEOLOGY: RESURRECTING OSIRIS* The path of Mystical Awakening and the Keys to Immortality NEW REVISED AND EXPANDED EDITION!   The Ancient Sages created stories based on human and superhuman beings whose struggles, aspirations, needs and desires ultimately lead them to discover their true Self. The myth of Aset, Asar and Heru is no exception in this area. While there is no one source where the entire story may be found, pieces of it are inscribed in various ancient Temples walls, tombs, steles and papyri. For the first time available, the complete myth of Asar, Aset and Heru has been compiled from original Ancient Egyptian, Greek and Coptic Texts. This epic myth has been richly illustrated with reliefs from the Temple of Heru at Edfu, the Temple of Aset at Philae, the Temple of Asar at Abydos, the Temple of Hathor at Denderah and various papyri, inscriptions and reliefs.   Discover the myth which inspired the teachings of the *Shetaut Neter* (Egyptian Mystery System - Egyptian Yoga) and the Egyptian Book of Coming Forth By Day. Also, discover the three levels of Ancient Egyptian Religion, how to understand the mysteries of the Duat or Astral World and how to discover the abode of the Supreme in the Amenta, *The Other World* The ancient religion of Asar, Aset and Heru, if properly understood, contains all of the elements necessary to lead the sincere aspirant to attain immortality through inner self-discovery. This volume presents the entire myth and explores the main mystical themes and rituals associated with the myth for understating human existence, creation and the way to achieve spiritual emancipation - *Resurrection.* The Asarian myth is so powerful that it influenced and is still having an effect on the major world religions. Discover the origins and mystical meaning of the Christian Trinity, the Eucharist ritual and the ancient origin of the birthday of Jesus Christ. Soft Cover ISBN: 1-884564-27-5 $24.95

19. *THE EGYPTIAN BOOK OF THE DEAD MYSTICISM OF THE PERT EM HERU* " I Know myself, I know myself, I am One With God!–From the Pert Em Heru "The Ru Pert em Heru" or "Ancient Egyptian Book of The Dead," or

Conversation with God

"Book of Coming Forth By Day" as it is more popularly known, has fascinated the world since the successful translation of Ancient Egyptian hieroglyphic scripture over 150 years ago. The astonishing writings in it reveal that the Ancient Egyptians believed in life after death and in an ultimate destiny to discover the Divine. The elegance and aesthetic beauty of the hieroglyphic text itself has inspired many see it as an art form in and of itself. But is there more to it than that? Did the Ancient Egyptian wisdom contain more than just aphorisms and hopes of eternal life beyond death? In this volume Dr. Muata Ashby, the author of over 25 books on Ancient Egyptian Yoga Philosophy has produced a new translation of the original texts which uncovers a mystical teaching underlying the sayings and rituals instituted by the Ancient Egyptian Sages and Saints. "Once the philosophy of Ancient Egypt is understood as a mystical tradition instead of as a religion or primitive mythology, it reveals its secrets which if practiced today will lead anyone to discover the glory of spiritual self-discovery. The Pert em Heru is in every way comparable to the Indian Upanishads or the Tibetan Book of the Dead." $28.95   ISBN# 1-884564-28-3 Size: 8½" X 11

20.   *African Religion VOL. 1- ANUNIAN THEOLOGY THE MYSTERIES OF RA* The Philosophy of Anu and The Mystical Teachings of The Ancient Egyptian Creation Myth Discover the mystical teachings contained in the Creation Myth and the gods and goddesses who brought creation and human beings into existence. The Creation myth of Anu is the source of Anunian Theology but also of the other main theological systems of Ancient Egypt that also influenced other world religions including Christianity, Hinduism and Buddhism. The Creation Myth holds the key to understanding the universe and for attaining spiritual Enlightenment. ISBN: 1-884564-38-0 $19.95

21.   *African Religion VOL 3: Memphite Theology: MYSTERIES OF MIND* Mystical Psychology & Mental Health for Enlightenment and Immortality based on the Ancient Egyptian Philosophy of Menefer -Mysticism of Ptah, Egyptian Physics and Yoga Metaphysics and the Hidden properties of Matter.   This volume uncovers the mystical psychology of the Ancient Egyptian wisdom teachings centering on the philosophy of the Ancient Egyptian city of Menefer (Memphite Theology). How to understand the mind and how to control the senses and lead the mind to health, clarity and mystical self-discovery. This Volume will also go deeper into the philosophy of God as creation and will explore the concepts of modern science and how they correlate with ancient teachings. This Volume will lay the ground work for the understanding of the philosophy of universal consciousness and the initiatic/yogic insight into who or what is God? ISBN 1-884564-07-0 $22.95

22.   *AFRICAN RELIGION VOLUME 5: THE GODDESS AND THE EGYPTIAN MYSTERIESTHE PATH OF THE GODDESS THE GODDESS PATH* The Secret Forms of the Goddess and the Rituals of Resurrection The Supreme Being may be worshipped as father or as mother. *Ushet Rekhat* or *Mother*

Mystical Answers to the Important Questions of Life

Worship, is the spiritual process of worshipping the Divine in the form of the Divine Goddess. It celebrates the most important forms of the Goddess including *Nathor, Maat, Aset, Arat, Amentet and Hathor* and explores their mystical meaning as well as the rising of *Sirius,* the star of Aset (Aset) and the new birth of Hor (Heru). The end of the year is a time of reckoning, reflection and engendering a new or renewed positive movement toward attaining spiritual Enlightenment. The Mother Worship devotional meditation ritual, performed on five days during the month of December and on New Year's Eve, is based on the Ushet Rekhit. During the ceremony, the cosmic forces, symbolized by Sirius - and the constellation of Orion ---, are harnessed through the understanding and devotional attitude of the participant. This propitiation draws the light of wisdom and health to all those who share in the ritual, leading to prosperity and wisdom. $14.95 ISBN 1-884564-18-6

23. *THE MYSTICAL JOURNEY FROM JESUS TO CHRIST* Discover the ancient Egyptian origins of Christianity before the Catholic Church and learn the mystical teachings given by Jesus to assist all humanity in becoming Christlike. Discover the secret meaning of the Gospels that were discovered in Egypt. Also discover how and why so many Christian churches came into being. Discover that the Bible still holds the keys to mystical realization even though its original writings were changed by the church. Discover how to practice the original teachings of Christianity which leads to the Kingdom of Heaven. $24.95 ISBN# 1-884564-05-4 size: 8½" X 11"

24. *THE STORY OF ASAR, ASET AND HERU:* An Ancient Egyptian Legend (For Children)   Now for the first time, the most ancient myth of Ancient Egypt comes alive for children. Inspired by the books *The Asarian Resurrection: The Ancient Egyptian Bible* and *The Mystical Teachings of The Asarian Resurrection, The Story of Asar, Aset and Heru* is an easy to understand and thrilling tale which inspired the children of Ancient Egypt to aspire to greatness and righteousness.   If you and your child have enjoyed stories like *The Lion King* and *Star Wars you will love The Story of Asar, Aset and Heru*. Also, if you know the story of Jesus and Krishna you will discover than Ancient Egypt had a similar myth and that this myth carries important spiritual teachings for living a fruitful and fulfilling life. This book may be used along with *The Parents Guide To The Asarian Resurrection Myth: How to Teach Yourself and Your Child the Principles of Universal Mystical Religion.* The guide provides some background to the Asarian Resurrection myth and it also gives insight into the mystical teachings contained in it which you may introduce to your child. It is designed for parents who wish to grow spiritually with their children and it serves as an introduction for those who would like to study the Asarian Resurrection Myth in depth and to practice its teachings. 8.5" X 11"   ISBN: 1-884564-31-3 $12.95

25. *THE PARENTS GUIDE TO THE AUSARIAN RESURRECTION MYTH:* How to Teach Yourself and Your Child   the Principles of Universal Mystical

Conversation with God

Religion. This insightful manual brings for the timeless wisdom of the ancient through the Ancient Egyptian myth of Asar, Aset and Heru and the mystical teachings contained in it for parents who want to guide their children to understand and practice the teachings of mystical spirituality. This manual may be used with the children's storybook *The Story of Asar, Aset and Heru* by Dr. Muata Abhaya Ashby.   ISBN: 1-884564-30-5 $16.95

26. *HEALING THE CRIMINAL HEART.* Introduction to Maat Philosophy, Yoga and Spiritual Redemption Through the Path of Virtue   Who is a criminal? Is there such a thing as a criminal heart? What is the source of evil and sinfulness and is there any way to rise above it? Is there redemption for those who have committed sins, even the worst crimes?   Ancient Egyptian mystical psychology holds important answers to these questions. Over ten thousand years ago mystical psychologists, the Sages of Ancient Egypt, studied and charted the human mind and spirit and laid out a path which will lead to spiritual redemption, prosperity and Enlightenment.   This introductory volume brings forth the teachings of the Asarian Resurrection, the most important myth of Ancient Egypt, with relation to the faults of human existence: anger, hatred, greed, lust, animosity, discontent, ignorance, egoism jealousy, bitterness, and a myriad of psycho-spiritual ailments which keep a human being in a state of negativity and adversity   ISBN: 1-884564-17-8 $15.95

27. *TEMPLE RITUAL OF THE ANCIENT EGYPTIAN MYSTERIES--THEATER & DRAMA OF THE ANCIENT EGYPTIAN MYSTERIES*: Details the practice of the mysteries and ritual program of the temple and the philosophy an practice of the ritual of the mysteries, its purpose and execution. Featuring the Ancient Egyptian stage play-"The Enlightenment of Hathor' Based on an Ancient Egyptian Drama, The original Theater -Mysticism of the Temple of Hetheru 1-884564-14-3 $19.95   By Dr. Muata Ashby

28.   GUIDE TO PRINT ON DEMAND: SELF-PUBLISH FOR PROFIT, SPIRITUAL FULFILLMENT AND SERVICE TO HUMANITY Everyone asks us how we produced so many books in such a short time. Here are the secrets to writing and producing books that uplift humanity and how to get them printed for a fraction of the regular cost. Anyone can become an author even if they have limited funds. All that is necessary is the willingness to learn how the printing and book business work and the desire to follow the special instructions given here for preparing your manuscript format. Then you take your work directly to the non-traditional companies who can produce your books for less than the traditional book printer can. ISBN: 1-884564-40-2 $16.95 U. S.

29.   *Egyptian Mysteries: Vol. 1, Shetaut Neter* What are the Mysteries? For thousands of years the spiritual tradition of Ancient Egypt, S*hetaut Neter*, "The Egyptian Mysteries," "The Secret Teachings," have fascinated, tantalized and amazed the world. At one time exalted and recognized as the highest culture of the world, by Africans, Europeans, Asiatics, Hindus, Buddhists and other

cultures of the ancient world, in time it was shunned by the emerging orthodox world religions. Its temples desecrated, its philosophy maligned, its tradition spurned, its philosophy dormant in the mystical *Medu Neter*, the mysterious hieroglyphic texts which hold the secret symbolic meaning that has scarcely been discerned up to now. What are the secrets of *Nehast* {spiritual awakening and emancipation, resurrection}. More than just a literal translation, this volume is for awakening to the secret code *Shetitu* of the teaching which was not deciphered by Egyptologists, nor could be understood by ordinary spiritualists. This book is a reinstatement of the original science made available for our times, to the reincarnated followers of Ancient Egyptian culture and the prospect of spiritual freedom to break the bonds of *Khemn*, "ignorance," and slavery to evil forces: *Såaa* . ISBN: 1-884564-41-0 $19.99

30. *EGYPTIAN MYSTERIES VOL 2:* Dictionary of Gods and Goddesses This book is about the mystery of neteru, the gods and goddesses of Ancient Egypt (Kamit, Kemet). Neteru means "Gods and Goddesses." But the Neterian teaching of Neteru represents more than the usual limited modern day concept of "divinities" or "spirits." The Neteru of Kamit are also metaphors, cosmic principles and vehicles for the enlightening teachings of Shetaut Neter (Ancient Egyptian-African Religion). Actually they are the elements for one of the most advanced systems of spirituality ever conceived in human history. Understanding the concept of neteru provides a firm basis for spiritual evolution and the pathway for viable culture, peace on earth and a healthy human society. Why is it important to have gods and goddesses in our lives? In order for spiritual evolution to be possible, once a human being has accepted that there is existence after death and there is a transcendental being who exists beyond time and space knowledge, human beings need a connection to that which transcends the ordinary experience of human life in time and space and a means to understand the transcendental reality beyond the mundane reality. ISBN: 1-884564-23-2 $21.95

31. *EGYPTIAN MYSTERIES VOL. 3* The Priests and Priestesses of Ancient Egypt This volume details the path of Neterian priesthood, the joys, challenges and rewards of advanced Neterian life, the teachings that allowed the priests and priestesses to manage the most long lived civilization in human history and how that path can be adopted today; for those who want to tread the path of the Clergy of Shetaut Neter. ISBN: 1-884564-53-4 $24.95

32. *The War of Heru and Set:* The Struggle of Good and Evil for Control of the World and The Human Soul This volume contains a novelized version of the Asarian Resurrection myth that is based on the actual scriptures presented in the Book Asarian Religion (old name –Resurrecting Osiris). This volume is prepared in the form of a screenplay and can be easily adapted to be used as a stage play. Spiritual seeking is a mythic journey that has many emotional highs and lows, ecstasies and depressions, victories and frustrations. This is the War of

Life that is played out in the myth as the struggle of Heru and Set and those are mythic characters that represent the human Higher and Lower self. How to understand the war and emerge victorious in the journey o life? The ultimate victory and fulfillment can be experienced, which is not changeable or lost in time. The purpose of myth is to convey the wisdom of life through the story of divinities who show the way to overcome the challenges and foibles of life. In this volume the feelings and emotions of the characters of the myth have been highlighted to show the deeply rich texture of the Ancient Egyptian myth. This myth contains deep spiritual teachings and insights into the nature of self, of God and the mysteries of life and the means to discover the true meaning of life and thereby achieve the true purpose of life. To become victorious in the battle of life means to become the King (or Queen) of Egypt. Have you seen movies like The Lion King, Hamlet, The Odyssey, or The Little Buddha? These have been some of the most popular movies in modern times. The Sema Institute of Yoga is dedicated to researching and presenting the wisdom and culture of ancient Africa. The Script is designed to be produced as a motion picture but may be addapted for the theater as well. $21.95 copyright 1998 By Dr. Muata Ashby ISBN 1-8840564-44-5

33. *AFRICAN DIONYSUS: FROM EGYPT TO GREECE:* The Kamitan Origins of Greek Culture and Religion ISBN: 1-884564-47-X FROM EGYPT TO GREECE This insightful manual is a reference to Ancient Egyptian mythology and philosophy and its correlation to what later became known as Greek and Rome mythology and philosophy. It outlines the basic tenets of the mythologies and shoes the ancient origins of Greek culture in Ancient Egypt. This volume also documents the origins of the Greek alphabet in Egypt as well as Greek religion, myth and philosophy of the gods and goddesses from Egypt from the myth of Atlantis and archaic period with the Minoans to the Classical period. This volume also acts as a resource for Colleges students who would like to set up fraternities and sororities based on the original Ancient Egyptian principles of Sheti and Maat philosophy. ISBN: 1-884564-47-X $22.95 U.S.

34. *THE FORTY TWO PRECEPTS OF MAAT, THE PHILOSOPHY OF RIGHTEOUS ACTION AND THE ANCIENT EGYPTIAN WISDOM TEXTS* <u>ADVANCED STUDIES</u> This manual is designed for use with the 1998 Maat Philosophy Class conducted by Dr. Muata Ashby. This is a detailed study of Maat Philosophy. It contains a compilation of the 42 laws or precepts of Maat and the corresponding principles which they represent along with the teachings of the ancient Egyptian Sages relating to each. Maat philosophy was the basis of Ancient Egyptian society and government as well as the heart of Ancient Egyptian myth and spirituality. Maat is at once a goddess, a cosmic force and a living social doctrine, which promotes social harmony and thereby paves the way for spiritual evolution in all levels of society. ISBN: 1-884564-48-8 $16.95 U.S.

35. **THE SECRET LOTUS:** *Poetry of Enlightenment*

Mystical Answers to the Important Questions of Life

Discover the mystical sentiment of the Kemetic teaching as expressed through the poetry of Sebai Muata Ashby. The teaching of spiritual awakening is uniquely experienced when the poetic sensibility is present. This first volume contains the poems written between 1996 and 2003. **1-884564--16 -X $16.99**

36. The Ancient Egyptian Buddha: The Ancient Egyptian Origins of Buddhism

This book is a compilation of several sections of a larger work, a book by the name of African Origins of Civilization, Religion, Yoga Mysticism and Ethics Philosophy. It also contains some additional evidences not contained in the larger work that demonstrate the correlation between Ancient Egyptian Religion and Buddhism. This book is one of several compiled short volumes that has been compiled so as to facilitate access to specific subjects contained in the larger work which is over 680 pages long. These short and small volumes have been specifically designed to cover one subject in a brief and low cost format. This present volume, The Ancient Egyptian Buddha: The Ancient Egyptian Origins of Buddhism, formed one subject in the larger work; actually it was one chapter of the larger work. However, this volume has some new additional evidences and comparisons of Buddhist and Neterian (Ancient Egyptian) philosophies not previously discussed. It was felt that this subject needed to be discussed because even in the early 21st century, the idea persists that Buddhism originated only in India independently. Yet there is ample evidence from ancient writings and perhaps more importantly, iconographical evidences from the Ancient Egyptians and early Buddhists themselves that prove otherwise. This handy volume has been designed to be accessible to young adults and all others who would like to have an easy reference with documentation on this important subject. This is an important subject because the frame of reference with which we look at a culture depends strongly on our conceptions about its origins. in this case, if we look at the Buddhism as an Asiatic religion we would treat it and it's culture in one way. If we id as African [Ancient Egyptian] we not only would see it in a different light but we also must ascribe Africa with a glorious legacy that matches any other culture in human history and gave rise to one of the present day most important religious philosophies. We would also look at the culture and philosophies of the Ancient Egyptians as having African insights that offer us greater depth into the Buddhist philosophies. Those insights inform our knowledge about other African traditions and we can also begin to understand in a deeper way the effect of Ancient Egyptian culture on African culture and also on the Asiatic as well. We would also be able to discover the glorious and wondrous teaching of mystical philosophy that Ancient Egyptian Shetaut Neter religion offers, that is as powerful as any other mystic system of spiritual philosophy in the world today.

37. The Death of American Empire: Neo-conservatism, Theocracy, Economic Imperialism, Environmental Disaster and the Collapse of Civilization

This work is a collection of essays relating to social and economic, leadership, and ethics, ecological and religious issues that are facing the world today in order to understand the course of history that has led humanity to its present condition and then arrive at positive solutions that will lead to better outcomes for all humanity. It surveys the development and decline of major empires throughout history and focuses on the creation of American Empire along with the social, political and economic policies that led to the prominence of the United States of America as a Superpower including the rise of the political control of the neo-con political philosophy including militarism and the military industrial complex in American politics and the rise of the religious right into and American Theocracy movement. This volume details, through historical and current events, the psychology behind the dominance of western culture in world politics through the "Superpower Syndrome Mandatory Conflict Complex" that drives the Superpower culture to establish itself above all others and then act hubristically to dominate world culture through legitimate influences as well as coercion, media censorship and misinformation leading to international hegemony and world conflict. This volume also details the financial policies that gave rise to American prominence in the global economy, especially after World War II, and promoted American preeminence over the world economy through Globalization as well as the environmental policies, including the oil economy, that are promoting degradation of the world ecology and contribute to the decline of America as an Empire culture. This volume finally explores the factors pointing to the decline of the American Empire economy and imperial power and what to expect in the aftermath of American prominence and how to survive the decline while at the same time promoting policies and social-economic-religious-political changes that are needed in order to promote the emergence of a beneficial and sustainable culture.

38. The African Origins of Hatha Yoga: And its Ancient Mystical Teaching

The subject of this present volume, The Ancient Egyptian Origins of Yoga Postures, formed one subject in the larger works, African Origins of Civilization Religion, Yoga Mysticism and Ethics Philosophy and the Book Egypt and India is the section of the book African Origins of Civilization. Those works contain the collection of all correlations between Ancient Egypt and India. This volume also contains some additional information not contained in the previous work. It was felt that this subject needed to be discussed more directly, being treated in one volume, as opposed to being contained in the larger work along with other subjects, because even in the early 21st century, the idea persists that the Yoga and specifically, Yoga Postures, were invented and developed only in India. The Ancient Egyptians were peoples originally from Africa who were, in ancient times, colonists in India. Therefore it is no surprise that many Indian traditions including religious and Yogic, would be found earlier in Ancient Egypt. Yet there is ample evidence from ancient writings and perhaps more importantly, iconographical evidences from the Ancient Egyptians themselves and the Indians themselves that prove the connection between Ancient Egypt and India as well as the existence of a discipline of Yoga Postures in Ancient Egypt long before its practice in India. This handy volume has been designed to be accessible to young adults and all others who would like to have an easy reference with documentation on this important subject. This is an important subject because the frame of reference with which we look at a culture depends strongly on our conceptions about its origins. In this case, if we look at the Ancient Egyptians as Asiatic peoples we would treat them and their culture in one way. If we see them as Africans we not only see them in a different light but we also must ascribe Africa with a glorious legacy that matches any other culture in human history. We would also look at the culture and philosophies of the Ancient Egyptians as having African insights instead of Asiatic ones. Those insights inform our knowledge bout other African traditions and we can also begin to understand in a deeper way the effect of Ancient Egyptian culture on African culture and also on the Asiatic as well. When we discover the deeper and more ancient practice of the postures system in Ancient Egypt that was called "Hatha Yoga" in India, we are able to find a new and expanded understanding of the practice that constitutes a discipline of spiritual practice that informs and revitalizes the Indian practices as well as all spiritual disciplines.

39. The Black Ancient Egyptians

This present volume, The Black Ancient Egyptians: The Black African Ancestry of the Ancient Egyptians, formed one subject in the larger work: The African Origins of Civilization, Religion, Yoga Mysticism and Ethics Philosophy. It was felt that this subject needed to be discussed because even in the early 21st century, the idea persists that the Ancient Egyptians were peoples originally from Asia Minor who came into North-East Africa. Yet there is ample evidence from ancient writings and perhaps more importantly, iconographical evidences from the Ancient Egyptians themselves that proves otherwise. This handy volume has been designed to be accessible to young adults and all others who would like to have an easy reference with documentation on this important subject. This is an important subject because the frame of reference with which we look at a culture depends strongly on our conceptions about its origins. in this case, if we look at the Ancient Egyptians as Asiatic peoples we would treat them and their culture in one way. If we see them as Africans we not only see them in a different light but we also must ascribe Africa with a glorious legacy that matches any other culture in human history. We would also look at the culture and philosophies of the Ancient Egyptians as having African insights instead of Asiatic ones. Those insights inform our knowledge bout other African traditions and we can also begin to understand in a deeper way the effect of Ancient Egyptian culture on African culture and also on the Asiatic as well.

40. The Limits of Faith: The Failure of Faith-based Religions and the Solution to the Meaning of Life

Is faith belief in something without proof? And if so is there never to be any proof or discovery? If so what is the need of intellect? If faith is trust in something that is real is that reality historical, literal or metaphorical or philosophical? If knowledge is an essential element in faith why should there by so much emphasis on believing and not on understanding in the modern practice of religion? This volume is a compilation of essays related to the nature of religious faith in the context of its inception in human history as well as its meaning for religious practice and relations between religions in modern times. Faith has come to be regarded as a virtuous goal in life. However, many people have asked how can it be that an endeavor that is supposed to be dedicated to spiritual upliftment has led to more conflict in human history than any other social factor?

Conversation with God

Music Based on the Prt M Hru and other Kemetic Texts

Available on Compact Disc $14.99 and Audio Cassette $9.99

Adorations to the Goddess

Music for Worship of the Goddess

**NEW Egyptian Yoga Music CD
by Sehu Maa
Ancient Egyptian Music CD**

Instrumental Music played on reproductions of Ancient Egyptian Instruments– Ideal for <u>meditation</u> and reflection on the Divine and for the practice of spiritual programs and <u>Yoga exercise sessions.</u>

©1999 By Muata Ashby
CD $14.99 –

**MERIT'S INSPIRATION
NEW Egyptian Yoga Music CD
by Sehu Maa
Ancient Egyptian Music CD**

Mystical Answers to the Important Questions of Life

Instrumental Music played on reproductions of Ancient Egyptian Instruments– Ideal for meditation and reflection on the Divine and for the practice of spiritual programs and Yoga exercise sessions.
©1999 By
Muata Ashby
CD $14.99 –
UPC# 761527100429

ANORATIONS TO RA AND HETHERU
**NEW Egyptian Yoga Music CD
By Sehu Maa (Muata Ashby)
Based on the Words of Power of Ra and HetHeru**
played on reproductions of Ancient Egyptian Instruments **Ancient Egyptian Instruments used: Voice, Clapping, Nefer Lute, Tar Drum, Sistrums, Cymbals –** The Chants, Devotions, Rhythms and Festive Songs Of the Neteru – Ideal for meditation, and devotional singing and dancing.
©1999 By Muata Ashby
CD $14.99 –
UPC# 761527100221

SONGS TO ASAR ASET AND HERU

Conversation with God

NEW
Egyptian Yoga Music CD
By Sehu Maa

played on reproductions of Ancient Egyptian Instruments– The Chants, Devotions, Rhythms and Festive Songs Of the Neteru - Ideal for meditation, and devotional singing and dancing.

Based on the Words of Power of Asar (Asar), Aset (Aset) and Heru (Heru) Om Asar Aset Heru is the third in a series of musical explorations of the Kemetic (Ancient Egyptian) tradition of music. Its ideas are based on the Ancient Egyptian Religion of Asar, Aset and Heru and it is designed for listening, meditation and worship. ©1999 By Muata Ashby

CD $14.99 –
UPC# 761527100122

HAARI OM: ANCIENT EGYPT MEETS INDIA IN MUSIC
NEW Music CD
By Sehu Maa

The Chants, Devotions, Rhythms and Festive Songs Of the Ancient Egypt and India, harmonized and played on reproductions of ancient instruments along with modern instruments and beats. Ideal for meditation, and devotional singing and dancing.

Haari Om is the fourth in a series of musical explorations of the Kemetic (Ancient Egyptian) and Indian traditions of music, chanting and devotional spiritual practice. Its ideas are based on the Ancient Egyptian Yoga spirituality and Indian Yoga spirituality.

©1999 By Muata Ashby
CD $14.99 –
UPC# 761527100528

Mystical Answers to the Important Questions of Life

RA AKHU: THE GLORIOUS LIGHT
NEW
Egyptian Yoga Music CD
By Sehu Maa

The fifth collection of original music compositions based on the Teachings and Words of The Trinity, the God Asar and the Goddess Nebethet, the Divinity Aten, the God Heru, and the Special Meditation Hekau or Words of Power of Ra from the Ancient Egyptian Tomb of Seti I and more...
played on reproductions of Ancient Egyptian Instruments and modern instruments - **Ancient Egyptian Instruments used: Voice, Clapping, Nefer Lute, Tar Drum, Sistrums, Cymbals**
– The Chants, Devotions, Rhythms and Festive Songs Of the Neteru – Ideal for meditation, and devotional singing and dancing.
©1999 By Muata Ashby
CD $14.99 –
UPC# 761527100825

GLORIES OF THE DIVINE MOTHER
Based on the hieroglyphic text of the worship of Goddess Net.
The Glories of The Great Mother
©2000 **Muata Ashby**

Conversation with God

CD $14.99 UPC# 761527101129`

Mystical Answers to the Important Questions of Life

Order Form

Telephone orders: Call Toll Free: 1(305) 378-6253. Have your AMEX, Optima, Visa or MasterCard ready.

   Fax orders: 1-(305) 378-6253 E-MAIL ADDRESS: Semayoga@aol.com

Postal Orders: Sema Institute of Yoga, P.O. Box 570459, Miami, Fl. 33257. USA.

     Please send the following books and / or tapes.

ITEM

_____Cost $_____

_____Cost $_____

_____Cost $_____

_____Cost $_____

_____Cost $_____

           Total $_____

Name:_____

Physical Address:_____

City:_____ State:_____ Zip:_____

Sales tax: Please add 6.5% for books shipped to Florida addresses

_____Shipping: $6.50 for first book and .50¢ for each additional

_____Shipping: Outside US $5.00 for first book and $3.00 for each additional

_____Payment:_____

_____Check -Include Driver License #:

  _____

_____Credit card: _____ Visa, _____ MasterCard, _____ Optima, _____ AMEX.

Card number:_____

Name on card:_____ Exp. date:_____/_____

Copyright 1995-2005 Dr. R. Muata Abhaya Ashby
Sema Institute of Yoga
P.O.Box 570459, Miami, Florida, 33257
(305) 378-6253 Fax: (305) 378-6253

www.ingramcontent.com/pod-product-compliance
Lightning Source LLC
Chambersburg PA
CBHW071217080526
44587CB00013BA/1411